Peter Titelman, PhD
Editor

Clinical Applications of Bowen Family Systems Theory

Pre-publication
REVIEWS,
COMMENTARIES,
EVALUATIONS . . .

"This book continues the vigorous extension of Murray Bowen's landmark accounts of the emotional evolution of an individual in the family. This volume focuses on the vicissitudes of the self in struggling to become more mature while being able to project more adaptive behaviors to those around you. The rich accounts of the struggle of 'self' are well described in an array of intriguing and thoughtful case descriptions."

Norman L. Paul, MD
Lecturer in Psychiatry,
Harvard University

"The opening chapters of this book by Titelman and Meyer are enough by themselves to justify the publication and purchase of this book. The summary of Bowen theory is so clear and concise that it will be both an excellent review to the experienced therapist and a fine introduction to the new therapist. The chapters that follow represent concrete examples of the use of this theory in practical case situations."

Thomas F. Fogarty, MD
Pulham Manor,
New York

Clinical Applications of Bowen Family Systems Theory

HAWORTH Marriage and the Family
Terry S. Trepper, PhD
Executive Editor

Marriage and Family Therapy: A Sociocognitive Approach
by Nathan Hurvitz and Roger A. Straus

Culture and Family: Problems and Therapy by Wen-Shing Tseng and Jing Hsu

*Adolescents and Their Families: An Introduction to Assessment
and Intervention* by Mark Worden

Parents Whose Parents Were Divorced by R. Thomas Berner

The Effect of Children on Parents by Anne-Marie Ambert

Multigenerational Family Therapy by David S. Freeman

101 Interventions in Family Therapy edited by Thorana S. Nelson
and Terry S. Trepper

Therapy with Treatment Resistant Families: A Consultation-Crisis Intervention Model
by William George McCown, Judith Johnson, and Associates

Developing Healthy Stepfamilies: Twenty Families Tell Their Stories
by Patricia Kelley

Propagations: Thirty Years of Influence from the Mental Research Institute
edited by John H. Weakland and Wendel A. Ray

*Structured Exercises for Promoting Family and Group Strengths: A Handbook
for Group Leaders, Trainers, Educators, Counselors, and Therapists*
edited by Ron McManus and Glen Jennings

*Making Families Work and What to Do When They Don't: Thirty Guides
for Imperfect Parents of Imperfect Children* by Bill Borcherdt

*Family Therapy of Neurobehavioral Disorders: Integrating Neuropsychology and Family
Therapy* by Judith Johnson and William McCown

*Parents, Children, and Adolescents: Interactive Relationships and Development
in Context* by Anne-Marie Ambert

*Women Survivors of Childhood Sexual Abuse: Healing Through Group Work: Beyond
Survival* by Judy Chew

Tales from Family Therapy: Life-Changing Clinical Experiences edited by Frank N.
Thomas and Thorana S. Nelson

*The Practical Practice of Marriage and Family Therapy: Things My Training Supervisor
Never Told Me* by Mark Odell and Charles E. Campbell

The Therapist's Notebook: Homework, Handouts, and Activities for Use in Psychotherapy
edited by Lorna L. Hecker and Sharon A. Deacon

The Web of Poverty: Psychosocial Perspectives by Anne-Marie Ambert

101 More Interventions in Family Therapy edited by Thorana S. Nelson and Terry S.
Trepper

Stepfamilies: A Multi-Dimensional Perspective by Roni Berger

Clinical Applications of Bowen Family Systems Theory by Peter Titelman

Clinical Applications of Bowen Family Systems Theory

Peter Titelman, PhD
Editor

Routledge
Taylor & Francis Group
New York   London

Cover design by Jennifer M. Gaska.

Library of Congress Cataloging-in-Publication Data

Clinical applications of Bowen family systems theory / Peter Titelman, editor.
     p.   cm.
  Includes bibliographical references and index.
  ISBN 0-7890-0469-0 (alk. paper).(ISBN: 0-7890-0468-2)
  1. Family psychotherapy. 2. Bowen, Murray, 1913-1990. I. Titelman, Peter.
RC488.5.C583 1998
616.89'156—dc21

                                    98-6169
                                       CIP

Dedicated to my wife, Tink

CONTENTS

PART I: BOWEN FAMILY SYSTEMS THEORY, ASSESSMENT, AND THERAPY

Chapter 3. Bowen Theory As a Basis for Therapy   **69**
    Patricia Hanes Meyer

PART II: CLINICAL APPLICATIONS

Chapter 4. Marital Fusion and Differentiation   **119**
    Phil Klever

ABOUT THE EDITOR

Peter Titelman, PhD, maintains a private practice in clinical psychology, specializing in Bowen family systems therapy, consultation, training, and supervision in Northampton, Massachusetts. Dr. Titelman consults to family businesses as a principal in LaForte & Titelman Associates, also based in Northampton. He is the editor of *The Therapist's Own Family* (Aronson, 1987), in which he and the other contributors illustrate the application of Bowen's concept of differentiation of self to the therapist's own family as a means of working toward personal and professional responsibility. Dr. Titelman has also taught and supervised professionals and graduate students in several New England graduate and professional schools.

CONTRIBUTORS

Katharine Gratwick Baker, DSW, is a Principal, Working Systems, Inc., Washington, DC, and is in private practice in Washington, DC, and Williamsburg, Massachusetts.

Edward W. Beal, MD, is Clinical Professor of Psychiatry, Georgetown University Medical School, Washington, DC, and faculty member, Georgetown Family Center, Washington, DC. Dr. Beal is in private practice in Psychiatry in Bethesda, Maryland.

Stephanie J. Ferrera, MSW, is a faculty member, Center of Family Consultation, Chicago, Illinois, and is in private practice in Oak Park, Illinois.

Brian J. Kelly, EdD, is in private practice in Fairfield, Connecticut.

Phil Klever, MSW, is in private practice in Kansas City, Kansas.

James C. Maloni, PhD, is a clinical psychologist specializing in individual, couples, and family therapy. Dr. Maloni's private practice includes supervision, training, and consultation in Pittsburgh, Pennsylvania.

Anne S. McKnight, LCSW, is a faculty member, Georgetown Family Center, Washington, DC; staff member, Arlington County Bureau of Substance Abuse, Arlington, Virginia; and is in private practice in Arlington, Virginia.

Patricia Hanes Meyer, LCSW, is in private practice in family therapy, including consultation and lecturing, in Reston, Virginia.

Sydney K. Reed, MSW, is a faculty member, Center for Family Consultation, Chicago, Illinois, and is in private practice in Evanston, Illinois.

Donald J. Shoulberg, ThM, PhD, is Adjunct Assistant Professor, Department of Human Development and Family Life, University of Kansas; Adjunct Assistant Professor, Department of Child Development and Family Studies, Kansas State University; and Director,

Menniger Family Therapy Training Program in Kansas City. Dr. Shoulberg is in private practice in marriage and family therapy in Prairie Village, Kansas.

James B. Smith, MS, is a faculty member, Western Pennsylvania Family Center, Pittsburgh, Pennsylvania, and is in private practice in Pittsburgh, Pennsylvania.

Bennett I. Tittler, PhD, is in private practice in clinical psychology in Beverly, Massachusetts. Dr. Tittler is Consultant, The Cape Cod Bowen Study Group, Falmouth, Massachusetts, and Instructor in Behavior Science, The Family Practice Residency, Beverly Hospital, Beverly, Massachusetts.

Foreword

As Peter Titelman mentions in his introduction to this book, *Clinical Applications of Bowen Family Systems Theory,* and as many of the book's contributors note, Murray Bowen was leery of books and articles describing the application of his theory to clinical work. His principal concern, I believe, was that readers would get the impression from such articles that family systems was not a new theory—an alternative to Freudian theory—but a new method of therapy.

During the 1970s and 1980s, many of the publications by family therapists focused on how to do therapy. A consequence of the emphasis on therapy over theory was the splintering of groups into a number of "schools" of family therapy. Each school represented somewhat different ideas about how families function, but the major differences between schools were in therapeutic approach. Most family therapists credited Bowen with contributing important new ideas to the field, but few recognized that his ideas comprised a comprehensive and radically new theory. Most thought Bowen had primarily developed a unique method of family therapy that focused on the multigenerational family, and they regarded his "approach" as another school within the field. The misperception of his ideas was a key factor influencing Bowen to focus more on theory and less on therapy in his presentations and publications.

Another reason Bowen emphasized theory over therapy was his observation that therapists entering the family field were liable to adopt a therapeutic technique they had heard or read about without examining the basic assumptions about human behavior held by the person espousing that technique. Consequently, trainees were not challenged to examine their own preexisting assumptions about the forces governing human behavior; they would simply incorporate the technique into their preexisting assumptions.

Common examples of family therapy trainees incorporating a technique without examining its underlying assumptions were the trainees that attempted to "differentiate a self" in their families of origin by "getting the feelings out." These trainees felt compelled to express their hurts, angers, and disappointments to the family and pressured their parents and other family members to do the same. The effort, sometimes planned to be accomplished over a weekend or in a large family meeting, often involved confrontations with parents and other family members over emotionally charged issues. Not surprisingly, the confrontations could precipitate a major relationship cutoff with one or both parents. Another outcome was a catharsis of feelings that generated a temporary surface calm, but invariably, the trainees and their families would revert to old patterns.

The approach of externalizing feelings is not based on an underlying assumption of Bowen theory but is a legacy of Freudian theory. A central assumption of Freudian theory is that clinical problems are linked to the repression of feelings. Many people inhibit the overt expression of their own and others' feelings, and many people reflect little on their own feelings; however, from the perspective of Bowen theory, what family members feel and how they manage the feelings reflect the operation of the underlying family emotional system, a concept that is not part of Freudian theory. For example, if a son berates his father for not affirming him and insists his father admit it, the son may feel better, but he is no doubt reinforcing an old triangle (the basic molecule of an emotional system) that involves the son and his two parents. The son's effort to externalize the feelings can tighten the parental triangle rather than foster differentiation. Thus, if a trainee is to use the techniques of Bowen theory effectively, he or she must first compare Bowen theory's assumptions about human behavior with his or her own assumptions.

I have known Peter Titelman since his family training days with Paulina McCullough and her Pittsburgh Bowen Theory group. We have crossed paths at dozens of meetings over the years, and I do not think we have ever been at a meeting together and not found some time to exchange ideas. He has been an enthusiastic supporter of my interests in biology, evolutionary theory, and cancer. He has supported my interests for a number of reasons, one of which is that he is fascinated by these areas himself. We have talked frequently about his long-standing belief, Murray Bowen's view notwithstanding, that more needed to be written about the clinical applications of Bowen theory. He knew Bowen did not agree with him on this point, but it was clear that Peter Titelman would stick to his beliefs—and so he has with the publication of this book.

I do not think Dr. Bowen was opposed to clinical description as a means of teaching theory because he himself wrote about clinical applications. When he wrote a paper about his own family, he structured it so that he left no doubt that every "move" he made in his family was grounded in theory. He carefully thought through every letter, every phone call, and every visit before he did any of them. He had spent twelve years getting almost nowhere in his family. It took the theory coming together into a whole before it was possible for him to make contact with his family system and not get "stuck" in the emotional process. Despite the pitfalls of writing about therapy, I suspect Bowen would have written more about clinical applications if he had had the time to do it. I think he only had so much writing in him, and he opted to devote it to writing about theory. He would leave the writing about applications to others, and hopefully those who undertook the task would fully comprehend the importance of theory to the effort and be aware of the pitfalls.

I have known most of the authors in this book as long as I have known Peter Titelman. I was not fully aware of their wide-ranging interests until I read the book. Similar to myself, they are all primarily clinicians, and the clinical arena is where their experience is most extensive and their skills most refined. They write from years of careful observations made both in the clinical setting and in their own families. I think it is valuable that they have the forum Peter Titelman has provided with this book. Something that I believe comes through in each person's writing is the importance of a broad perspective on the human condition. None of them gained that perspective from just sitting in an office and doing family therapy. All have heeded Bowen's challenge to think beyond the human family to the larger society and to think beyond human societies to the societies of all living things.

When I spoke at Murray Bowen's funeral in October 1990 in Waverly, Tennessee, I said that one of the characteristics that I thought was special about him was his having the rare combination of a "can do" mentality that seeks solutions to problems, not assuming that the problem is too big and that nothing can be done, and the unusual ability to step back from human problems and think broadly about them. He believed the family movement's main contribution to the future would be a new theory of human behavior, but he also believed that the method he developed of differentiation of self in one's own family was one of his most important contributions. This book mirrors that importance.

Michael E. Kerr, MD
Director, Georgetown Family Center,
Washington, DC

Acknowledgments

The late Murray Bowen, MD, is gratefully acknowledged for having created the theoretical foundation upon which this book rests.

Thanks are extended to all of the contributors for their effort and patience during the lengthy process from the conception to the completion of this book.

Jim Smith, MS, deserves thanks for his thoughtful comments on Chapter 12.

Dan Pender, MA, deserves thanks for his editorial comments on Chapter 1.

Special thanks are offered to Katharine G. Baker, DSW, for her generosity and valuable suggestions regarding the organization, style, and clarity of the editor's chapters and for her overall enthusiasm and belief in the value of this book. I want to acknowledge her invaluable work as the "shadow" editor of this book during the last two and one-half years.

Introduction

Peter Titelman

This book presents the application of Bowen family systems theory to a variety of clinical issues. All of the contributors share a common theoretical foundation. However, they provide their own versions of Bowen theory filtered through their personal lenses. From a Bowen perspective, theory and therapy are reciprocally intertwined. Therapy will always be a somewhat personal endeavor; however, Bowen theory provides a map for guiding clinicians and clients through the emotional process of therapy.

Just as there are different ways to learn Bowen theory, there are various ways to present and teach it. As Bowen continued to develop his theory and his way of teaching it, both evolved. Early on, his focus was on the application of theory in clinical practice. Later, he concentrated on the therapist's effort to differentiate a self in the family of origin. Still later, Bowen turned his focus in teaching to locating his theory in the context of evolutionary biology and related natural systems thinking.

Some teachers and students of Bowen theory may favor one approach in teaching or training. I believe that all three perspectives—theory in clinical practice, the therapist's own family, and natural systems thinking—are important and necessary. They interlock to form the fullest learning complement. The best source for understanding the place of theory in clinical practice is the collected papers of Bowen (1978), *Family Therapy in Clinical Practice*. The relationship between Bowen theory and natural systems thinking is illuminated in *Family Evaluation: An Approach Based on Bowen Theory,* Kerr and Bowen (1988), and *Bowen Family Systems Theory,* Papero (1990). Also, *The Therapist's Own Family: Toward the Differentiation of Self,* Titelman (1987), is a useful source for illustrating the application of Bowen's conception of differentiation of self to the therapist's own family as a means of working toward personal and professional responsibility.

The thirteen contributors whose work is included in this book all had significant contact with Dr. Bowen. They are senior clinicians whose connections with Bowen theory all exceed twenty years. Nine contributors were trained at the Georgetown Family Center, Washington, DC, under the direct auspices of Murray Bowen, MD. One contributor received his training in Bowen theory at the Georgetown Family Center subsequent to Bowen's death. Three contributors received their training from a student of Bowen's, Paulina McCullough, MSW, originally at the Western Psychiatric Institute and Clinic and later at the Western Pennsylvania Family Center, Pittsburgh, Pennsylvania.

The contributors, whose professional backgrounds include psychiatry, psychology, social work, and counseling, are all involved in the clinical practice of family systems, and all of them use Bowen theory in their training and consultation work. Two are on the faculty of the Georgetown Family Center, Washington, DC; two are on the faculty of the Western Pennsylvania Family Center, Pittsburgh, Pennsylvania; two are on the faculty of the Center for Family Consultation, Evanston, Illinois; one is on the faculty of the Kansas Family Institute, Kansas City, Kansas; and six contributors are involved in training professionals in their independent practices and through university affiliations.

This book is divided into two parts: (1) *Bowen Family Systems Theory, Assessment, and Therapy* and (2) *Clinical Applications,* with the former providing the theoretical foundation upon which the latter rests. In the first chapter, Titelman describes the historical evolution of Bowen's theoretical-therapeutic system. In Chapter 2, Titelman presents a version of family systems assessment based on Bowen theory. In Chapter 3, Meyer describes the application of Bowen's theory in clinical practice. Chapters 4 through 8, in the part on clinical applications, are presented in a life-cycle order for organizational purposes: Klever on fusion and marriage, focusing on differentiation in the context of marital therapy; Maloni on child-focused families, centering on the parents as primary change agents; Reed on a family with a child with a special problem, with the focus on the mother as the differentiating one; Kelly on young adults in college making early efforts toward differentiation; and Smith on family process with the elderly, with the focus on the wife as the differentiating one.

Chapters 9 through 15 focus on the following particular clinical dysfunctions and issues: Tittler discusses a family systems perspective on depression; Shoulberg tracks an individual's phobia in the context of the emotional process in a family system; McKnight focuses on family systems with alcoholism; Titelman presents a family systems perspective on incest; Beal describes the process of child-focused divorce; Baker describes the use of the Bowen approach in treating a remarried family; and Ferrera discusses the process of bridging emotional cutoff from a former spouse.

The contributors vary in the way they apply and present Bowen theory to clinical phenomena. Two, Ferrara and Reed, include material about the therapist's own family as it is relevant to the clinical material they are presenting. Reed and Titelman integrate important material from natural systems theory with Bowen theory and clinical case material. Klever, McKnight, and Smith present extensive versions of Bowen theory and relate it to their clinical applications. Baker, Kelly, Maloni, Shoulberg, and Tittler each have their own ways of contextualizing their clinical applications in the Bowen theory.

In Titelman's chapter, "Overview of the Bowen Theoretical-Therapeutic System," the reader will become familiar with Bowen's view that family therapy is a term that refers to the effort to modify the relationship system, be it with multiple family members, the spouses together, or one family member. In this book, the majority of the case material involves the coach/therapist working with one family member. However, included in this volume are the contributors' efforts in working with the following combinations of family members: individual adult, individual spouse, both spouses, one parent, both parents, parent(s) and child(ren), one child, individual young adult, divorcing parent(s), and divorced parent(s).

Eight of the twelve chapters in the clinical application section describe a single family. One chapter describes two families. The other four chapters consist of a number of clinical vignettes or case studies. The specifics of the clinical case material presented in this book have been modified in order to protect the confidentiality of the families.

In this volume, I believe the contributors' versions and application of the theory provide another access for communicating Bowen's theory. In this regard, I will cite a comment of Bowen's that I believe applies to this present volume. In a foreword to Carter and McGoldrick's book, *The Family Life Cycle: A Framework for Family Therapy* (1980), Bowen wrote:

> I think the best way of communicating family systems ideas is through the orientation and the self of the teacher. A teacher who has not mastered the concepts for self will be less effective in communicating these ideas to others. A good teacher will find his or her own ways for communicating the concepts and dealing with the communications blocks. There are no right or wrong ways for accomplishing the mission. A right way is one that works and a wrong way is one that does not work. (pp. xviii-xix)

It is the hope of this editor that this book will provide a useful source for illustrating Bowen theory in clinical practice.

REFERENCES

Bowen, M. (1978). *Family Therapy in Clinical Practice.* New York: Jason Aronson, Inc.

Bowen, M. (1980). Foreword. In Carter, E. and M. McGoldrick (Eds.), *The Family Life Cycle: A Framework for Family Therapy.* New York: Gardner Press, Inc.

Kerr, M. and Bowen, M. (1988). *Family Evaluation: An Approach Based on Bowen Theory.* New York: W.W. Norton and Company.

Papero, D. (1990) *Bowen Family Systems Theory.* Boston: Allyn and Bacon.

Titelman, P. (Ed.) (1987). *The Therapist's Own Family: Toward the Differentiation of Self.* Northvale, NJ: Jason Aronson, Inc.

PART I:
BOWEN FAMILY SYSTEMS THEORY, ASSESSMENT, AND THERAPY

Chapter 1

Overview of the Bowen Theoretical-Therapeutic System

Peter Titelman

INTRODUCTION

This chapter describes the relationship between Bowen family systems theory and Bowen family systems therapy. Its purpose is to provide a theoretical framework for understanding the application of Bowen theory in the diverse arena of clinical practice.

This chapter is divided into the following sections: (1) the relationship between theory and therapy, (2) historical development of Bowen theory and its relation to Bowen family systems therapy, (3) differentiation of self, (4) Bowen's perspective on the therapeutic relationship, (5) the role of the therapist or coach, and (6) functions of the therapist or coach.

THE RELATIONSHIP BETWEEN THEORY AND THERAPY

What does the term *theory* refer to in Bowen's thinking? Theory as "science" can refer to an organized body of knowledge within the framework of the natural sciences. At another level, theory can refer to Bowen's understanding that all individual and family behavior must be understood in terms of a variation of natural systems theory. Darwin's theory of evolution was the foundation for the development of Bowen theory. At times the term theory, for Bowen, served as a shorthand reference to natural systems theory in general and Darwinian evolutionary theory in particular. According to Bowen (1981), "Evolutionary biology accounts for process and the relationship system [conceptualized in the eight concepts of Bowen theory] accounts for content." And theory in its most concrete form can be a reference to Bowen's eight clinical concepts, the theory of differentiation, and the paradigm of the family as an emotional unit that underlies his theory.

In Bowen's (1978) *theoretical-therapeutic system:* " . . . the term *family therapy* is derived from the way the therapist thinks about the family. It refers to the effort to modify the family relationship system, whether the effort is with multiple family members, the two spouses together, or only one family member" (p. 310). In other words, family therapy is defined by the way in which the therapist thinks about the family, and the therapy is designed to help bring about change in the family, whether the change is brought about through one or more family members (Bowen, 1978, p. 212).

Bowen therapy follows a blueprint based on Bowen theory, as theory always guides therapy. Bowen was antitechnique. He opposed using therapeutic techniques separated from a solid theoretical foundation. The therapist's efforts are based on two factors: One factor involves the therapist's efforts toward defining a self in his/her own family. The second factor is based on the therapist's understanding of Bowen theory and its relationship to natural systems theory.

Bowen theory is antithetical to models that view the human predicament in terms of health versus pathology and in terms of discrete, differential diagnosis. For Bowen, the issue of diagnosis involved perceiving emotional problems along a continuum, with quantitative differences existing between families and between individuals. A focus on the phenomenology of symptoms is secondary to the underlying issue with which all individuals and families are struggling—the balance of the instinctual, emotional forces of individuality and togetherness. Bowen (1978) defined differentiation in the following way: " . . . the degree to which people are able to distinguish between the *feeling* process and the *intellectual* process (p. 355). . . . The concept defines people according to the degree of *fusion*, or *differentiation* between emotional and intellectual functioning" (p. 362). In contrast, traditional theories place individuals in discrete diagnostic categories from normal to psychotic, with other categories in between.

The goal of Bowen family systems therapy is to increase the capacity of one or more members to adapt to and deal with the vicissitudes of life. Graefe (1995) describes the differentiation effort using a metaphor from sailing: "You cannot change the velocity of the winds, but you can change the direction of the sails" (p. 2).

In other words, the Bowen approach is focused on facilitating the effort of the family member, *the differentiating one,* to gain the tools to be able to deal with the emotional process within one's self and in relation to one's family in the face of anxiety-provoking life situations and events both in the present and the future. This focus on emotional process is in contrast to approaches that focus on content, that is, the alleviation of concrete specific symptoms or problems. From the Bowen perspective, in order for differentiation of self to take place, anxiety has to be reduced to a manageable degree. Predictably, presenting symptoms or problems begin to modify or disappear as anxiety decreases. This in turn creates the opportunity for working toward solid change.

HISTORICAL DEVELOPMENT OF BOWEN THEORY AND ITS RELATION TO BOWEN FAMILY SYSTEMS THERAPY

The central focus in Bowen theory is the family, which is conceived of as a multigenerational emotional unit occuring in the context of nature. The following stages in the evolution of the Bowen theory will be explored: (1) the movement from the concept of the "undifferentiated family ego mass," to the nuclear family emotional systems and extended family emotional systems, to the family conceived of as a multigenerational emotional unit; (2) the movement from the concept of the triangle to the concept of interlocking triangles; and (3) the movement from focusing on fusion to focusing on the interlocking process of fusion and cutoff.

The Family As a Multigenerational Emotional Unit

Bowen initially spoke of how the child and adult are embedded in an emotional oneness that he described as the "undifferentiated family ego mass." He later abandoned this term for several reasons: First, he believed that the term was not consistent with the terms of evolutionary biology. Second, although Dr. Bowen believed that the term "undifferentiated family ego mass" described the sticky fusion of individuals within their nuclear family, he believed the use of the term ego was too psychological and psychoanalytic and, unfortunately, would cause people to perceive Bowen theory as a psychological theory rather than as one grounded in evolutionary biology. Third, as Bowen's theory became more and more clear in its multigenerational focus—expanding beyond the three generations that consisted of the nuclear and immediate extended family systems—he chose to replace the term undifferentiated family ego mass, and then nuclear and extended family emotional systems, with the concept of the family as a multigenerational emotional unit or system. The latter includes the individual's evolutionary descent and relationship to all biological life; his/her level of differentiation and functioning position, both within the context of the evolution of the multigenerational family, as a part of all life, with its variability and stability; and the multigenerational transmission process in which an individual exists like a grain of sand on a beach. Just as each grain of sand is unique yet similar to all other grains of sand in relation to its origin, each family member is unique but still shares similarities with all other members of his/her family.

From a Bowen perspective, differentiation, as a phenomenon of life and as a process, is both formed and modified in relation to one's family of origin and one's multigenerational extended family. It is based on instinctual emotion, as Kerr and Bowen (1988) describe it:

> Saying that human relationship process is rooted in instincts has much in common with what occurs in other forms of life, and has a function in evolutionary terms . . . This way of thinking about what "energizes" the phenomenon being described is contained in the concept of the family emotional system. (p. 11)

In addition to describing the family as an *emotional system,* based on instincts that are shared with all animals and that are the basis of the natural history of man's emotional reactivity within the family, the concept of *functioning position* is central to the evolving focus on the family as a multigenerational emotional system. People are born and are fitted into functioning positions based on a number of variables: gender, birth order, family patterns, and nodal events occurring in the multigenerational family. Extreme nodal events such as disease, death, unemployment, and emigration can modify a functioning position. Typical functioning positions are: "responsible oldest," "irresponsible youngest," "leader of the clan," "family historian," "mediator," "sick one," and "smart one."

Kerr and Bowen (1988) define the concept of functioning position in the following manner:

> [It] predicts that every family emotional system generates certain functions. These functions are performed by certain individuals in the system. When one individual performs certain functions, other individuals will not perform them. An individual is born into a sibling position. By virtue of being born in a specific position, the individual takes on the functions associated with it. An individual's personality is shaped, to some extent, by being in a certain functioning position in the family. An oldest child for example, functions in certain predictable ways in relationship to his parents and younger siblings. The nature of his functioning shapes the development and nature of his personality, and his personality, as it develops, shapes the nature of his functioning. (p. 315)

Toman's research proves that the predicted relationship between personality development and functioning position exists (Kerr and Bowen, 1988, p. 315). A person's functioning position has a significant influence on his/her beliefs, values, attitudes, feelings, and behavior. To some extent, these expectations are built into the situation, for example, for an oldest child to feel responsible for younger siblings. Even if parents try not to make the oldest child responsible for younger siblings, the process is so automatic that it will likely occur anyway (Kerr and Bowen, 1988, p. 55). Functioning positions operate in reciprocal relationship to one another; for example, the interplay between overfunctioning and underfunctioning and pursuit and distance.

From Triangles to Interlocking Triangles

A second concept that Bowen elaborated on was *interlocking triangles*. As this author wrote previously (Titelman, 1987):

> The evolution and the broadening of the concept of differentiation of self, from the focus on the nuclear family emotional system to a focus on marital fusion, and then to the current focus on each spouse's unresolved attachment to his or her family of origin, involved several phases. Initially, the focus was on the concept of fusion/undifferentiation in the context of the nuclear family emotional system. A second phase emerged with the clarification of the concept of the emotional triangle; with this came a shift of focus, theoretically and clinically, toward the marital pair. (pp. 17-18)

The concept of interlocking triangles is:

> ... the phenomenon that emerges when, anxiety having overloaded the system, and the initial triangle is unable to stabilize the situation, others are triangled into the process, thus forming a series of interlocking triangles. (Titelman, 1987, p. 19)

Two-person, three-person, and multiperson relationships are stable, or unstable, depending on the relationship between two variables: level of differentiation and anxiety. A two-person relationship can be open and stable until a certain level of stress is experienced, and then triangulation ensues. When a triangle is formed, it temporarily functions as if it were a stable structure. In general, a three-person system handling stress is somewhat more stable than a two-person system, given the same level of differentiation of the members of that system.

The triangle is characterized by a rigid or fixed dysfunctional stability involving a lack of openness among all three members and a relative lack of differentiation. The triangle is similar to a three-legged stool that is more stable than an overly stressed and fused dyad. The latter cannot stand; it collapses. However, when the triangle is overloaded by the combination of stress and undifferentiation, the distancing between two of its members, or the fusion between two members, is akin to pulling out one leg from the three-legged stool; the triangle becomes unstable.

When differentiation is relatively high and stress is low, three people operate as a "threesome" or an open three-person system. An open three-person system consists of three relatively differentiated one-to-one relationships. This open system is characterized by functional stability, openness of communication, and differentiation among all three members. A threesome or an open three-person relationship is a very stable and functional structure. Theoretically, a differentiated three-person relationship is more stable and flexible than an open, two-person differentiated relationship: when normal nodal events, stressors, and life-cycle events unfold, there is more flexibility and possibility for coping with stress when it is more widely distributed.

The three-person unit is the basic building block of the family both biologically and psychologically for several reasons: (1) it takes a male and a female to create a child; (2) differentiation is best accomplished when the young adult leaves home through leaving a stable twosome, for whom he/she does not have to caretake, and then proceeds to form a new twosome; and (3) conflict between one parent and a child is automatically modified by the soothing contact with a nonanxious, nontriangled second parent.

According to Bowen (1974), "In a calm threesome the togetherness is always moving around and a good percentage of the communication in each twosome is about self to the other self" (p. 17). For example, if a teenage son and his mother argue over any given issue, and it is not a recurring pattern, the father, if he is not emotionally reactive to either the perspective of his wife or that of his son, may defuse their conflict by his nonreactive presence or position.

If a three-legged stool, or a three-person system, has more potential for being a stable structure than a dyad, is a four-legged stool or a four-person system even more stable? The answer is yes, theoretically, if the foursome has a relatively good functional level of differentiated, one-to-one relationships; that is, each of the four family members would have a relatively open, direct, and clear relationship with the other three members of the family. Finally, if the family is characterized by open and direct relationships among its members, the family of origin and extended family, in conjunction with the nuclear family, is a better family structure for handling nodal and life-cycle events and stress in general because there are more avenues or possible relationships in which emotional process can be directed, bound, and resolved.

The emotional viability of the twosome, threesome, foursome, and larger groups ultimately rests on the level of differentiation of the individuals within that family and their capacity and willingness to deal with the anxiety elicited by the nodal and life-cycle events in which they are engaged.

From Fusion to the Interlocking Process of Fusion and Cutoff

A third conceptual development involved Bowen seeing, describing, and defining the concept of emotional cutoff. Bowen realized that triangles in the nuclear family interlocked with triangles in the extended family systems. He then linked the concept of interlocking triangles with the interrelated process of fusion and emotional cutoff; this shifted the focus of the theory and therapy from marital fusion to each spouse's unresolved attachment to his/her family of origin. From a focus on the fusion in the nuclear family, Bowen's therapy shifted to "bypassing the nuclear family," focusing on the family of origin and the wider extended family.

Bowen described emotional cutoff as the flip side of fusion. Emotional fusion and emotional cutoff constitute an interrelated, multigenerational phenomenon. One of the most significant clinical implications of understanding that fusion and cutoff are intertwined is the family systems postulate that states, *to the degree that there is fusion in one or more relationships in a single generation there is correlative emotional cutoff in one or more relationships in another generation.*

Summary

This section has described the evolution of three concepts in Bowen theory: (1) the family as an emotional unit or system, including functioning position; (2) interlocking triangles; and (3) the interlocking of fusion and cutoff. It demonstrates that what was initially spoken of in terms of the nuclear and extended family emotional systems is more consistent with evolutionary biology when contained in the concept that *the multigenerational family is an emotional unit or system.*

The clinical implications that have unfolded and paralleled the shifts of Bowen theory are as follows: first, Bowen family systems therapy focused on exploring and seeking to modify fusion in the nuclear family; second, the focus changed to exploring fusion in the marital dyad and the triangles within the nuclear family; third, the focus shifted to exploring and attempting to modify interlocking triangles involving the nuclear and extended family emotional systems; and fourth, the focus shifted to include emotional cutoffs and functioning positions spanning many generations.

Clinically, these movements lead from a focus on the theory of triangles and various means for de-triangling self, to a broader focus on emotional reactivity and efforts to become more neutral. This includes an effort to understand humankind's place in the natural world with the help of Bowen theory and input from evolutionary biology and other natural systems theory. The development and shifts in focus of Bowen theory culminate in a therapeutic focus on the principles and processes of differentiation of self.

DIFFERENTIATION OF SELF

The Principles of Differentiation of Self

The hallmark of Bowen theory and therapy is the concept of differentiation, which is a way of characterizing the balance/imbalance of two life forces or instincts: the force for togetherness and the force for individuality. Differentiation is used to describe an individual's ability to separate his/her instinctually driven emotional reaction from his/her thoughtfully considered goal-directed functioning. Individuals reside on a continuum constituted by this universal characteristic. At the level of the nuclear family, the concept of differentiation refers to the various patterns through which the nuclear family members exhibit their emotional oneness/separateness. Bowen used the term nuclear family emotional system to describe the patterns that family members manifest in being part of an emotional amalgam, including the various means through which they attempt to manage the interplay of the forces of togetherness in the face of anxiety (marital distance or conflict, dysfunction in one spouse, or projection onto one or more children).

Finally, Bowen's concept of differentiation refers to the relation between an individual and his/her parents in terms of the degree of unresolved/resolved attachment to the family of origin: "The degree of unresolved emotional attachment is equivalent to the degree of undifferentiation" (Bowen, 1978, p. 534).

From a Bowen perspective, the focus on differentiation is directed toward the therapist as well as the family. The therapist must work at being a separate self, and the main goal of therapy is to help the client and the family become more differentiated. The therapist is encouraged to do his/her own family-of-origin work in order to facilitate his/her efforts to be nonblaming and objective and to keep from being either emotionally fused or cut off from the clinical family. The therapist's main tool is himself or herself; being as differentiated as possible creates a space, an opening or invitation, for the client to improve his/her level of differentiation.

Bowen therapy does not seek a "united front" on the part of the parents against the child(ren). According to Bowen, parental "we-ness" is an emotional amalgam against which the child has difficulty developing an individual relationship with each parent (Bowen, 1978, p. 478). Bowen (1980a) noted the difficulty in seeing one's parents as separate beings: "It takes a long time before one can hear one's parents with their differences." Bowen (1978) wrote:

> On a clinical level, the "parental we-ness" presents the child with a parental amalgam which is neither masculine nor feminine and it deprives the child of knowing men by having an individual relationship with his father, and knowing women from the relationship with his mother. From the standpoint of triangles, the "parental we-ness" presents the child with a locked-in "two against one" situation which provides no emotional flexibility unless he can somehow manage to force a rift in the other side of the triangle. From a theoretical standpoint, the poorly defined selfs of the parents fuse into a common self and it is this that becomes the "parental we-ness." (p. 497)

From a Bowen perspective, the goal of therapy is to guide one or more family members (or parents) to become a more solid, defined self in the face of the emotional forces created by the marriage, children, and/or family of origin, in order to gain the clarity and conviction to carry through one's own positions. From Bowen's perspective, working on differentiation in relation to one's family is the "royal road" to becoming a more responsible and higher functioning individual. Working on self through traditional individual therapy avoids the reality that one's family, rather than the therapeutic relationship, is the crucible for becoming a higher functioning individual: "You were born into a *birthright* and you never give it up; all other relationships are transient" (Bowen, 1984). Bowen (1978) commented on a crucial difference between a social relationship and a family relationship: " . . . The nonfamily relationship may provide a reasonably comfortable existence as long as the relationship is calm, but it has a low tolerance for stress" (p. 539).

The concept of "differentiation of self" evolved as Bowen developed his theory in interaction with his clinical work and his own efforts to modify his position in his own family—his Promethean efforts to develop, apply, and live the theory in his own differentiation efforts.

According to Bowen, in the early 1960s, the working notion was that if one de-triangles from one's own parents that would be sufficient for a successful effort for differentiating a self. However, the problem, as Bowen discovered, was that one cannot differentiate from parents alone because parents are part of a "gigantic amalgam" originating in the past (Bowen, 1980a).

Bowen spent many years developing a one-to-one relationship with each parent. To do this, one has to go back several generations and compile a multigenerational history. Three generations is the absolute minimum, but four to seven generations is necessary. Bowen (1984) said, "Know the times they lived in." The researcher needs to obtain the vital statistics: births, deaths, cutoffs, marriages—the who, what, when, and where of the multigenerational family history.

From a theoretical standpoint, it is possible to de-triangle self from one's parents, but from a practical standpoint, one is much more than a product of one's parents (Bowen, 1980a). The primary triangle is embedded in the total family. One knows one's mother and father by knowing their families (Bowen, 1980a). One's ancestors faced the same issues as those existing in one's family of origin and in one's nuclear family. In the effort to define self to both parents, there will be many difficulties. If you could revive all that went on with parents it would be great, but it is virtually impossible to do. Bowen (1984) suggested getting to know as many people in your family as possible.

Bowen (1984) encouraged the differentiating one to:

> Study the immaturities of both parents [knowing] one is always an absorber of the triangle . . . being as objective as possible about the parents and the part one absorbed . . . self will rush in and be an "absorber" or a "cut-offer" . . . one reason that differentiation of self from parents is a difficult goal is because they are bigger "pretenders" than self . . . Anytime you run away with the immaturity, you put it in the next generation.

Bowen (1978) wrote of the depth, historically, in which a self is embedded:

> In only 150 to 200 years an individual is the descendent of 64 to 128 families of origin, each of which has contributed something to one's self. With all the myths and pretense and emotionally biased reports

and opinions, it is difficult to ever really know "self" or to know family members in the present or recent past. (p. 492)

Nevertheless, Bowen (1984) has said that, "Every person who dies has left tracks; if not facts, multiple opinions." And, according to Bowen (1984), "The more you know about the past, the more you know about you. . . . The feelings in the family, they are in all alive members."

Bowen (1978) described how gaining more objective knowledge about one's distant relatives helps an individual:

> . . . one become[s] aware that there are no angels or devils in the family; they were human beings, each with his own strengths and weaknesses, each reacting predictably to the emotional issue of the moment, and each doing the best he could with his life course. (p. 492)

Bowen (1984) described how he had been doing extended family work in his own family for twenty years. He found common ancestors back to 1730. Two people emigrated to the United States and from them came a multitude of descendents. Bowen believed that, "When you have a relationship with all those people, your functioning will be unbelievable. . . . To be human, not to build them up, or to tear them down. They are human and you are. Attempt to be more objective."

According to Bowen (1984), "The incidence of symptoms in the extended family will go down when one person stays in contact with the whole group." Bowen (1978) found that the successful effort that is directed " . . . toward improving the frequency and quality of emotional contact with the extended family, will predictably improve the family's level of adjustment and reduce symptoms in the nuclear family" (p. 538).

By 1967, Bowen's goal was to develop an "open relationship with every living relative," a goal he believed would do more for enhancing a solid self than anything else he could do in his whole life (Bowen, 1980a). In Bowen's words (1978), the process of differentiation:

> involves establishing a person-to-person relationship with each parent. In the extended family this process is equivalent to establishing personal communication between two spouses. The person-to-person relationship is one in which it is possible to talk about self as a person to the parent as a person. (p. 236)

Bowen (1984) said that if one was able to say anything he/she feels or thinks to his/her spouse, an individual would not have to go back to the extended family in order to modify one's relationships in the family of procreation. Bowen (1978) speculated about the efficiency of defining self in one's parental family:

> One speculation is that it is easier to make valid observations of emotional forces in the removed, but equally important, parental family, than in the nuclear family in which one's needs are more intimately embedded. It is also easier to take an action stand in the parental family than in the nuclear family. (p. 519)

Bowen (1978) described an "open relationship system" in contrast to a family system characterized by emotional fusion or cutoff: "[It] . . . is one in which family members have a reasonable degree of contact with one another" (p. 537). Openness reduces anxiety but does not in itself increase differentiation. However, it does allow for opportunities for motivated family members to increase their level of differentiation.

What does it mean to be a self in one's own family? Bowen's response was that one has to know and respect one's family. According to Bowen (1980a), "The family member that stays in contact with the family becomes a different person," but the goal is "being present and accountable." From this perspective, being emotionally attached or running away are both problems. The effort involves a move from "*changing* family to *making contact* with them" (Bowen, 1980a).

The basic goal of a differentiation of self effort has to be directed at changing self. Bowen (1984) was adamant in teaching that an individual attempting to differentiate self does not go back to "fix" the family. A differentiating effort will only be successful if it is undertaken for "self" alone. Bowen (1978) described why the differentiation effort must be for self rather than to change another family member or the family as a whole:

> If it is done for self alone and the effort is successful, the system automatically benefits also. If it is done primarily to help others or with the expectation that other will approve and express appreciation, then the effort was for togetherness and not for differentiation; an emotional system does not appreciate such stressful nefarious maneuvers in the service of togetherness. (p. 518)

Bowen (1984) believed that the differentiating one is perceived as an attractive person to the family when he/she can interact with the family when anxiety is high and still be neutral. Bowen (1984) said, "Proceed just for self. Then you will become known for what you did . . . If you work for self, the family will say thanks."

The work of the differentiating one must be done privately. It should not be shared with any other family member, including one's spouse.

As was described in a prior section, Bowen theory moved from focusing on fusion in the nuclear family to focusing on the interlocking process of fusion and cutoff. The process of differentiation of self takes place in the context of the family of origin and the larger extended family. Bowen (1980a) spoke of how the differentiating one needs to move from seeking to change his/her family to making contact with them. There are family members who are easy to contact and people who are difficult. One can reduce cutoff, but not completely, and there are two sides to a cutoff. Bowen (1978) defines emotional cutoff in the following terms:

> . . . emotional distancing, whether the cut-off is achieved by internal mechanisms or physical distance. . . . The person who runs away from home is as emotionally attached as the one who stays at home and uses internal mechanisms to control the attachment. The one who runs away does have a different life course. He needs emotional closeness but is allergic to it. He runs away kidding himself that he is achieving "independence." The more intense the cut-off with his parents the more he is vulnerable to repeating the same pattern in future relationships. He can have an intense relationship in a marriage which he sees as ideal and permanent at the time, but the physical distance pattern is part of him. When tension mounts in the marriage, he will use the same pattern of running away. He may go from one marriage to another, or through multiple living-together arrangements, or his relationships may be even more transient. An intense example of this is the relationship "nomad" who moves from one relationship to another, each time cutting off emotional ties to the past and investing self in the present relationship. (pp. 535-536)

Bowen (1978) described those people who use internal mechanisms to achieve emotional distance as utilizing another means of expressing emotional cutoff. They are more prone to dysfunction within self such as depression, alcoholism, and physical illness (p. 536). Bowen also pointed out that a majority of people draw upon various combinations of mechanisms to " . . . deal with the unresolved emotional attachments to their parents" (p. 536).

Bowen stated that in the beginning of a differentiating effort an individual can fool himself or herself into believing he/she is not being emotionally reactive to the family. However, as Bowen wrote, "Distance and silence do not fool an emotional system" (1978, p. 491).

The Process of Differentiation

The process of differentiation has two main steps: (1) developing a person-to-person relationship and (2) de-triangling. The capacity to accomplish those steps involves having and increasing an attitude of objectivity and neutrality in relation to, and in the midst of, one's family on the part of the differentiating one. The goal is to become a more differentiated self by developing person-to-person relationships with as many members of one's extended family as possible. The action process for accomplishing this is de-triangling. In order to make de-triangling moves, one has to understand the family system accurately by becoming a better observer and controlling one's emotional reactivity. De-triangling will be described in a later section, "Detriangling: Basic Principles of the Process." Bowen (1978) described the process of what goes into a person-to-person relationship as follows:

> It is one in which two people can relate personally to each other, without talking about each other, without talking about others [triangling], and without talking about impersonal "things" (p. 540). . . . A person to person relationship is conceived as an ideal in which two people can communicate freely about the full range of personal issues between them. (p. 499)

In the process of working on person-to-person relationships in one's family, one learns who fuses and who cuts off: ". . . one learns about emotional systems, the way people cling together, the way they drift apart in periods of anxiety, and the power of the emotional process between people who reject and repel each other" (Bowen, 1978, p. 540).

In Bowen's own differentiation work, he went from a painstaking effort to understand and modify patterns in his nuclear family to correlating those patterns with those he observed in his family of origin. After many years, Bowen (1978) enlarged the sphere of his effort:

> The new plan was to define myself as a person as much as possible and to communicate individually to a wide spectrum of extended family members; I tried to establish as many individual relationships within the family as possible. (p. 499)

Bowen found that research families did better in psychotherapy than families who were only seen for psychotherapy. After that discovery, Bowen sought to make every family he saw clinically into a research family (Bowen, 1978, p. 246). According to Bowen:

> Subtle and important things take place when the therapist functions as a "therapist" or a healer, and the family functions passively, waiting for the therapist to work his magic. Equally subtle and im-

portant factors are involved in getting a therapist out of his healing or helping position and getting the family into a position to accept responsibility for its own change. (1978, p. 246)

The researcher, or differentiating one, needs to gain control over his/her emotional reactivity to his/her own family, frequently visiting the parental family, especially during nodal events, and seeking to become a more objective observer in his/her family (Bowen, 1978, p. 531). The research effort is aimed at helping the trainee or motivated family member get a little bit "outside" the family emotional system in order to acquire a broader view of the human phenomenon, and it helps one move beyond blame and anger (Bowen, 1978, p. 541).

The work involved in achieving person-to-person relationships as well as in becoming a better observer and controlling one's own emotional reactiveness "helps create a more open relationship and reactivates the emotional system before one's cutoff from it" (Bowen, 1978, p. 542).

At this point, de-triangling, the other major component in the process of differentiation, is possible:

Now it is possible to see the triangles in which one grew up, and to be different in relation to them. . . . The overall goal [of de-triangling] is to be constantly in contact with an emotional issue involving two other people and self, without taking sides, without counterattacking or defending self, and to always have a neutral response. (Bowen, 1978, p. 542)

Bowen (1978) believed that one part of the process can be accomplished simply by placing oneself in the middle of the family during an emotional situation and being more objectively neutral or less reactive than the others (p. 542). Important natural events that serve as opportunities for the differentiating one to define self are the following: illness, death, homecomings, holidays, and other gatherings or rituals (Bowen, 1978, p. 542).

Bowen (1980a) applied a variety of principles to the operational process of de-triangling:

1. Work toward a person-to-person relationship with each person in the extended family.
2. Avoid emotional reactivity in returning to the family (again and again).
3. Recognize that the primary triangle is the most significant (the parents are fused, with one being the spokesman); set out to develop a one-to-one relationship with each parent separately.

4. Put more emphasis on resolving intensity with mother prior to resolving intensity with father; meet and get to know one's mother's important relatives—go to the periphery, then one's relationship to one's mother becomes softer and more viable; usually one can spend more time with the mother's side; this is culturally determined.

5. There are times when when one is emotionally "locked into" the parental triangle; focus instead on a triangle consisting of one parent, a family member who is emotionally important to the parent, and self; when the differentiating one is locked into the parental triangle, sometimes the block can be productively approached through a sibling (Bowen, 1978, p. 543).

6. Do not spend too much time differentiating from siblings; it is more useful to go back to the extended family.

7. Go home frequently and when anxiety is high (anniversaries, weddings, birthdays, and funerals); the goal is to get as much individual time with each member as possible; it can be difficult getting individuals alone, when one is working against family fusion; revive the family system and take responsibility for self.

8. Do the work for self, not to change the family; accept responsibility for self and for being a responsible family member.

9. Avoid confrontation; confrontation says more about the confronter trying to square the ledger; the expression of negative feelings to counter togetherness usually only leads to short-term gains.

10. When the parents are dead, go to the emotional field; you can obtain valuable information from cousins and other more distant family members; at times, contact with cousins can be more fruitful than contact with the nuclear family ("societies of cousins" can provide a magical connection); if the whole family is dead, go back to friends of the dead family.

11. Use approaches specific to explosive and peace/agree families: with peace/agree families, one has to stir up a "tempest in a teapot," and in a reactive family, one has to spend considerable time calming one's own reactivity; just be less reactive than the others.

Differentiation is the reverse process of triangling. According to Bowen (1978), if one takes steps toward a higher level of differentiation and stays in contact with the family, then one member of the family followed by another will take steps toward differentiation:

This chain reaction is the basis for the principle that change in the central triangle is followed by automatic change throughout the family system. The change in all others takes place automatically in the living situations of everyday life. Change is most rapid when the initial triangle involves the most important people in the system. (p. 218)

Specific de-triangling methods and techniques will be presented in a later section of this chapter, "Functions of the Therapist or Coach." They are applicable both to the efforts of the coach/therapist and the individual making an effort to modify his/her position in the family as part of a differentiation-of-self effort.

Clinical Approaches to Differentiation of Self

Bowen (1978) described three clinical approaches to differentiation of self: (1) psychotherapy with both spouses, (2) psychotherapy with one family member, and (3) psychotherapy with one spouse in preparation for a long-term effort with both spouses. The choice of approach depends upon family configuration and motivation (p. 223).

In 1960, Bowen (1978) began to exclude the child from ongoing family psychotherapy sessions with the parents (p. 244). He explained his rationale to the parents in the initial interview:

> . . . my conviction [was] that the basic problem lay in the relationship between the parents, and if the parents could define and modify their relationship, the children's problems would automatically disappear. A high percentage of parents readily accepted this working premise. (p. 245)

The present method of working with both spouses started about 1962, after Bowen had sufficiently developed the concept of the triangle and used it in clinical operation (Bowen, 1978, p. 247). This method is designed to *work* with the two most important members of the family, with the therapist replacing the triangled child. The therapist becomes a target for the family's efforts to involve or triangle a third person. The therapist's effort is to maintain meaningful contact with each member of the family without becoming an emotional part of the communication (Bowen, 1978, p. 312).

Bowen described the second clinical approach to differentiation of self, psychotherapy with one motivated family member, in the following terms:

> It works best with oldest children who usually feel more responsibility for their families and who are more motivated for such an effort. It requires that the single members be self-supporting, or else they never develop the emotional courage for change that might threaten

the family attitude about them. An optimum distance from the extended families is about 200 to 300 miles, which is close enough for frequent contact and far enough away to be outside the immediate emotional sphere of the family. . . . The average well-motivated young person will spend about 100 hours spread over a period of four or five years at such an effort. (1978, p. 482)

A third clinical approach involves family psychotherapy with one spouse in preparation for a long-term effort with both spouses. The motivated spouse is seen alone until the other spouse is willing to become a part of the effort. This approach is similar in the initial phase to family psychotherapy with a single family member:

The goal is to teach the family member about the functioning of emotional systems, to discover the part that self plays in the system and especially toward the other spouse, and to modify the system by controlling the part self plays. (Bowen, 1978, p. 237)

If the motivated spouse is successful in lowering his/her emotional reactivity toward the antagonistic spouse, the latter often asks to participate in the sessions. At that point, the method is identical to that used for both spouses.

Bowen (1978) found that the family of origin approach was more productive in a shorter period of time, with fewer sessions, than traditional family therapy appointments focused on the emotional interdependency of the marriage. In this regard, Bowen wrote the following: "Overall, for a motivated person, half a dozen one hour appointments a year are more productive than weekly formal family therapy appointments between the spouses" (p. 547).

Bowen (1978) came to the conclusion, based on his personal experience and clinical work, that:

. . . families in which the focus is on the differentiation of self in the families of origin automatically make as much or more progress in working out the relationship system with spouses and children as families seen in formal family therapy in which there is a principal focus on the interdependence in the marriage. (p. 545)

Change in Bowen Family Systems Therapy:
Formats, Phases, and Stages

This section describes the modification of Bowen's clinical approach, the phases that characterize a differentiation of self effort, and the stages that typify a family's reaction to an individual's effort to differentiate a self in relation to his/her family.

Changes in the Format of Bowen
Family Systems Therapy

Bowen initially worked with the nuclear family—methods he described as *family group therapy* and *multiple family group therapy* (when a number of families were seen together)—with hospitalized schizophrenics and their families at National Institutes of Mental Health (NIMH) from 1954 to 1959. In that phase, Bowen was guided by the theoretical assumption that a modicum of differentiation could be achieved through loosening the glue of the "undifferentiated ego mass," the emotional fusion in the nuclear family, particularly the symbiosis between the diagnosed schizophrenic offspring and his/her mother.

The second form of Bowen's therapy was directed at the nuclear family emotional system. Bowen worked with the two spouses or parents seeking to lessen emotional fusion and facilitate differentiation of self from the marital fusion. This form of differentiation work was made possible by Bowen's conceptualization of the triangle, in 1959, and became established between 1962 and 1964. In 1965, a variation of the focus on the two spouses/parents was multiple family therapy. The focus was on both the nuclear family and extended family emotional systems. Between 1966 and 1967, understanding and development of the concept of interlocking triangles led to a breakthrough in which the therapeutic focus became the effort to coach a motivated individual to differentiate a self in the context of his/her unresolved attachment to parents and the larger extended family.

Initially, when Bowen (1978) began to work with the couple, toward the end of his research project on hospitalized schizophrenics and their families, the following clinical method was used:

> . . . analysis of the intrapsychic process in one and then the analysis of the corresponding emotional reaction in the other. They continued the family therapy sessions three times a week for 18 months for a total of 203 hours. The result was far better than would ordinarily be expected with 600 hours of psychoanalysis for each. This family has been followed periodically by letter and telephone during the 12 years since the therapy was terminated, and their life course has been ideal. (p. 195)

With a clearer understanding of the concept of the emotional triangle in the mid-1960s, a method was designed to be effective for short-term therapy, and it could be applied to long-term therapy as well:

This method is designed to put the two most important family members into therapy with the therapist, which makes the therapist a target for family efforts to involve a third person. Progress in therapy depends on the therapist's ability to relate meaningfully to the family without becoming emotionally entangled in the family system. (Bowen, 1978, p. 312)

Bowen (1978) described the previous method as being effective as a short-term, middle-term, or long-term process. The length of therapy is determined by the motivation of the family. Bowen described short-term "cures" in as few as five to seven sessions (p. 316). Middle-term good results usually involved twenty to forty sessions " . . . when symptoms have subsided and the togetherness-oriented spouse exerts pressure to discontinue" (p. 316).

In discussing the criteria for positive outcome with this approach, Bowen (1978) wrote the following:

An orderly termination is reached when both have achieved a reasonable level of differentiation of self from each other, and from their families of origin; when they know enough about family systems so that one or the other of them has developed the capacity to handle crises; and when they have some kind of reasonable plan and motivation to continue working toward differentiation in the years ahead. (pp. 254-255)

In 1966, Bowen adapted his method of family systems therapy with two people for multiple family therapy. The therapist sees four families, with each family receiving a thirty-minute minisession while the other three families are nonparticipant observers. Bowen found that the average family in multiple family therapy made faster progress than those families who had one-hour individual sessions. He stated, "The difference appears related to the ability 'to hear' and learn from the other families without reacting emotionally" (1978, p. 317).

As a result of his experience with multiple family therapy, Bowen spread therapy over longer periods of time, with less frequent appointments. Bowen spoke of holding the majority of the sessions monthly. Long-term families continued for an average of five years. This included about sixty multiple family sessions and only thirty direct hours with the therapist (Bowen, 1978, p. 317). Bowen's favorable experience with seeing families monthly in the multiple family group led him to reduce the frequency of appointments with all families, " . . . whether therapy with multiple families or single families, to once every two weeks. An increasing number are seen once a month, and a small experimental group of families are being seen once every three months" (Bowen, 1978, p. 257).

According to Bowen, differentiation involves "a certain amount of time on the calendar." In Bowen's (1978) words:

> The families are able to accept responsibility for their own progress and to use the sessions for the therapist to supervise their efforts (p. 317). . . . Families are more on their own, made to be more resourceful and less dependent on therapy to provide working solutions. This also fits with my conviction that it takes a certain amount of time on the calendar for families to change, and the length of time necessary for change is not decreased by increasing the frequency of appointments. (p. 257)

Bowen (1978) described how his effort to differentiate a self in his own family and the presentation of that work in his teaching and therapy led to a turning point in his therapeutic method, with the focus turning toward *the differentiation of self in one's own family.* As has been described in the previous section:

> The method involved a detailed family history for multiple generations in the past and developing a personal relationship with all important living relatives. This activates old family relationships grown latent with neglect. Then, with the advantage of objectivity and the knowledge of triangles, the task is to detriangle old family triangles as they come to life. . . . It is easier to "see" self and modify one's self in triangles a bit outside the immediate living situation than in the nuclear family. (pp. 317-318)

With this approach, a person who is actively working can utilize coaching sessions about once a month. Bowen (1978) found that individuals who had access to teaching sessions did not even need private sessions, or only needed them infrequently. Some individuals who came from a great distance were only seen three or four times per year (p. 318). Although working on extended family is urged as a part of all family therapy, it often cannot be undertaken until anxiety is substantially reduced. Bowen described the possibility of success with extended family work as involving motivated people whose families are fairly intact but have drifted apart (p. 318). Those who have the least success in working on defining self in the family of origin:

> . . . are those who are repulsed with the idea of contacting extended family and those whose families are extremely negative. In between

are all different levels of motivation and families with varying degrees of fragmentation and distance. There is not a serious problem when parents are dead if there are other surviving relatives. Reasonable results are possible with those who have no living relatives. (Bowen, 1978, p. 319)

Phases in Bowen Family Systems Therapy with Both Spouses or Both Parents

Bowen described therapy as having certain predictable phases: In the first or early phase, the couple come to know each other better, some quickly and others gradually. When families are motivated to continue, the process facilitates each spouse beginning to differentiate a self from the other, proceeding in alternating small steps (Bowen, 1978, p. 253).

Each small step in the process of differentiation " . . . stirs emotional disharmony in extended families and other interlocking emotional systems, which is generally easier to handle than the disharmony between the spouses" (Bowen, 1978, p. 253). After the coach/therapist helps lower the anxiety of the family by working to stay emotionally neutral in the presence of the clinical family's emotional field, the first phase of differentiation begins when one spouse begins to take responsibility for self and begins to blame the other less. Then the other evokes the togetherness forces:

> The togetherness pressure includes accusations of lack of love, indifference, not caring, and lack of appreciation. When the differentiating one is sure enough of self to proceed calmly on course, in spite of the togetherness pleading in the other, without defending self or counterattacking, and without withdrawing, the attack subsides and the differentiating process passes through its first major nodal point. (Bowen, 1978, pp. 315-316)

This first phase takes approximately one to two years. The second phase involves a period of calm and a new higher level of adjustment in both spouses. In the third phase, the second spouse begins similar differentiating efforts to change self, and in turn, the first spouse begins to be the promoter of togetherness.

However, new cycles in the alternating spousal differentiation process take less time and are less clearly defined than the initial efforts. The forces of individuality emerge slowly, and in the beginning, the forces of togetherness drive the couple back to a tenuous but more stabilized emotionally fused position (Bowen, 1978, p. 316). According to Bowen (1978), the family system automatically moves to restore itself to its former symptom-free emotional equilibrium, following either a disturbance caused by the regression of a family member or the movement of a family member toward a slightly higher level of differentiation (p. 495).

Phases in Bowen Family Systems Therapy
with One Family Member

Working on differentiating a self in one's family of origin and the larger extended family can also be described as going through a number of phases. They are not clearly linear; they are mutually interdependent.

The first phase involves understanding self in one's family emotional system (nuclear, family of origin, and larger extended family). During this phase, there is a lowering of acute anxiety and a lessening in symptoms presented by the differentiating one. The second phase involves efforts to modify one's position in one's family. The third phase focuses on dealing with the ripples from the family's reaction to the individual's differentiating efforts. The fourth phase involves other family members making efforts to differentiate a self in relation to the family.

In making efforts to differentiate a self in one's family of origin, one tends to go through predictable phases. Initially, there is the elation of the first contact; the second phase involves the gritty one-to-one contact with family members; and finally, there is a shift to focusing on one's own challenge to be a self (Bowen, 1981).

Stages in a Family's Reaction to an Individual's Effort
to Differentiate a Self

There are three predictable stages through which the family passes when responding to any small step toward differentiation on the part of the differentiating one: (1) "You are wrong"; (2) "Change back"; and (3) "If you do not, these are the consequences." These steps can be expressed in many different ways, but they are so predictable that if they do not follow a differentiating effort then that effort probably was not successful (Bowen, 1978, pp. 216,495).

Bowen (1978) described the differentiating one as responding in one of two ways; either within self or in response to the family. Within self, the symptoms can involve emotional, social, or physical dysfunction. The responses to the family can typically include the following: merging into the family togetherness within hours of the family's reaction; fighting back; silence and withdrawal; or running away, never to return. These responses on the part of the differentiating one are all a part of the "family reaction-response system" (Bowen, 1978, p. 216). However, if the differentiating one can control his/her automatic emotional reactivity, it interrupts the "chain reaction," and differentiation can slowly occur (Bowen, 1978, p. 216).

BOWEN'S PERSPECTIVE ON THE THERAPEUTIC RELATIONSHIP

According to Bowen (1978), Freud defined the basic theory underlying the therapeutic relationship. In this regard, Bowen wrote:

> The growing multitudes of mental health professionals who use all the different theories and therapies still follow two of the basic concepts of psychoanalysis. One is that emotional illness is developed in relationship with others. The second is that the therapeutic relationship is the universal "treatment" for emotional illness. (p. 339)

Based on family research, Bowen (1978) identified some characteristics of emotional systems that place the therapeutic relationship in a broader perspective: " . . . the successful introduction of a significant other person into an anxious or disturbed relationship system has the capacity to modify relationships within the system" (p. 342). Bowen also believed that the individually oriented psychotherapist can be a significant other who can modify relationships within a system. If he/she can manage the intensity of the transference and if the patient stays in "viable contact with the family, it can calm and modify relationships within the family" (p. 342).

From Bowen's perspective, problems occur when the therapist and the patient become so intensely involved with each other that the patient withdraws from emotional contact with the family, and in turn, the family becomes more disturbed. This represents a triangle in which the therapist and patient are an overly close twosome with the family being the distant outside leg of the triangle. Bowen believed that many therapists, without raising it to a thematic awareness, have ways of handling the intensity of the therapeutic transference. According to Bowen (1978), "Some choose to intensify the relationship into a therapeutic alliance, and to encourage the patient to challenge the family" (p. 343). Bowen believed that the most important variable is the assumed, assigned, or actual importance of the significant other, and there are all kinds of distorted importance attributed to the significant other by the patient. Bowen pointed out that psychoanalysis has subtle techniques to increase transference. At one end of the continuum of increasing transference, the significant other evangelizes and makes promises regarding the things he/she will produce if he/she is invited in. At the other extreme, according to Bowen (1978):

> ... the significant other enters the system only on solicited invitation and with a contract either verbal or written that comes closer to defining the reality of the situation of the time. (p. 344)

One factor in the success or failure of the involvement of the significant other depends on whether the family member devotes a reasonable amount of thinking-feeling energy to the relationship without becoming emotionally preoccupied (Bowen, 1978, p. 344). According to Bowen (1978):

> The more the relationship with the significant other is endowed with high emotionality, messianic qualities, exaggerated promises, and evangelism, the more the change can be sudden and magical, and the less likely it is to be long term. (pp. 345-346)

Bowen believed that high levels of emotionality are elicited by the majority of therapists from their patients.

Bowen's approach was to avoid transference, knowing that all therapists are subject to being drawn into an emotional system. He did this by attempting to eliminate assumed and assigned importance from the therapeutic relationship. Successful management of transference in schizophrenia served as a model for Bowen, and it made it easier to:

> ... manage the milder transferences of the neuroses. The change to family research provided a new dimension for dealing with the therapeutic relationship. It became theoretically possible to leave the intensity of the relation between the original family members, and bypass some of the time consuming detail. I began to work toward avoiding the transference. (1978, p. 346)

Bowen's position was that if a therapist has knowledge of family systems, and particularly a working understanding of triangles, he/she can deal, for the most part, in the realm of facts and "eliminate much of the emotional process that usually goes into transference" (1978, p. 346). Bowen stated that all therapists, even those trained in the systems approach, are vulnerable to automatically falling back into the emotionality of transference. Bowen constantly used mechanisms to reduce assumed and assigned overimportance, such as charging standard fees and not evoking his status as a pioneer in the field of family therapy.

Bowen (1984) described the problem that arises when there is an "unconscious breach of promise." This involves the therapist making an implicit promise that seeing an individual is going to make the problem better, when in fact the problem might actually get worse. If a therapist can be clear about what he/she can or cannot do, the client makes better progress. Bowen spoke of trying ". . . to be predictably present"; the therapeutic contract should be based on " . . . what you can reasonably deliver" (Bowen, 1984). Bowen (1995) articulated clearly, as far back as 1956 when he was involved in carrying out his NIMH research on schizophrenia, the need to have a way of dealing with "Patients' expectations beyond the reality capacity of the staff" (p. 26). Bowen (1995) described his experience in the following way:

> Experience with this brought an acute awareness of how much the average patient implicitly expects from his psychiatrist, how much the psychiatrist implicitly expects he can do for the patient, and how long the situation can go without becoming openly recognized and stated. It also brought an awareness of how little a psychiatrist can guarantee to the patient. He cannot realistically promise that he can understand, that his efforts will be helpful, or even promise that he will continue to be interested in trying to help. Eventually a concise way was developed for dealing with the unstated and unreal expectations of the patients. This was for the psychiatrist to work toward changing the implicit into an explicit request, to make explicit clear statements to meet only the demands he could fulfill with certainty, to live up to his agreed promise with meticulous certainty, and to openly refuse any request he could not fulfill to the letter. The clarification of this issue was a turning point. It was the experience that the patients did not expect the impossible and they were very secure with a clear concise statement of what the doctor would and would not do. The staff was then free to set the limits at what could be realistically provided rather than according to the patient's anxiety. (p. 27)

The guiding premise for Bowen was staying outside the transference or automatic emotional relationship within the family. As Bowen (1978) states, "It is accurate to say there is some emotionality in any relationship, but it is also accurate to say that the emotionality can be reduced to a low level through knowledge about emotional systems" (p. 347). Bowen (1978) believed that he differed from the other mainstream family therapists because he learned more about the complexity and details of the therapeutic relationship from being involved in designing and carrying out family research (p. 348). He adopted a "research attitude" to maintain distance from overinvolvement in the intensity of the therapeutic relation-ship. He was able to stay out of the transference through his evolving knowledge of triangles and how they operated and by keeping the work between the family member and his/her family. Understanding the concept of triangles provides a blueprint for reading automatic emotional respon-siveness and thereby allowing the coach to control his/her own participa-tion in the emotional process. Bowen called this process of staying outside the transference de-triangling. No one ever stays outside completely, but one can do reasonably well with a knowledge of triangles, while maintain-ing emotional contact with the family. When one family member is moti-vated to learn about and control his/her emotional reactivity, he/she can influence the entire family unit (Bowen, 1978, p. 349).

The assumption is that the individual and the family know what they need. A Bowen therapist respects the family members as persons who need to define themselves as separate individuals. The Bowen therapist takes the position, "I stand here and you stand there," and from that position, "I am able to hear you."

The therapist who follows Bowen theory seeks to be a neutral observer, knowing that he is frequently unable to maintain that detachment and has to work toward it. Therapy based on Bowen theory seeks to be neutral and de-triangled from the client and his/her emotional entanglements within his/her family. In this regard, the Bowen-oriented therapist does not emo-tionally side with one family member in therapy against other members of the family. The therapist seeks to be neutral and equally open to all family members, seen and unseen, without emotionally fusing with, or cutting off from, any one family member or any segment of the family. Systems thinking is neutral, nonblaming, nonreactive, and nontriangling; it seeks to see things the way they are, not the way they should be.

THE ROLE OF THE THERAPIST OR COACH

Just as the differentiating one attempts to avoid being a fixer of his/her family, so the effort of the therapist is to avoid trying to fix or change the clinical family. The most important variable in doing therapy depends on the therapist's own emotional functioning—the capacity to remain neutral when working with an emotional system. The therapist has to avoid being drawn into the family's emotional fusion. Bowen (1984) made the follow-ing comment about staying out of the fusion, or what he described as "clumpiness":

> People tend to "clump" themselves and the subhuman world tends to fuse together. Each nuclear family "clumps" together. Standing up

for self in relation to the group is central. Seeing the whole group increases "clumpiness." How are you going to "unclump" with another person? The problem is the therapist "clumping" with the "clump." Differentiation of self involves staying out of the feeling world. Leave the "clump" alone and stay outside of it; the "clump" automatically decreases its "clumpiness."

Over time, as the focus shifted from modifying fusion in the nuclear family toward focusing on one or more individuals' efforts to differentiate a self in relation to the nuclear and/or family of origin, Bowen began describing the therapist by the term "coach." In broad terms, the position of the family systems therapist is that of coach, consultant, supervisor, researcher, learner, and questioner. Bowen (1978) believed that the term coach "is probably the best in conveying the connotation of an active expert coaching both individual players and the team to the best of their abilities" (p. 310). This author (Titelman, 1987) described the choice of the term coach and its analogical implications in the following way:

> Like a football coach, the Bowen family systems coach is on the sidelines. Both serve as teachers/consultants who prepare the player(s)/client(s), but the player(s)/client(s) need to translate the learning into action on the playing field and family turf . . . The systems coach and the sports coach both teach the client family members(s) or team member(s) the theory, application, and long-term conditioning for how the sport or family operates. (p. 22)

When the coach functions as a therapist, he/she is indirectly supporting the family's passivity insofar as he/she supports its waiting for the therapist to do his/her "magic."

In this book, the term *therapist* will be used synonymously with the term *coach*. Therapist tends to be used more frequently when referring to work with more than one family member in the consultation. Conversely, *coach* is used more frequently when referring to the consultation process with one family member.

Significant progress is possible when a therapist/coach forgoes a helping or healing position and encourages the family to accept responsibility for its own change (Bowen, 1978, p. 246). The coach seeks to help one or more family members work on differentiation of self rather than seeking to change one or more family members.

From the perspective of the Bowen theoretical-therapeutic system, family systems therapy is generated from the way the coach thinks about the family, " . . . whether the effort is with multiple family members, the two spouses together, or only one family member" (Bowen, 1978, p. 310).

Common Misunderstandings of the Bowen Approach

In many ways, the Bowen approach and method is often misunderstood. Some family therapists have portrayed the Bowen perspective as overly focused on history and not adequately focused on changing the family in the present through action. Actually, the Bowen approach focuses on dealing with the multigenerational family emotional system through themes, patterns, functioning positions, and symptom eruptions, as they have emerged from the past but are encountered in the present, in relation to the nuclear family, family of origin, and larger extended family. More than any other family therapy approach, Bowen's theoretical-therapeutic system sponsors the differentiating one in going back into the family and making contact with it in the present, whether the issues involve fusion or emotional cutoff, including all the manifestations in which those two faces of undifferentiation interlock and express themselves.

Another fundamental misunderstanding of the Bowen theoretical-therapeutic system is the often-heard characterization that it is an overly intellectualized or cognitive approach that supports emotional distancing among family members. Rather, the Bowen approach supports, guides, and teaches members of a family to seek repeated contact with the important and less important members of the actual multigenerational family during times of calm, but particularly when the family is going though important nodal events, such as births, weddings, illnesses, deaths, rituals, as well as holidays, important milestones, and achievements on the part of one or more members or segments of the family. The Bowen approach never wavers in its efforts to support a family member's effort to deal with the emotional forces in the family. Rather than sponsor direct emotional exchange, catharsis, or confrontation among family members, the Bowen approach seeks to help one or more family members find ways to react more neutrally in the face of the emotionally charged force of togetherness.

Other significant differences between Bowen's theoretical-therapeutic system and other types of individual and family therapies involves Bowen's work with the "strength" versus the "weakness" of the family emotional system; with the "top of the system" versus the "bottom of the system"; and with the "pursuer" rather than the "distancer" in that system. In regard to working with the strength in the family, Bowen (1978) wrote the following:

> One of the most difficult changes has been finding ways to relate to the healthy side of the family instead of the weak side. It is a slow

laborious task to improve the functioning of the weakest family member. It is many times more effective to work through the healthy side of the family. Opposing this are the family forces to create the patient and the popular notion that psychiatrists are to treat mental illness. . . . The search for the most responsible, most resourceful, and most motivated part of the family can be elusive. It is best determined from knowledge of the family emotional process and the functioning patterns in the past and present generations, in collaboration with the family. The potential source of family strength can be submerged in an emotional impasse with a nonproductive family member. (p. 310)

Bowen believed that therapy—an effort toward differentiation of self—is faster and includes a higher level of motivation when it involves the coaching of an oldest son or an oldest daughter who feels responsible for family problems and can stay in reasonable contact with his/her family. On the other hand, Bowen (1978) indicated that younger children can work toward differentiation of self, but the effort takes longer because they ". . . are more inclined to expect the environment to change for them and . . . are slower to grasp the idea that they have the capacity to change family patterns if they so desire" (p. 236).

A general rule of thumb, from a Bowen perspective, is that the coach seeks to work with the "top of the system," rather than the "bottom." In other words, the therapy effort bypasses focusing on the symptomatic child and focuses instead on the architects of the family, the parents. However, he occasionally included children in sessions for special reasons. According to Bowen (1978):

This approach has never been successful with a young adult still financially dependent on his family. They have an aptitude for quickly understanding family emotional systems, but they lack the courage to risk family displeasure in the differentiation process. (p. 235)

FUNCTIONS OF THE THERAPIST OR COACH

Bowen described the role of the coach in family systems therapy with two spouses or both parents as consisting of the following four functions: (1) defining and clarifying the relationship between the spouses; (2) keeping self de-triangled from the family emotional system; (3) demonstrating differentiation by taking an "I position" stands during the course of the therapy, which in turn allows one or both of the spouses to establish I positions between themselves; and (4) teaching the functioning of emotional systems and encouraging one or both of the spouses to work toward differentiation of self in relation to his/her family of origin (1978, pp. 247,481).

Defining and Clarifying the Relationship Between the Spouses

From a Bowen perspective, therapy/coaching aims first to lower anxiety, thereby reducing symptoms. Symptoms are anxiety binders. Bowen (1979) believed that the two major ways of reducing anxiety are drugs and relationships. Relationships in the family, and outside of it, tone down anxiety. The next goal is to help one or more family members gain a higher level of differentiation of self—a more solid self. When the therapist/coach begins to help one or more family members define and clarify the family emotional system, anxiety lessens, and symptom reduction occurs automatically as a consequence.

In the initial period of working with both spouses, Bowen focused on having each spouse "externalize intrapsychic process." Somewhat later, Bowen focused on the relationship system. The emphasis was on the careful discrimination between thoughts and feelings, since spouses tended to overreact to the communication of feelings (Bowen, 1978, p. 225). Finally, the present approach involves the therapist/coach maintaining a role of an interested clinical investigator asking about the details of the problem. For every answer there are more questions. Bowen (1979) left "the impression that if these questions are to be answered, someone in the family will have to become a better observer" (p. 225).

Very early in the development of this version of systems therapy, Bowen (1978) ". . . discouraged spouses from attempting to talk more at home; and after about 1962 I stopped suggesting that they talk directly to each other in the family therapy sessions" (p. 248). The goal is to maintain a structure of communication in which the spouses talk to the therapist instead of directly to each other (Bowen, 1978, p. 230).

In defining and clarifying the relationships between the spouses, the goal is to get them to *think and talk about* the feeling, rather than expressing it. It is important to define the *emotional triggers;* they consist of the negative stimuli, mannerisms, gestures, facial expressions, and tones of voice of one spouse that generate negative emotional responses in the other (Bowen, 1978, p. 250). This stimulus-response system, utilizing any of the five senses, is beyond the intellectual conscious awareness of the spouses so the therapist helps each spouse become less reactive to unconscious stimuli from the other (Bowen, 1978, p. 249).

The principal method for helping the two spouses or parents clarify their relationship system involves providing a structure in which each spouse talks directly to the therapist/coach in a relatively factual, calm voice:

> It is talking about emotional process, rather than communication of emotional process. The therapist avoids a structure in which family members talk directly to each other. Even when the emotional climate is calm, direct communication can increase the emotional tension. This one technique is a major change from earlier methods in which emotionally distant family members were encouraged to talk directly to each other. (Bowen, 1978, p. 313)

The therapeutic principle involves a focus on process rather than on content to keep tension low (Bowen, 1978, p. 229). A typical session involves the therapist eliciting a comment from one spouse and then, to avoid possible triangling, getting the other spouse to respond with his/her thoughts about the other's comments. When either of the spouses' comments are minimal, the therapist asks a series of questions to elicit a clearer view of that spouse's thinking. The therapist/coach seeks a summary of thoughts and ideas, avoiding feelings or subjective responses. In Bowen's (1978) opinion, "this process of externalizing the thinking of each spouse in the presence of the other is the epitome of the 'magic of family therapy' " (p. 314). Spouses are fascinated to learn about how the other thinks and they feel challenged to be as expressive and articulate as possible (Bowen, 1978, p. 314).

When a spouse responds emotionally toward the other spouse:

> The therapist increases the calm questions to defuse the emotion and to focus the issue back to him. The therapist is always in control of the sessions, asking hundreds of questions and avoiding interpretations. By considering each new family as a research project, the therapist always has so many questions there is never time to ask more than a fraction of them. (Bowen, 1978, p. 315)

The process of getting the spouses to communicate their thoughts and ideas sets the stage for differentiation of self; they begin to achieve an awareness of self and the other and of their differences that was not possible before. In this way, "A line of demarcation begins developing between the spouses and they clarify the beliefs and principles that differ one from the other" (Bowen, 1978, p. 225). When either spouse begins taking action stands based on principles, they then face the predictable emotional reactions, described in a previous section, associated with the steps in the differentiation of self. According to Bowen (1978), "The emotion that accompanies differentiation is contained within the twosome, it is cohesive rather than disruptive, and it is followed by a new level of more mature togetherness" (p. 227).

De-Triangling: Basic Principles of the Process

All methods and techniques in Bowen family systems therapy represent specific efforts on the part of the therapist/coach and the differentiating family member(s) to move toward defining a self in the family, and therefore, they are in the service of de-triangling. De-triangling, according to Bowen (1978), is emotional nonparticipation; it means staying out of the family emotional system and gaining:

> . . . some control over taking sides with any family faction . . . (p. 192)
> . . . . become nonparticipant observers . . . and . . . regard the family as a phenomenon (p. 191) . . . a tension system between two people will resolve itself in the presence of a third person who can avoid emotional participation with either while still relating actively to both (p. 190)
> . . . . Emotional nonparticipation or staying out of the family emotional system does not mean the therapist is cold or distant, or aloof. Instead, it requires the therapist to recognize his own emotional involvement when it does occur, to gain sufficient control over his emotional system to avoid emotional side-taking with any family member, to observe the family as a phenomenon, and to be able to relate freely to any family member at any time. (p. 192)

Bowen broadly described de-triangling in the following statement:

> When there is finally one who can control his emotional responsiveness and not take sides with either of the other two, and stay constantly in contact with the other two, the emotional intensity within the twosome will decrease and both will move to a higher level of differentiation. Unless the triangled person can remain in emotional contact, the twosome will triangle in someone else. (p. 480)

De-triangling takes many forms, such as expressing neutrality-objectivity, humor, reversal, systems questioning, and avoiding fusion by putting the other together with the other or phantom other. These techniques are used both to elicit and clarify the emotional system and to de-triangle from it.

From the perspective of Bowen theory:

> The therapeutic system is directed at modifying the functioning of the
> most important triangle in the family system. If the central triangle
> changes, and stays in contact with others, the entire system will auto-
> matically change. . . . In even the most "fixed" triangle, the positive
> and negative forces shift back and forth constantly. The term *fixed*
> refers to the most characteristic position. (Bowen, 1978, p. 479)

A basic principle in de-triangling states, "If one can modify the functioning of a single triangle in an emotional system, and the members of
that triangle stay in emotional contact with the larger system, the whole
system is modified" (Bowen, 1978, p. 245). At a practical level, there are
two ways to modify the function of triangles. The first method involves
putting two people from a family emotional system into contact with a
third person who understands how triangles operate and who does not get
caught up in the predictable moves of the "familiar twosome" (Bowen,
1978, pp. 24-26). The second way to modify the function of a triangle is
through the efforts of one family member:

> If one member of a triangle can change, the triangle will predictably
> change, an entire extended family can change. Thus, an entire family
> can be changed through one family member, if this motivated family
> member has sufficient dedication and life energy to work toward his
> goal in spite of all obstacles . . . *An entire family can be changed
> through the effort of one person.* (Bowen, 1978, p. 246)

The basic principle in Bowen's (1978) theoretical-therapeutic system is
that ". . . the emotional problem between two people will resolve automatically if they can remain in contact with a third person who can remain free of
the emotional field between them, while actively relating to each" (p. 229).
As Bowen (1983) said, "For every issue there is an opposing issue. And
systems helps you see the opposing sides and triangles means getting hung
up one side."

In the 1980s, the latter years of his career, Bowen expressed considerable
concern that too much focus was being placed on therapeutic technique
rather than on knowledge of Bowen theory, natural systems theory, and the
effort needed for the therapist to differentiate a self. Bowen still acknowledged that triangles are the blueprint for understanding and modifying a
family member's position in the family emotional system, but that he " . . .
doesn't bother with triangles . . . just sit with the family and be less reactive" than they are." For Bowen, technique became less focused on an
active intervention and more characterized by "what one believes . . . what

are the things one's responsible to" (Bowen, 1980b). This effort on the part of the therapist/coach to define self to the family will be described in a later section on "I-positions."

Expressing Neutrality and Objectivity

Staying emotionally neutral is the first priority of the therapist. Bowen (1984) asked the questions "How do you go about relating to the emotional system without being a part of it?" and "How do you go about relating to the emotional system in a neutral way, without rejecting it or joining it?" Bowen's posing those questions is a way of saying that neutrality is a very difficult task; it is also a way of saying that this effort must be accomplished by each therapist alone. There is no formula for achieving the capacity to be neutral and objective. The therapist must avoid taking sides, while being in contact with all members of the family, and still be able to discuss emotional issues (Bowen, 1978, p. 224). Each therapist has to find his/her own way of maintaining emotional neutrality. It may involve sitting in a certain position, writing notes on a pad in order to disengage visually, addressing the family members as Mr., Ms., Mrs., Dr., and referring to oneself using one's professional title or credential, among other devices. Bowen (1987a) provided the following explanation of the value of addressing family members by their proper names in order to maintain neutrality and avoid confusion with the family process:

> I think anytime you use first names it automatically pulls the therapist into part of the emotional process going on in the family. . . . I think one of the hardest things to do is to use a proper name with a schizophrenic person, because people with low level functioning are acting so much like children that they literally force you to use first names. . . . That is a very difficult one to do. I worked on that damn thing for years. . . . And if you can stay with proper names the whole emotional process goes better. The family can keep it more within them and I can keep it more within me. That's the process of the therapist getting mixed up in the family thing.

Bowen's (1978) best operating emotional distance was that position from which he was able to see emotional process flowing back and forth among the family members (p. 313). In speaking about the relationship between anxiety and neutrality, Bowen (1984) said if the therapist or coach " . . . can relate neutrally you are the greatest asset to the family—most therapists are either oversympathetic or rejecting—then you can be the figure they can use to pull up—priceless. How do you relate to them without rejecting them?" Feeling sorry for family members is a trigger that indicates that the coach/therapist has lost his/her position of neutrality (Bowen, 1974, p. 45). And, if the coach/therapist is unable to think of what to say—draws a blank—he/she is emotionally entangled and has lost a neutral/objective position.

Bowen (1988) asked another pithy question pertaining to neutrality: "Am I there because I want to be there or because the patient wants me to be there?" A therapist knows that he/she is being neutral in the clinical setting when he/she (1) can walk out of therapy without inheriting the family's problems, and (2) can be with the family without merging with it—relate to it, but be apart from it. And, Bowen (1984) answered his question, "What do you do to stay neutral?", with the comment, "Listen." Bowen (1984) emphasized that neutrality is expressed by trying to stay in contact with, and relate to, the grown-up part rather than the infant part of the family members. One way Bowen (1979) would evoke the grown-up side of a family member was to say, "Give me a few minutes of your most objective thinking." In this way, the therapist/coach seeks to bypass the conflict or anxiety.

The Use of Humor, Seriousness, and Reversal

The use of humor and reversal are two techniques that deintensify an emotionally loaded situation in a family. The "reversal," or paradoxical comment, is a technique that focuses on the opposite side of an issue. The comment neutralizes a polarizing statement or position held by one or more family members. These techniques can only be used effectively when the therapist or coach is able to communicate from a neutral or objective perspective. These techniques function in the service of the efforts of the therapist/coach to de-triangle from the family. Bowen (1978) tried to find the right balance between seriousness and humor which would communicate to the family that he was neither taking their dilemmas too seriously or too lightly, in order to facilitate the process in the family (p. 250). In Bowen's (1978) words:

> If the family goes too serious, I have an appropriate humorous re-
> mark to defuse the seriousness. If the family starts to kid and joke, I
> have an appropriate serious remark to restore neutrality. An example
> was a wife going into detail about her critical, nagging, bossy moth-
> er. The husband was indicating his agreement. If the therapist per-
> mitted them to believe he also agreed, he would be in the emotional
> process with them. His comment, "I thought you appreciated your
> mother's devotion to you," was enough to change the seriousness to
> a chuckle and defuse the emotional tension. (p. 313)

A casual comment or reversal is an effective way of defusing or decompressing an emotionally intense situation, helping the therapist/coach maintain a neutral position and offering a clear message to the family that the coach/therapist is not overinvolved. If the therapist/coach is emotionally overinvolved with the family, the reversal is heard as an expression of sarcasm or hostility, and the effort fails (Bowen, 1978, pp. 251,313,315). For example, if the coach says to a family member, who is reacting emotionally to a mother who is intrusively offering advice, "Your mother certainly goes out of her way to be helpful," the comment may be heard either as hostile or sarcastic if the timing or tone of the reversal is tinged with emotional reactivity on the part of the coach.

Adopting a Research Attitude and Systems Questioning

The therapist maintains the role of researcher, an interested clinical investigator who has many questions to ask the family. Bowen assigned the family tasks of becoming "research observers" of their own families. And a major part of each therapy session was spent on their report on their efforts to see self as it functions in the context of the family (Bowen, 1978). As Bowen wrote, "A goal of this therapy is to help the other make a research project out of life" (Bowen, 1978, p. 179). The therapist seeks to keep the tone of the session objective and the discussion directed toward facts and efforts to define self and toward a more defined position on the part of one of the spouses. The therapist opens the session by asking the family what they want to discuss. It may also be left to the therapist to raise an issue for discussion. The therapist has one spouse present a clear picture of his/her thinking and then gets a response from the other spouse and then a response to the response, continuing on in this vein. He/she may say to the spouse who is listening to the other spouse, "What were you thinking while your wife (or husband) was talking? What is your impression about this situation? What is your reaction?" (Bowen, 1978, p. 226). Bowen describes the effort to soothe feelings. In response to tears on the part of a wife, Bowen (1978) would say, "What were the thoughts that ticked off the feeling? Did you notice your wife's tears? What did you think when you saw them?" (p. 227).

The family systems therapist or coach places responsibility on the family for bringing about change. Questioning is one of the chief ways of de-triangling. The therapist or coach maintains the role of researcher or an interested clinical investigator who has a stream of unending questions to ask the family. The list of questions increases rather than diminishes with each session. Change involves understanding based on developing a map, or a family diagram, illustrating the multigenerational family emotional system. The functions of the question in family systems therapy include the following: (1) to understand the who, what, when, where, and how in relation to the history of the family; (2) to call attention to a process or pattern of behavior in the family; (3) to de-triangle through detoxifying hot issues; avoiding attacking, defending, or withdrawing; lowering reactivity and anxiety; and avoiding giving advice; and (4) to increase the ability to observe.

In the past, interpretations were eagerly awaited by the family and they avoided finding their own answers (Bowen, 1978, p. 215). Bowen (1978) described the clinical use of questions in the following way:

> About a fourth of the comments by the therapist are designed to detriangle the situation when a family member invokes the emotional process in a session. In the background are questions about events since the last session. . . . One parent usually spends much time thinking about the family problem, and the other has thought little about it. The therapist is always interested in who has been thinking, how much he has thought, what was the pattern of the thoughts, and what kinds of working conclusions came from the thinking. The therapist implies with questions that it is the family's problem to solve. He asks if they have made progress, if they have any ideas about how to get past the blocks, if they have any plans to speed up progress, and many other questions of this nature. (p. 225)

Putting the Other Together with the Other

Bowen (1987b) described a technique he used—"putting the other together with other"—in his efforts to differentiate from the fusion in his professional family, the family of family therapists. This involved his efforts to differentiate a self from other family therapists. These efforts were highlighted at three national meetings on family therapy in Philadelphia, in 1967, in San Francisco, in 1977, and in Phoenix, in 1986, and they were aimed at differentiating a self from important colleagues and their theoretical positions, namely, Whitaker, Ackerman, Erickson, Bateson, Haley, Minuchin, and others, as well as all the current therapists who represented their descendent "relatives."

In order to stay out of the emotional process of his own family and his professional family, Bowen sought to disengage from every person in his family and every person at large professional gatherings. The technique (Bowen, 1987b) involved "taking every person you meet and bring in a third person . . . You can get out of the fusion by putting the other together with the . . . other." Bowen put each person together with an other in order to de-triangle himself. With his own family, he "put the other together with another family member," and in his efforts with his professional family, he did the same. Bowen (1987b) said, "When you bring someone together with another . . . you are doing it, compared to it being done to you." An example of Bowen's putting one family member together with another, to escape the emotional fusion of being triangled, is the following effort Bowen described in getting outside of the triangle with his parents. Bowen's mother would share negative "stories" about his father in letters to Bowen. His (Bowen, 1978) response was:

> In the next mail I wrote to my father to say that his wife had just told me this story about him, and I wondered why she told me instead of telling him. He shared the letter with her, and she fussed about not being able to trust me. Several letters such as this, plus similar exchanges when I was with both parents had been reasonably effective at detriangling me from them. During that period, mother made comments about my reading too much between the lines, and I made comments about her writing too much between the lines. (p. 506)

Bowen's referring in his letter to his mother as his father's wife was a device that helped create more objectivity and suggested, in an indirect way, that the "story" his mother told Bowen about his father was more suitable for a husband-wife discussion. This further helped him get out of the middle of the parents' relationship as a couple.

Bowen spoke of spending more time getting people not to take his side, rather than seeking well-meaning alliances. He tried to remain separate from others, taking one on after the other, without letting the relationships go stale by always remaining in emotional contact with all members involved. Bowen's (1987b) humorous style of "putting the other together with the other" is seen in the following examples: "Does your mother know you're loose today?" and "I'm glad your mother let you out today." These comments were made to individuals and also to therapists who were part of the "fused mass" of family therapists at these conferences.

Defining an I Position

Bowen's experience in working in large hospitals and in clinical and research settings provided opportunities for him to see that the emotional forces at work in the administrative environment, the professional family, and the therapist's own family together create the environment in which emotional process occurs. Bowen wrote, "He [the therapist] must have a working plan and operating positions for dealing with anxiety in his administrative and professional environment before he can start clinical work in family psychotherapy" (1978, p. 209).

The "I position" is the action manifestation of the underlying differentiating force; it is the counterbalancing force to togetherness. In Bowen's (1978) words:

> The differentiating force places emphasis on "I" in defining the foregoing characteristics. The "I position" defines principle and action in terms of, "This is what I think, or believe" and, "This is what I will do or not do," without impinging one's own values or beliefs on others. It is the "responsible I" which assumes responsibility for one's own happiness and comfort, and it avoids thinking that tends to blame and hold others responsible for one's own unhappiness or failures. The "responsible I" avoids the "irresponsible I" which makes demands on others with, "I want, or I deserve, or this is my right, or my privilege." A reasonably differentiated person is capable of genuine concern for others without expecting something in return, but the togetherness forces treat differentiation as selfish and hostile. (p. 495)

The therapist/coach continuously defines his/her self to the families. This process begins from the initial contact that defines the Bowen theoretical-therapeutic system and how it differs from other approaches. The therapist proceeds to define his/her self throughout the therapy in relation to all types of life issues. The therapist defines important I positions by taking "action" stands regarding "what I will do and what I will not do." The Bowen-based therapist believes that the therapist/coach should not ask a family to do something he/she is unwilling to do on behalf of self. Bowen (1978) suggests that when a family is progressing slowly in the process of differentiation, there is some important, unclear and ambiguous area in relation to which the therapist/coach has failed to define him- or herself (p. 177).

The I position is typically very useful early in therapy, when the family's anxiety level is high. The therapist's use of the I position at that stage both lowers anxiety by its being a de-triangling technique and models for the family how the process of differentiation can proceed. Taking I positions can be fruitful throughout the course of therapy, whenever the opportunity avails itself to the therapist (Bowen, 1978, p. 252). When the therapist takes the opportunity to define his/her own beliefs and principles in the course of family therapy, the spouses, in turn, begin to take I positions, defining self in relation to each other (Bowen, 1978, p. 230). The process of defining self through taking I positions, as Bowen (1978) describes it, involves an interlocking progression:

> When one member of a family can calmly state his own convictions without criticism of the beliefs of others, without becoming involved in

emotional debt, then the other family members will start the same process of becoming more sure of self and accepting of others. (p. 252)

Teaching How Family Emotional Systems Operate

According to Bowen (1978) some teaching is necessary in all kinds of psychotherapy. With Bowen family systems theory and therapy " . . . which explains the human phenomenon in special terms, and which utilizes intellectual concepts, to guide the effort to modify emotional systems, teaching is even more necessary" (Bowen, 1978, p. 251). From Bowen's (1978) perspective, "This kind of knowledge provides the family with a way of understanding the problem, and a framework in which they can direct their energy on their behalf" (p. 316).

In the final phase of Bowen's evolution of his theoretical-therapeutic system, he increasingly taught families and therapists about how one's family emotional functioning was best understood in the context of evolutionary and other natural systems theory. Not only does this theoretical framework provide the widest context for understanding the functioning of the family as a multigenerational emotional unit, but a framework based on evolutionary biology is useful in helping the family therapist obtain a broader focus, be a better observer, and lower emotional reactivity in order to become more emotionally neutral. Using evolutionary theory in this way provides the family therapist with a broader theoretical context in the effort to become more objective.

The utilization of natural systems theory becomes an active means for the therapist to de-triangle from the nitty-gritty content that obscures his/her ability to see emotional process in both the nuclear and extended families. It helps keep the therapist from being fused into one or more triangles and the emotional system in general.

Teaching is done indirectly when anxiety is high, more directly when anxiety is somewhat lower, and directly when either the individual being coached or those family members being seen are in a calm state. According to Bowen (1978):

> Early in therapy, when family anxiety is often high, instructional communications are put in terms of the "I-Position," by parables, illustrated by successful clinical solutions of similar problems in other families. Still later, when there is little anxiety, the teaching can successfully be quite didactic. (p. 252)

Bowen's use of indirect teaching through parables and stories is described as a technique by Pendagast (1974) as "the use of displacement stories," a term she attributes to Guerin, a systems therapist trained by Bowen. In the 1960s, Bowen began teaching families about how other families handled their problems. Parables and "displacement stories" are a way to teach the family about emotional systems when anxiety is very high, enabling family members to hear without emotional reactivity. An example of a displacement story would be the therapist describing how another family had dealt with an emotional situation similar to that confronting the family in the consultation. The therapist may describe how another family had dealt with an unruly adolescent by defining clear I positions in regard to making objective rules and applying them without becoming emotionally reactive.

When therapy has progressed sufficiently, with a new level of differentiation attained on the part of the differentiating one(s), attending conferences and training sessions may be useful (Bowen, 1978, p. 316). Teaching about systems, when tension is low, is used when both spouses are present and often with one motivated spouse. The latter involves the short-term goal of instruction about how the system is operating in order to reduce anxiety and emotional reactiveness, so that the "antagonistic" spouse can participate with the other spouse in a long-term effort in therapy (Bowen, 1978, p. 234). According to Bowen (1978), "The goal is to teach the family member about the functioning of emotional systems, to discover the part that self plays in the system, and especially towards the other spouse, and to modify the system by controlling the part self plays" (p. 237).

Teaching directly, when anxiety is low, is of course a major part of Bowen family systems therapy with one family member. The initial sessions are devoted to teaching the motivated family member about the emotional functioning of family systems—prior to the family member formulating the part he/she plays in the family—undertaking supervised visits back to check the accuracy of his/her formulations, doing a multigenerational family history, and defining self in relation to the family in a variety of settings.

SUMMARY

In this chapter, an overview of the Bowen theoretical-therapeutic system was presented. The author began by contextualizing the notion of theory in Bowen's work. This was followed by a section on the historical development of Bowen's thinking. The next sections presented the principles, processes, and clinical approaches of differentiation of self. Finally, the chapter concluded with a section on the role and functions of the therapist or coach in Bowen family systems therapy, including the following topics: defining and clarifying the relationship between the spouses, de-triangulation, defining an I position, and teaching how family emotional systems operate.

REFERENCES

Bowen, M. (1974). "Bowen on Triangles." Edited and transcribed by K. Terkelsen. *The Family,* 2 (2): 45-48.

Bowen, M. (1978). *Family Therapy in Clinical Practice.* New York: Jason Aronson.

Bowen, M. (1979). "Anxiety and Emotional Reactivity in Therapy." Videotape produced by the Georgetown Family Center, Washington, DC.

Bowen, M. (1980a). "Defining a Self in One's Family of Origin—Part 1." Videotape produced by the Georgetown Family Center, Washington, DC.

Bowen, M. (1980b). "Defining a Self in One's Family of Origin—Part 2." Videotape produced by the Georgetown Family Center, Washington, DC.

Bowen, M. (1981). "A Day with Murray Bowen, MD." Lecture. Sponsored by the Family Living Consultants of the Pioneer Valley, Northampton, Massachusetts, November 4, 1981.

Bowen, M. (1983). "Violence as a Human Problem." Videotape from conference titled "Violence as a Family and Societal Problem," Cosponsored by Fort Sam Houston and Brooke Army Medical Center, Houston, Texas.

Bowen, M. (1984). "Two Days with Murray Bowen, MD." Workshop. Sponsored by The Western Psychiatric Institute and Clinic, University of Pittsburgh, Pittsburgh, PA.

Bowen, M. (1987a). "Bowen Clinical Conference." Transcribed by L. S. Keeton. From videotape produced by the Georgetown University Family Center, Washington, DC, November 16, 1984.

Bowen, M. (1987b) "Triangles and Differentiation." Videotape produced by the Western Pennsylvania Family Center, Pittsburgh, PA.

Bowen, M. (1988). "A Day with Murray Bowen, MD." Workshop. Sponsored by the Center for Family Consultation, Chicago, Illinois, May 7, 1988.

Bowen, M. (1995). "A Psychological Formulation of Schizophrenia." *Family Systems: A Journal of Natural Systems Thinking in Psychiatry and the Sciences,* 2 (1): 17-47.

Graefe, S. (1995). "In the Fullness of Time: Reflections on Bowen Theory as a Compass to Navigate a Life Cycle." Journeys and Detours: Retrospectives and Prospectives in Bowen Family Systems Theory," Seventeenth Pittsburgh Family Systems Symposium. Sponsored by the Western Pennsylvania Family Center, Pittsburgh, Pennsylvania, June 8, 1995.

Kerr, M. and Bowen, M. (1988). *Family Evaluation.* New York: W.W. Norton and Company.

Pendagast, E. "The Use of Displacement Material in Family Therapy." *The Family,* 1 (2): 14-19.

Titelman, P. (Ed.) (1987). *The Therapist's Own Family: Toward the Differentiation Self.* Northvale, NJ: Jason Aronson.

Chapter 2

Family Systems Assessment Based on Bowen Theory

Peter Titelman

INTRODUCTION

Family assessment from a Bowen theory perspective starts with obtaining the facts and patterns that comprise the family system. This material becomes a map that provides the basis for planning intervention. In gathering the material, one begins to fill in blanks in one's knowledge and to understand the part that each individual plays in the family system.

This chapter is divided into the following sections: (1) the multigenerational family emotional system, (2) gathering a multigenerational family history, (3) components in Bowen family systems assessment, (4) specific factors to look for in Bowen family systems assessment, and (5) implications of Bowen family systems assessment for planning and implementing family systems therapy.

THE MULTIGENERATIONAL FAMILY EMOTIONAL SYSTEM

Figure 2.1, the Multigenerational Family Emotional System, illustrates Bowen's conception that the family is composed of interlocking emotional fields of the nuclear and extended families.

The term *emotional* is used to denote that the family is a system that automatically—below the level of feelings—responds to changes in "togetherness" and "individuality" within and among the membership of the extended family. The interrelationship between these evolutionary, instinctual forces energizes or drives the relationship processes within the family system.

The term *field* is used to describe the constant fluidity of movement, of emotional action and reaction, that occurs within and across the subsystems that constitute the family as a multigenerational system. It is not merely the relationship between an individual and his/her parents that is essential to the field; the family of origin also provides an emotional field

FIGURE 2.1. Multigenerational Family Emotional System

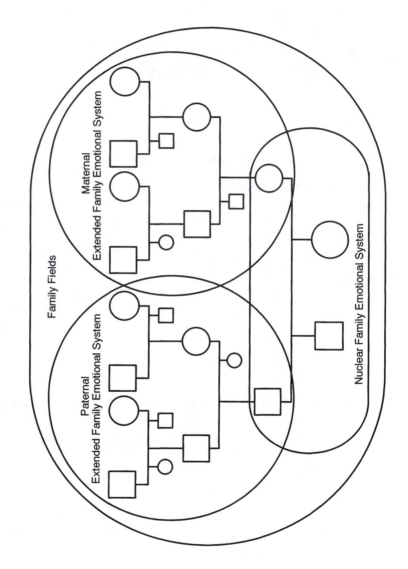

that an individual is connected to, fused with, or cut off from, which influences him/her and which he/she in turn influences.

M. Kerr and M. Bowen (1988) provide the following description of an emotional field:

> The emotionally determined functioning of the family members generates a family emotional "atmosphere" or "field" that, in turn, influences the emotional functioning of each person. It is analogous to the gravitational field of the solar system, where each planet and the sun, by virtue of their mass, contribute gravity to the field and are, in turn, regulated by the field they each help create. One cannot "see" gravity, nor can one "see" the emotional field. The presence of gravity and the emotional field can be inferred, however, by the predictable ways people behave in reaction to one another. (p. 55)

For Bowen, the concept of "the family as a system" means that the context to be considered is at least three generations, preferably more. The nuclear family—mother, father, and children—constitutes one emotional field. The father's family of origin—he, his siblings, and parents—constitutes another emotional field, and the mother's family of origin—she, her siblings, and her parents—constitutes another extended family system with yet another emotional field. The nuclear family and the families of origin of both spouses/parents, including the respective extended family systems, constitute three interlocking emotional subsystems.

These emotional fields "interlock" because what occurs in one of the subsystems affects the functioning of the connecting subsystems. They are also interlocking because the father/spouse of the nuclear family is also a son in his family of origin and a grandson/nephew/cousin in the extended family; the mother/spouse in the nuclear family is a daughter in her family of origin and also a granddaughter/niece/cousin in her extended family; and the children in the nuclear family are also grandchildren and cousins in the extended family.

GATHERING A MULTIGENERATIONAL FAMILY HISTORY

Gathering a multigenerational history can take several sessions, but the basic information can be obtained in the first one or two sessions. The full family systems assessment profile is obtained over time because it is a continuing process of gathering material and refining an understanding of the family.

It is easier to do a multigenerational assessment with a couple or one spouse, parent, or single adult than to include children. However, it can also be done with children participating. With an individual or couple, I sketch the family diagram, always explaining what I am doing. With children, I sometimes follow the procedure initiated by Bradt and Moynihan (1971) of making a poster-sized family diagram that I put on the wall, where it can be easily observed. The use of a large pad or blackboard for constructing the family diagram are other ways of facilitating active participation and learning for the family. The use of colored pencils or markers to highlight a variety of factors on the family diagram was introduced by Bradt (1980). A key for the symbols used in constructing a family diagram can be found in the Appendix at the end of this chapter.

The therapist sets the stage for inquiry by being direct and interested in each new family. An attitude of respectful neutrality and objectivity creates a research atmosphere that helps the family explore the presenting problem in the context of three or more generations of multigenerational family emotional process. The therapist explains that it is valuable to gather a multigenerational family history and create a family tree or diagram. While the therapist or coach is gathering history, he/she is attentive to the family's need to share pertinent information about what brings them to therapy now and the immediate concerns with which they are dealing.

Specifically, gathering family history, using the outline of the Survey of Family Fields presented in Table 2.1, begins with finding out who makes up the nuclear and extended families and the gender, ages, names, occupation/ school, and other basic identifying data of individual family members.

Next, the focus of the interview moves to the individual or couple's view of the presenting problem(s), including dates of the onset of symptoms and prior dates and history of previous symptoms or problems.

This is followed by gathering a history of the *nuclear family emotional system.* The therapist asks the individual or couple, getting the perspectives of both partners, about their courtship, such as when, where, and how the couple met and the major events during that period. Then the assessment moves to gathering material about the wedding, such as when, where, and who attended and the attitudes of the families of origin of both spouses. This is followed by asking about the major events, year by year, since the marriage began; geographical moves, illnesses, births, deaths, divorces, and job changes are noted on the family diagram.

The therapist then turns to the *extended family emotional systems,* beginning with asking each spouse about the major events between leaving home and getting married. Questions are asked about dating patterns, goal and career development, and education. This line of questioning is followed by gathering material involving the major events in both families of origin prior to and after leaving home. The family diagram is expanded for

TABLE 2.1. Survey of Family Fields

I. Current Situation

A. *Presenting Problems:* include date of symptom onset

B. *Early History of Problems:* date of prior symptoms

II. Nuclear Family Emotional System

A. *Courtship:* where, when, how did couple meet; characteristics; major events during this period

B. *Marriage:* when, where, who attended; attitude of families of origin

C. *Major Events:* year by year since the marriage; make family diagram of nuclear family; include moves, illnesses, births, deaths, divorce, jobs, etc.

III. Extended Family Emotional Systems

A. *Major Events Between Leaving Home and the Marriage:* include relationship with the extended family for both husband and wife; dating patterns; goal and career development; education

B. *Major Events in Both Families of Origin Prior to Home and Since Leaving Home:* make a family diagram for the husband and the wife with dates and major changes; include sibling history and description of important triangles

C. *Parents' Relationship:* meeting, marriage, history of major events in their lives; include family diagram for each parent

the husband and the wife. Questions are directed toward obtaining dates and major changes, including the histories of the siblings and the important triangles. Then the therapist/coach obtains material about the couple's parents' relationship. Questions are asked about how the parents met, their marriages, and the history of the major events in their lives, resulting in an expanded family diagram for each parent.

COMPONENTS IN BOWEN FAMILY SYSTEMS ASSESSMENT

According to Bowen theory, the family system assessment serves as a framework for organizing clinical data into a coherent picture of the emotional functioning of a family. It is not quantitative, nor is it a checklist. Rather, it serves as a qualitative guide to help the clinician understand a family and as a blueprint for the clinician to develop a therapeutic direction with one or more individuals to modify their position in the family.

The components of Bowen family systems assessment are contained in Table 2.2. These components can help the clinician understand the relationship between the symptom or presenting problem and the family as a multigenerational system.

Drawing from the summary of Table 2.2, section II, each component will be discussed separately, even though there is much overlap in content.

The components of (A) Symptom development in the nuclear family: eruption and chronology and (B) Stage in the family life cycle refer to the nuclear family. The components of (C) Nodal events that evoke anxiety in the family fields (nuclear and extended family emotional systems), (D) Patterns and themes interwoven in the family emotional fields (nuclear and extended family emotional systems), and (E) Level of differentiation within the family fields (nuclear and extended family emotional systems) refer to an interlocking of the nuclear and extended family systems. Also, symptom eruption and chronology of symptom development should be correlated with dates of nodal events and changes in the family life cycle.

Although Bowen (1970) does not explicitly refer to family life cycle and its stages as a theoretical component, it is clearly part of his thinking. For Bowen, the addition or subtraction of a family member can be a key modification in the structure of a family, and naturally it has profound implications for the family's functioning and potential dysfunctioning. In Bowen's terms, the first stage would be marriage—the marital dyad and the issues of the original fusion; the second stage is the addition of a child; the third stage would be the complete nuclear family. The nuclear family is solidified when all children have been added. The fourth stage of the nuclear family is when the children begin to move out; the departure stage lasts until the youngest child leaves. A fifth stage is when the marital dyad age, and a sixth stage is when they die. Each stage involves significant triangles in relation to both families of origin and includes persons outside the family. But specifically, each stage represents the addition or subtraction of members to the nuclear family around which triangles of the nuclear and extended families revolve.

Nodal events that evoke anxiety in the family fields refer to those significant events that are central to the life course of the multigenerational family system. Bowen (1978) uses the term *nodal points* to refer to the intersection of the onset of symptoms in the child with dates of nodal events in the parental relationship (p. 172). Bradt and Moynihan (1971) were the first to elaborate upon Bowen's use of the term nodal event. Bradt and Moynihan (1971) call these events nodal "because at these points there is the clustering of phenomena which stimulates the family organism to take on qualities of greater openness, closeness, or to fly apart explosively" (p. 5). The following

TABLE 2.2. Bowen Family Systems Assessment

I. **Components of Bowen Family Systems Assessment**
   A. *Symptom Development in the Nuclear Family*
      1. Presenting problems (including date of symptom eruption)
      2. Early history of problems (including chronology of symptom development)
   B. *Stage in the Family Life Cycle of the Nuclear Family*
      1. Marriage
      2. Addition of a child
      3. Complete nuclear family (including the addition of each subsequent child)
      4. Departure of child (including each subsequent child)
      5. Retirement
      6. Aging and death
   C. *Nodal Events That Evoke Anxiety in the Nuclear Family*
      1. School initiation
      2. School change
      3. Family migration
      4. Marital separation
      5. Divorce
      6. Remarriage
      7. Job stress
      8. Unemployment
      9. Retirement
      10. Physical changes
      11. Illness
      12. Death
   D. *Nuclear Family Emotional System*
      1. Functioning positions
      2. Sibling position and marital choice
      3. Boundaries:
         a. From differentiated (open) to undifferentiated relationship (fused/cut off)
         b. Cohesive versus exploding family
      4. Significant triangles
      5. Symptom typology—pattern(s) of handling and undifferentiation in the presence of acute or chronic anxiety:
         a. Marital distance/marital conflict
         b. Physical, social, or emotional dysfunction in one spouse
         c. Projection to a child
      6. Family projection process
      7. Family themes (including myths and secrets)

TABLE 2.2 *(continued)*

E. *Level of Differentiation of Self of Individuals in the Nuclear Family and Level of Differentiation of the Nuclear Family as a Whole Unit*
   1. Amount and quality of individual goal-directed behavior versus amount and quality of adaptive, nongoal-directed behavior
   2. Amount and quality of differentiated "I-positions" versus amount and quality of undifferentiated "We-position"
   3. Amount and quality of emotional reactivity versus amount and quality of thinking-objectivity

F. *Extended Family Emotional Systems: Maternal and Paternal*
   1. Functioning positions
   2. Capsule summaries of the functioning of both parents and each sibling
   3. Nodal events in the extended family
   4. Symptom typology—pattern(s) of handling and undifferentiation in the presence of anxiety:
      a. Marital distance/marital conflict
      b. Physical, social, or emotional dysfunction in one spouse
      c. Projection to a child
   5. Boundaries:
      a. From differentiated (open) to undifferentiated relationships (fused/cut off)
      b. Cohesive versus exploding family
   6. Significant triangles
   7. Family projection process
   8. Family themes (including myths and secrets)
   9. Level of differentiation of individuals in the extended family and of the extended family as a whole unit

II. **Summary of Relationship Between Symptom Development in the Nuclear Family and the Multigenerational Family Emotional System**

   A. Symptom development in the nuclear family: eruption and chronology
   B. Stage in the family life cycle
   C. Nodal events that evoke anxiety in the family fields (nuclear and extended family emotional systems): Including multigenerational interlocking of symptom typology, fusion and emotional cutoff, significant triangles, and multigenerational transmission of the projection process and of family themes
   D. Patterns and themes interwoven in the family fields (nuclear and extended family emotional systems): Including multigenerational interlocking of symptom typology, fusion and emotional cutoff, significant triangles, and multigenerational transmission of the projection processs and of family themes
   E. Level of differentiation within the family fields (nuclear and extended family systems)

are the main nodal events: (1) school initiation, (2) school change, (3) family migration, (4) marital separation, (5) divorce, (6) remarriage, (7) job stress, (8) unemployment, (9) retirement, (10) physical change (menses, puberty, menopause), (11) illness, and (12) death. In addition, certain religious rituals of transition or other events that are more idiosyncratic can be nodal events for certain families. Births are categorized as nodal events by Bradt and Moynihan (1971) and along with deaths are considered the two most significant forms of nodal events for a family system.

The interaction of nodal events, patterns, themes, and levels of differentiation are explored as they reveal relationships between the nuclear and extended family emotional systems. Nodal events are not only correlated with symptom eruption and family life cycle stage, but they are also correlated between extended and nuclear families. Patterns and themes that characterize the functioning of both nuclear and extended family emotional systems are interwoven. Symptom typology, fusion and emotional cutoff, significant triangles, the projection process, and transmission of differentiation/undifferentiation need to be integrated in order to properly assess the family system.

The level of differentiation within the family fields (nuclear and extended family systems) is difficult to define due to the "borrowing" and "lending" of the properties of pseudoself or functional self among family members, that is, the overfunctioning-underfunctioning reciprocity that constantly takes place within the family. It is easier to assess the functional level of self than the solid level of self due to the give-and-take of adaptation between family members and the current effects of life stage and nodal event stress. The level of basic or solid self-differentiation must be charted over a long period of time. For clinical assessment, a picture of the level of differentiation is obtained by examining the history of the life course to date, including family relationships, social relationships, and educational and occupational history. Specifics to look for include the amount and quality of individual goal-directed behaviors versus the amount and quality of adaptive, nongoal-directed behaviors; the amount and quality of differentiated I positions versus the amount and quality of undifferentiated "we positions"; and the amount and quality of emotional reactivity versus the amount and quality of thinking and objectivity.

The intersection of eruption of symptom development, stage in family life cycle, nodal events, patterns and themes, and levels of differentiation in the nuclear and extended family systems can be illustrated by the following clinical example and the diagram in Figure 2.2.

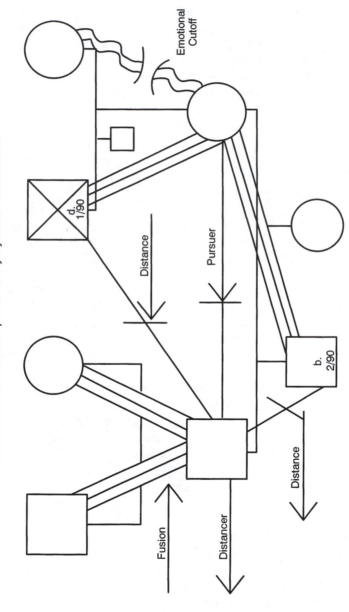

FIGURE 2.2. Clinical Example of Family Systems Assessment

Symptom development: Maternal overconcern with child's emotional functioning

Stage in family life cycle: Addition of first child

Nodal event: Death of maternal grandfather

Family typology: Child–focused family

Following the death of her father, with whom she was emotionally fused, a woman gives birth to her first child, a son. He becomes the immediate focus of the projection process. The woman's relationship to her husband is characterized by emotional distance, he being the distancer and she, the pursuer. The original interlocking triangle would have involved the woman and her father in an overly close position with the woman's husband being in the outside position. The current triangle interlocks with the woman being in the overly close position with her newborn son and her husband being in the distant, outside position. Husband and wife remain in their characteristic positions within the interlocking triangles in the nuclear family and the wife's family of origin. The game is an old one, with a substitution for one player; the woman's father is replaced by the woman's son. In regard to level of differentiation, it can be hypothesized that since the woman was the recipient of the brunt of the projection process in her family of origin her level of differentiation is lower than that of her sibling. Her relatively low level of differentiation of self is expressed by the degree to which she is fused both with her father and her son and by her efforts to pursue and fuse with her husband. However, since individuals marry other individuals who are at basically the same level of differentiation of self, the husband's operative position as a distancer represents his way of being reactive to his wife, due to the uncomfortable closeness of relationships. It is his way of trying to avoid falling prey to the forces of fusion to which he is also subject, based on his experience in his own family of origin.

In this clinical vignette, the eruption of the symptom was a woman's anxiety about her infant son's emotional functioning in the context of the "addition of the first child" stage in the life cycle. It is a child-focused family. The most significant nodal event was the death of the woman's father. This event created much anxiety for the woman and is likely responsible for tripping off the projection process directed toward the infant son when he began manifesting some minimal sleep difficulties. The interlocking triangles make sense in the context of life stage, nodal event, and the pattern of daughter-father and wife-husband relationships. The relatively lower level of differentiation of self of the woman in comparison to her brother's level of differentiation is an important component in understanding the movement of anxiety, pursuit, projection, and fusion within this family at the time this young woman presented for consultation.

SPECIFIC FACTORS TO LOOK FOR
IN BOWEN FAMILY SYSTEMS ASSESSMENT

The following are a number of specific factors that are useful in planning and implementing a direction for therapy based on a family systems assessment:

- Look for nodal events that correlate with dates regarding the current situation. However, families may discontinue therapy if the therapist overtly focuses on the correlation between events (Bowen, 1978, p. 184).
- Information about the feelings and fantasy experiences of various family members on the day symptoms began may prove important (Bowen, 1978, p. 181).
- Check on the early development of the projection process by asking what the mother's fantasy was before and during pregnancy and at birth (Bowen, 1978, p. 182). If the mother's concern has been fixed on the child since pregnancy, the projection process is much more intense and the prognosis for therapy is more guarded than for a family involved in a projection process that started later as a response to a family nodal event, for example, a death (Bowen, 1978, p. 182).
- Triangling in the nuclear family is similar to triangling in the families of origin and the therapeutic triangle.
- Sibling position and the general level of family functioning make it possible to postulate, with a good deal of accuracy, an individual's personality profile (Bowen, 1978, p. 183).
- The lifestyle developed in the family of origin will operate in the nuclear family and in family therapy based upon an interlocking paternal and maternal multigenerational transmission process (Bowen, 1978, p. 183).
- The more emotional cutoff from the family of origin, the more symptoms develop and continue to reside in the nuclear family.
- If symptoms develop rapidly, they are probably a response to a disturbance in the extended family. The prognosis for restoring family functioning quickly, in these situations, is good. If symptoms develop slowly, over a long period of time, they are usually the product of a disturbance that has developed over a long period of time in the nuclear family (Bowen, 1978, p. 173).
- The lower the general level of differentiation in a family. the greater is the frequency and intensity of the emotional shock wave phenomenon, that is, the presence of a series of anxiety-provoking nodal events that reverberate through the family system.

- The lower the level of differentiation, the more difficult it is to motivate an individual, or more than one individual, to work on basic change because he or she is living more in a feeling world than a thinking world. There is more emotional dependence on others and less capacity to transcend "here and now" comfort for principled positions based on understanding the past and being able to consider future consequences.
- In regard to symptom typology, the pattern of handling undifferentiation in the presence of anxiety, there are only a few families in which only one pattern of handling fusion is present:

   1. The poorest prognosis involves either all of the projection process going to one child or to the development of illness in one spouse (when the degree of the projection process is intense).
   2. When the family's mode of handling undifferentiation is located in one mechanism, the therapeutic prospect tends to be poor (Bowen, 1970).
   3. When there is a fluctuation among the three patterns of handling undifferentiation in the face of anxiety, the immaturity is spread out—not so fixed—and it is a better indicator for change (Bowen, 1970).

- The best prognosis for basic change is when there is potential for open communication and relatedness to the family of origin.
- The best prognosis for obtaining change in a family system involves working with:

   1. the highest functioning individual(s);
   2. the one who wants to modify his/her position within the family systems; or
   3. the one who is the pursuer, rather than the distancer, in the relationship system.

IMPLICATIONS OF BOWEN FAMILY SYSTEMS ASSESSMENT FOR PLANNING AND IMPLEMENTING FAMILY SYSTEMS THERAPY

The following are some of the general implications and rationales for using a family systems assessment in therapy:

- The consultative process of doing a family systems assessment detoxifies problems by locating and contextualizing them in a three- or four-generational field.

- The family systems assessment helps the clinician determine who is most motivated to work and what level of change can be attempted (symptomatic or basic).
- With the aid of a Bowen family systems assessment, determination of an accurate prognosis is greatly increased due to the clinician's ability to comprehend the relationship between the course of the symptom, its eruption and development, and the emotional process in the nuclear and extended family fields. The clinician's ability to achieve an accurate prognosis about the outcome of therapy is also greatly enhanced by the ability to relate the presenting problem to the nodal events and current stage of family development in the nuclear family and the patterns and themes interwoven within the (nuclear and extended) family fields.
- By connecting symptom development and the complex functioning of the family as a multigenerational system, the clinician can plan interventions that may deal directly with the nuclear family, or he/she may decide to focus on the extended family in order to resolve nuclear family problems. For example, when symptom development occurs rapidly, a family systems assessment often shows that it is a response to nodal events in the extended family. If the clinician focuses on issues in the extended family, the prognosis for improving or restoring nuclear family functioning is improved.
- Bowen family systems assessment provides a scheme for exploring the levels of functioning of the individuals within the family and of the family as a whole (level of differentiation). These levels include the responsiveness to stress, that is, the level of anxiety that is triggered or evoked by significant nodal events; the flexibility or rigidity of the family system in the face of transition into or out of a stage of the family life cycle; and the range of fixity of symptom typology, family projection process, triangles, and boundaries (fusion, emotional cutoff or interlocking fusion and cutoff), among other patterns and themes in the family fields.

SUMMARY

Family assessment from a Bowen theory perspective is a guide for the clinician, providing access to understanding the phenomena of family life in terms of the clinical theoretical foundation of Bowen theory. The broadest theoretical postulate is the conception of the family as a multigenerational emotional unit, comprising interlocking family fields—the nuclear family field and the two extended family fields.

Through the components, Bowen family systems assessment provides a way in which the systems therapist can integrate Bowen theory with the events in the life of the multigenerational family emotional system, thus implementing an effective systems-based course of treatment.

APPENDIX:
A KEY FOR THE FAMILY DIAGRAM SYMBOLS

Males are drawn as squares, females as circles:

Male = □   Female = ○

Dates of birth and death are written above the person's symbol.
Age is shown within the square or circle. Death is indicated
by an × through the symbol.

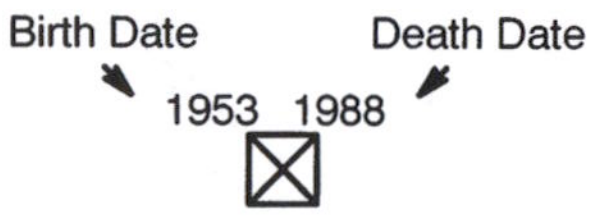

Birth Date   Death Date

1953 1988

⊠

Couples are shown by a line connecting their symbols
as follows, with the relevant dates written on the line:

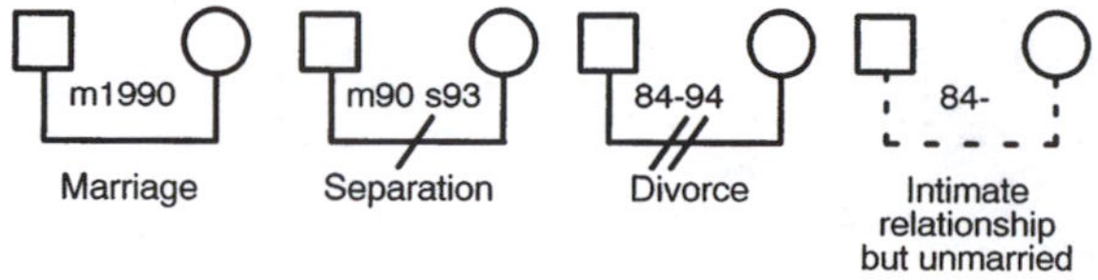

m1990
Marriage

m90 s93
Separation

84-94
Divorce

84-
Intimate
relationship
but unmarried

Children are shown left to right, oldest to youngest:

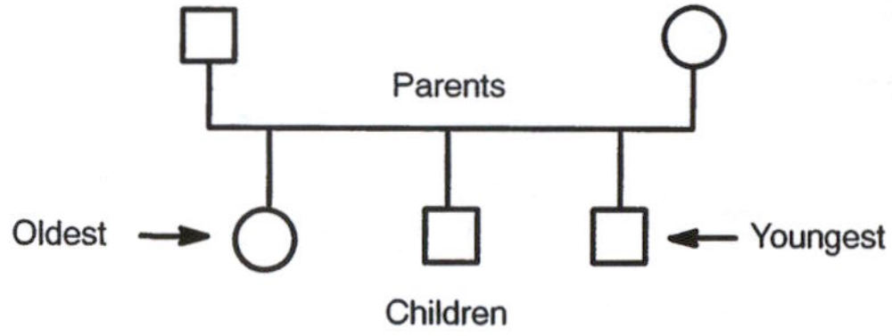

Parents

Oldest

Children

Youngest

66

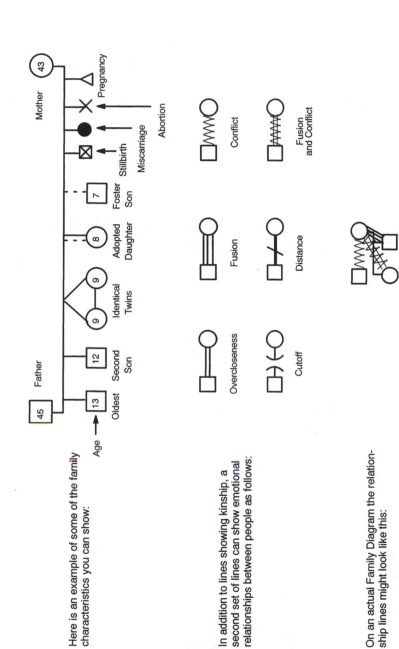

Here is an example of some of the family characteristics you can show:

In addition to lines showing kinship, a second set of lines can show emotional relationships between people as follows:

On an actual Family Diagram the relationship lines might look like this:

Mother

Father

Age

Oldest
Son

Second
Son

Identical
Twins

Adopted
Daughter

Foster
Son

Stillbirth

Miscarriage

Abortion

Pregnancy

Conflict

Fusion
and Conflict

Fusion

Distance

Overcloseness

Cutoff

REFERENCES

Bowen, M. (1978). "The Use of Family Theory in Clinical Practice." In Bowen, M. (Ed.), *Family Therapy in Clinical Practice*, New York: Jason Aronson, pp. 147-181.

Bowen, M. (1970). "Multigenerational Transmission and Sibling Position." Videotape produced by the Georgetown Family Center, Washington, DC.

Bradt, J.O. (1980). *The Family Diagram: Method, Technique and Use in Family Therapy*, Washington, DC: Groome Center.

Bradt, J.O. and Moynihan, C.J. (1971). "Opening the Safe: A Study of Child-Focused Families." In J.O. Bradt and C.J. Moynihan (Eds.), *Systems Therapy, Selected Papers: Theory, Technique, Research*, Washington, DC: Georgetown Family Center.

Kerr, M. and Bowen, M. (1988). *Family Evaluation: An Approach Based on Bowen Theory*. New York: W.W. Norton and Company.

Chapter 3

Bowen Theory
As a Basis for Therapy

Patricia Hanes Meyer

INTRODUCTION

Murray Bowen, MD, devoted his years in psychiatry to the discovery of the most fundamental patterns of human functioning that could be verified through study of the human family. Bowen theory (Bowen, 1978; Kerr and Bowen, 1988) places the functioning and dysfunctioning of individuals in the context of the larger emotional systems in which they live, both past and present. Knowledge of human functioning enables discovery of repeating patterns that are present in a dilemma confronted by an individual. Knowledge of patterns permits the establishment of predictability. Predictability provides the possibility for preparation to confront a dilemma. Prediction of potential patterns and preparation provides the opportunity to prevent those automatic patterns of response and action.

Dr. Bowen developed an aversion to discussion of therapeutic technique. He believed that there were few mental health professionals who were driven to fully understand the human phenomenon. Rather, many were impatient, wanting to quickly "fix" a human dilemma, showing disrespect for the complexity of human functioning and the endurance of patterns of functioning in multiple generations of a family. After the early years, Bowen avoided expressing his thoughts on the application of theory.

The problem with refusing to discuss technique is that it encouraged some individuals to view therapy based upon Bowen theory as following from charisma or magic. In other words, if you know theory, change will follow. It doesn't! Change is a two-step process. Without knowledge of human functioning, knowledge of individual patterns of functioning, and knowledge and respect for environmental factors, change is not possible. This is so because the individual is unknowingly reacting to emotional forces and emotionality experienced in the family of origin. However, knowledge of human functioning and family patterns does not in and of itself change anything. It is necessary to be able to act on the knowledge effectively. Individuals who have attempted to begin to use their knowledge about functional patterns become respectful of how difficult it is to resist old patterns and to create new ones. An individual can know that attempting to avoid parental disapproval through avoiding certain topics of discussion uses mechanisms of distance (e.g., not remaining alone with a parent long enough for a certain question to arise) and causes anxiety in self and a feeling state of preventive "flight." Attempting to reverse that tendency with a statement about self and by not overreacting to the predictable response or attack of the other is no easy thing. Meticulous knowledge about what will predictably occur and what will be necessary to reverse the pattern is required.

As with all efforts to write about Bowen theory, this chapter is presented with deep gratitude for the opportunity to have been trained and personally challenged by Dr. Bowen.

Theory As a Framework for Studying Man

Attempts made to understand any life problem by studying *only* the individual in whom it occurs places the observation in isolation. Further, when an understanding of the nature of a problem is based upon an individual's "feelings" about the problem, the understanding will be subjective, affected by emotional reactivity. An accurate understanding of the problem, therefore, is not possible. For example, it is common for a marital partner to announce in a session that he or she is no longer sexually attracted to his or her mate. Often, this announcement comes with the further assumption or conclusion that, therefore, the marriage is no longer viable. The case may be that the male partner has relinquished a responsible functional position within the marriage, leaving the raising of children and the handling of the family finances to his wife. Feeling overburdened by all the responsibility, the wife may turn to nagging and criticism. She has now begun to relate to her husband as a frustrated mother, nagging her young son. The husband, understandably, does not view his wife as a sexual partner; rather, she is experienced as a nagging mother. Any therapist who views this family situation as a sexual problem or proceeds with the therapeutic focus on the feelings of the husband will miss the mark of the problem completely and decrease the chance of solid change by failing to focus on the broader arena of dysfunction in the couple.

Bowen theory addresses the ways in which generations of a family manage their emotional attachment to one another. The general level of maturity of the individuals within a system will determine, to a great extent, how many and how extreme the functional mechanisms will be that develop to manage floating anxiety in the system and in self. Maturity can be thought of as the degree to which an individual knows the difference between fact and feeling in responding to emotional issues and has the ability to act on the *facts* rather than respond automatically to the *feelings*. It is about containment, being able to be centered within self (knowing what self believes about a situation and acting objectively in response) while surrounded by the emotionality of important others. This ability constitutes solid differentiation. Bowen theory focuses on the functional characteristics of the individual that have emerged during the developmental years. For example, does the individual function as a youngest child, depending on others to solve problems and contributing little to the functioning of the system? Can the individual contain high levels of emotion without attempting to draw others into the emotion as a way to calm self down? Can the individual resist the subtle efforts of important others to draw self into his or her emotionality? Maturity is being able to bring a dilemma directly to the person or persons who are connected to the dilemma, resisting the urge to relate to others who could be counted on for support. It is determining to what degree a parent may gain or lose self and a sense of well-being, based on the success of his or her children. For example, the parent whose life focus and sense of personal accomplishment is based on the visible success of his or her athletic son is less mature. There is nothing in the father's own life or accomplishments in which he finds passion or pride or excitement; those factors are provided by the visible success of the son.

What this factual approach to understanding family and individual functioning requires is the scientific reporter's approach to information gathering. It requires evaluating functioning through a meticulous lens, searching for facts (who, when, how, where, what, for how long, reason for change) and avoiding an evaluation based on assumption, memory, or feelings.

The therapist will be required to use a method for organizing and visualizing vast quantities of information about numerous generations of a family. The family diagram is the method of systematically organizing data used by most family therapists. No two women organize their kitchen in the same way, nor do any two therapists organize their diagrams in the same way. However, it is critical that a therapist have an organized method to make information accessible and visible, with patterns and triangles highlighted. Therapists who do not gather and then thoroughly organize large quantities of information into theoretical categories with clearly defined patterns will be limited in their ability to make change possible for a family or individual and will be vulnerable to transference. When a therapist listens to heavily laden emotional material without the clarity and accuracy of the factual assessment described previously, the likelihood of getting caught in feelings of sympathy, sadness, irritation, or reactivity is extremely high. I do not believe that solid change is possible for any individual who has not proceeded through this laborious journey of building a thorough knowledge of patterns of human functioning, family functioning, and self-functioning.

Individuals learn in different ways and with different momentum. For some, frequent sessions are necessary in the beginning for the person to begin to discover the functional patterns in self and the system. For others, frequent sessions can clog up thinking; more time is needed between sessions to master the ideas being presented. However, there are some generalities about the phases that all individuals will proceed through, to one degree or another, in learning about their emotional functional system. Those phases will be described in subsequent sections. First, however, this chapter will discuss the importance of using theory to establish predictability.

Theory As a Framework for Establishing Predictability

Predictability is critical anytime change is sought in human functioning. Knowledge of what can be expected to occur, factually and in emotional response, makes it possible to know how an individual needs to function differently, providing the framework for establishing a plan. Such a plan must be based on knowledge of the complex family patterns. Predictability also provides a framework for understanding failures in attempts to bring about change.

The purpose of therapy is to provide an environment in which change is possible. Such change may include seeking symptom relief, calmness, some change in the environment, or building solid change in self.

Change in functioning can be expected to precipitate anxiety in self and in those in the system. Anxiety activates difficult forces, creating discomfort in self and in the system. In self, the anxiety flows toward fears of rejection, a loss of belonging, and fears of being attacked by important others who will not appreciate the family member's change in functioning. Change in one person in a system automatically creates the *possibility* of shifts occurring in all significant relationship systems, but it does not predict nor guarantee change in others. The clarity in thought and action of the changed member may create a calmer environment in which others can function better. However, for other family members to change, the same individual journey of gaining knowledge about human functioning, the functioning of one's extended family, and the functioning of self must be accomplished.

Mature individuals can say and do whatever is necessary to fulfill personal responsibilities or accountability to others. Mature individuals accept that others will react to some of those actions and that there will be disapproval. Disapproval is a part of life, even when lived responsibly and fully. Immature individuals will resist and be reactive to actions that will cause potential disapproval or make self stand apart. The fear of standing alone or feeling disapproval can be a driving force to take actions that will reduce discomfort and increase comfort. One mechanism immature individuals will use to reduce discomfort is to make a move toward someone else, to establish a new connection with another as an ally, an assurance. This is the concept of triangulation in Bowen theory that speaks to the constant flow of human emotionality, as individuals automatically seek connection with another based on the discomfort felt with an individual with whom there is a difference of opinion or threat to connection. One of humankind's ultimate fears is that of being alone, not belonging to others, or being seen as different. This experience of disapproval from others can be a major discomfort. The greater the degree of an individual's immaturity, the greater the fear and intolerance of disapproval. The greater the maturity, the greater the tolerance for disapproval. You cannot be your own person, saying and doing what you believe to be correct, if you cannot risk the disapproval of important others. In many ways, this is one of the basic human struggles, if not *the* human struggle, that is played out in every individual's daily life.

The freedom to say and do what is accurate for self is not limited by the reactivity of others. One sixty-year-old man found himself in the tenth year of a cutoff from his only sibling, an older sister. He had grown up in the position of "golden boy" to an older sister whose niche was that of the daughter who could do nothing right. The wealthy mother sent a $30,000 check to her son. Now wise about the triangle of mother, "golden boy," and "defective sister," he inquired whether his sister had also received a $30,000 gift. The mother responded, "Of course she will, once my medical bills have been paid." As the accountant to his mother, the son knew the mother could buy the hospital to which the bills were owed. Immediately, he wrote a check to his sister for $15,000, one-half the amount of the gift. He then wrote to his mother, sympathizing with her financial plight and saying that he knew she would be pleased for the daughter to receive payment also. The prickly relationship continues between the mother and the daughter. However, the son can now move "out" of circumstances in which he is the "golden boy" and sustain an active relationship with both mother and sister. Although the relationship between the mother and her two children is much the same, the actions of the son are now based on his knowledge regarding the triangulation process.

Theory provides the ability to evaluate efforts to define a self that have failed. It has already been mentioned that humans have a fear of standing alone. Fear of failure is another strong force in many lives. Fear of failure can make it difficult to take responsible risk. Far more important, it can make it impossible to learn from a failed effort, and if you cannot learn from experiences of failure, change is not possible. Rather, repeating the same pattern of action or reacting in an opposite pattern is predictable. According to Walter Toman (1969), it is predictable that patterns which are not known and respected (as to their power and persistence) will be repeated over and over in the same or in an opposite presentation, "all things being equal."

Therapists who value failure as a vehicle for change with individuals and families will be able to use unsuccessful outcomes to develop additional knowledge about human functioning. Therapists who are comfortable focusing on failed attempts with families will find that Bowen theory provides five areas of evaluation:

1. *A Theoretical Structure for Observation.* A theoretical structure for observation is based on knowledge of human functioning needed to understand a particular family's functioning.

2. *A Theoretical Structure for Developing Hypothesis.* Bowen theory provides an hypothesis about the functional patterns that are observed in the system and the individual. This structure of theory acts as the foundation, the "roadmap," to all therapeutic focus that will follow.

3. *A Theoretical Structure for Determining Needed Change.* Theory provides clarity about the source and severity of dysfunction. Therefore, there is automatic focus on development of new knowledge as well as where change in functioning must occur.

4. *A Theoretical Structure for Evaluating Attempts at Change.* Theory provides a structure for evaluation of the quality of the thinking and effort of an individual to change the functional patterns of self. Was the paradigm of what needed changing accurate? Were the individual's efforts executed well?

5. *A Theoretical Structure to Evaluate Reactivity in the Individual.* Theory provides a structure to determine how an individual reacted to the predictable reaction of others, the predictable disapproval of his or her efforts. Many a successfully executed effort to break a pattern in self has been lost when the definer becomes reactive to the predictable reaction of important others, either seeking approval for his or her actions or attacking others for being reactive.

By using these five areas of evaluation, it becomes possible to determine where a failure to change self occurred. Was it that the observations of the characteristics of the system were not accurate or were major pieces of fact missed? Were major triangles in the system not understood? Was the hypothesis about where change was needed inaccurate or incomplete? Did the individual misfire because of a lack of understanding of human functioning or concepts of the theory? Was the individual so anxious regarding what was being attempted, walking straight into disapproval, or so distant from the system that others reacted to the distance rather than to the issue being focused upon? Was the defining individual unprepared for disapproval or unable to control automatic reactivity in self to the other's reactivity?

THE FOUR PHASES OF THERAPY

Viewing Therapy in Phases

All individuals enter the therapy process with some degree of reactivity, anxiety, fixed-focus motivation, and a belief or lack thereof in a capacity to significantly gain control over dilemmas in life. When a therapist has the knowledge and ability to accurately access the presence of each of these forces in an individual and his or her system, it becomes possible to speak directly to the emotionality of the family.

The process is one of connection or disconnection between a therapist and a family system. When a therapist's questions do not connect with the family's emotionality, the therapist is unable to teach, and the family is unable to learn. The therapist may view the family as uncooperative, resistant to issues, or unmotivated. Consequently, the therapist's conclusion as to the basic level of differentiation (basic level of maturity) of the individual and his or her family may be inaccurate. This may lead a therapist to conclude that a family is of a low level of maturity and incapable of change.

For a family beginning the therapeutic process with a therapist whose questions do not connect to their emotionality, there is often frustration and distress. The family may feel that they are providing data for a therapist who is "writing a book." After all, the therapist may have asked many questions concerning the functional history of the individual and family yet not be connecting the answers to the factors that led the family to enter therapy. The therapist may be viewed as having little understanding or concern for the family's anxious focus. Such a therapist may well be viewed as being irrelevant to the individual who sits anxiously in the therapist's office. Such failures of the therapist to hear and acknowledge the anxious focus of a family can occur when there is a disconnection between a therapist's paradigm of the family and the family's emotional state and anxious focus.

A different picture emerges in therapy when the questions of a therapist connect with the emotionality of the family and its anxious concerns, when the questions and focus of the therapist are on target for the family or individual. Individuals frequently respond to a connected question with a comment such as "that is a very good question" or "I have never thought about that before." There is an immediate thoughtfulness, although not necessarily a lasting thoughtfulness, at this early stage. Individuals frequently leave initial sessions visibly calmer, knowing that there is someone who has connected to their anxious concerns and connected in a way that is objective and neutral. The therapist has positioned himself or herself in this way to provide individuals with an opportunity to *think* about a problem in their families about which they have felt frantic and to *discover* their patterns of emotionality and their families' patterns of emotionality, in the context of knowledge about human functioning. The therapist's office, a neutral classroom, creates an environment in which individuals can be productive "learners," capable of building solid change.

Phase One: Observation of Family of Origin

The task of phase one is to stimulate curiosity in the individual about family history, the presence of family myths (i.e., family stories that illustrate one side of a reciprocal relationship, such as the *saint* grandfather and *villain* grandmother), the presence of family secrets, and a general lack of knowledge about one's own history. This environment of curiosity is created through taking a thorough family history, asking a multitude of factual questions that create a focus on the patterns of the multigenerational family. Questions address two arenas of information: what, in fact, happened in past years, and what was the impact of those occurrences?

The initial focus begins with the establishment of a thorough family diagram. Drawing the multigenerational history of a family consistently and thoroughly creates a "picture" of family history that can act as a road map, a framework for the ideas and concepts that will be explored in sessions to come. Many therapists fail to complete this step effectively, creating a diagram that is incomplete and incomprehensible at a glance and that does not readily reflect multigenerational patterns. To maximize usefulness, diagrams need to be thorough, meticulous, readable, and coded to bring visibility to the largest amount of information possible.

The diagram illustrates functional indicators of each individual's life: age, health, education, religious experience and current practice (can be a good indicator of family reactivity), for whom each individual was named and why, work history, unique nodal events, disappointments (wanted to go to Harvard), overall competence, achievement, satisfaction, and the effect of each of these factors on the individual and system.

A diagram reflects the manner in which a nuclear or extended family related (e.g., frequent contact, no contact, depth of quality of connection, degree of teamwork around nodal events). Functional patterns in the individual and nuclear and extended family systems are all traced. Is there a pattern in the way marital fusion was managed in the family? Is it similar to, the opposite of, or different from the way that marital fusion is managed in the individual's marriage?

Finally, the search for understanding of a family's functioning assesses the impact of nodal events. What was the impact of a particular death in the family? What was the impact of an uncle not becoming a general in the U.S. Air Force? What has been the impact of a particular chronic illness on functioning in the family. In other words, what difference, if any, did an event make on a family's functioning and on the individual's functioning? Many therapists do not adequately pursue *impact* information. They gather information that a family member was diagnosed with rheumatoid arthritis, but they may ask nothing else. Therefore, it is impossible to assess whether a particular fact is critical or insignificant to a family. Knowing *how* a chronic disease affected an individual's ability to rely on normal life functioning and *whether* the impact on the individual affected the family and its functioning makes it possible to evaluate that fact's importance.

When phase one is vigorously pursued, most individuals will automatically begin to focus on self, making comments such as "the more I see the pattern of cutoff in my family, the more I see the very same pattern within myself." The more mature the individual who can focus on difficult facts in the midst of emotion—the sooner subtle and nonsubtle patterns will become visible. The individual who cannot rise above his or her emotionality to know the difference between connectedness of events and his or her feelings toward them will not be able to build a framework for significant change in basic or functional levels of self. Therapy for such an individual may well provide an environment in which he or she may be calmer. Calmness does not equate to change, nor does it provide greater control over a person's life, but it does make it easier to be more constructive and less emotional. In some chaotic families, in which solid change is not possible, providing the opportunity for a calmer state of mind should be considered a significant therapeutic accomplishment.

Phase Two: The Functional Patterns of the Individual

In many ways, phase two is a rerun of phase one, but with a specific focus on those identified family patterns that manifest in the individual.

How, if at all, is the pattern defined in the mother's family present in the individual's own functioning as well?

Phase two is the phase in which the individual accepts responsibility for his or her life, for the dilemmas and difficulties with which self struggles. If this personal acceptance does not occur, the individual will blame "others" or the "environment" for the problems of self. Building more control over one's life course will not be possible for the individual who remains in a blaming stance toward life. One common version of this stuckness can be seen in the individual who views self as a "victim." Whether this state of "victimhood" is due to some perceived or real deprivation in life (absence of love, money, opportunity, among others) or a perceived or real abuse (sexual, physical, financial), there can be a dominating conviction that life has not been fair to the individual. There is no position in human functioning that is more dys-functional than that of a *victim* because a victim is an innocent individual to whom something "happened." Therefore, an individual has no ability to gain control or to prevent future dilemmas. It is similar to being on the beltway in a car with four flat tires and trying to drive forward. As soon as an individual accepts responsibilities for some part of a problem or pattern, whether through contributing to an environment in which an event developed or by actively participating in the event itself, it is possible to begin changing what the individual views as unacceptable.

Change is not possible for the person who continues to view self as an innocent victim. Acceptance of participation in the evolution of an environ-ment in which a problem occurred or of participation in the problem itself, does not mean that destructive events did not occur, that the individual was not traumatized, nor that the events should have occurred. It does provide a framework through which forgiveness of self for involvement in a destruc-tive experience is possible. Further, acceptance of playing some part in a problem provides objectivity about the problem, which in turn provides a framework for understanding another's contribution as well. No therapy or theory can erase trauma from a person's past. It can, however, provide the opportunity for emotional closure of the bitter blame and anguish that has kept alive an event that may have occurred years ago. Once such an emo-tionally laden event is presented in the most neutral, factual context, *clo-sure,* an acceptance and respect for all of the operating forces, becomes possible. Such was the case for a female in her thirties who, as a young girl, was fondled by the man next door. She could not move beyond feelings of shame and guilt, knowing that she had walked to his house each day, making the fondling possible. However, when she began to focus on the fact that this neighbor was the only adult who showed interest in her school work by encouraging her to do better, she was able to begin to forgive herself for interacting with the neighbor and to "let go" of the paralyzing feelings.

In *all* cases, individuals need to be validated for the hurtfulness of events and their effects. Individuals need to be freed to "move on" by defining and accepting those thoughts and actions that bring closure to emotions associated with hurtful memories and events. This may include communication to involved others; it may include gaining information and a new way of thinking about a buildup of events; it may include forgiveness of self and of others. What will be required is an acceptance that individuals do the best they know how. No one foregoes functioning on a better level by casually choosing to function less well. Human beings have often limited mechanisms for coping with strong emotional reactions. This can lead to humans functioning in truly destructive ways. Such destructive behavior can be validated when used to increase an individual's objectivity about the forces operating in a system at the time of the dysfunctional occurrences. There are few more satisfying experiences for a therapist than watching an individual "let go" of memories and emotions from a trauma as a result of becoming informed about the complex emotional forces of the family and the complex forces operating on those involved. That individual can now begin to focus on his or her unique characteristics and opportunities to become a responsible, capable, achieving individual who lives in the present and future and not in the past.

Phase two involves the individual determining the part that self has played in the development of problems, but only the part that self played, not the parts played by others. It can be a difficult phase. The individual can now see patterns repeating, sometimes even predicting their occurrence. Yet, there is insufficient knowledge to break the pattern. Some individuals become distressed and very impatient during this phase. Reversing a pattern of reaction that has been in place for years takes great clarity of thought and great determination. A beginning understanding will not be sufficient to reverse the pattern; time and more complex understanding will be required.

The responsibility of the therapist in phase two is to assist the evolution of a thoughtful focus, a sharpening awareness of the presence of patterns within self, and to bring the awareness of those patterns into connection with broader family patterns. All of this is then balanced with the conviction that human beings usually try to do their best.

As with the end of phase one, many individuals will begin to automatically move out of phase two. There will be observations and comments reflecting the need to amend a reaction or pattern. The more respect developed for a pattern, the quicker change begins to occur naturally. As with phase one, the individual who cannot separate fact from feeling and who cannot develop increased objectivity about a system and its problems will not be able to achieve the task of seeing clear patterns and the path to reverse them.

Phase Three: The Formulation of a Strategy for Personal Change

For most individuals, it will take many months of work in therapy to reach this point. Formulation of a plan for personal change will be centered on theory and intensive data gathering about human, extended family, and personal functioning.

The formulation of a strategy for change is a completely different process than "technique," which is a specific action for a specific situation. Strategy is a plan of action based on life principles that *guide* an individual to think, decide, and act. These principles can provide guidelines throughout an individual's life. *How* a specific decision is carried out is a *technical* question; *what* decision is appropriate is a *theoretical* question. Examples of life principles might include:

1. *Whenever possible, attend every family nodal event.* Nodal events often involve significant family emotion. Therefore, participating in the events in the lives of important others is critical. It is particularly important to attend funerals of significant family members. Deaths are often the most emotionally significant event in families so participation is critical. Family systems are the most open and factual in the immediate hours and days following an important death. Gaining knowledge about the system and developing a deeper connectedness to family members may be possible for only a brief time. During this time, individuals may communicate intimate, private thoughts, feelings, and memories about the deceased member, the extended family, and the system. Unless a stronger connection, private and personal, with another family member has been established in this brief period of openness, subsequent communication will return to a more normal, less private level.

2. *Act to correct an error in functioning in relation to another whenever there is action available to take.* When individuals know they have erred in their functioning in relation to another, it is critical that an effort at correction be made (what action is the *technical* question).

3. *Respect and thoughtfully plan "exits" and "entrances" into and out of important systems.* Exits and entrances into or out of a system (births, deaths, graduations, weddings, retirements, relocations) are always critical.

Exits and entrances are so pivotal that it is important to put energy and thought into how to enter or depart from a system. The process involves "honoring" those who have contributed to one's growth, learning, and actual accomplishments in any significant system, including friendship, work, school, and of course, family. Often, someone leaving a system is a one-way process—the system recognizes the individual, and, too often, the departing individual focuses exclusively on his or her promising future elsewhere. Honoring reverses this process. Believing that an individual's future will be attended to in future days, the individual's responsibility now is to acknowledge and recognize all those whose functioning has "eased" or "increased" functioning of self while in the system. Individuals honoring a system have left framed mementos, an object such as a clock or floor plant, or dollar contributions honoring the *system*. Others have presented pastries at the coffee area on a final day of work, accompanied by a note of gratitude and good wishes to the "staff." More elaborate efforts have included luncheon foods brought in for colleagues with whom one has worked directly and closely. Such efforts honor a system; there still remains the honoring of the individuals in the system.

Complete closure involves acknowledging anyone who has directly permitted or enhanced the functioning of self. Sometimes this includes notes to individuals for whom one's "feelings" may be negative but who have nevertheless contributed to one's functioning. The principle is to be accurate. A note may say no more than "thank you for what you have contributed to my work." It does not say "thank you for being wonderful" to someone who has not been wonderful, nor does it say "I will miss you" when, in fact, that is not so. Notes written to those for whom there is deep gratitude evoke strong emotional feelings of loss, mourning, joy, exhilaration, and excitement for those individuals who have touched the formation of self. It is as if life stands still for a moment and self remembers joining a work system, an athletic team, or a class. In such situations, often another helps make possible a visible transformation of self. All individuals who experience, in the midst of striving for a goal, significant interaction with a mentor may find the self changed. The change may have been the result of the mentor's passion for one's ability or his or her unique ability to teach and demands for excellence that have left a strong mark on the departing individual.

When his or her journey of departure is completed with deep thought, effort, and integrity as to who must be acknowledged, there is powerful closure to a chapter of one's life. With such focused closure, the honoring of those now left behind and their contribution to self, a burst of energy is released within self that creates future success.

Knowledge about the predictable functioning of systems is critical for a strategy of change; it leads to an understanding of what in a system tends to increase and/or decrease emotional reactivity and tightness. Increased anxiety tends to encourage polarization, heightened reactivity, and decreased thinking. Thoughtful actions will calm and loosen the system.

Once an individual discovers the "truth" in life principles, there follows a flow of creativity as life dilemmas are confronted. Because the creativity grew out of the individual's own emotional thinking system, developing respectful knowledge about human functioning is a natural consequence. It is not an arbitrary response "borrowed" from another (i.e., the therapist). For this reason, therapists who provide an environment that teaches *how to think objectively* about dilemmas can assist individuals to become more thoughtfully in control of their life courses. Enduring effectiveness requires that thinking and strategy be consistent and accurate within the system in which they are carried out.

Most individuals have personal principles. However, these principles may have long ago been buried under high anxiety (an automatic response of yielding to discomfort over many years) or the force for "sameness" with, and approval from, important others. One purpose of therapy is to provide an individual with an opportunity to rediscover those long-buried principles.

The rediscovery process can be aided by questions such as "Prior to having children, what were your beliefs about responsible parenting?" or "If you were to write a brochure on guidelines for effective parenting, what guidelines would you include?" In pursuing these questions, it is productive to focus on the differences between the ideas that individuals would include in the brochure and their actual parenting practices with their own children. In the process of thinking through such questions, the forces for belonging, for sameness, of projection to children, and of protection from travail become readily visible.

The task of raising children illustrates the thinking and strategy required in an effective nuclear family system. It requires that parents have knowledge about emotional systems, about the specific system into which they were born and in which they confronted the dilemmas of maturity, and about the reality of their child. Effective parenting requires meticulous awareness of personal principles, responsibility *for self,* responsibility *to the child,* and the boundaries that exist between the two generations. The process between parent and child will include providing for, protection of, and preparation of the child. A parent who has moved into a phase three ability to think and build strategy will have the capacity to distinguish between the responsibility that belongs to the parent and the responsibility that belongs to the child at various stages of growth and development of the young family member.

Children who develop in family systems that are strong in each area become effective functioning adults. They have been "provided for" with the emotional validation, material goods, opportunities, and successes necessary to be free of automatic responses of having been a "have not" or of having been "deprived." They have had "enough" and are grounded and grateful. This response is not necessarily based upon objective reality. Poor families who believed that life was hard but whose needs were met can produce children who feel "provided for." On the other hand, children from "plenty" may have grown up in families that "felt" they did not have as much as others, as much as they should have had. In other words, how children "feel" they were provided for will influence their emotionality in adulthood.

Protection concerns literal safety in the environment, from natural physical harm (learning to crawl, walk, ride a bike, drive a car, among others), and using preventive medicine. It further concerns emotional protection from environments and relationships that are destructive or harmful. However, it can be difficult to distinguish those dilemmas when a parent should protect a child from the environment from those when, in fact, permitting the child to cope with a difficult environment would be excellent "preparation" for life.

One measure for determining whether to protect a child is the appearance of a destructive force in the emotional functioning of another. For instance, an athletic coach can pressure players with strong demands for work ethic and excellence. This stress is significantly different from the stress of a player who plays for a coach who, when frustrated, will demean and humiliate his or her players. Athletes can become very confident and successful playing for the first coach, but players who must perform for the demeaning coach may produce out of fear but may seek a new team. Players who can remain detached and calm in the presence of a coach who is out of control have developed a significant life skill. However, beyond a deep self-confidence, there may be little to gain from remaining permanently in such an environment.

The third, and hardest, function of parents is to "prepare" their children for high-functioning independent adulthood. This phase begins in childhood but becomes paramount during adolescence. It is hardest because it is the antithesis of the other two tasks—to provide for and to protect. The preparation phase represents a transition and the ultimate end of providing for and protecting dependent children. The parental role shifts now to teaching (the family kitchen becomes a classroom) a maturing child about the nature of human emotion and about effectively responding to dilemmas such as the "out-of-control coach." The parent teaches knowledge of functioning and the critical importance of "boundaries," where the realities of self end and those of another begin. For example, an individual may be involved in dilemmas in which he or she has no role. Honoring boundaries would dictate that the individual remove himself or herself immediately from future involvement. In the dilemma of the "out-of-control coach," parental teaching would focus on the appropriate range of responses of the player toward his or her coach. The responsibility then resides with the adolescent to respond appropriately.

In other cases, parents have to watch and allow their children to make mistakes or poor decisions and, in some cases, fail. Until children are given the opportunity to test for themselves the outcome of their decisions, they will not have personal conviction about the laws of solid functioning. What must be learned for solid adult functioning is that being "casual" about principles of personal responsibility and accountability yields lost functioning and lost self. This reality becomes unquestionable only when discovered as a "truth" by the adolescent. It has to be taught (by parents or other adults), but must be discovered by self as true. Parents' inability to "prove" functional truth to their child (as they once could provide an inoculation from disease) can be a source of deep distress and frustration. Should parents be unable to remain detached, when appropriate, leaving their child's dilemmas to the child, the ultimate development of maturity (differentiation) in the child will be impaired. The child may be unable to distinguish between fact and feeling, to act on facts not feelings, to know without question where his or her own boundaries reside, to be accountable for his or her failures toward others, and to have the courage and ability to "correct" self when there is a failure in responsibility.

During phase three, the individual continues to study the system and observe patterns in the functioning of the human in his or her emotional system and self. The part that self plays in functional difficulties has become clear. Once known principles have been rediscovered, and new knowledge about human functioning has been uncovered. As phase three moves toward completion, the individual will have formed an overall strategy for change in self-functioning based on knowledge about human functioning.

Phase Four: The Work of Changing Self

For the individual who enters the fourth phase, the role of the therapist changes dramatically. Previously, the therapist was the beacon for thinking, providing a thoughtful focus through questions and representing knowledge about general patterns of human functioning. From this foundation, the individual could ponder the realities of his or her own multigenerational family emotional field and knowledge of human functioning in the therapy process. Now, the individual has discovered *subjectivity* for self—the automatic emotionality and lack of objectivity that are part of humans. Further, substantial knowledge about the patterns of his or her own emotional system over many generations has been discovered. There is a respectful knowledge about that individual's own functional patterns and their strengths and weaknesses. Now a resource and coach, the therapist can act as a mirror in which to check for accuracy and objectivity. The individual who has moved to phase four has no difficulty differing with the therapist's view concerning his or her system or actions, now having the ability to refute the therapist's thinking based on facts. The individual might say, "In this case, I don't believe that approaching it the way you suggest would be productive because. . . . " The individual is now free to function and to "say what he or she means and mean what he or she says." There is freedom to look at self accurately, to acknowledge failure, to be responsible and accountable, and to have the courage and conviction to correct self. As the individual moves through his or her life journey, there is an ability for full functioning. The individual can distinguish between feelings and facts and can act effectively based upon the facts of the dilemma.

For success in phase four, several factors are required. The work of phases one through three must be thorough and accurate. Partial completion will not yield change in basic self, although it can yield significant improvement in certain specific arenas in which the individual learned a particular pattern very well and was successful at amending it. In that specific arena, the individual will find new freedom to function. Because of the difficulty of amending powerful and complex emotional patterns, celebration of improvement in any arena of life functioning is appropriate. However, that new freedom is only an increased ability to say and do what is important to self *in a specific arena*. Changing self in the broadest context is the attempt to know all of the major and moderately important patterns of functioning in self. Further, it is a respectful watchfulness for those patterns in self and in the extended system. It becomes a lifetime effort to be aware of the functioning of self on a daily and long-term basis. It is having the integrity and determination to see self accurately and the integrity and willingness to reckon with and correct slippage in functioning.

There is no graduation from a serious focus on the functioning of self. Every day, the individual confronts the flowing forces of stress and its predictable anxiety as well as the task of managing multiple responsibilities and relationships. Balancing these forces is required for solid functioning. This is no easy task for the most mature, and a burdensome task for those with less maturity.

Summary of Four Phases of Therapy

The therapy process is a vehicle through which an individual can move to bring predictable change and create a new level of freedom. It is a freedom to say and do all those things that are necessary to have a deep sense of inner peace, pride in one's own life journey, and conviction. There is an acceptance that self creates its own destiny. Further, there is acceptance that the only route to emotional freedom is to function accurately (based upon facts) rather than to "look the other way" or at someone else's functioning. Deep peace, internal tranquillity, and pride are only possible for the individual who believes that he or she has faced the dilemmas in his or her path honorably and constructively and has been a contributor in those arenas in which he or she lives. Fun, excitement, and activity can be created without conviction about how one is living or a belief in self. But an individual can only know tranquillity when he or she faces, constructively and decisively, the dilemmas in which he or she lives every day. For individuals who attempt to honorably reckon with dilemmas that confront them, the passage of years is simply part of the reality of the journey. There is a sense of appropriateness to life's flows, such as the emergence of gray hair in middle age. Individuals who have not become objective about self, their strengths and weaknesses, and who have not "squared off" honorably concerning their life issues feel panic as they approach nodal events (thirtieth, fortieth, fiftieth birthdays, among others). The panic stems from feelings of a lost future, and in fact, the feeling is accurate. This individual's life journey passes by, and he or she knows that self is not accurately "saying what it means, meaning what it says." Rather, the self dismisses, avoids, denies, or blames others for life's potholes. The solid self of the individual knows better, and there is a feeling of depression for the lost, incomplete self.

The phases that have been described are not cast in concrete; they are general processes through which any individual must pass in order to become knowledgeable, humble, and respectful of human functioning, the functioning of family, and the functioning of self. The first phase requires observation of multiple years of functioning of the family. All individuals carry some myths of their family that include heroes, angels, and villains. These actors often have scripts filled with blame, judgment, and an absence of understanding of the important life forces that another has experienced, hence, the requirement for lengthy observation and curiosity about the broad story of one's family. There must be substantial understanding of general human functioning as the framework for viewing one's own family. Into this fabric comes the slow weaving of facts about the functioning of self, consistent with general human functioning, in response to and in connection with one's nuclear and extended family patterns and history.

From all of this knowledge grows a humble respect for what it will take to amend one's own lifelong patterns. If such respect is matched with a powerful passion to live differently, as a "self-defined" self rather than an "approval-seeking" self, then the lifelong journey to live with high levels of responsibility ends only at death. The determined focus on self-functioning has to be sustained without lengthy vacations. There has to be continual awareness of the factors that will increase (or decrease) personal functioning. Such factors cannot be ignored for long without the consequences of lowered functioning and increased anxiety.

The four phases of therapy do not flow perfectly, nor with the same timing in every individual. However, in general, there is a flow from significant new knowledge (about human functioning, one's family patterns, and the patterns of self) that changes assumptions about family to curiosity and increasing respect for the patterns that have influenced and shaped one's own history. This leads, for the first time, to choice. If patterns are known and predictable, planning and choosing whether to yield to the patterns, do the opposite, or "choose a different response" become possible.

Discoveries about family functioning and the functioning of self continue as long as the individual seeks to observe them. The discovery of a new pattern can throw the individual back into the observation-knowledge–gathering stage. Once processed, it becomes part of the emotional fabric about which the individual seeks to become accurate. These "journeys" back into earlier phases can be short visits because they are built on an acceptance of human functioning and knowledge of other patterns in the extended family and of patterns in self. That knowledge and understanding does not have to be rebuilt. Rather, the new observation is added to that which is already known and understood and can often be processed quickly for use. This process, and that of "slippage" factors (e.g., exhaustion, cumulative difficult dilemmas, inability to function on the level that is consistent with self-expectations), can lead to a decline in functioning, appearance of symptoms, and increased anxiety. In such a case, knowledge has to be "remembered" and returned to, much like riding a bike after many years of not doing so. No one is immune to loss of functioning or to the lifelong battle against internal forces that resist being accountable for self.

SOLID PERSONAL CHANGE IN CONTRAST TO BEHAVIORAL SHIFTS

The Application of Theory

Many therapeutic processes as well as much of the popular self-help literature focus on change as a vehicle to shift a particular situation or feeling through a particular behavior. The focus centers on a specific problem and a specific series of acts to remedy the situation. There is little focus on gathering historical information concerning the evolution of a problem and little respect for the multitude of factors that may be operating. Uncertainty is not a comfortable state for humans; it breeds anxiety, which creates a state of discomfort. Discomfort is avoided by many humans, who automatically respond with behavior to reduce it as quickly as possible.

Bowen theory can be seen as an orderly process to permanently counter emotional forces that foster dysfunction. In this sense, a specific action is but one brick placed in a foundation of many other bricks, all of which are necessary to build a solid structure for functioning. Emotional issues and relationships can now be acted upon in a carefully defined new way.

The differences between behavioral shift or solid change can be seen in the following comparison between techniques of symptom relief and techniques for solid change.

Techniques for symptom relief focus on immediate lowering of discomfort and anxiety. They:

- bring immediate relief;
- are focused on short-term goals only—often, simply feeling better; and
- usually represent a singular action.

Techniques for solid change focus on managing life decisions based on fact and personal accountability. They:

- are based on unchanging life principles that are present in a dilemma;
- increase, not decrease, immediate tension in self about a dilemma;
- are but a part of a larger plan to amend functional patterns in self;
- emerge from a focus on one's personal responsibilities and accountabilities; and
- are based on knowledge of human functioning and the prediction that it provides.

Therapeutic techniques based on a broad understanding of theory emerge through a natural evolution of clarity, understood in theoretical terms. The accurate and appropriate response often becomes clear on its own. For instance, as a complex pattern of cutoff becomes clear, ways to move toward connectedness and to resolve those forces that influenced the cutoff pattern become apparent. In this view, therapeutic techniques are linked intricately to the theoretical concept that explains the evolution of the dysfunctional pattern.

Acceptance of Personal Immaturity

An understanding of the complexities of change is clearly observable when the therapist refuses to engage in quick and early declarations or make statements such as "Based on what you have said, I think a separation is called for." Rather, comments might include, "It is too early to know what will be appropriate for you"; "You don't yet know enough to move toward such a decision"; "I know you are uncomfortable; however, it will be necessary for you to continue to be uncomfortable for several months while you determine the primary forces that are operating in this situation"; "Are there other factors influencing this family at this time that you have not yet focused upon such as financial difficulties, job dissatisfaction, or elderly parents who are ill?" There is no focus yet on *doing* anything.

A therapist would be remiss in refusing to address the dilemmas that are on the minds of a family concerning a crisis in which they may find themselves. However, focus on actions that precede broad understanding of the functional patterns of self and of the family must be clearly defined as short-term efforts. Such actions will not bring change to a family. They may, however, provide a temporary calm, ease a specific conflict, or provide immediate direction to a floundering family unit or individual.

For the individual who goes through this process with a willingness to learn, observe, and accept facts that require an ability to acknowledge immaturity in self and in the family, there will be a natural evolution of clarity of the functional patterns that must be changed if the individual is to function better. It is at this point that specific techniques can productively begin to be taught because:

- the individual has developed knowledge about human functioning, the functioning of his or her multigenerational family, and the functioning of self, and
- the individual has discovered repeating patterns in the system and in self.

Armed with this knowledge of theory, the prediction and development of a broad strategy for change of self now becomes possible. Theory-based knowledge of family makes it possible to define:

- how patterns operate,
- what patterns need to change,
- how the system will respond to change, and
- how self will respond to the system as it responds to changes in the individual.

The individual now has built a theoretical basis for selecting techniques that will become part of a larger plan of changing self—a project for the remainder of life.

Differentiation: The Balance of Base and Functional Levels in Individuals

Differentiation can be considered the cornerstone of Bowen theory. The concept of differentiation places all human beings on one spectrum of emotional solidness—those with little emotional maturity and those with significant levels of emotional maturity. Those with minimal maturity are incapable of distinguishing fact from feeling. The automatic emotional response is believed to be factual truth. Those with significant maturity can readily distinguish fact from feeling; feelings are "felt." However, the individual can be thoughtful about the facts that stimulate feelings and can think through actions, despite powerful feelings. This capacity, the ability to distinguish fact from feeling, will govern the nature of an individual's life journey. The greater the emotional response to life events, the more readily "potholes" will impede self, detouring self from steady accomplishment of any goal. The greater the ability to respect the "facts" of a situation and to act on those facts, the more an individual can bypass falling into old, familiar functional patterns.

There can be enormous force from a clustering of factors that occur in a brief time period. No individual, no level of maturity, is immune to a significant clustering of potent factors. There is no greater marker of differentiation, in my opinion, than the speed and quality of *recovery* from a symptom or return of an old pattern. In my opinion, many clinicians place too much emphasis on the development of a symptom in an individual or family as the "marker" of differentiation. This view frames knowledge about and efforts to increase one's personal level of differentiation as some kind of "insurance policy" from symptoms. Such a view represents a lack of respect for the impact of a cluster of factors on human beings.

Basic level of differentiation reflects the balance in a self between an automatic pull to belong, to be the same as others and not be seen as different, to experience approval and avoid disapproval, and the ability to stand alone, detached from approval in the face of important dilemmas. Intellect permits a focus on facts—the realities of a situation. In every individual, one force or the other, the automatic emotional responses or the opposition of the intellect, will guide the individual's response to, and management of, the dilemmas in which he or she finds himself or herself.

Functional level of self concerns an individual's management of daily life responsibilities and dilemmas at any given period of time. In a calm period of life, the individual may function very well. However, once problems occur and anxiety increases, the basic level of differentiation may begin to emerge. Although thoughtful in calm "waters," some individuals shift into automatic emotionality in troubled waters. Others remain firm to "facts," even in troubled waters. The world of athletics often brings out both phenomena. A coach may be fair and stay well within the bounds of the game rules, until a championship playoff and then "anything goes." In the world of sports recruiting, should a very good player become available, fair rules of recruiting may be bypassed. When emotionality becomes heightened, either subjective automatic emotion or fact-based principle will guide behavior. Individuals with higher levels of maturity who can distinguish between fact and feeling (I would love to grab that player, but taking a player who is pursuing you at the start of a season from another coach is neither fair nor reasonable) can remain consistent to their beliefs regardless of how tempting it would be to do otherwise.

Many who read about the difference between basic and functional level of differentiation become reactive to the concept of base level because many perceive a "helplessness," a predestined nature, in the concept. The fact is that one's life course can be changed specifically because of:

- a developed respect for one's own basic level differentiation, one's well-patterned tendencies of functioning, and
- thorough knowledge about the predictable patterns of one's multigenerational system and those of self.

Through knowledge of forces, patterns, and chronic levels of anxiety, it becomes possible to predict the arenas in which an individual will have difficulty in remaining thoughtful and making decisions based on the facts. A clinician who has difficulty with a certain type of family or individual (because of automatic emotionality) can excel, with determination and hard work, when working with the very individual who activates his or her most common weakness. How can this be? Meticulous awareness and knowledge about predictable patterns in self make it possible to choose an action rather than to respond with reaction. Without this knowledge, the individual acts upon automatic emotional process without being aware of the cues to which he or she is responding.

"Choice" in action can be seen in the individual who has the tendency to withdraw from an emotional system once anxiety reaches a certain peak. Through discovered knowledge about self, the individual can learn to know *what* escalates anxiety, *when* anxiety escalates, and *when* the trigger to withdraw occurs. Armed with this self-knowledge, he or she can plan his or her own actions so that the automatic withdrawal never happens. For example, individuals can preplan to control the occurrence of those factors that escalate anxiety. They can learn that when anxiety increases, they must act to create contact at the very point from which they might otherwise automatically begin to withdraw. The gut reaction signals to withdraw and the individuals' knowledge-based awareness signals to go to the phone and make contact. This is proactively choosing a different action before automatic emotionality activates.

This choice is relinquished anytime there is a failure to monitor the system, that is, not paying attention to what is happening. The only time when one can "go on vacation" from paying attention to the environment is when one is on vacation—if then!! Further, too many commitments, fatigue, or illness can compromise one's ability to choose to avoid functional tendencies, releasing automatic emotionality, at least for the moment.

It is not possible to say enough about the impact of anxiety on human functioning. As anxiety levels rise, it becomes more difficult for even the most mature to continue operating out of cognitive respect for facts, realities, and accuracy. Automatic reactivity is always waiting to emerge!

TECHNIQUES AND CHANGING SELF

Therapeutic technique, the application of theory, is a vehicle for eliminating irresponsible patterns in self and for the development of responsible patterns; it is change based on principles of a responsible life course (actions and behaviors about which an individual feels deep pride, personal honor, and self-dignity) rather than a solution to a specific problem or the process of "taking a stand." Many a trainee in Bowen theory has thought that taking a visible or "loud" action is "being a self." Being a "self," in my opinion, is having the courage to be accurate about self-functioning in such a manner as to honor what self believes and thinks.

In this section, techniques will be divided into two broad categories: foundation techniques and supportive techniques. Foundation techniques act directly to enable an individual to build new patterns of functioning that reflect greater thoughtfulness and maturity. The function of supportive techniques is to enhance foundation techniques through actions that loosen the system or keep self calm.

Foundation Techniques

Acting as vehicles to enable an individual to increase his or her functional level of differentiation (maturity), foundation techniques guide the

individual on the path toward change. A solid self knows about and respects boundaries; there is clarity regarding what is "you and yours,"
what is "mine," and what is factual reality. This self does not bother with
"I wish" for that which is not. Rather, actions are based on the facts of the
situation. Foundation techniques include the I position, Not Bailing the
Other Out, and De-Triangulation.

The I Position

Being a solid self requires knowing who self is in relation to all important issues in life such as important dilemmas, relationships, and life goals.
It requires exquisite respect for boundaries, knowing what is accurately
mine and what is "another's," and the ability to act consistently on that
clarity. In the process, many statements about self are spoken and, more
important, acted upon. The process of becoming a solid self is, in the long
run, action that brings change in a system, rarely discussion. It is *what* is
done. The calm, quiet action "speaks," and the solid principle is "heard"
by others.

For solid action to be taken, the actor must be free from needing approval and support for his or her actions, free from avoiding disapproval
from important others. Becoming a solid self is a process of building
clarity, acting on it objectively, not seeking approval from others nor
avoiding disapproval, and then "letting go." "Letting go" is acceptance of
an outcome, knowing that self has made every effort to carry out a responsible action. No effort is expended to convince others about an action nor
to defend its connectedness. It is an acceptance, without explanation or
attack, of the understanding or misunderstanding others may have of one's
action. It is often, in fact, the lack of response or the obvious detachment
from needing others that communicates most clearly the depth of one's
conviction to the principles that self was operating upon all along.

The individual who has the clarity to develop and follow a defined
course of action, most of the time, will experience several impacts:

1. It will be possible for the individual to define and pursue lifelong
   goals without being detoured by emotional forces. The task is to
   know self. As Dr. Bowen used to say, "It is doing what you say and
   saying what you do." Consistency is that ability to know what you
   are about, coupled with the discipline and motivation to act accord-
   ingly.
2. The individual who can live a consistent, self-defined life will experience emotional calmness as a result. Clarity about life goals and
   principles limits doubt about one's response to life's dilemmas and

challenges. The absence of needing to convince others of the merit of one's thinking frees an individual from "cat fights" with others over whose viewpoint is correct. It also frees self from the urge to set another straight, pointing out how another's way of thinking is "off," and from *needing* to let someone else know that his or her actions or way of thinking is reactive. Reactivity does not want to let go; it has a natural pull to be "right," to ensure that the other knows that the individual's position is right.

3. The individual will experience a clarity of self-identity. There will be a clarity about how one wants to spend free time and with whom it is important to have contact to ensure personal responsibility to others and the good functioning of self. There is a clarity about how, and in what ways, money is important. There is a clarity about what provides personal well-being. Physical fitness is seen by some as critical to well-being. Being in tune with nature, plants and animals in the environment, is important for others. What is critical is that the individual knows what factors in his or her life are critical to good functioning. Contrast this individual with the individual who gets confused and drawn toward the interests, focuses, and goals of others; he or she will experience doubt, as someone else's goals or values become confusing.

4. Finally, the individual will find it possible to establish and maintain close, consistent, interpersonal relationships because of lessened reactivity. The individual will have a greater capacity to tolerate disagreement and disapproval from important others. This enables one's focus to remain on facts and issues, making problem solving possible. When an individual cannot tolerate disagreement with an important other, it isn't possible to confront issues. Rather, they are lost in the emotional turmoil of intolerance for the present tension.

The process of defining self has been divided into four phases. The specific task of each of the phases must be accomplished in order to define self and be free of the need for approval. The process has moved from fact gathering about functioning that the individual considers to be unacceptable to good functioning. Fact gathering, if thorough, creates clarity. Clarity, if broadly developed, yields arenas that require action. I focus much less on reporting a position to others for two reasons. First, because of respect for the speed with which human reactivity develops, announcing a future action makes it potentially more difficult to carry through. Second, needed energy for a difficult action can be diluted or lessened through "talk." Nevertheless, there are times when an announced decision about an action or inaction is required. Phase four is the completion of the action.

A well-developed respect for another's reality and viewpoint in taking an action is critical. This respect can aid in the avoidance of polarization that the position of self is right and that of others is wrong. In human functioning, "right" is action that permits self to be fully accountable for one's outcome and commitment to others. The "right" action may be equally right for no one else.

The final phase, letting go, may be the most difficult. Enormous work has gone into gathering data, defining a position for self, and carrying through an action. It can be difficult, therefore, not to be praised for the action and courage that has been required and even more difficult to experience intense criticism. What a great reward for such a difficult journey! Paradoxically, the reward really is great, but in an opposite way. The journey of defining a self, and experiencing the predictable reaction, leaves self feeling very much alone. There is an impending sense of doom and feeling of exile from important others. The individual who can remain calm and consistent in his or her defined beliefs at such a point experiences a sense of internal calm and emotional strength—an exhilaration that is deep and private.

Not Bailing the Other Out

Another technique concerns not bailing others out. Defining self also requires reporting what self will *not* do. All concerned parents know the difficulty of this process. It means letting another you care deeply about make a mistake and not offering the obvious solution to a problem. We humans get caught in this process in two ways. There is the desire in all of us to be important, to be needed by others, or to be the strong one with the answers others seek. We reach out with a solution and feel better about our own ability. The other may not yet have gained new knowledge about functioning or developed new personal competence. In fact, the other may feel less capable and more dependent on the wisdom of the strong one. Meanwhile, the energy used in being "strong" for the other is not directed at the strong individual's own accountability and areas of responsibility. In most cases, no one has "won" in the area of personal responsibility. The "strong one" has not focused on self, and the "weak one" is now more convinced of the need for assistance from others.

Bailing out another fails, in the long run, because most individuals fight accepting responsibility for a dilemma until the burden sits unarguably in their own laps. When parents invest in the anxieties of their children's successes, the children feel assured by the parental energy and focus. The sense that this is my problem and I must do something about it does not exist. The child who is permitted to "let life teach him or her" begins to experience reality in a way that can promote maturity. Maturity represents the ability to access facts in a situation and to be aware of not liking the facts, but to act responsibly toward those facts nevertheless. Immaturity responds to the feelings of not liking facts and gives self permission to ignore them.

Attempting to live one's life accurately requires constant focus on boundaries. Not bailing others out focuses specifically on not being the "answer" for another's dilemmas. Being strong for another's weaknesses can bring feelings of self-importance. It is, however, a destructive process for two reasons. First, it takes so much time and energy to live one's own life responsibly that it is not possible to function well as a self and still represent the "answer" to another's dilemmas. Therefore, the strong one, overfunctioning for another, is underfunctioning for his or her own self. The overfunctioning individual's life journey will be lessened, as his or her focused energy on the realities of his or her own life is drained by functioning as another's answer.

Second, the life journey of the dependent other will be lessened and drained as well. Other individuals, whether one's own mate, child, parent, or co-worker, cannot function responsibly, acting factually on their own dilemmas, if a strong, helpful other worries, thinks, and provides solutions for them. There is an initial sense of relief and release when a dilemma is removed. However, with each and every event in which self is confronted with a dilemma, but does not determine a responsible action for self, there is loss of self. What is lost is an inner sense of being in control of one's own destiny, a loss of confidence to face what challenges life may bring. This sense of self-honor, self-knowledge, and calm confidence is limited, if not destroyed, when a strong other functions for self. The weak self remains a child to the parentlike other.

Such was the case of a young adult floundering in all areas of his life. His erratic behavior made the management of his finances difficult. Realizing he was far behind in his credit card payment, he asked his father for a loan of the required amount. The father agreed to make the needed payment after hearing the son's repayment proposal. However, when the bill arrived, the father discovered that the required payment was much higher. Rather than pay the bill, the father mailed the bill back to his son with a note that said, "I am happy to discuss making loans to you that appear reasonable. However, I will not participate in the role of banker unless the information provided is accurate and consistent." Somehow, the son managed to satisfy the credit card officials. The young adult continues to struggle with his financial management. However, he does so with ever-increasing wisdom and restraint. How differently his future might have evolved had the father automatically paid the higher amount. It is fair to assume that the son would have felt less urgency to manage any aspect of his own functioning.

De-Triangulation

Another major process that is important to understand is the avoidance of de-triangulation. Referring back to the discussion of the parent who is called upon to provide a solution to his child's problem, the latter is being "triangled," or pulled in, by the child into a problem that belongs entirely to the child.

Reactivity is human nature. It is inescapable. During periods of calm, with little pressure and the absence of emotional issues, it is possible for two individuals to interact without experiencing any significant level of reactivity. However, as soon as tension is introduced, anxiety in the individuals will begin to escalate. In the most mature individuals, there will be an awareness of the anxiety, but they are able to remain focused and thoughtful. Discussion about differences, such as a work issue that has to be solved, will be possible.

In less mature individuals, the *fact* of a difference of opinion begins to create discomfort. That there is a disagreement may be enough to disrupt the relationship. How can there be a relationship if the two individuals do not think alike? It can become a question of whose authority or knowledge is accepted. Each individual may find himself or herself fighting for a position on an issue as if serious loss will be experienced if his or her view does not prevail. Loss of what is the question. For less mature individuals, disagreement on an issue may mean that they, themselves, are not credible. It becomes a personal focus rather than a factual one. Feelings are easily hurt and the discussion becomes very personal. With more mature individuals, discussions of difference of opinion can, in fact, be very exciting and stimulating, with each individual seeking to present the most compelling facts. Each person can proceed with great respect for the other and with strong conviction about his or her own viewpoint. The discussion is factual. Although it may become vigorous, it may not ever become personal. After all, these two individuals respect the knowledge and convictions of the other. Neither needs to agree with the other. Disagreement must become strong before these two individuals are truly uncomfortable.

Individuals at lower levels of maturity will become uncomfortable much earlier. The process can automatically lead to efforts to regain comfort for self. One route to such comfort would be to discuss the disagreement in the first relationship with another, hoping that a third individual will vigorously agree with one's view. Also, the individual can seek agreement on the issue from an authority, such as *Oprah*, the Bible, one's mother, or the family therapist. Every family therapist has known moments when a family member is unhappy because he or she has heard another family member "quote" some statement that the therapist supposedly made. One couple spent years taping newspaper articles and columns on their kitchen cabinets to "make the point to the other" and "set the other straight." Neither in the pair has changed his or her thinking on any issue but both continue to cut out articles anyway. Their automatic effort to prove their truth has created a circular polarization in which neither can be objective, neither can hear the other, and neither can think about the facts involved. The only avenue to short-circuit this pattern is for one or the other to no longer need agreement, to become self-contained in his or her beliefs, and now able to listen to difference.

The driving force in triangling is *automatic discomfort* resulting from a lack of agreement on an issue. The process becomes one of substitution. Rather than resolve the discomfort in the two-person relationship in which it exists, one or both individuals seek assurance through agreement with another individual or source of authority. The original problem or dilemma remains and, in fact, most often grows in complexity. Over a lifetime, the load can become heavy. If every individual carries behind him or her a "wagon" full of the issues and relationships that remain unresolved over a lifetime, the burden becomes immense. Issues and unresolved emotionality do not go away. Only closure, facing facts, being accountable to one's own contributions to problems, not blaming self for being imperfect, and not blaming others for what they are not able to do better can protect a life journey from old, heavy, negative baggage that is carried until death. Such closure is not possible unless issues and unresolved dilemmas are kept between the two individuals with whom they belong. This is only possible when the two have the emotional strength to stand in the midst of personal discomfort and the discipline not to seek approval and agreement from outsiders. It is only possible to build solid, personal relationships when triangulation can be avoided and reckoning with issues becomes possible.

The absolute respect for boundaries has been discussed throughout the chapter. It is the simplest of concepts, but perhaps the most difficult challenge in daily life to honor. For the individual seeking to function at high levels of responsibility and effectiveness, there will be a focus on all the decisions and dilemmas the day has brought. The focus will constantly seek to answer four questions: (1) Does this dilemma have to do with me? (2) Is there an action required of me? (3) Have I acted already, by commission or omission, in a reactive way? and (4) If I have acted in a reactive way, what correction is required?

Supportive Mechanisms

I positions are actions that represent an objective statement of what self believes and what self can be expected to do; they are a serious reflection of important principles of living. No individual can take an I position on every aspect of life. Rather, I positions are reserved for those issues that will compromise personal functioning should an individual not act consistently with his or her beliefs and convictions. If the individual did not act consistently with what he or she believed, there exists a sense of lost self, a compromise of honor and pride. Such principles cannot be ignored without paying a high price in self-esteem. However, I positions are so difficult and require so much energy that it is not possible to define a self on every issue, nor is it appropriate. For example, a young adult may strongly disagree with his or her family's plan to put grandmother in a nursing home, but may have neither the living space nor extra money for home care to offer as an alternative. An I position may also not be appropriate when one is a guest of another family whose functional decisions are not respected. Most of life has to do with much lesser concerns—concerns more appropriately thought of as life preferences. Many an individual has experienced confusion between personal principle and personal preference. Personal principle cannot be sacrificed without loss of self. Personal preference, on the other hand, represents areas for compromise as two individuals maneuver through the shared life of a relationship. Personal preference could apply to decisions such as where to vacation, at what restaurant to dine, the color of furniture. What is critical is that an individual knows which is which. Personal principle applies to decisions such as religious conviction, parental philosophy, or career choice.

Two mechanisms can prove to be useful in dealing with dilemmas in which an I position is not possible. These mechanisms are banter and reversal. Banter and reversal represent a "play on words," which actually represents a play on paradigms. Unless used when the speaker is very calm, clear, and respectfully knowledgeable about emotional reality, each mechanism can be destructive, leading to a significant increase in reactivity—the opposite outcome that is sought.

Bantering

Bantering is the use of humor to deal with a dilemma. Humor, a light touch, can loosen up a polarized or polarizing situation. Tightness breeds polarization, heavy reactivity, an inability to hear another's viewpoint, and a perceived sense of truth. It is frozen emotionality that focuses on a given viewpoint. Bantering, if done at the right time and in the right way, can ease tension and create a more relaxed environment. When humans are calm and relaxed, it becomes more possible for them to think about facts (as opposed to their own experience or viewpoint) and to hear how another can think in a different way.

Bantering is a thought-out response that can be used to loosen an uptight environment, when there is no position to take, or it has already been taken. However, the uptightness is interfering with smooth functioning of the relationship or system. Such would be the case with children in a family with structured curfews whose friends have no curfews. The children with curfews see themselves as "being in prison." Parents who hold to their family's rules can experience reactivity from their children. Rather than being defensive, parents have found that bantering, referring to self as the "warden" and the children as "jailbirds," can loosen things up. Such light humor in response to the children's attacks can take the passion out of the dilemma. The children may not appreciate the humor, but nevertheless, they will be less angry and intense in their objection as their parents play along with their angry attack rather than defending it.

This is the wonderful gift of humor. It is a release valve for passionate reactivity that can permit a return to thinking and listening. The humor itself does not solve a dilemma. It does, however, create an environment in which a solution can be reached because individuals are able to listen.

Reversals

Reversals are statements made by an individual that convey the opposite message from what is felt or meant. These statements can act to loosen up a situation or communicate a message that would not be heard otherwise.

Reversals are mechanisms that can be destructive if they are not done with great care, timing, and accurate understanding of the situation. I have seen many reversals done poorly, without understanding or respect for reactivity. I rarely use this mechanism, nor do I choose to teach it. Instead, I believe in giving a straight statement to another and working hard to balance one's own opinion with an understanding of the other's.

Most individuals will have more ability to hear thoughts they do not seek to hear if those thoughts are presented as opinions rather than as truth. Further, most individuals will be more respectful of ideas which they are asked to "consider" rather than ideas which they are expected to accept. Communication of difficult material can be enhanced by stating up front that an opinion will be expressed which the other does not want to hear. In my practice and in my personal dealings, I have found this approach to be very effective. This is not to say that there is never a situation in which a reversal is appropriate or that I do not on occasion use the mechanism of reversal. I do, but it is always with enormous respect for the emotionality that surrounds the dilemma.

There are also situations in which every attempt to communicate to a reactive other has failed. In such cases, a reversal may be appropriate. Such was the case when a gentleman recommended to his recently retired friend that he move to a retirement/nursing center. This recommendation came after months of depression, during which the gentleman had made every effort to support, encourage, and advise his depressed friend. Nothing penetrated the depression. The only action that remained was to directly challenge the believed hopelessness by validating the perceived hopelessness as realistic. Therefore, the retirement/nursing center was recommended, triggering a reaction of fury in the depressed retiree. After a brief period of anger, the depressed man returned to an adequate level of functioning. At last report, the once depressed man had not forgiven the gentleman for his suggestion and had not spoken to him again. The possibility of reactive cutoff had been understood by the gentleman, but nevertheless, he chose to make this final effort to aid his friend, "letting go" of the outcome.

Another example is a young athlete afraid of failure during competition. When words of encouragement and an accurate review of the capabilities of the athlete did not provide relief, the father told the son that the athletic demands were too hard for him and he should quit. The response to the recommendation, as with the depressed retiree, was fury. However, the young athlete, in his fury, broke through the paralysis and began to play competently. Father was forgiven.

The risk of using a reversal is not the fury of the other. On the contrary, the freedom to responsibly "say and do" whatever an individual believes is necessary is a requirement of living maturely, with consistent personal accountability. Maturity is the ability to tolerate loss of relationship, approval, and belonging as a result of acting on what self believes to be accurate and responsible. The risk, rather, is that the individual making the reversal statement is not calm or neutral when the communication is made. If the statement is made instead at a point of anger and high reactivity in self, the statement may be heard as sarcasm or worse, and the outcome is destructive. Such is the case of a wife reactively stating to her husband, who she thought was overreacting to a mess made by the dog, "Why don't you beat him?" The dog was beaten.

It is out of respect for possible destructive outcomes that can arise from the use of a reversal that this mechanism is regarded with such strong caution. There are rare occasions when there is no other alternative. In such situations, the reversal represents a final "letting go" after every responsible step has been taken.

Summary of Techniques for Changing Self

Solid change becomes possible when an individual has knowledge of human functioning, the functional patterns of one's family, and the functional patterns of self. It is an acceptance that one's self is responsible for the creation and solution of one's own life problems. Solid change evolves from a knowledge of theory. Techniques are based on decisions that apply theoretical knowledge. Foundation techniques are actions that directly encourage attempts to increase differentiation. Supportive techniques keep a system calm. Five techniques have been discussed: the I position, refusing to bail the other out, de-triangling, bantering, and reversals.

APPLICATION OF THEORY

This section of the chapter will discuss two emotional systems: the emotional system of the therapist and the emotional system of a family in therapy. It is a discussion of reactivity within one's own emotional system, to another's emotional system, and between the two interacting systems. The purpose of this section is to focus on actions that can counter, diminish, or resolve reactivity, permitting therapeutic process maximum effectiveness.

The Therapist's Emotional System

Therapy Without a Theoretical Foundation

The quantity of content in therapy sessions that a therapist listens to is tremendous. Without the framework of theory, there can be no factual or consistent way to evaluate content for importance or to determine priorities of focus. Bowen theory provides a context in which to view symptoms in an individual. By knowing the characteristics and patterns of a system, the individual's family, and of the individual, prediction becomes possible. On the basis of this knowledge, a therapist has a foundation for building a plan for therapy with short-term and long-term goals.

When there is no plan, a couple processes may develop:

1. The direction of sessions may come from the family's focus. Hence, the emotional system of the family directs the focus of sessions.
2. Therapy without a plan can become a drifting process. This lack of direction may create anxiety in the therapist and family alike. The

therapist may distance himself or herself from the uncomfortable process. A family may react to distance in the therapist and end therapy as a result. The drift is, of course, in the therapist.

Communication Out of Phase with a Family's Reality

All families enter therapy with reactivity, anxiety, a fixed focus, and belief in, or lack thereof, their capability to gain control over life dilemmas. The more a therapist can assess and be respectful of these forces, the greater the possibility for an effective therapeutic environment.

The issue is one of connection or disconnection. When a therapist's questions are consistent with the state of the family's or the individual's motivation, anxiety, and hope, then change is possible. Further, the likelihood that the family can "hear" the questions greatly increases. Questions that are understood open the lens of an individual's understanding, creating objectivity and a growing distinction between fact and feeling. On the other hand, it is when a therapist moves toward change in a family, making suggestions for actions to bring about change without first "building the context," that disconnection occurs. Such would be the case in discussing change of self with an individual who is still vigorously focused on symptoms.

When disconnection occurs, a family does not "feel" understood by the therapist. In fact, the therapist appears irrelevant to their distress. This can lead a therapist to view the family as uncooperative, resistive, unmotivated, and at a low level of functioning. All of these outcomes can occur when a therapist is unaware or disrespectful of the process of the family.

The Lack of Personal Conviction

When a therapist has not gone through the efforts to counter forces against change in his or her own system, it becomes difficult to coach another to do so. Hence, the therapist's lack of personal experience with the struggle to define a self in his or her own family greatly lessens his or her ability to provide a therapeutic "classroom" that fosters development of solid differentiation.

Coaching a Family with the Characteristics of Low Levels of Differentiation

Characteristics of a family that represent low levels of differentiation include multiple major life problems, long duration of symptoms, severity of symptoms, and high levels of anxiety. Awareness of these characteristics can cause a therapist to have little expectation for change in a family, lessening his or her thoughtful observation and minimizing attempts to communicate ideas and concepts. Therefore, a therapist may fail to learn those forces that prevent this family from functioning better. Human functioning can be seen most clearly in an immature, highly reactive family system because patterns and characteristics are so visible. It is also possible that the therapist's early assessment of low-level functioning of the family is inaccurate. Functional strengths of the family may have been missed or ignored or the family's functional weaknesses overemphasized. Further, the therapist may be observing a family in an episodic low level of functioning, which may well prove to be temporary. Finally, personal motivation to live differently can be a powerful force, resulting in progress that the therapist might not have predicted. The longer a therapist is in practice, the more respect he or she has for the subtle complexities of human functioning that make it difficult to distinguish between functional and base levels of an emotional system. Extensive knowledge about a family system is necessary to determine its basic and functional levels of differentiation.

Therapeutic Decisions Based on a Therapist's Comfort

When decisions about therapy—who in the family will come or the frequency of sessions—are made on the basis of the therapist's comfort rather than based on theoretical concepts, the ultimate impact of therapy will be significantly diminished. A therapist must remain detached from a family's anxious approval and disapproval. Effectiveness requires an ability to focus on any topic, interact with any member, and schedule sessions as frequently as necessary for maximum family thoughtfulness and leadership.

Responsibility for Change

Every therapist is faced with the dilemma of defining a position for himself or herself regarding what and who will change a family. Due to anxiety, families will express expectations that the solution for the problem will come from the therapist. Such expectations may be communicated through "helplessness" in the family, through a directly expressed expectation of the therapist, or through flattery of the therapist for being an expert. Most therapists have experienced such strong approval from a family and have acted to demonstrate that expertise. One family, with whom I had refused to continue working but with whom there was still contact, kept returning with messages that no other therapist was as effective. A therapist can easily get caught up in responding to such flattering communication.

Should the therapist accept responsibility for the family's functioning and change, solid change will not be possible for the family. Therapists must avoid trying to "save" a family from itself. Only the family, through the efforts of one or more individuals, can change ingrained patterns.

Should a therapist react to the expectations of a family, a negative power struggle will evolve. A therapist may find that he or she has reactively distanced from the family or may find himself or herself attacking the family for being irresponsible. *Until a family is left with its own quandary, it is not possible to know how responsible it can be.*

The wise therapist, on guard for automatic forces in a family to place its problem in his or her hands, can remain outside the system and its expectations. Being detached from a family system, the therapist knows he or she can neither save nor change the family. Such detachment allows the therapist to connect with each member of the family. The individual has the opportunity to accept that he or she is the "author" of his or her own life course, its successes and dilemmas. The individual now has the opportunity to become a defined self.

Polarization with the Family's Emotional Process

Struggling against the symptom focus of a family. The task of assisting a family to de-focus the presenting symptom and instead to widen its lens of understanding is required for a family to change. Knowing this, therapists can be vulnerable to fight the symptom focus, sometimes refusing to discuss it. The result can be a disconnection between therapist and family and a probable early end to the therapy process.

General resistance in families. "Blocking" in a family can take many forms. A family may directly refuse to discuss certain topics; it may dismiss specific questions as irrelevant (discussing my sister has nothing to do with this situation); it may inform the therapist that he or she is not providing that for which the family is paying.

Rather than *fight* reactive forces, a therapist can pursue them through a process that I call "buying the block." The process involves talking about the reactivity thoroughly with the individual. For example, a female is having difficulties in her relationships with siblings. When asked about them, she appears to be flooded with emotion toward the family. Yet she is vehement that she is not affected by her family's behavior. Rather than forcing her to acknowledge distress, she could be asked, "Many individuals having this kind of difficulty with their siblings would tend to get reactive. What keeps you from doing so?" A parental pair, distressed over a rebelling teenager and unwilling to discuss marital functioning, could be asked, "How have you managed the discomfort of living with a rebellious child without tension developing between you?" A couple experiencing marital tension but denying experiencing anxiety could be asked, "Most spouses experiencing marital tension report high anxiety as well. What has enabled you to remain free of spiraling anxiety?" A young adult denying discomfort about a lack of life direction could be asked, "Many in your circumstance would experience considerable discomfort. What has kept you from such discomfort?"

Individuals who are too anxious about an emotional reality to discuss it are calmed by a therapist's agreement that they are free of the feared emotional reality. Often, they respond with an admission that they did not mean to say they "never feel anxious," and they may be comfortable enough now to describe moments of the anxiety that earlier could not be acknowledged. In the process, the family has had the opportunity *to discuss topical material to which they are reactive.* Such discussion will be required if they are in fact to change. The therapist must keep the family focused on the content until reactivity is reduced and a dilemma, resolved. This requires that the therapist neither distance, react, nor attack the tendency in the family to avoid an anxious focus. Unless a family has been freed to move beyond the "block," solid change is impossible. Change in an individual or a system is not possible without every aspect of the multigenerational functioning of a family being available for inspection and thorough discussion.

A therapist will affect a family's possible reactivity through the nature of the questions in therapy, whether content or process. Focusing on process, repeating patterns of functioning and emotionality, the therapist pursues facts about emotional material. Thus begins an interweaving of current content with historical facts. It is in the discovery of predictable processes and patterns of a system that solid change becomes possible.

Seeing More than One Family Member

Whenever more than one family member participates in a course of therapy with the same therapist, the challenge for the therapist to maintain meticulous boundaries with each individual as he or she deals with the emotionally laden material can be grueling. This is particularly true when one spouse or family member appears to "hear" theory, and the other, to "react" to theory. A therapist is vulnerable to becoming triangled, allied in understanding with the family member who appears to hear and reactive to the one who does not.

There are many similarities between athletics and psychotherapy—"that agility to move around a defense." In psychotherapy, several therapeutic skills (discussed earlier in the chapter) permit a therapist to remain outside a family's (whether one family member or several) emotional process.

Bantering. Bantering is the use of humor to relax family members about issues that escalate anxiety. For instance, a therapist might say to a conflictual couple who cannot agree on each other's descriptions, "Are you two sure that you live in the same house?"

Abstracting. Abstracting is the use of discussion about other families to introduce information. Concepts and expressions of opinion can be introduced without either attempting to "sell" an idea or to be seen as agreeing with one family member. The therapist might comment:

- "There are theories that suggest . . ."
- "I have known families who . . . "
- "Many individuals in your situation would react by . . . "
- "However, your family may be the exception."

Such statements by a therapist permit a family to focus on ideas disconnected from the family's own functioning, thereby avoiding a connection that could create reactivity.

Most couples who engage in serious effort to learn Bowen theory will eventually do work alone. This is because work on increasing differentiation, raising one's level of maturity, and moving beyond seeking approval requires so much hard work that sharing sessions with a mate becomes constricting. There is so much to discuss and consider about family history and functioning that sharing session time with one's mate's agenda creates frustration. Some couples never reach this point in their progress and never seek individual work time. One couple called to schedule therapy sessions. Upon sensing tight fusion, I insisted that I have an initial session with each individually. Because the couple focused so intensely on "we," it was important to determine whether this "each divorced/premarital" couple could negotiate the discomfort of being seen individually. They could not, would not, and decided not to schedule appointments.

Although the work of changing self involves individual focus and effort, there are major benefits to seeing as many family members or other important individuals as possible. However, no matter how many family members are seen, or who they are in the system, the manner in which the potential forces for being "triangled" are addressed by the therapist will determine:

- whether a polarization develops, with one member for therapy and another against therapy,
- whether family members actively working toward change will continue this work, and

- whether nonmotivated family members can reach a point where changing self becomes important.

Therapists Who Are Triangled with the Theory

Beginning to understand the concepts of Bowen theory can be an emotional as well as a cognitive experience, as descriptions of human functional patterns become visible in the individual's own environment. For many, there will be a struggle to move beyond fusion or dependency on the theory to a clarity of each concept, an ability to explain and describe the concepts in one's own words and from one's own observations. It is a commitment to Bowen theory, based on the accuracy of the concepts verified from his observations. Personal ownership of theory is not an attachment to a theory nor to the therapist. Rather, it is the ability to describe theoretical process in one's own words and to differ with a theory or theorist on fact or opinion.

Whether one remains triangled with theory, or develops a conviction of belief and commitment to it, will be important both for a therapist and for an individual attempting to be a self.

When a theory and the therapist are seen as the same, reactivity to an idea can become reactivity to the therapist as well. For instance, polarization (when one individual is right and the other wrong) can occur. A family may conclude that the only path for change with this therapist will not be successful.

The same concepts about a dilemma can be conveyed without creating vulnerability to polarization. For instance, the following phrases can be used to introduce an idea: "I don't know whether this would apply to your family . . . "; "There are theorists who believe . . . "; or "Some families have come to believe . . . " What is important is that the therapist has developed methods to introduce broader and broader facts that pertain to the situation. A family is freed to hear ideas or concepts, without the reactivity that would have occurred had the focus been on the family's reality. Potential reactivity, avoidance, disagreement, and disconnection have been bypassed. The potential to move beyond reactivity to critical process and content has been created.

When a therapist is attached to the theory, the theory becomes an "answer" for the therapist. A therapist will refer to theory without having thought through, defined, or described the presenting phenomena from his or her own perspective. Bowen theory provides factual direction for pursuing the evolution of a symptom. Development of factual hypotheses resides with the therapist. Commitment to a particular theoretical framework can, at worst, represent a professional "social group" (this can be so for any group to which one belongs). A therapist trained in Bowen theory may make assumptions about the life and work of another trained in the same theory. It is as if one can assume how another thinks or what another believes. Such assumptions can occur when a therapist has become attached to a theory. It may be a fact that both therapists studied a certain theory, but *how* each individual understands the theory and *how* that individual applies the theory as a therapist or in his or her daily life may differ.

The Emotional System of a Family

The goal of Bowen theory, as a basis for psychotherapy, is to provide an individual with the opportunity to learn about human functioning and the functioning of self. For the motivated individual seeking to function at a more thoughtful level, this therapeutic process can make such change possible. With every individual, there are obstacles that can end forward motion of the process. The skilled therapist must know, respect, and anticipate these obstacles in the therapy process. Five potential obstacles will be mentioned: symptom relief; decreasing focus on children; reporting emotional information; change in the functioning of the therapist; and a worsening picture for the family.

Symptom Relief

Symptom relief becomes a problem when a therapist has failed to broaden the focus and understanding of a family from the specific anxious focus that brought them into the office. Individuals should gradually move from an anxious focus to a curious focus about human functioning, knowledge of self-functioning patterns, and the possibility of functioning more effectively and responsibly. For the individual or family who remains focused on initial symptoms, symptom relief ends the motivation for continuing to work on the family functioning. For the family that has become a "student" of human functioning, of its own strengths and weaknesses, relief of the original symptom represents *freedom* to focus on broader arenas of functioning. The journey has become very exciting and energizing. Such is the case for a woman who arrived in my office for the first time, functioning minimally, following a marital separation. Three years later, she has completed her first semester of undergraduate school with straight As at the age of fifty-one! Amid the loss, fear, and sadness of an ended marriage, she began to study the functional history of her own life. What emerged was a reality that her own identity, her self, had received little energy, time, or focus over the years. Rather, she had sought to find her place of belonging, her identity, through marriage relationships that ended, each of the three, in divorce.

Decreasing Focus on Children

Two "negative" outcomes are possible when parents succeed in reducing their overfocus on a child. First, the child may initially increase symptoms of acting out. This can be understood, in part, as a loss of connectedness for the child. Such flare-ups will usually be followed by a significant reduction in acting out, new levels of calmness within the child, and more order in his or her life if the parents commit to their change. The second possible negative flare-up, if in fact there is a reduction in child focus, is a new level of marital conflict and tension. This occurs because part of the mechanism of child focus is an avoidance of issues between the parents, such as disappointments, unresolved expectations, or lingering reactivity. Neither has known how to successfully address dissatisfaction with the other. Hence, energies and focus were diverted automatically away from distressful aspects in the marital relationship. Diversions can be work, hobbies, sports, or children's activities. Further, they can include symptoms such as affairs, chemical dependency, or illness. These diversions represent mechanisms to avoid unfulfilled needs for comfort or lack of satisfaction between the partners. Neither can solve the unresolved dilemmas or has the ability to withstand the conflict necessary to reckon with and solve the issues.

Once child focus is lessened, the negative energy may automatically appear between the partners. The couple may now view the therapy with great apprehension, remembering that when they walked through the door there was a problem with their child and now they have a marital problem as well.

The knowledgeable therapist will be expecting this shift in focus and can calmly walk the not-so-calm couple through unexpected tension into a position for finally reckoning with those long-unsolved conflicts between them. Humor can be very useful with such a couple. Assurance that they now have the opportunity, after all of these years, to build a genuine closeness they have never known can be calming. Such satisfaction comes from personal clarity about significant issues, a new, factual understanding of the other, and respect for the impact of nodal events on the evolution of the marriage.

Disclosure of Emotional Information

Disclosure of highly emotional personal information (incest, infidelity, premarriage pregnancy) can set off several different destructive reactions. Feelings of shame, embarrassment, and disloyalty can lead to an assumption that the therapist has lost respect for the individual as a result of the disclosure. The individual may respond by missing the next scheduled session or never returning.

The knowledgeable therapist will address these possible "automatic reactions" in the same session so as to dissipate them *before* the individual leaves the office. For instance, the therapist might ask, "What has it been like to finally discuss this material?"; "What has been the impact of not being able to discuss this all of these years?"; or "How can this new information make your efforts here more productive?" Each of these questions allows the individual to begin to process the emotional reactions of having disclosed the material and to discuss the reactions thoughtfully. Statements by the therapist that discuss the disclosure as a positive action rather than negative action might include, "I believe that you will find the discussion of this material will provide you with new freedom to reckon with your concern."; "If not discussing something makes it impossible to solve it, then is it not disloyal *not* to discuss the area?"; or "Your courage in talking about this material will be discussed in your sessions for a long time to come and will become one of the most important things you will have said in here as you work to change your life." Rather than filled with shame, the individual now leaves the office feeling that he or she has accomplished something very difficult to the benefit of self and the family.

Change in the Functioning of the Therapist

Therapists who continue to work on their own functional level of maturity, accountability, and personal responsibility will continue to increase their own functioning. The gains in self will increase their effectiveness with families. Gains in personal clarity and increased definition in one's own family can provide a new "looseness" in thinking, sharper communication, and new clarity to focus in the therapy process. Some families will be aware of the enhanced detachment in the therapist. They may react silently, make comments that the session has been different, or make a direct statement that the therapist has changed. These reactions result from the therapist's newly clarified self and a sharper awareness of his or her own boundaries. The individual in therapy is now left to manage his or her own need for approval and to focus on the task to resolve dilemmas through an enhanced awareness of what is truly self.

The knowledgeable therapist will be aware of this new detachment in himself or herself, expecting possible reaction from the families. Awareness and knowledge provide the opportunity for prediction; prediction provides the opportunity to plan ahead. Preparation permits competent, effective functioning when common obstacles occur in the therapy process.

A Worsening Picture of the Family

Families that experience a worsening problem can feel hopeless, want to give up, and become angry at the therapist. Reactivity can be focused on the therapist, with strong blame and accusation. Such was true of a wife who found herself in a separation and divorce after a several-year therapy course. For much of a year, she made frequent comments such as, "But you said, if I did 'such and such,' the relationship would likely work out. I thought that coming here was to avoid a divorce, not cause one." It is as if coming to a therapy office acts as a form of "life insurance" that will protect the family from negative outcomes.

It is hard work to validate accurately the continuation or beginning of new problems within a family while keeping a focus on the process of long-term differentiation and change. Life is, in my opinion, starting on the Oregon Trail at one end in a covered wagon and attempting to get to the other end before the end of life's journey. Wheels fall off, axles break, disease occurs, Indians attack, and weather beats down. This is human life, not a smoothly paved, modern road on which one achieves and acquires. The family that comes to believe in the Oregon Trail concept can ride through and over obstacles, strengthened in the process. In fact, there is an acceptance of the struggle that represents human functioning and an awareness of the victory for self each time a dilemma is constructively confronted and resolved.

Summary

Discussion of the therapy process has suggested that:

- knowledge of reactivity within self and within a family system can provide a prediction of those occurrences that will create reactivity in families and failure of solid change;
- prediction of family reactivity and reaction in self allows for preparation and action that can counter this potentially destructive reactivity;
- the goal for the therapist is to operate in objective, neutral, and thoughtful ways that permit a family to disengage from reactivity;
- an individual can become knowledgeable about human functioning and observant of functional patterns in his or her own family and in self; and
- it is then possible to take actions to change self-functioning in those arenas one has defined.

THE PROCESS OF CHANGE
IN THE BOWEN THEORETICAL SYSTEM

Bowen meticulously focused on theory in his life work, not on technique. His determination kept him from discussion of technique after the early years. He was concerned that focus on technique would encourage an individual orientation (rather than a broad, systems focus) to human functioning; dysfunction would be understood as residing within the individual, outside a connection to the emotional and historical system in which the individual was born and developed; and there would be a disrespect for the complicated and vast processes of human emotional systems that yield the functional patterns of a self.

However, if Bowen theory accurately describes human functioning, then there has to be a way to discuss therapeutic techniques based upon theory without becoming individually oriented or focused on techniques separate from theory. It is the purpose of this section of the chapter to discuss therapy that is connected and is indeed an outgrowth of theory.

Change

Understanding the nature of change may well have bothered humankind since evolving the capacity to observe. Certainly, it has been a question for study and hypothesis since the origin of psychiatry and other disciplines associated with mental and physical functioning.

In order to discuss and describe change, it is necessary to first discuss the difference between shift and change in functioning. A shift will be defined as a temporary, sometimes opposite, fluctuation in functioning. Change will be defined as consistent, predictable new patterns of action as an individual negotiates emotional fields within self, within family, and with others.

Characteristics of Change versus Shifts in Functioning

A functional shift seeks to avoid discomfort and to gain approval; it is usually of short duration and is based on feeling. Solid change, on the other hand, is based upon principles that are followed consistently, endure under stress and risk, and are based on facts rather than feelings.

Shifts in behavior are a form of change familiar to all of us. The shift may result from a change in the environment. It may also be the product of a good intention, or a "New Year's resolution," that is not grounded in personal accountability—an intention fueled with the desire to change.

Examples of a shift in functioning might include solving a child's classroom problems by changing the teacher rather than accurately confronting the problem. A shift can come from solving an unresolved frustration with one's life or work by creating a new focus, such as a new baby, new house, or moving to a new town. It feels different, as if the original frustration or discomfort is now resolved. It is, rather, the solving of a dilemma, a dependency on another, or dysfunction in one arena of life through the substitution of another focus or dependency. It is impossible to think about shifts in functioning without discussing the concept of the *triangle*. Shifts occur as the result of fluctuations in triangles. In therapy, an individual's functioning can shift as a result of the establishment of a relationship with a therapist—as if the person's life has now become stable. It only takes a break in this important relationship, even a temporary break, for the superficial nature of the shift to be apparent. The relationship is, of course, a manifestation of emotional fusion.

Change in human functioning is a different process. Permanent change requires knowledge of those forces that influence functioning. This knowledge acts as a foundation for developing solidness, the ability to define life principles, goals, and objectives and the ability to stay on course through fluctuations in emotionality of important others. It is making decisions for self based upon facts, not upon the approval or disapproval of important others. Permanent change results from the development of life principles that can act as a guide for life. It requires a long-term effort, continual awareness of emotional forces, and a willingness to work toward individuation and self-definition in the midst of compelling togetherness forces.

Observing the Process of Change

Change is a phenomenon that can be factually observed. It is a fact that an individual can effectively define boundaries—say "no" and stick to it—on issues for which they could not do so before. It is a fact that an individual can define principles in life dilemmas (e.g., when self has participated in a problem, being able to see that role objectively, and to act to correct it). The process of change is being able to "see" the operation of emotionality in self. It is knowing that a particular action will create reaction in others. It is being prepared for reactivity with acceptance of the strong discomfort that will occur. Finally, it is an automatic focus on responsibility for self and to others in all areas of life. As Dr. Bowen so often said, "It is saying what you mean and meaning what you say, doing what you say and saying what you do." Living objectively, focusing on the facts, creates a consistency that brings deep tranquillity in self and respect from others. This respect is above and beyond agreement, or dis-agreement, with a viewpoint or action.

Individuals often ask about the nature of change and what is required to create it in their own lives. Over the years, I have drawn a spectrum to describe the process of change. At the far left is pretherapy—symptoms with no successful action to resolve them. Individuals who enter therapy with a Bowen-trained therapist will first enter a phase of observation (developing knowledge of human functioning, the patterns of one's own family, the functional patterns in self, and societal anxiety). During this phase, symptoms remain essentially unchanged. However, a family may now be calmer because of the focus on facts about human functioning. Individuals are encouraged to "sit back and take their shoes off" because it will be a while, an uncomfortable while, before they are capable of effectively countering the symptomatic patterns, due to their lack of knowledge about functioning. Those who are curious and motivated enough to work at this phase will complete several tasks. Myths about the "heroes and villains" in one's own family will be broken. The patterns in self that are dysfunctional, or in the very least not effective, will be stud-ied. The part self has played, through omission or commission, in the problems faced today will be discovered. The symptoms that caused the individual to make the first call to the therapist have been resolved. On the change spectrum, this state is in the middle and is neutral. Many will have no further motivation to continue work on self, since the discomfort has abated. For those who are caught, unable to stop observing, being curious, and working at self, the fun has only begun. No longer focused on "prob-lems," the individual begins to focus on every aspect of his or her life (personal responsibility, the use of time, money, opportunities, resources). With a lens on the nature of emotionality, the honoring and dishonoring of boundaries, and the outcomes for self in being accurate, enormous possi-bilities are created. This focus, working every day to know who self is and attempting to live accurately, becomes a lifetime effort. For some, infre-quent visits to the therapy office will occur over many years. Such "check-ups" result from respect for the ability in all individuals to lose clarity, without knowing, until old, unwelcome symptoms from the past or a new version of some symptom appear.

Change *does not* mean that the family or problem has changed. Bowen theory is not an insurance policy or a promissory note that, if certain actions are taken, those around self will finally change or be set straight! What it means is that *self* can change by the way in which a relationship or dilemma is reckoned. Freedom is the ability to find closure and to feel deep peace and tranquillity about one's actions. There is a feeling of completeness and a lack of regret about an outcome. The self has represented full accuracy to another or to a system through action concerning an issue.

SUMMARY

Life is not a smooth paved road upon which an individual works to achieve and then acquire. It is rather the Oregon Trail on which self travels in a covered wagon encountering obstacles all along the way. A mature self will confront those dilemmas fully, taking the risk of discomfort and disapproval. There will be the courage to be accurate to self and to pay an enormous price in discomfort. There will be acceptance of the fact that problems and patterns do not go away; rather, they act like bacteria, festering and growing. Many a family has reexperienced a family issue twenty-five years later, as the eldest marries and the parents find themselves confronting a passionate issue from their own wedding just as "hot" as the issue had been a quarter-century earlier. Either issues are confronted by self, going to the furthest point to be accurate and responsible, or they take on a life of their own, growing like a kitten into what can be a life-threatening three-hundred-pound cat. Either emotionality and personal irresponsibility are faced or their effects will ultimately govern the outcome of one's life!

REFERENCES

Bowen, M. (1978). *Family Therapy in Clinical Practice.* New York: Jason Aronson.

Kerr, M. and Bowen, M. (1988). *Family Evaluation: An Approach Based on Bowen Theory.* New York: W. W. Norton and Company.

Toman, W. (1969). *Family Constellations,* Second Edition. New York: Springer Publishing Company.

PART II:
CLINICAL APPLICATIONS

Chapter 4

Marital Fusion and Differentiation

Phil Klever

What contributes to a well-functioning marriage? The way a clinician answers that question directs the clinical work with a marital problem. For example, if the clinician views marital functioning as a product of the husband's and wife's individual personalities, the clinician works with the psychopathology within the individual. If the clinician sees communication as the key to marital functioning, communication skills are assessed and taught. The lens of Bowen theory expands the view of marriage beyond the individuals and the marital dyad to the interlocking relationships in the family. From this theoretical perspective, marital process is regulated by the individuals, the couple, and the family relationships.

This chapter first presents a natural systems and Bowen family systems theoretical view of marriage. Then, application of Bowen theory to a marital problem is discussed, followed by presentation of a case example.

THEORY

A Natural Systems View of Marriage

Bowen believed the human has much in common with other life forms because of our evolutionary inheritance. One pathway to understand the human is to examine the similarities and differences between our evolutionary ancestors and our own species. Marriage from this perspective is seen to be in part a product of evolution, and this section aims to explain that viewpoint.

The mating strategies for males and females within a species (polygamy or monogamy) and the nature of their attachment (pair bonding or lack of involvement) are adaptations to perpetuate individuals' genes. The male-female relationship is a response to the demands of the environment, the morphology of the animal, and the survival of the offspring. In most species, especially mammals, males and females are not monogamous and seldom form pair-bonds. Instead, males compete for dominance, with the highest-ranking males winning the rights of reproduction. In polygamous species, the females usually benefit from having the hardiest males provide genes for their offspring (Betzig, 1986). A male seldom assists the female in care of her young unless it aids survival of his offspring or earns him favor with the female for future mating.

Monogamy is often selected for when the survival of the offspring is enhanced by the male and female joining forces to face the challenges of the environment and/or the demands of parenting. Monogamy occurs in most birds, about 3 percent of mammals, and 16 percent of primates (Kleiman, 1977; Konner, 1982). Variations in monogamy between species range from a male and female who have little association other than sharing territory and mating, to a male and female in a pair-bond who share care of offspring and mate exclusively. A pair-bond or emotional attachment is formed to ensure the partnership lasts. The pressures that select for formation of monogamy and a pair-bond are defense against predators, scarce or difficult nesting sites or lodging, offspring feeding demands, weaning, prolonged offspring dependence and delayed offspring sexual maturation (as compared to related species), and weight of the young (Kleiman, 1977; Whitten, 1987; Wilson, 1975). In most pair-bonded species, males and females share care of offspring and have similar or identical morphology, less role differentiation, and less intense sexual interaction as compared to polygamous species.

What kind of species is the human? The human's primary mating strategy is monogamy, the pair-bond is semisynchronous, and care for offspring is somewhat biparental. Although many human cultures are polygamous, the spoils of this mating system are reserved for the top 10 percent of males. The remaining 90 percent form monogamous pair-bonds. But humans are not the most monogamous species, as evidenced by their frequent infidelity, with reports of infidelity ranging from 25 to 72 percent (Fisher, 1992).

The human pair-bond or emotional attachment is semisynchronous or less than perfect, as compared to more pair-bonded species. The human male and female have more inherent differences between them. For instance, although the human male and female are somewhat similar in morphology, they are not as identical as compared to other species. Perhaps pair-bonding in the human is half-baked in the evolutionary oven (Maraskin, 1994).

With humans, care of offspring is usually provided primarily by the mother, with the father providing an assistant role in all cultures across the globe. As in other species, the father's involvement with offspring is sensitive to his relationship with the female. When the pair-bond is stable, the male is usually more involved with the offspring. The human is capable of much variation in this basic evolutionary blueprint, providing interesting exceptions to monogamy, pair-bonding, and biparental care.

BOWEN THEORY AND FACTORS INFLUENCING MARITAL FUNCTIONING

Differentiation of Self

Differentiation of self is a cornerstone concept in Bowen theory. Variation in adaptiveness among individuals is predicted by varying levels of differentiation. Differentiation of self is the ability to be an individual while staying connected with others or the ability to be separate while remaining engaged. At higher levels of differentiation, people are responsible for themselves and to others, capable of clear thinking in the midst of emotional situations, guided by a well-defined set of principles and goals, and tend to have minor or few physical, emotional, or social symptoms and more stable marriages. At lower levels of differentiation, people are underresponsible for themselves and/or overresponsible for others, guided primarily by emotions or impulses with little to no reliance on thought, consumed by relationships with little energy left for self-direction, and tend to have major physical, emotional, or social symptoms and more marital disruption.

Bowen (1978) believed that fusion reaches its greatest intensity in the togetherness of marriage. This fusion is at the core of marital disruption and clinical work with couples. Marriages vary in their level of fusion or differentiation. Figure 4.1 (Kerr and Bowen, 1988) graphically represents this range in marriage, showing the degree to which the self is determined through the spouse, or the balance between individuality and togetherness. The no fusion illustration does not occur in humans at this point in their evolution. Couples at the highest levels of differentiation fall between moderate and no fusion.

FIGURE 4.1. The Range of Fusion in Marriage

High fusion   Moderate fusion   No fusion

Couples that are most fused have the least individuality available and are mostly governed by the marriage relationship. These couples are highly dependent on each other, over- and underreact to each other, are more easily threatened by changes or differences in the other, fight about or avoid their differences, more frequently misinterpret each other, are more overtly emotionally intense and/or distant, or are unclear or inconsistently rigid about their positions on important issues in the marriage. Sometimes the fusion expresses itself through one spouse regularly accommodating the other so much so that they operate more as one individual than as two. Positively fused couples may report being very content, but their bond is more vulnerable and unstable as stressors increase or as the oneness is threatened.

In contrast, couples that are the least fused have the most individuality which allows for a more steady, stable togetherness. These couples tolerate and accept differences, are more self-directed, allow more room for the husband and wife to be themselves, have lower levels of dependence, have a wider range of personal and emotional topics that they can talk about, have clearly defined positions on important issues in the marriage, are guided by thought rather than emotion, can distinguish when to compromise and when to maintain a bottom line, sustain a sense of humor, and adapt to stressful events with fewer symptoms.

Anxiety

The level of anxiety influences marital functioning. Anxiety is the response to real or imagined threats. Each individual has a basic or chronic level of anxiety that is rooted in one's family relationships. The more unstable or emotionally reactive the family of origin was/is and the more dependent one was/is on the family, the more chronic anxiety an individual has to manage over a lifetime. One's position in the family also affects how much of the anxiety one absorbs. Couples with higher levels of chronic anxiety experience more reactivity in their marriage and have more difficulty distinguishing between real and imagined threats. In addition to the chronic anxiety is the acute anxiety that is rooted more in pressures of day-to-day living. Acute anxiety, unlike chronic anxiety, fluctuates as stressors such as job changes, geographical moves, and family transitions ebb and flow. Stability in a marriage often fluctuates with the shifts in acute anxiety.

Triangulation

Togetherness pressures and anxiety are not distributed evenly in a family so some members get more and others less. This process is dynamic and governed by the laws of the triangle. All marriages involve a third party in managing marital stress, but vary in the intensity and frequency of the triangulation. Some marriages project their emotional sensitivity and anxiety away from the marriage and onto a child or other family member (Bowen, 1978; Klever, 1996). This projection makes the marriage look better than it is and the child worse than he/she is. The projection process can also work within the marriage, with one of the spouses being the target of the projection. For example, the take-charge wife and her children vacillate between worry and anger with the alcoholic, jobless husband. The primary focus of concern is not the marriage but the husband. In other marriages, instead of projecting, the couple absorb the family sensitivity and anxiety, with the husband and wife overfocused on each other and the problems in the marriage. Marital functioning is more likely to be compromised when this pattern is dominant. At higher levels of differentiation, the spouses do less projecting and absorbing. They therefore contain marital stresses within the marriage and let others take appropriate responsibility for their lives.

Multigenerational Family

A husband and wife replicate the degree of fusion each had/has with his/her own family of origin. The ability to be a self with one's mother, father, and siblings is the same as the ability to be a self with one's spouse. The amount of energy that went into avoiding, accommodating, or fighting one's parents is equal to the amount of energy invested in managing the relationship with one's spouse. The exact style of relationship orientation may vary, but the degree of relationship sensitivity is the same. For instance, a husband may have fought bitterly with his parents and is now devoted to his wife through accommodation and avoidance of differences. Although the relationships are different, they are similar in their degree of focus on the other. The greater the fusion between the spouse and his/her family of origin, the more vulnerable the marriage is to instability.

Marriage is another step in separation. Marriages are sometimes formed to escape the intensity of emotions with one's parents. The illusion is created that one has found a way to break free of the unresolved issues with one's family, only to find that the same emotional intensity reappears in the marriage. The more one manages parent-child intensity through distance, the greater the marital dependency, and the more the marital expectations go beyond what the partner can realistically provide. A spouse cannot be a mother, father, brother, sister, and grandparent. A marriage inevitably cracks from the weight of those dependencies and expectations. When a husband and wife do have viable relationships with the families of origin, more resources are available to the couple to handle marital fusion. The families potentially provide historical perspective, more objectivity to understand marriage, the family, and self, and more pathways to manage anxiety.

Another way multigenerational fusion may manifest itself is not through distance, but by an overt dependency on the family of origin. The spouse with this type of togetherness with the parent reports being best friends, having no differences, keeping frequent contact, relying on the parent for decision making, receiving financial help, or feeling very close. This togetherness between a spouse and his or her family may stabilize a marriage as long as the other spouse accepts being in the outside position. The other spouse may even be adopted into the family as though he or she has no family of his or her own. But when the other spouse expects to have an inside position with his or her partner or when his or her partner's fusion with the family is no longer so cozy, marital turmoil usually erupts.

The multigenerational family also influences marital functioning through its anxiety about marriage and male-female relationships. Indicators of marital anxiety are marital instability, separation, divorce, and never marrying. The more prevalent these indicators are in the husband's and wife's families, the more likely the symptoms show up in the marriage instead of the children or individual adults. Women whose parents divorced before the women were sixteen years old had a 59 percent greater chance of divorcing than women from intact families. Men whose parents divorced had a 39 percent greater chance of divorcing than men from intact families (Beal and Hochman, 1991). These statistics support the idea that marital anxiety may be passed from one generation to the next. However, children from divorced families can have stable marriages, and children from intact families can get divorced. Due to the dynamic nature of the triangle, the primary storage site for togetherness and anxiety can shift from one generation to the next, but the overall level of functioning between generations is similar.

One's sibling relationships also influence marital functioning. Marriage as a relationship between peers is in some ways more similar to the relationship between siblings than the relationship between the parent and child. (Over two years, in 60 percent of my clinical cases presenting with a marital problem [50 cases], one or both spouses were an only child or a functional only child with six or more years between him/her and his/her adjacent siblings. These only children generally had less experience in cooperating, sharing space, and affiliating with a peer in the family than those with siblings.) Sibling relationships are another arena in which to balance self and other. The degree of differentiation between siblings is similar to the level of differentiation between the parent and child. Siblings intensify (through projection) and/or tone down (through putting the parent in the outside position) the parent-child fusion by inevitably being a part of the interlocking triangles in the family. Siblings with higher levels of relationship orientation engage in more competition, conflict, distance, accommodation, or reciprocal functioning. Siblings who are more competitive with one another often enter marriages in which they are likely to get caught in struggles for control or dominance. The more a spouse had joined with the parents to focus on his/her "inadequate" or acting out sibling, the more likely the spouse projects onto his/her spouse or child. And likewise, the more a husband or wife was the primary target of projection by his/her siblings and or parents, the more vulnerable he/she is to becoming a symptom bearer in his/her marriage and nuclear family. The amount of energy left over in sibling relationships for self-direction, or the room available to be an individual in the sibling relationships, is similar to the degree of individuality one has in a marriage.

THERAPY

Couples reduce their symptoms of marital conflict through a reduction in the level of stress (the unemployed husband finds a new job); a new response to the stress (rather than fighting about spending and saving, the couple decides to have separate accounts and split the expenses); a new stress that joins the couple together (a distant couple joins forces to care for a sick child); resumption of a previous cozy togetherness or positive fusion (the falling-out-of-love couple separates then realizes how much they love each other and recommits to show their love and appreciation to each other more); or developing greater differentiation. The last way to reduce marital conflict or distance provides the most solid path to long-term marital stability. Initial reduction in marital symptoms usually occurs through any of the first four, which are ways to reduce anxiety in the couple. Sometimes couples are satisfied with this reduction in symptoms and lack motivation to address their underlying interdependency. The step of raising one's level of differentiation is a long-term project that goes beyond the marriage to the interlocking triangles with children and extended family.

DEFINING THE EMOTIONAL PROCESS IN THE MARRIAGE

The first step in therapy with a couple problem is defining the emotional process in the marriage. This involves clarifying the patterns of emotional sensitivity between the couple. These patterns reflect the degree of fusion and anxiety in the marriage. The ways of thinking and feeling about self and the spouse, as well as the types of reactive behaviors, spell out the particular emotional dances for each couple. The most frequent marital patterns or symptoms are distance, conflict, reciprocal functioning, and/or a disruptive triangle (e.g., an affair or in-law). In assessing these patterns, gathering facts about the marriage and its symptoms is useful for the clinician's assessment and for injecting some objectivity into an emotionally charged situation. Some of the facts to gather are length of engagement and living together, planning of the wedding, those who did or did not attend the wedding, the families' reactions to the marriage, and timing of the marriage with other family changes—deaths, moves, births, etc.

Defining the emotional process in the marriage involves two parts:

- Assessing the frequency, duration, and intensity of the distance, conflict, reciprocal functioning, or triangulation
- Clarifying the interplay between the spouses that contributes to the marital symptom

Assessing Distance and the Marital Interplay

Emotional distance is almost always a component of the emotional process in a marriage. Distance is an instinctual flight response to emotional intensity. Couples vary in their ability to engage with each other about emotional issues, and assessment examines this range of distance and the contribution of the marital interaction to this variation.

Ability to Be Open About Emotional, Personal Issues

This is the most important indicator of emotional distance in the marriage. During the course of therapy, the degree of distance is usually revealed. As a client responds to a clinician's questions, the spouse may say, "I have never heard that before." or "This is the first time we have talked about this issue." Or the clinician asks, "What happens when you talk about this with your partner?" The response: "We do not talk about it." Other related questions that elucidate the degree of distance are, "How often do you have a personal discussion with each other? Who usually initiates the discussion? Who does more of the talking? What percentage of your thoughts and feelings about yourself, your spouse, and your relationship with each other do you tell your partner? Is there a time in your marriage when that percentage would have been more or less? Are there issues you do not talk about with each other? What are they?"

Ability to Listen to and Understand Each Other

How a spouse responds to what the partner said indicates the ability to hear and understand the other. With more emotional issues, couples often misinterpret each other's position. One may hear the partner criticizing his or her character when the message is instead about a particular behavior or incident. This aspect of assessment determines the spouse's ability to have an objective view of the partner.

Awareness of Thoughts and Feelings

Some people know what they think and feel but keep it to themselves. Others have so much relationship focus that they do not know what they think or feel. Distance rooted in the latter is generally more entrenched than the former. This lack of awareness shows itself in the clinical process when the client does not have a position about the issues being discussed.

Number of Hours Together a Week

Couples vary in the time they spend together and apart. One extreme are the couples who spend almost no time together because of conflicting work schedules or persistent avoidance. Finding time to set up a joint appointment can often be difficult or impossible. Distant couples often display a fair degree of difficulty in finding time to be together and knowing what to do or say if they are together, or when they are together, the intensity is so great that they again retreat to their opposite corners. The other extreme are couples who spend almost all of their time with each other and cannot imagine being apart. Both extremes suggest an imbalance in the togetherness/individuality forces.

Frequency of and Satisfaction with Physical Affection and Sex

At one end of the continuum are couples who have practically no physical affection or sexual contact. These couples often do not sleep together and are "allergic" to physical or sexual closeness. Physically distant couples may or may not be distant in other areas of the relationship. At the other extreme are couples who have a constant focus on touching and sex. The sexual relationship may be the main bond in the marriage and often a primary way to manage anxiety. Both of these ends of the continuum reflect higher degrees of fusion.

The Interplay Between the Spouses
That Contributes to the Distance

Distance is a reaction to the other in a relationship. When it is a chronic response predating the marriage, the couple may see it as part of the person's personality or inherent in the individual's nature. Another way to conceptualize the distance is to see it as a result of family relationships or as a chronic reaction to intense relationships in childhood. Distance in the marriage is a way of managing one's sensitivity to the other. The following questions are one way to stimulate thinking about the distance as part of the interdependence: "What do you do or think when he is distant with you? When you pursue her, what does she do? What do you or your partner do that contributes to you being more open or personal? If you were to respond to your partner's intensity differently, what do you think would happen? How does your distance affect your partner? What makes you anxious about contact with your partner?"

Assessing Conflict and the Marital Interplay

Conflict can be a part of the husband, wife, and marriage moving forward when it is an outgrowth of the effort to define a self in the marriage that is done with respect for the partner. Another characteristic of healthy conflict is the ability of the couple to have thinking guide self in the midst of a conflictual interaction. The ability to deal with differences effectively is in fact an indicator of more stable mariages (Gottman, 1994). But when conflict is rooted in an effort to change the other and driven primarily by emotion, it becomes more of a problem and reflects the emotional sensitivity in the marriage.

Assessing the Frequency, Duration, and Intensity
of the Conflict

The following questions help to assess the conflict: "How often do you fight or bicker? When you fight, how long does it last? How loud does it get? How do you stop? Does it get out of control? How often have you called each other names? How often have you thrown things at each other, threatened, shoved, or hit each other? Have you been injured? How often have the police been called? Do drinking or drugs make the fight worse? Was there a time in the marriage that you fought more or less than you do now?" The greater the intensity and threat, the more important it is to meet with the husband and wife separately.

The Degree of Focus on the Other

In conflictual marriages, each spouse is fixed on the weaknesses or the negative characteristics of the other and loses sight of the partner's strengths. This usually surfaces at the beginning of therapy, when the person describes the marital problem as the spouse's fault, and most of the initial time is spent giving a detailed picture of the spouse's deficits. With a conflictual couple, each spouse holds the belief or conviction that if only the partner would change the marriage would be much better. "If only he would start telling me what he feels, if only she wouldn't spend so much money, if only she were more sexually responsive, etc., our marriage would improve." or "I feel so sorry for my husband. He must have deep emotional problems for him to blow up at me like he does. I sure hope you can help him. Maybe he needs medication." These statements may shed light on a part of the problem, but they do not recognize the essential interplay that operates in the marriage. This way of thinking—that the problem is in the other and the other must change—fuels the cycle of conflict. The following are questions that highlight the interdependence and stimulate more thinking in the marriage: "When he/she gets angry with you, what do you think and do? How does he/she respond to your anger? How are you able to get your spouse so upset? What would be difficult or easy about arguing with you or living with you? How are you at discussing your differences thoughtfully? What helps you to be less reactive to your differences with each other? How does going along with your husband's abuse affect the pattern? What would it take for you to reach your bottom line with your husband's beating you?"

Defensiveness and Ownership of the Problem

Persistent or intense focus on the spouse as the problem usually generates a defensive response with a conflictual couple. Defensiveness is a signature characteristic of conflictual marriages (Gottman, 1994). Even with physical violence, the abused spouse is usually defensive in her interaction (Gottman et al., 1995). This finishes the cycle in the conflictual marriage—"You are the problem." "No, I'm not; you are the problem." Again, this is usually evident early in the clinical course as the couple responds to questions to define the problem bringing them into therapy. In addition to observing the defensiveness in the session, the clinician may ask, "How often are you or your partner defensive? What happens if you are not defensive? How do you manage to stir such a reaction in your spouse?" Persistent defensiveness is a way to manage the intense focus of another on one's self and reflects an inability to take ownership for one's own part in the problem, see the other's contribution at the same time, and manage one's emotional reactivity effectively.

Assessing Reciprocal Functioning

Reciprocal functioning in marriage reflects the borrowing and trading of self that results in one spouse functioning better overall than the other spouse. The dysfunctional spouse has more physical, psychological, and/or social problems. Bowen theory hypothesizes that people marry another who is at a similar basic level of differentiation. But through projection and triangulation, one spouse absorbs more of the anxiety and undifferentiation and manifests more symptoms, while the other spouse does better. Often these couples do not see the marriage, but rather the symptom of the spouse, as the main problem. While in the conflictual couple each focuses on the other and is defensive, in reciprocal functioning, one spouse sloughs his/her anxiety to the other and the other accepts it by becoming symptomatic. The "competent" spouse focuses on the incompetent side in the other and the "incompetent" one acts dependent upon or gets reactive to the "competent" side of the other. Although this process may be conscious, it usually occurs on a more automatic level.

Assessing the Frequency, Duration, and Intensity of the Reciprocal Functioning

This involves a thorough assessment of the physical, psychological, or social symptoms in each spouse. Part of the assessment includes onset, frequency, severity, and duration of the symptom; degree of limitation; how the symptom affects functioning at work, home, and in the community; degree of responsibility taken to manage the symptom; how much the symptom affects one's self-direction and responsibility to others; and how much the community or family is involved in managing the symptom—health care professional involvement, hospitalizations, medications, or police or court involvement.

Clarifying the Interplay Between the Spouses That Contributes to the Reciprocal Functioning

With reciprocal functioning, assessment of the mature and immature side of each partner develops more objectivity about the husband's and wife's basic functioning. To explore the cognitive aspects of this dynamic, the clinician examines how each person thinks about self and the other's strengths and weaknesses and the degree of focus on the other and self. Feeling states such as feeling sorry for, angry with, or responsible for the spouse or feeling inadequate or invulnerable about self also reflect reciprocal functioning. Assessing the behavioral interplay between spouses and their emotional sensitivity to each other develops an even clearer picture of this borrowing and trading of self. The following questions highlight this interdependence: "When he looks depressed, what do you usually do? When she pays the bills for you, what do you observe in yourself? How does his complaining about your drinking influence you? What is your position about your husband's not contributing any income over the last two years?"

DEFINING THE INTERLOCKING TRIANGLES

Assessing the interplay between just the husband and wife produces an incomplete picture of the emotional process in the marriage. A marriage inevitably involves others in the management of its emotional reactivity because every marriage reaches a point at which the anxiety and relationship sensitivity is too much to contain within the marriage. In assessing the triangulation process, it is helpful to examine the following aspects.

Location of the Symptoms in the Nuclear Family

Because physical, psychological, social, and marital symptoms are hypothesized to be a by-product of triangulation, identifying who is symptomatic is a way to identify who is absorbing more of the undifferentiation and who is projecting it.

Who and How the Spouse Talks with Others About the Marriage

Talking with others about the marriage is usually a way for the spouse to feel better temporarily. Assessment of the intensity of the triangle examines how much the spouse relies on that interaction to manage the marital stress and the degree to which the interaction joins the two together against the other spouse. Two factors affecting this are the ability of the spouse to see the husband's and wife's mutual responsibility for the problem and the ability of the third party to maintain a neutral stance and put the focus on the tension back in the marriage.

Who Is Involved with Whom

Although talking is a behavior to track in triangulation, the triangle operates primarily on nonverbal levels. Patterns of contact or affiliation are key aspects to help define who is in and who is out. For example, if a mother spends almost all of her time with her children and almost no time with her husband, who is busy on the Internet, the triangle in the nuclear family is the mother and children together and the husband on the outside. These patterns of affiliation often shift and reflect the dynamic nature of the triangle. The challenge for assessment is to determine the most pre-dominant patterns and be aware of their changing nature.

How the Marriage Is Affected

Another area to assess is how much the triangle seems to calm or agitate the marriage. This may fluctuate with the degree of pressure with which the couple is dealing. For instance, the husband who can become over-whelmed by his wife's need to talk may be glad that his wife sees her mother as her best friend and primary affiliation. However, when he is stressed and wants more involvement with her, he may start to complain about the time she spends with her mother.

Assessing Affairs

Affairs create an emotional storm in most marriages. Couples usually want to focus primarily on the affair and have varying degrees of interest in viewing the affair in a larger context. First, assessing the degree of compulsion, attachment, and intensity of the affairs offers some objectiv-ity. For instance, a one-time-only "one-night stand" with an anonymous partner is a different kind of an affair than multiple affairs throughout the marriage or a three-year emotional and sexual attachment with a family friend. Each reflects a different degree of impulsiveness in the individual and a different degree of anxiety in the marriage and family.

Couples have varying perspectives of who is responsible for what in an affair. Sometimes the betrayed party is primarily upset with the "affairee," as reflected in statements such as "My spouse would not have had this affair if this person did not seduce him/her." Other times, the spouse who had the affair blames the affair on the other spouse for being too critical or sexually distant. Most typically, the spouse who had the affair is viewed by his/her partner and the larger social network as the "bad" person. Sorting out this blame game is part of viewing the emotional process in the marriage more clearly. Although the person who had the affair is responsible for the affair, not the other spouse, the husband and wife are usually mutually responsible for the conditions of the marriage. Assessment of each person's ability to take responsibility for his/her own part of the pattern and to see the interplay with the other tells the clinician about the couple's ability to move beyond the affair.

The Influence of Multigenerational Triangles

The marital relationship is embedded in a larger family system. Any solid effort to understand a marital problem expands the lens to include relationships with the extended family, especially the primary triangle— the spouse, his/her primary caregiver (usually mother), and the caregiver's primary attachments. The primary triangle is then influenced by the interlocking triangles with siblings, grandparents, aunts and uncles, and others. The assessment examines the nature of the primary attachment and how other relationships influenced that attachment, as well as how the primary attachment influenced other relationships in the family.

As the clinician asks questions about these relationships, a broader view is developed, which reduces the glare of the husband's and wife's over-focus on each other. Bowen found that psychiatric residents who worked on their family of origin relationships improved their functioning in their nuclear families more than the residents who were in therapy working primarily on nuclear family problems (Bowen, 1978).

The following three areas provide a framework for assessment of multigenerational relationships:

* The degree of fusion or differentiation in the primary triangle and the extended family, as expressed in overt dependency or distance and cutoff
* The degree of fusion or differentiation in sibling relationships
* The stability in multigenerational marriages and male-female relationships

One example of a common intergenerational triangle that is presented clinically is troublesome relationships with in-laws. The problem in the in-law triangle can manifest in different ways, but usually the conflict surfaces between the wife and her husband's parents (usually his mother) or the husband and his wife's parents. This then creates conflict between the husband and wife because the husband often takes a mediator position between his mother and wife, while the wife wants the husband to support her against his mother. The key relationship in this triangle is the relationship of the husband with his mother and the other relationships that surround that unresolved attachment. The wife conflicts with the mother when the husband cannot define himself clearly enough to his wife and his mother, when the mother is overattached to her son, and when the wife becomes overresponsible for her husband in this triangle.

DEFINING HOW ANXIETY AND STRESS INFLUENCE THE EMOTIONAL PROCESS IN THE MARRIAGE AND THE INTERLOCKING TRIANGLES

Stressors and changes in relationships are a primary cause of fluctuations in marital problems. Couples vary in their awareness of the effects of stress and how their responses to stress affect the marriage. Chronic distance or conflict usually intensifies as anxiety increases. Thus, identifying when a symptom emerged is important to identify what stressors and changes were occurring during that time. The assessment goes beyond the direct effect of the stressor on the individual—a job promotion creating increased feelings of responsibility—and looks at how the stressor created a shift in relationships—with the job promotion the spouse became more distant and irritable and his older sibling became more competitive and critical. Humankind's complex social nature makes humans especially sensitive to shifts in relationships, even when they are not consciously aware of these shifts. These changes in relationships throughout the life cycle affect symptoms in and out of the marriage. The individual's and couple's responses to stress are also important to assess, and questions such as the following should be asked: "How do you think about the stressor? How have you responded to the increase in your wife's distance and your brother's criticalness? How have you handled this challenge? What ideas guide you in dealing with this anxiety? What helps you to think clearly about the anxiety?" Questions are also asked to identify stressors, the shifts in the relationships, and the effects on marital process.

DIFFERENTIATING A SELF IN THE MARRIAGE AND THE EXTENDED FAMILY

Clients working on differentiation take their best understanding of the marriage and family, develop and implement a plan for self, and learn from observations of self, others, and the relationships. Differentiation is more than insight; it is also action.

Most couples come to therapy hoping to resume a comfortable togetherness by changing the spouse, communicating more, or compromising better. However, developing a more stable marriage is about individuality as well as togetherness. Developing one's individuality is the counterbalance to relationship fusion. Managing relationship sensitivity and emotional reactivity in the marriage is futile without defining a clearer self-direction and I position in the marriage and family. Differentiating a self in the marriage first arises from a systems understanding of the relationship and a knowledge of the interdependence in the marriage and family. With this new way of thinking, new actions sometimes emerge automatically. Other behavioral changes require more planning and thoughtful effort. What is involved in the effort to differentiate a self, by definition, is unique to the individual and determined by the individual. This effort usually involves the individual taking more responsibility for his/her own functioning by being a keen observer of self and others, working on his/her own emotional sensitivity and reactivity, being a responsible individual in family relationships, gathering facts about the family, and maintaining steady one-to-one involvement with family members.

Differentiating a self in the marriage may mean developing a position for self on important, emotional issues in the marriage. This is especially applicable to the spouse who is critical of the partner's way of handling an issue but has no proposal based on his/her goals or values. This spouse maintains a reactive rather than a proactive position. In contrast, for the spouse who has taken an overresponsible position, differentiating a self may be less about presenting his/her viewpoint for the hundredth time and more about redefining his/her level of responsibility for his/her actions and about understanding the partner's position. A common comment with couples in therapy is for one partner to ask the other, "How do you want me to change?" Although the question and answer have value in understanding the other, more self-defining questions are, "What are my standards for being a good husband/wife?"; "How do I evaluate myself at the end of a day, month, or year on being a good spouse?"; and "What are the factors that I take into account to know if I am doing my best?"

Another part of differentiating a self in marriage is not about the marriage, but about the individual working on his/her set of principles, goals, and direction for living. The less self-directed a person is, the more he/she takes direction from others or gives direction to them. Therefore, one way to reduce the relationship sensitivity is to reduce the dependency or other-directedness in the marriage.

Differentiation is not distance. A common misdirected application of differentiation is for a spouse to pull away from the intense influence of his/her partner in order to be more of an individual. Escaping the emotional pressures in the marriage may in fact help a person to be more self-aware and feel better away from the spouse, but differentiation is the ability to be a self while engaged with the other. The self-actualizing person may report that the spouse could not handle the person's independence, but often the spouse is reacting more to the distance than the independence.

Marital symptoms are affected even more when one moves beyond the marriage to develop one's individuality with mother, father, siblings, and extended family. Efforts to work on the original symbiosis with mother and the interlocking relationships pay double because parent-child symbiosis is replicated in the child's marriage. Being an individual while staying responsibly involved with the family is a long-term project. Identifying the emotional issues (religion, alcoholism, mental illness, money, divorce, death, among others) in the family and learning to define a self on those issues with the family is usually a worthwhile challenge. With a marital symptom, it is useful to gain a clearer understanding of the parents' marriage—facts such as length of courtship and age of marriage, families' reactions to the marriage, their patterns of reactivity, hot issues in their marriage, similarities and differences between the parents' ages and the client's, the client's place in the marital triangle, reasons for divorce, and effect of the divorce on the client and other relationships in the family. This same understanding about siblings, grandparents, and aunts and uncles is also useful.

THE CLINICIAN-CLIENT RELATIONSHIP

The Clinician's I Position

To promote differentiation of self, the clinician works on differentiating a self with the client. The client's transference with the therapist is part of the togetherness force in the therapy relationship. The client may push for the therapist to agree with him/her, seek the therapist's approval, ask for advice or direction, or become critical or angry with the clinician. These are just some of the manifestations of the client's dependency or relationship sensitivity. The other part of the clinical fusion is the therapist's countertransference, which may express itself in distance, yawning, falling asleep, forgetting an appointment, telling the client what to do, criticizing the client, losing a sense of humor, seeking the client's approval or agreement, worrying about the client, or being too personal.

The clinician's I position provides some separateness in the midst of the togetherness. The I position is the clinician defining a self in words and actions with the client or staying connected yet detached. In differentiating a self, the therapist sees the client as the expert on how to live his/her life. The clinician sets the structure for therapy and balances asking questions to gather information and to stimulate the client's thinking with stating the therapist's viewpoint of the client's situation through stories, metaphors, humor, or direct comments. The therapist creates a thoughtful environment and redirects the processing of emotional issues back to the family system.

Generally, when both spouses are present, each spouse talks to the therapist while the other listens. This tends to decrease reactiveness during the session, encourage listening, stimulate thinking, and demonstrate one-to-one interaction. When the couple's reactiveness is high in the session or when the couple is abusive, meeting with the husband and wife separately is necessary. Sometimes marital problems are worked on in therapy by only one member of the couple. Although some balk at this, an individual working on self in the marriage and family can have a noticeable effect within the family system.

Managing the Marital Triangle

Getting caught in triangles is a part of any therapy, but it is especially prevalent with therapy involving marital problems. Each party makes subtle or direct invitations for the therapist to take his/her side. Some examples are:

- a wink of the eye, a look, a smile or frown, as if to say, "*We* know what's really going on here";
- a funny story of the "incompetent" spouse that draws the therapist into laughing with the client;
- flattery for the therapist or being a "good" patient who is motivated to apply theory, while the spouse could care less; and
- directly saying or asking, "Obviously, our marriage was doing fine until she had an affair. You do not think it's okay for a wife to be unfaithful, do you?" or "I have thought more about what you said last time about the distance in the marriage. I would agree that my husband's inability to communicate has been the main problem." or "I am wondering how you and I can help my husband with his problem with anger."

Managing the triangle effectively means maintaining contact with both spouses if both are involved in a session, staying focused on process rather than content, and maintaining a keen awareness of the dynamic of the triangle throughout therapy. When the clinician is thinking systemically and monitoring his/her countertransference, neutrality is automatic, and the course of therapy takes a more thoughtful direction.

CASE EXAMPLE:
THE GARCIAS—DISTANCE, CONFLICT,
AND TRIANGULATION

The following case example illustrates the author's application of Bowen theory to a marital problem. See Figure 4.2 for a diagram of the Garcia family.

Mr. Garcia, thirty-five years old, and Mrs. Garcia, twenty-six years old, initiated consultation for marital difficulties. Mr. Garcia was an engineer, and Mrs. Garcia was an office worker in her mother's small business. Mr. Garcia came from a Mexican-American family and Mrs. Garcia from an Italian-American family. They had three daughters, four years old, two years old, and four months old. Mr. and Mrs. Garcia dated for six months before they lived together. They lived together for two years and then married. The wife's first pregnancy was part of the impetus for their decision to marry. This was Mr. Garcia's third marriage and Mrs. Garcia's first marriage.

Emotional Patterns in the Marriage: Distance, Conflict, and Triangulation

In the first session, Mr. Garcia said that he did not love his wife as he used to and that he was avoiding the marriage by staying at work longer. He was unsure if he wanted to continue with the marriage, but did not want to divorce either. He reported that he started to withdraw from his wife when their second child was born because his wife was giving too much attention to the children, and he was left out. He did not talk about it with her and hoped she would see that he was unhappy and needed more attention.

Mrs. Garcia acknowledged that she had become less attentive in the marriage due to getting overinvolved at work to please her mother, meeting the demands of mothering, and assuming her husband could adapt to less attention. She usually kept her thoughts and feelings to herself, if she thought it would disappoint her husband. She also reported his decline in physical affection and sex. She wanted sex about three times a week, and he wanted sex about once every two weeks.

They also both described persistent conflict. Mr. Garcia said that they did not talk to each other, but if they did talk, 100 percent of the time it turned into an argument with no resolution. He said it was hard to deal with differences, so they just avoided them. Mrs. Garcia said the arguments were occasionally "verbally abusive" and about twice a year he shoved her. One time she called the police.

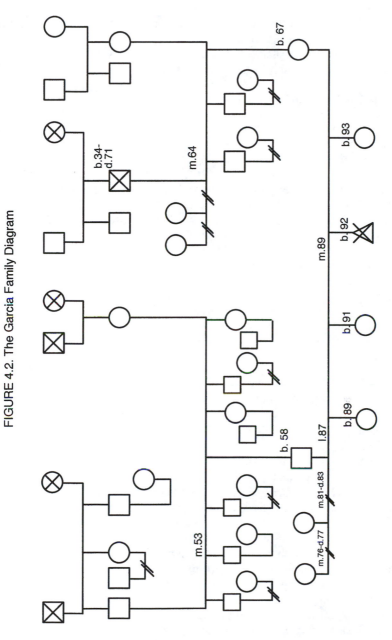

FIGURE 4.2. The Garcia Family Diagram

The stressor that pushed Mrs. Garcia to call for a consultation was her husband getting involved with a secretary at his workplace. Between the second and third consultation, Mr. Garcia told Mrs. Garcia that the relationship with his secretary, which he had stopped, was both a friendship and a sexual relationship that lasted three months.

The Influence of Other Relationships

Mr. Garcia's cutoff from his family of origin intensified his dependency on and emotional reactivity with his wife. Mr. Garcia reported being quite distant with his parents and siblings, and he had no contact with his grandparents or aunts and uncles. All of his family lived in other states. He had superficial contact with his parents and one of his siblings once a month and with the rest of his siblings, one to three times a year. Throughout his childhood, he said, his father was gone most of the time due to his work, and his mother was a housewife who was spread too thin having to care for seven children. When Mr. Garcia came into therapy, he had only one friend and considered his wife as his main and sole support.

Mrs. Garcia's overt dependence on her mother, cutoff from her father's family, and distant, overresponsible position with her brothers all contributed to her distance and criticalness with her husband. Mrs. Garcia reported being very close to her mother, with each being the other's stability. Her father died from cancer at thirty-six years old, when she was three years old. Mrs. Garcia had almost no contact with her father's family after his death. Her mother never remarried or dated. Mrs. Garcia's mother also had little involvement with her own brother and parents. The closeness between Mrs. Garcia and her mother was reinforced by these factors. Mrs. Garcia's older brothers both were financially dependent on their mother and abused drugs. Mrs. Garcia vacillated between helping them and staying away from them.

Mr. Garcia's difficulty with marriage was related in part to anxiety stemming from his previous two divorces and marital problems in his family of origin. Mr. Garcia described his parents' marriage as being cold and distant. He never remembered them touching or talking to each other, and they seemed to lead separate lives. They once had a separation, and his mother still alluded to wanting a divorce. Three of his six siblings had been divorced at least once, but he had little knowledge about any of his siblings' marriages. Neither his maternal nor paternal grandparents had divorced or separated. His paternal aunt was divorced. His previous two marriages lasted about one to two years. He started those marriages being "very much in love," followed by his becoming angry with each spouse and pulling away. In each case, the wife left him after several months of that behavior.

Mrs. Garcia reported being anxious about relationships with men, in part due to her view of men in her family and the prevalence of divorce. Mrs. Garcia's father was married and divorced two times before he married her mother. Mrs. Garcia had no knowledge of those marriages. Her parents had a conflictual marriage, according to her mother. Mrs. Garcia's father was critical and blamed his wife for physical and behavior problems the two older sons were having. He is suspected of having had an affair during the marriage. Both of Mrs. Garcia's older brothers have been divorced. Mrs. Garcia's mother frequently told Mrs. Garcia that she didn't have much use for men and that men cannot be counted on.

The Stressors

The primary chronic stressor in this family was the level of fusion. The fusion in the husband's family expressed itself in distance; the fusion in the wife's family expressed itself in overt dependency and reciprocal functioning. The husband and wife reported that a significant portion of their well-being was based on the mood and approval of the other. Managing this dependency and the accompanying sensitivity was an ongoing burden for both partners.

Another stressor in the nuclear family was the birth of children, particularly the second and third children. This couple reported difficulty in adapting to the shifting relationships created by the needs of children. With children to care for, Mrs. Garcia became less focused on her husband, and Mr. Garcia became more sensitive to the lack of attention from his wife. Another stressor was the husband's work. He did not like his work and usually came home from his job irritable. He wanted to start his own business but felt stuck in how to do that.

The Therapy and the Clients' Work on Self and Relationships

This couple attended fourteen sessions in 1993, two sessions in 1994, and thirteen sessions in 1995. Sixteen of those sessions were individual sessions and thirteen were couple sessions, all initiated by the clients. The process of clarifying the emotional process in the marriage, the interlocking triangles, and the stressors and their influence on the marriage was ongoing. The questions and conversations about these areas provided a framework for the therapy process, stimulated thinking in the couple, and laid the foundation for a plan for self.

A major focus of half of the sessions was the husband's two affairs— one at the beginning of therapy and one later in 1995. Mrs. Garcia wanted to talk about the affairs and found herself "obsessing" on why they happened and whether she could trust him. Mr. Garcia wanted to put the affairs behind him by not talking about them and going on. These polarized approaches to dealing with an affair are common. I commented on the polarization and suggested that they try to better understand the factors that contributed to the affairs and determine how to put the marriage on more solid footing. I asked, "What do you think will happen if you both maintain your pole positions? What contributed to your having an affair? What would have happened to you or your marriage if you had not had the affair? How did you decide to stop the affair? How did the marital tension affect the affair? What would you each need to do to make your marriage more immune to an affair?" Mr. Garcia was able to talk about factors that led to the affairs, and Mrs. Garcia was able to answer her questions and ease her anxiety. Each person's efforts gradually loosened up the polarization between them and helped them to go beyond the affairs to emotional patterns in the marriage and other relationships. Mrs. Garcia examined her tendency to overaccommodate and began to think more about her "bottom lines." They both made occasional attempts to monitor their tendencies to withdraw and become critical and argumentative.

Another important triangle in the marriage was Mrs. Garcia's relationship with her mother. In the first session, Mr. Garcia stated that one of their main arguments was about his mother-in-law's interference. Mrs. Garcia was employed by her mother from 1991 to 1993 and often turned to her mother for advice and as her primary support. During the first session, Mrs. Garcia admitted that she was overinvolved with her mother and often caught between her mother and her husband and that she needed to reduce her dependency on her mother. Mrs. Garcia changed jobs and made efforts to be more involved with her husband. Although this change had some positive effects, it also increased her expectations and dependency on her husband—expectations that he was unable to meet. She found that shifting her dependency to her husband was not the same thing as developing her individuality.

Mrs. Garcia developed more awareness of her fusion with Mr. Garcia and her mother. In 1994, she reported, "He waits for me to be happy, so he can be happy. And I wait for him to give me attention, so I can be happy." With that insight, she made some attempts to define herself and her responsibility more clearly concerning emotional issues in the marriage such as child care and household responsibilities. She also discussed some of her personal goals to clarify her self-direction and started her own business in 1995.

In her relationships with her mother and brothers, she became less responsive and helpful regarding their dependence and started to report to them more of her own struggles with her marriage and parenting. She also learned more about her mother's family. Her mother's parents' marriage was one in which Mrs. Garcia's grandfather was seldom home because of work-related travel, and Mrs. Garcia's grandmother made every effort to accommodate her husband. Mrs. Garcia identified that she and her mother shared a belief that, "Men won't come through." So another part of Mrs. Garcia's work was sorting her view of men from her mother's view. This meant gathering more facts about the underfunctioning of most of the men in her family and the overfunctioning of most of the women. She also wrestled with a persistent thought that she would be better off to do what her mother did, raising her three children on her own. She recognized that such a path was more familiar to her than raising children with a man.

The couple developed greater awareness of how stress affected their reactivity with each other. Mr. Garcia's dissatisfaction with work tended to make him view his wife more negatively and critically, and he would pull away from her. Mrs. Garcia's pressure of being an overresponsible parent, employee, and child fueled her distance and irritability with her husband. In 1995, a series of stressful events spawned the second affair for Mr. Garcia. His paternal grandparents died within three days of each other; two weeks later Mr. Garcia's best male friend, forty years old, died of a sudden heart attack; when he comforted his friend's widow, Mrs. Garcia's antennae went up and she started to complain. This led to his spending more time with the widow, which in turn led to the affair. The emotional power of this process was so great that for several weeks they demonstrated almost no ability to think or slow down their automatic reactions.

When the affair stopped (Mrs. Garcia eventually drew her bottom line—"Stop the affair, or I file for divorce") and the intensity died down, Mr. Garcia saw this episode as a "wake-up call." He had thought that the previous affair was just a fluke. Now he had more motivation to work on the factors that contributed to the problem. He started to realize the ways in which he had lost his individuality in his marriage and began to reduce his overaccommodation. He also saw that he had very few people with whom to process emotional issues. The death of his grandparents highlighted this, when he observed that he did not/could not talk to anyone in the family about his sense of loss or his grandparents' lives. Realizing this, he began to increase the frequency of contact with his mother and a couple of his siblings. In therapy he discussed his observations of his thoughts, feelings, and behavior and his family members' responses. He also began to gather more information from his mother to understand the distance in himself and his family.

Over the three years of therapy, the marriage improved temporarily, when they reestablished a previous positive fusion by paying more attention to each other and being more positive with each other. During these periods, the couple reported that the marriage was much better, but that they were generally avoiding difficult issues. The marriage also improved in a more steady way, as each spouse accepted more responsibility for his/her emotional reactions, developed his/her individuality, and began to work on the fusion with the family of origin. This couple was doing better when they stopped therapy, but with an increase of stressors, a shift in family relationships, and the ongoing fusion in their marriage and families, this couple is still quite susceptible to marital turmoil.

CONCLUSION

A couple living in a house with cracked walls may want to plaster and wallpaper over the cracks, which provides a short-term solution to the problem. Another direction the couple may choose is to fix the foundation before they wallpaper so the walls do not crack—a more solid, long-term approach. Likewise, a person with marital problems can work to reestablish a positive togetherness or he/she may also choose to work on himself/herself and his/her emotional reactiveness and personal responsibility. Bowen theory provides a map for thinking about marital problems. This framework examines not just the togetherness of the couple, but also the degree of individuality in the marriage and extended family. For the clinician, this theory provides a framework for how to think about the problem, the person, and the family and how to manage the clinical relationships with the couple and their family system.

REFERENCES

Beal, Edward and Hochman, Gloria (1991). *Adult Children of Divorce.* New York: Delacorte Press.

Betzig, Laura L. (1986). *Despotism and Differential Reproduction, A Darwinian View of History.* Hawthorne, NY: Aldine de Gruyter.

Bowen, Murray (1978). *Family Therapy in Clinical Practice.* New York: Jason Aronson.

Fisher, Helen (1992). *The Anatomy of Love.* New York: W.W. Norton and Company.

Gottman, John M. (1994). *What Predicts Divorce?* Hillsdale, NJ: Lawrence Erlbaum Associates.

Gottman, John M., Jacobson, Neil, Rushe, Regina, Shortt, Joann Wu, Babcock, Julia, La Taillade, Jaslean J., and Waltz, Jennifer (1995). "The Relationship

Between Heart Rate Reactivity, Emotionally Aggressive Behavior, and General Violence in Batterers." *Journal of Family Psychology,* 9 (3): 227-248.

Kerr, Michael and Bowen, Murray (1988). *Family Evaluation.* New York: W.W. Norton and Company.

Kleiman, Devra G. (1977). "Monogamy in Mammals." *The Quarterly Review of Biology,* 52: 39-69.

Klever, Phil (1996). "The Study of Marriage and Bowen Theory." *Family Systems,* 3: 37-51.

Konner, Melvin. (1982). *The Tangled Wing.* New York: Harper & Row.

Maraskin, Merry (1994). "Monogamy and Society." Paper presented at Georgetown Family Center Symposium, Washington, DC, November 5.

Whitten, Patricia L. (1987). "Infants and Adult Males." In Smutz, Barbara, Cheney, Dorothy, Seyfarth, Robert, Wrangham, Richard, and Struhsaker, Thomas (Eds.), *Primate Societies.* Chicago, IL: The University of Chicago Press, pp. 343-357.

Wilson, Edward O. (1975). *Sociobiology.* Cambridge, MA: Belknap Press.

Chapter 5

Emotional Dysfunction in Children

James C. Maloni

INTRODUCTION

Emotional symptoms in one or more children are one way that dysfunction manifests itself in a family. Dysfunction is also related to the two primary factors that determine the occurrence of symptoms, according to Bowen family systems theory: chronic anxiety and level of differentiation. The child most susceptible or receptive to being affected by the family anxiety is the one least able to separate himself or herself from the parents, especially the mother. This usually begins early on and can be observed in the mother-child relationship. Sibling position, gender of the child, and parental and/or extended family anxiety at the time of this child's birth are a few of many factors that contribute to the level of differentiation of this child. This child is sometimes pampered, given special attention, which in turn hampers this child's growing to depend more on himself or herself to deal with everyday life problems. The parents, especially the mother, operate on the assumption that poor parenting has caused this problem. Often, the mother tries to compensate for this by giving more of herself to the child. This behavior is sometimes heavily reinforced by psychological theories that emphasize insufficient bonding as causing emotional problems in children, and therefore, extra attention is given to this child. This attention assumes various forms but in general creates an inflationary baseline in terms of what the parents, the child, and often other interested adults think he or she needs to function. It is as if this child becomes an "emotional gas guzzler," i.e., he or she gets less and less mileage from each gallon of "emotional fuel."

If life events in the nuclear and extended families remain fairly calm, emotional symptoms usually do not develop to any great extent in this child.

147

He or she may show temporary difficulties negotiating transitions and new situations such as starting or changing schools, but things settle down after new routines are developed. He or she may have difficulty developing or sustaining peer relationships, but this usually does not create undue concern when conditions are calm. However, if the emotional climate becomes tense and this persists for an extended period of time, emotional symptoms often appear in this heavily focused-upon child. The intensity of the focus has always been present to some extent, but up to this point, the intensity may have taken the form of a benign specialness. However, if significant stressors such as unexpected financial or health setbacks occur and persist in the nuclear or extended families, this intensity can take the form of a weighty urgency, and in a child-focused family, the intensity of focus can quickly be funneled toward the least-differentiated child. This child is not just a passive receptacle in this process. It is almost as if he or she reaches out and catches the tunnel of anxiety and seems willing to "run with it." This occurs with the assistance of most, if not all, family members but develops in an automatic rather than purposeful way. This vertically downward projection of anxiety toward the most emotionally susceptible child inadvertently keeps the marriage relationship and other family members relatively free of the anxiety and thus better able to function on an everyday basis.

Psychotherapy from a Bowen orientation usually involves working with the adult member of the family who is more motivated to work on self. This approach is difficult to implement in child-focused families, especially while symptoms are still present in the susceptible child. Over the course of the past fifteen years, this author has attempted to intervene with these families by coaching one or both parents to shift their reaction to the child. This may or may not involve direct contact with the child; sometimes it has been easier to reduce the focus of the parental anxiety toward the child by including the child in one or a few sessions. At the same time, however, the risk here is that the therapist can become more focused on the child and is then less able to coach the parents toward a broader view of the problem.

Whether the symptomatic child is included in sessions or not, finding a way to broaden the focus to have congruence between theory and intervention, while at the same time being able to help the parents find relevance in the focus, is the primary objective of therapy. Instructing parents about how their reactivity to the child's symptoms can have a bearing on the severity and duration of the symptoms is sometimes an immediate focus that parents find useful. Less entrenched symptoms can clear up rather quickly in this context, while others are more difficult to shift.

THE M. FAMILY

The M. family sought help for their seven-year-old daughter, Judy, who is a second grader. Numerous fears, bad dreams, immaturity in peer and family relationships, underachieving in school, stealing from mother and sister, and talking about death were the presenting problems. Judy is two and a half years younger than her sister. The older sister is described as brilliant, an early talker, and "always upstaging" her younger sister. On the other hand, the parents described Judy as clinging and not willing to be left alone as a young child. The older daughter and father are viewed as similar in terms of their brightness and intellectual orientation, while Judy and mother are linked together as being more emotional. (See the M. Family Diagram, Figure 5.1.)

Mr. M., age thirty-five, is an upwardly mobile professional. In his family of origin, he is the middle of three children, having an older sister and a younger brother. The younger brother is also a professional and is viewed as highly competitive; he was described as being rebellious as a child. Both siblings are married and have children. Both of Judy's paternal grandparents are in their early sixties and in good health. They live approximately three hours from the M. family. The grandfather passed up promotions to stay in a safe middle-management job, which was in contrast to his father and great-grandfather. Mr. M. sees himself as somewhat caught between his father, grandfather, and great-grandfather in terms of job aspirations. He admitted that he has been quite consumed with his work.

Mrs. M., age thirty-six, received a graduate degree not long ago and is in the midst of making a decision concerning her work. Similar to Judy, she is two years younger than her sister. Her sister is an unmarried professional who has had to deal with numerous anxieties for many years. Both of Judy's maternal grandparents are in their late seventies and live in the same general geographical area. Both have worked in professional positions. The maternal grandmother is the youngest of three sisters, making Judy at least the third generation of youngest sisters. Mrs. M. reported that as a child she remembers taking care of her older sister rather than vice versa.

The M. family was seen for a total of twenty-eight sessions, which extended over a sixteen-month period. Judy was seen in joint and individual sessions for the first part of the therapy. Her symptoms significantly decreased after a few months. As is often the case with child-focused families in which the symptoms are not too severe, a low-key intervention with Judy and her parents helped to calm the family system. Staying sufficiently outside the system, while at the same time enjoying Judy's intellectual curiosity and playfulness, made it possible for this therapist to view much of Judy's behaviors in a relatively benign way. Mr. and Mrs. M. were fairly

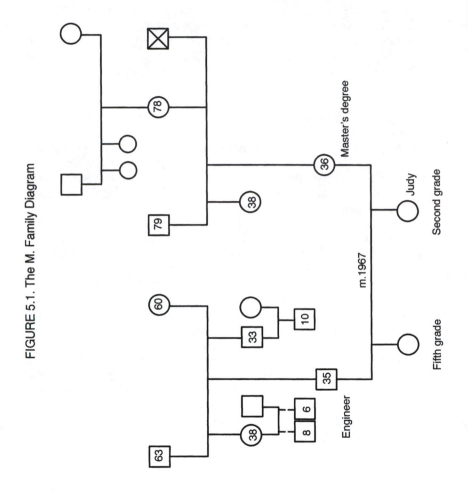

FIGURE 5.1. The M. Family Diagram

easy to engage in this manner. As is true with most parents, they were relieved and pleased that an outside person could emphasize their daughter's strengths while at the same time provide suggestions as to how they might contend with some of the problem areas. In an implicit manner, Judy and her parents were being taught not to focus so intensely on her deficits. This process evolved gradually over a period of several weeks and ran parallel with the general calming of the family system. The transition from an extended period of anxiety to relative calmness is necessary for this type of learning to occur.

The mother was seen alone for eight of the last ten sessions. During the first of these sessions, she reported, "I'm feeling less anxiety about things." Finding ways to think about what was going on appeared helpful to her. She described herself as becoming more independent. Since dependency had been a multigenerational theme for the youngest sisters, driving a vehicle held much significance for her mother and herself. The maternal grandmother never drove after she married the maternal grandfather. Mrs. M. learned to drive after her oldest child was born. Her mother, the maternal grandmother, taught herself to drive in between her two marriages. Mrs. M.'s work on self during the latter part of this intervention included examining how the details of her mother's first husband's death (not the maternal grandfather) played a role in the emotional process influencing the lives of all three generations of youngest daughters. As is frequent in child-focused families, Mrs. M. had difficulty sustaining her focus on her family's emotional history; her focus was more motivated by her feeling state rather than her curiosity and determination. She was able to observe, however, that "it helps my tension to look at it [family of origin]." Mrs. M. also realized that she had learned from her mother to keep a neat home and that this had required much of her energy and focus when the children were young, but she saw this as "more tied into my level of anxiety, rather than [being] out in the world."

Mrs. M. also discussed the blending of both her and her sister's patterns of functioning as they applied to both of her daughters' emotional processes. Although she was younger than her sister, Mrs. M. operated, at least partially, as a functional oldest. "I took care of her more than she took care of me . . . she had more fears than me. She was the one my father would compliment a lot for her academic skills. . . . I wasn't as smart." She also described her linkage with her mother, sharing the role of "keeping peace" while her sister was in the role of "triggering tension." It took both Mrs. M. and her mother to counterbalance the sister's antagonizing of the father. On the other hand, Mrs. M. described herself as being similar to her father in her nuclear family—"I tend to flare up a lot like my father."

Mrs. M. described the relationship issue of relative competence as stemming from her husband's family and also being operative in her marriage relationship. It appears that keeping "a lid on her professional aspirations" relates to her husband and herself as well as to the process from her family of origin. Apparently Mrs. M.'s overadaptive position in her family of origin was carried over into the marriage. Giving priority to the others, as well as intense questioning about relative competence, interfaced with consistent and efficient functioning. Mrs. M. found it difficult to separate herself from her husband in thinking about her goals: "I need to prove myself in relation to him." This comparative baseline for self was transmitted to her daughter Judy. True to form with multigenerational projection process, this pattern assumed a greater level of emotional intensity in Judy, which manifested itself in greater undifferentiation in her academic functioning.

Enjoying being with her daughters without her husband around also took on a new emphasis for Mrs. M. "He's traveling more lately. I'm feeling better, almost enjoying it—time by myself—confident being with the kids myself—before it was he and I and the kids—he had a relationship with the kids; I never felt I did." Mrs. M. also focused more specifically on her daughter Judy, "She is growing up a lot in the last few months . . . it reduces my need to push." The latter statement illustrates well how the child is an active participant in this emotional dance, rather than simply being a victim of the process.

Although Judy's symptoms were not as severe as sometimes seen, nevertheless, they had been well entrenched for an extended time. The multigenerational projection process can be observed quite readily in the M. family. What is useful in a family such as this, in which the child's symptoms of emotional dysfunction are not extremely severe, is the ability to observe the marital relationship and the functioning of each parent. Although Mrs. M. has been quite emphatic about women's issues prior to the birth of her children, she became caught in the same emotional process that guided her mother's accommodating to her husband. For the M. family, this occurred in spite of societal consciousness about women's issues, which was also subscribed to by Mr. M. This is a good illustration of how intellectual goals can be powerless in the face of more basic forces that have developed over a much longer period. This phenomenon of accommodating or overadaptiveness to the other can be seen in the three generations discussed here. One could hypothesize that, although Mr. M. and the older daughter are quite intelligent, the emotional forces in the family have allowed this perception to create a dichotomy whereby Mrs. M. and Judy find it more useful to "sit on" their abilities. If one cannot be as successful as the other, it might be better not to test one's productivity at all. Once again this is not done in a purposeful way but is part of the emotionality circulating in the family.

One of the more serious aspects of Judy's symptoms has been her preoccupation with death. Although this appears to have been triggered by the accidental death of a peer, the intensity of this preoccupation suggests the influence of the "vertical axis," the power of the older generation on the younger generation. As mentioned earlier, one area that seems important is the circumstances surrounding the death of the maternal grandmother's first husband. Not only are the events themselves important, but also of significance is the influence of these events on Mrs. M.'s mother's later life, including the time Mrs. M. was growing up in her family of origin. This appears to be a classic example of the potency of the emotional transmission process, particularly since it operates primarily at the "meta" level. It is as if the trauma of the past is sealed off, but somehow the fumes find a way to seep through the most minute "cracks and crevices."

To what extent intervention could ever reverse the effects of the "volcanic ashes" which apparently "sizzled" through the family emotional climate is unknown. Another way to capture the intensity of this process would be to draw on Bowen's descriptions of how death in a family can manifest itself as an earthquake does, whereby the aftershocks persist for an indefinite period of time. New damage can occur on a progressive basis from the aftershocks, which sometimes contribute to lower levels of differentiation.

As mentioned earlier in this discussion, it is more typical to approach these matters from one's feeling state than to decide on a course and stay with it for a long time. There is something natural about wanting to stop when the comfort level in self and family feels right. The paradox of this natural state of affairs is that stemming the tide of multigenerational emotional process requires going beyond this point. It is as if nature works against itself, in the sense that it is more natural not to invest a lot of time and effort. Whether this is any more true for families in which the emotional dysfunction is manifested in child symptoms is unknown to this author. It does appear, however, that the projection process that operates toward manifestation of symptoms in one or more children in a family is a highly insidious process. It seems to be similar to carbon monoxide in that it is so difficult to see, smell, or touch.

THE Z. FAMILY

The Z. family illustrates an even lesser degree of severity of child symptomatology but nevertheless portrays a family directing its anxiety toward a particular child. This particular child, Barbara, also seems to be made for this "dance," as her emotional cycles make no small contribution to her family situation. Barbara is ten years old and is in the fifth grade in school. She has a sister who is four years older and in the seventh grade. Mrs. Z. is forty years old and does not work outside the home. She is the youngest of three children and both of her siblings are married with children. Her mother is in her late seventies and in relatively good health. Her father died suddenly eighteen months ago; the cause was never determined. Mr. Z. is a forty-five-year-old professional. He is the oldest of two brothers. His parents are in good health and are in their middle seventies. Both his brother and parents live in a different geographic area from himself. Mr. Z. has been in excellent health all his life but had a temporary physical setback about one year ago. (See the Z. Family Diagram, Figure 5.2.)

Barbara is described as outgoing but more difficult than her sister and has periodic problems in school, and she is often sad and lacks self-confidence. The parents describe their older daughter as quiet and reserved but very self-confident, does well in school, and very active with friends. Mrs. Z. describes difficulty in her relationship with Barbara that parallels her past relationship with her mother.

The Z. family was seen for fifteen sessions, extending over a period of nine months. Most of the sessions were with the mother, but several were with both parents jointly. Barbara was never seen. The primary goal of this work, initially defined by Mrs. Z., was to help her gain more distance and perspective in thinking about and responding to her daughter Barbara. The task assigned to Mrs. Z. was to systematically monitor her own reactions to Barbara's behaviors. She could approach her husband for consultation (in contrast to supervision) on this matter to the extent that she found his advice useful.

Mrs. Z. was generally receptive to studying and working on her reactivity to her daughter. She had a lot of initial insight into what was happening between her and Barbara and how it reflected the earlier emotional dance with her mother. She also knew that working on her self-confidence would help her be more accepting of her daughter. Barbara's functioning in school became more productive and quickly stabilized, and Mrs. Z. reported that her daughter generally seemed happier and better able to deal with her self-doubts.

It is fairly apparent that Mr. Z.'s physical setbacks as well as Mrs. Z.'s father's sudden death were two factors that raised the anxiety level in the family for an extended period of time prior to their seeking professional help. Barbara also appears to be quite susceptible to her mother's anxiety and on occasion subtly assumes a caretaking role. Mrs. Z. had been attempting for some time to become more independent from her husband. She described herself as never having the opportunity to function independently in her family of origin or her marriage. Since Mr. Z. has always had definite ideas and opinions about things, they were well prepared for each other. After experiencing some depression a few years into the marriage,

FIGURE 5.2. The Z. Family Diagram

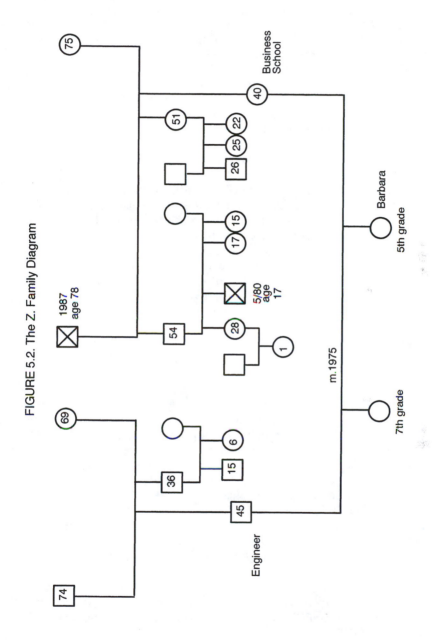

Mrs. Z. began to realize that her pervasive dependency and fusion with her husband were eroding her self-confidence. Although she did not want to jeopardize her marriage, she was determined to become more of a separate self in relation to her husband.

This earlier work on differentiation appeared to have some positive results for Mrs. Z., which in turn probably helped to contain her level of reactivity toward her younger daughter, even in the midst of increased anxiety. However, she knew that becoming more of a self in relation to her family of origin was a more difficult task and that the aftershocks from her father's death were still affecting the extended family system. She was able to separate herself somewhat from this but realized that it was affecting her despite her efforts.

Mrs. Z. is a determined person who may find the right opportunity to do more work on self in relation to the multigenerational emotional process. Her dedication to being a good mother includes an intuitive sense that Barbara's upcoming adolescence can benefit from her pursuing this work. Mrs. Z.'s determination and intuitive abilities are important ingredients. However, for her family to benefit, Mrs. Z. must also find a way to make choices that will organize her life more, thereby giving her a sense of control over what affects her. The multigenerational tide of depression is strong in this system and is lurking in various nooks and crannies.

THE J. FAMILY

The J. family consists of father, mother, two daughters, and a son, Robert. Robert is eleven years old and in the fifth grade. He has functioned inconsistently in school for several years and struggles with his confidence, which in turn leaves him more susceptible to peer pressure. He is in between his two sisters in age. He is only thirteen months younger than his older sister. Both sisters, especially the older, do well in school and participate in various activities that are satisfying to them. Mr. J., age forty-two, is a hard worker and dedicated husband and father but functions below his educational level. He is a low-key person who has a steadying influence on his family. His father died a year after Robert was born, and his mother is in her late seventies and in poor health. She has been in a nursing home for four years. Mr. J. is the youngest of four, and almost seven years separate him from the next oldest. All his siblings are married with children. Mrs. J., age forty-three, has worked part-time for eight years. She is the seventh of nine siblings, with the younger two being male and five of the older six being female. Her father died four years ago, two months after her mother-in-law went into a nursing home. Her mother is in her late seventies and in good health. Mrs. J. has worked tirelessly since childhood as a caretaker in her family of origin. She is able to describe numerous interlocking triangles that in recent years have involved her son Robert with various members of her extended family. Several of Mrs. J.'s siblings, especially her older brother, have been negatively reactive to Robert since he was a young child. Evidently they take offense at his rather direct and sometimes "asocial" manner of telling people what is on his mind. Since Robert has been in the picture, her caretaking focus has been on him in relation to other family members. Similar caretaking triangles have occurred for several years with his school. (See the J. Family Diagram, Figure 5.3.)

The intervention consisted of twenty-five sessions over a period of one year. This involved several sessions with father, mother, and Robert; several sessions with Mr. and Mrs. J.; a few sessions with Mrs. J. and Robert; a few sessions with Mrs. J. alone; and one session with Mrs. J. and her older daughter. The work included coaching Mrs. J. to identify and monitor her anxiety and overfunctioning in the family. It also involved engaging Mr. J. and Robert to think about their functioning. Robert has improved in his school functioning and has become more selective in his peer relationships. Mrs. J. is clearer about when and how she will intervene with and for her son. She is able to delegate some of this responsibility to her husband. It is as if Mrs. J. passed the overfunctioning "hot potato" to her husband. Since the intensity between father and son is at a different level than that between mother and son, Mr. J. and Robert do not get caught in as much of an overfunctioning/underfunctioning dance.

Mrs. J. will probably have to work hard to maintain her position of stepping back from the overfunctioner/caretaker role, especially when her son enters adolescence. She has learned some things about how her intensity in these matters relates to past and present issues in her family of origin. Although she has five older sisters, she was called on by others and by herself to mediate among other family members. There have been numerous difficulties in her family of origin. Divorce and alcoholism are pervasive in this family. Worrying about her son's lack of motivation and difficulty with self-confidence is anchored in what she has observed in many of her siblings and in her father.

THE O. FAMILY

The O. family manifests some variation of symptomatology in a child. They are a family of five, including father, mother, a daughter, and two sons. The daughter, Rose, age eleven, is the oldest of the three offspring and in fifth grade. Her brothers are two and five years younger. She is a

FIGURE 5.3. The J. Family Diagram

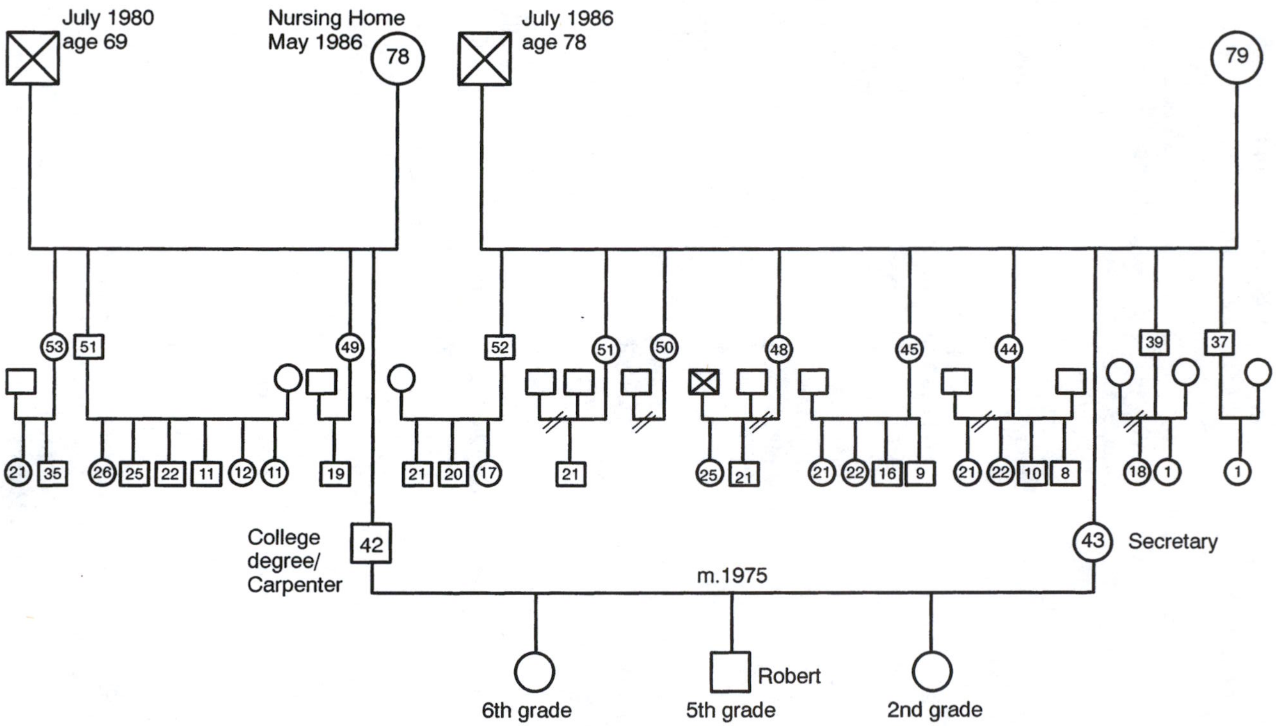

very bright and active girl who has been developing some classic neurotic symptoms related to perfectionism and the inability to risk failure. Some of her current activities, which began at a young age, such as dancing and gymnastics reinforce this perfectionism. However, she carries this behavior well beyond that of her peers who are involved in the same activities. Mr. O. is thirty-six years old and quite successful in his profession. He is the youngest of two children, having an older sister who is also married with children. She and her family live a few hours away. His father died suddenly one year prior to Mr. O.'s marriage. His mother is in her late sixties, in good health, and lives in the same geographic area. Mrs. O., also age thirty-six, is not currently working outside the home, although she once worked at a professional level. Her parents are both in their early sixties and live in the area. Her maternal grandparents are in their mid-eighties and are in relatively good health. Her father is in good health, but her mother has suffered from a chronic illness that has impaired her mental functioning since Mrs. O. was in her middle teens. Mrs. O. is the third of five siblings and the only female. All her siblings are married with children. (See the O. Family Diagram, Figure 5.4.)

Both Mr. and Mrs. O. experienced an early loss associated with the same-sex parent that helped create an above-average level of cautiousness in how they relate to their nuclear family roles. This would have been particularly operative in their early parenting of Rose, who is their first offspring. The premature loss of each of their parents, through death and mental illness, could have been transferred into their caretaking. It may have also been significant that their oldest child is female, particularly for Mrs. O. As a teenager, Mrs. O. was required to think for her mother. This early responsibility for her mother probably helped to emotionally program Mrs. O. toward an intense level of caretaking, especially with her firstborn daughter.

Emotional intensity related to letting go and risking failure is pervasive in Rose's behavior. This has decreased her efficiency in completing schoolwork as well as constricting her athletic efforts. This constricting pattern appears to be occurring on a more intense level with Rose than with her parents. However, it can also be observed in how Mr. and Mrs. O. have been working "overtime" to develop a successful and happy family life. This has made it difficult for them to accept the everyday conflicts and tensions that arise in families, especially as the problems apply to their children. Mr. O. has worked much overtime to gain the success he has achieved in his work. In general, it appears that he has sacrificed himself for his work and family. He is the primary agent of worry and concern over whether and how they have caused their daughter's problems. He voices both of their anxieties about properly caring for their daughter.

FIGURE 5.4. The O. Family Diagram

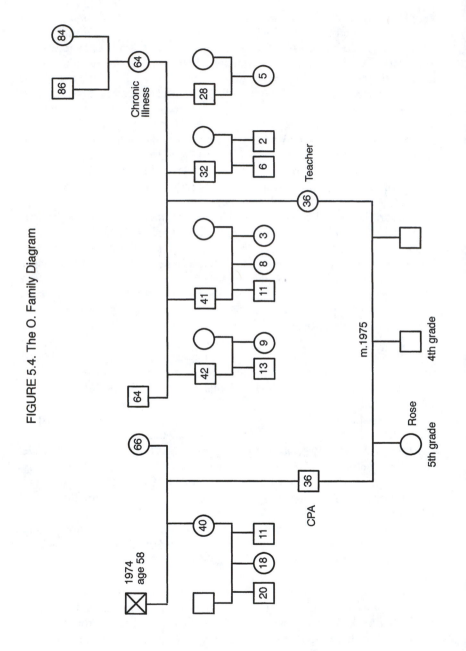

Intervention has focused primarily on Mr. and Mrs. O. both because of the provider's preferred way of operating as well as parental protectiveness of the daughter. They reported instant progress in a couple of areas of their daughter's behavior, but became easily frustrated when this progress did not occur in all areas. They are both sufficiently bright and motivated to understand, at least at the intellectual level, the importance of their reactions to their daughter. However, with the type of emotional process described previously, it is very difficult for these parents to significantly change their reactions. Rather, they tend to suppress their reactivity, which is bound to stir up new reactivity. Basic change in their reactions to Rose's symptomatic behaviors requires a different way of understanding themselves in relation to their daughter and family life in general. They illustrate well the downward projection of anxiety that leads to a constrictive way of living, which in turn generates new tension. This is coupled with the tension and anxiety that is generated by the high level of togetherness which they aspire to in their nuclear family.

Because it is difficult for Mr. and Mrs. O. to observe emotional process from their families of origin except in terms of cause and effect, the intervention with them had been limited to an intense focus on child symptoms. Therefore, the therapist was required to back up and find a way to broaden the focus in a way that Mr. and Mrs. O. could hear. This led to a subtle reframing of the problems in such a way as to highlight what each parent was doing with Rose that was working well. When seen alone, Mrs. O. was better able to separate herself from the family emotionality and focus more productively on areas of her life that she could do something about. This led to a gradual easing of the emotional intensity and a more relaxed lifestyle for the O. family.

Although the levels of differentiation of Mr. and Mrs. O. in relation to their families of origin and each other remained about the same, Mrs. O's shift of focus lowered the overall anxiety level in the family. Also, although Rose's level of functioning in relation to her parents did not change significantly, her mother's refocusing aided her in worrying less about doing everything so perfectly. When Mr. O. saw that both his wife and daughter were less anxious, he began to worry less about his family.

PROJECTION OF EMOTIONAL PROCESS

The previous four case studies have been presented to illustrate how emotionality and anxiety can be transmitted over generations. According to Bowen family systems theory, this can lead to family dysfunction that manifests itself in three forms: (1) physical or emotional symptoms in one of the marriage partners, (2) marital conflict, and (3) emotional symptoms in one or more children. This chapter addresses the third form of family dysfunction. According to Bowen theory, emotional symptoms in children are a very clear depiction of the multigenerational transmission of emotional process.

These case studies also emphasize the special role of the mother-child relationship in the development of symptoms. This is a very different process, however, from the popular notion that the mother did not love the child enough or was not sufficiently available for the child. Quite the contrary, the mother overfocuses on the child in these situations. This, however, is not what has caused the problem. In a way, the problem was there at the start; it was just a question of whether and how the problem would manifest itself in the nuclear family. According to this theory, problems manifest themselves as dysfunction in the nuclear family when chronic anxiety persists for an extended period of time and when family members have not resolved emotional issues with their families of origin.

Therefore, the mother is susceptible to transmitting chronic anxiety to one or more of her children to the extent that she has not emotionally defined herself in relation to her family of origin. The father, however, is also a primary agent in this process. According to the theory, his level of emotional differentiation from his family of origin is approximately the same as that of his wife. He contributes to the mother-child emotional dance both by his anxious reactions to this dance as well as by his own emotional dance with his wife.

In the case of the M. family, the three-generational youngest daughter/ sibling position, coupled with the toxic issue of how death occurs, was observed in the maternal extended family. The issue of relative competence was also observed in the paternal system. However, it appeared that this issue of competition as it related to Mr. O.'s brother, coupled with the paternal intergenerational emotionality related to career decisions, was significant. One could hypothesize that Mrs. M.'s own issues with relative competence caused her to maintain a low profile with her husband, which he found attractive and a relief in contrast to the obviously more intense process with his brother. This may also be one important ingredient in Mr. M.'s unwillingness to counterbalance the mother's and Judy's "obsessive" view of the older daughter's brilliance and the way she resembled her father. This may therefore be a vivid illustration of how Mr. M.'s continued fusion with his family of origin and with his wife contributed to the intensity of the mother-daughter relationship. Also apparent was his inability to consistently connect with his more playful younger daughter. This was partially related to his intense seriousness about and absorption in his work. Thus, his apparent distancing from his own playfulness and that of his younger daughter inadvertently contributed to the mother-daughter intensity.

In the case of the Z. family, the two-generational mother-daughter relationship was highlighted. On the one hand, Mr. Z. played an important counterbalancing role in terms of his ability to accept his daughter as she was. On the other hand, he became somewhat more intense in communicating this to his wife. His apparent need to be in the right in relation to his wife is a result of the fusion in their relationship that relates to each partner's relationship with his or her family of origin.

It was observed that Mrs. J.'s long-term mediating role in her family of origin had also manifested itself intensely in her relationship with her son. This intensity was focused on his school performance for several years. Mr. J.'s special position in his family of origin led him to become trapped for a period of time between choosing a career that would please his mother or something that he wanted for himself. Something similar to this was occurring between his wife and son in relation to the latter's school functioning. Although his low-key manner generally has a calming effect on the family, his inability to be clear in regard to his son's school issues may have been reflective of his unresolved emotional issue with his family of origin. More clarity as to his position regarding this matter was helpful to the mother-son process.

In the case of the O. family, the relationship between mother and maternal grandmother was reversed. This probably helped to intensify the early mother-daughter relationship. Mr. O.'s ability to help deintensity these matters at home varied. Factors affecting his ability included his overfunctioning at work as well as variation in his own anxiety about his daughter's vulnerabilities and/or a sometimes intense concern about the quality of the mother-daughter relationship. The overfocus on his daughter's vulnerabilities points to a protectiveness on the vertical axis that may be related, in part, to his father's sudden premature death. His ambition to succeed in his professional life is consistent with his overall intense focus on improvement, which assumes a perfectionistic quality.

Therefore, in all of the four case studies, the mother-child process is highlighted in terms of the multigenerational transmission process of emotionality. At the same time, however, the significant role of the father is discussed in terms of his level of ability to counterbalance the intensity of the emotional process, which is analyzed in terms of his current level of differentiation in relation to his family of origin and his wife, as well as the level of chronic anxiety affecting his functioning in general.

INTERVENTION ISSUES

Working with the parents to help them shift their reactions to their children's symptoms is based on the belief that parents are important therapeutic resources for their children. Coaching them on dealing with their own emotional reactions is an attempt to utilize the same natural energies and concerns that they have been using as parents. The coaching is intended to help them remove the negative patterns of reactivity from the family. Symptoms in one or more of their children provide a new opportunity to learn about the emotional forces that are operating within themselves. Becoming clearer about the "cards that one has been dealt" often provides a more objective view, which then allows the person to distinguish between intellectual and emotional functioning. Knowing when one's behaviors are more emotional rather than goal-directed can help to deintensify emotionally driven behaviors. The calmness provides an important nurturant function in one's family.

Therefore, the goal is to become more of a student of the emotional process that is impacting on one's behavior. Shuffling rather than changing the cards in your hand is a more manageable objective. Accepting one's history is an important ingredient for acceptance of oneself. Such acceptance provides a better chance at efficient and effective parenting. The latter is probably a byproduct of learning to view self in relation to family life in a clearer, broader, and more flexible way. This can be arduous work. Often the wife/mother is more motivated to do this work. It is as if the emotionality that initially fueled her fusion with the symptomatic child is being redirected toward more productive work. Often she can accomplish more outside the fused emotional climate that may exist between her husband and herself (in situations in which divorce or death has occurred, the details are different but the basic emotional forces are similar). Once she has done some of her own work with the family of origin, the wife/mother is often better able to deal with her husband. The chances are then better for him to become a contributing partner in this process.

Chapter 6

Treatment of a Family Whose Child Has a Serious Medical Problem

Sydney K. Reed

INTRODUCTION

When Mrs. Jones called to request therapy in February 1986, it came as no surprise. Her younger son, Michael, had been born with medical problems and had not been expected to live. The facts of Michael's medical problems were common knowledge in the community. His survival was seen as just short of a miracle.

This chapter will focus on the issues that are involved in the treatment of a family that includes a child with serious medical problems. The case study is primarily the treatment of the mother as she faced problems that frequently became life and death issues. The challenge for the therapist in such a case is to avoid becoming overwhelmed by the intensity of the problems and to keep an objective perspective that will be useful to the family.

First, I will summarize the history of the child's illness and the theories of the clinical treatment of Mrs. Jones. Second, I will outline the importance of the therapist's thinking and the work on self that the therapist does to prepare for the therapy. Third, the theoretical framework of Bowen family systems therapy will be discussed. Finally, an evolutionary perspective that grows out of the Bowen theory will be included in a section titled, "Adaptation and Survival in Families."

THE CLINICAL CASE

Michael's Medical History

Michael was born with a variety of heart problems. When he was two days old, the doctors successfully performed a balloon septostomy. He was to have surgery at five months old to change the configuration of his heart, but at this time, it was discovered that he also had a valve problem and a narrowing of the artery that goes from the heart to the lung. After frequent checkups and consultations, it was decided that surgery could be postponed until he was fifteen months old.

In 1980, heart surgery was still very experimental, and there was uncertainty about which procedures would be appropriate for Michael. Concern arose about the amount of time that it would take to make these corrections and the amount of time Michael could survive on a heart/lung machine. It was finally decided that some of the corrections could be postponed until Michael experienced some difficulty. In 1984, when Michael was five, a plastic valve was installed in his heart. This procedure was followed by frequent checkups. The parents were instructed to keep a watchful eye to determine if Michael was faring well. In August 1986, he appeared to be in trouble again. He was given medication to prevent blood clots. One month later, he suffered a small stroke from a blood clot. He was put in the intensive care unit (ICU) until he recovered from the numbness on his left side.

From 1986 to 1987, Michael experienced a gradual decline in health. In March 1987, he was in a state of congestive heart failure with an enlarged heart and enlarged liver. In August 1987, he underwent a highly experimental and risky procedure that involved putting a band on his heart. In the first two weeks, there appeared to be some improvement, but it then became clear that the procedure had not affected the basic problem. The Joneses were told that no further medical interventions were possible. This was a very sad and frightening time for the Joneses, as they faced the prospect of watching Michael die. After about a month, his doctor called with the news that a medical team in another city could consider Michael a candidate for a heart transplant, and by November 1987, Michael was the recipient of a new heart. After months of signs of rejection, his body stabilized and the heart was accepted. In these medical situations, there is the accompanying fear that the medicine given to suppress the immune system's functioning will not be able to protect the child. Transplant recipients are at risk of developing cancer at this stage of treatment. Michael recently celebrated his tenth year anniversary with his new heart.

Presenting Problem

When Mrs. Jones came in for therapy in early February 1986, eight years after Michael's birth, it was clear that living with the constant uncertainty of the outcome of Michael's rare medical problems had been a major stress in the family. However, the family had resolved to live as "normal" an existence as possible and had done a remarkable job of living full and productive lives without being completely focused on Michael. The Joneses had chosen to walk a very fine line: they needed to be alert for signs of medical deterioration in Michael, yet they determined that becoming overly focused on his problems would detract from their overall quality of life.

Mrs. Jones was concerned about problems she was having managing her life. She was suffering from TMJ (jaw pain), a painful and stress-aggravated condition. In addition, she felt that there was a great deal of tension in her relationships with her husband and children. She blamed herself for not being strong enough to handle life better. During the first few sessions, an extensive family history was taken. It became clear that there were numerous life events over the past eight years that had contributed to a very high level of anxiety in the families of origin of both herself and her husband. During the course of treatment, it was often necessary to review the facts on the time line to reestablish the significance of these stressful events.

Nuclear Family History and Evaluation

Mr. and Mrs. Jones met and married in a small college town where Mr. Jones was an assistant minister and Mrs. Jones was finishing her master's degree and teaching at a community college. Their first child was born in 1972. In 1978, Mr. Jones began work as a senior minister in a suburban church in a neighboring state. The family moved, and Michael, the second son, was born in this town. The Joneses' marriage could be described as a somewhat flexible reciprocal relationship at that time. Mrs. Jones was helpful to Mr. Jones as a sounding board for his work, and he encouraged her to become more emotionally expressive. However, during times of growing anxiety, Mrs. Jones would absorb all the anxiety in the system and begin to function in a one-down position to her husband.

The death of her mother-in-law the year before she entered treatment was a significant personal loss and also a sign of what was ahead in her own extended and aging family. Her husband's family was struggling to adjust to the loss. Mr. Jones made frequent trips to a neighboring state to help his father make important life changes. Also, Mr. Jones had entered a demanding graduate program in addition to his regular job, placing him in an overload position.

The older son, Joseph, was entering adolescence and high school, with the associated adjustments that entering a high-powered suburban high school entails. Mrs. Jones was able to look back at her own experience to gain some objectivity about Joseph's position in the family. She could identify with this son as the functional child who receives less attention.

Michael had become the "shining superstar" of the family. He seemed to have developed above-average physical and social skills for his age. He was a very outgoing, remarkable child.

This was a family with some degree of flexibility about how they handled their anxiety. During times of medical crisis, Mrs. Jones was able to function well in the medical system. Unending stress occurred over an eight-year period, overlaid with predictable developmental stresses. The family was experiencing emotional overload. Mrs. Jones occupied the most vulnerable position in the system by virtue of her tendency to respond in an overly responsible way.

Mrs. Jones's Family History

Mrs. Jones was the firstborn of a sibship of four females. Her sister Mary, now diagnosed schizophrenic, was born two years later. The third sister, Sue, was born eight years after that, and Emily, the youngest, was born with Down's syndrome when Mrs. Jones was twelve. (See the Jones Family Diagram, Figure 6.1.)

Her mother is the oldest of eleven children whom she helped raise. Her grandmother, whose mother had died when she was six, was the younger of two females. Her father is the third child in a sibship of thirteen. He is a retired minister. Her parents chose to keep the youngest child in the home despite the advice of many to institutionalize her. At age thirty-three, Emily requires constant care and supervision. The second daughter, Mary, had also lived at home except for four years, 1982 to 1986. She had participated irregularly in several treatment programs in the past and was beginning to show signs of destabilizing when Mrs. Jones entered treatment. How to relate responsibly as a daughter and a sister to this complicated family situation was one of Mrs. Jones's biggest concerns. Given the ages of her parents, seventy-one and sixty-eight, she worried about what her responsibility would be in her sisters' lives when their parents died. These issues had never been addressed in the family, and Mrs. Jones had been unable to choose a position for herself with which she was comfortable. Mrs. Jones was in fairly regular contact with her family, although from a distance; visits were a source of discomfort.

Mrs. Jones had evolved into a position of overfunctioning in her relationships, and the costs were beginning to show in her own functioning. She had managed the anxiety in the extended family by maintaining distance. Yet, she felt a tremendous pull toward her family; she couldn't just cut off from them. At the same time, they were a source of considerable anxiety for her. The anxiety with Michael's medical problems and within her nuclear family seemed more than she could handle. How to function

FIGURE 6.1. The Jones Family Diagram

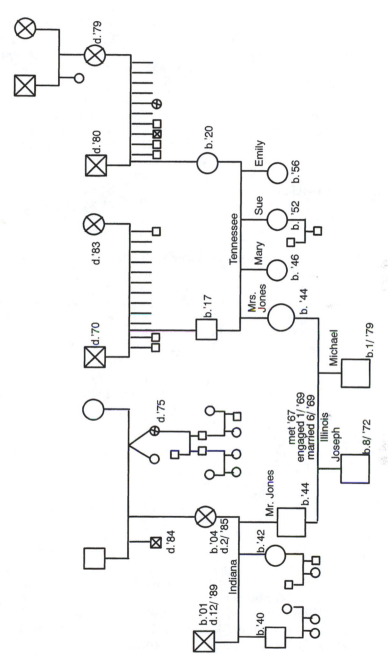

169

responsibly without being overwhelmed in this highly complex relationship network was the question she was facing. Mrs. Jones was convinced from some of the reading she had done that she could only answer that question by obtaining a clearer picture of how she functioned in her family relationships.

Achieving a clearer understanding about herself and her family would involve looking at the situation from a new perspective. She felt overwhelmed and inadequate to face this task. Looking at the facts of the family history was enough for Mrs. Jones to see that "overwhelmed" might be a very understandable response to the magnitude of stress in her life. She was willing to engage in a process of treatment that would lead to her gaining a sense of control over her life.

Mr. Jones's Involvement in the Treatment

Although the main focus on the therapy has been Mrs. Jones, Mr. Jones attended sessions as well. When family anxiety was heightened by concern for Michael's medical condition, Mr. Jones became worried about his wife and called the therapist with his concerns. It was important to neutralize this worry by broadening his perspective and lowering his anxiety through a series of thoughtful questions about the facts of the situation. This helped him gain some objectivity. Mr. Jones's investment in understanding the nature of the family as a system and his part in the process was unquestionably useful to Mrs. Jones and the entire process of treatment. However, his part of the treatment will not be discussed in detail in this chapter.

Mr. Jones was seen a total of six times individually in the two-year period, with about the same number of brief telephone contacts; Mrs. Jones was seen sixty-five times individually during this period; and they were seen ten times as a couple.

Treatment: Work with Client

The following material examines the engagement process in treatment and the first and second years of treatment. Mrs. Jones did work in defining herself in three areas: (1) as a daughter and sister in her family of origin, (2) as a wife in her marriage, and (3) as a mother in her nuclear family. This work was the focus of the first year and involved gaining some knowledge about the difference between facts and feelings. Once this could be determined, the client was more able to make choices for herself based on facts that would be in her best interest. These choices could then be made to fit her life goals instead of being automatic reactions fed by feeling states. Given the understanding of the principles of interlocking triangles (as has been described in Bowen theory), gains that Mrs. Jones made in any of these systems would have a carryover to other systems. The goal of treatment was to reduce Mrs. Jones's overall level of anxiety through some important changes in the way she thought about her problems and in the way she managed herself in her significant relationships.

Engagement Process

Gathering facts about the life events in the family was an important first step to establish the evidence that Mrs. Jones needed in order to believe that she had the right to ask for help in managing herself in the face of these difficult circumstances. In addition, she was able to trace her stoic nature to her family of origin. She recognized that it was both a burden and a blessing to her. As is true with many clients, the decision to enter treatment was her first task in defining a self. Looking at the facts and gaining some understanding about her own subjective relationship to those facts was a useful beginning for the process of lowering Mrs. Jones's anxiety. She was able to laugh at herself as she identified "stoic, overly responsible, firstborn-daughter" behavior.

The First Year

Mrs. Jones had announced in the first session that she was anxious about visiting her family during spring vacation. Exploring the source of her concerns revealed the areas of anxiety. One area of importance could be labeled "knowing the right way to be." Beginning with the assumption that both similarities and differences would be present, Mrs. Jones was asked to determine the ways in which she was the same as and different from her parents and sisters.

This is not easy when you have such obvious differences as a schizophrenic and a nonschizophrenic sibling in the family. Some newspaper articles about growing up in a family with a mentally ill member stimulated her to reevaluate the process of growing up as Mary's older sister. She identified the double bind of being the responsible oldest daughter and the expectation that she not be "too different" from Mary so Mary would not feel bad. During her visit home, she observed symptoms in herself that "seemed to really belong" in her sister Mary. She was able to look at the ways in which she might be similar to Mary and the ways she is different. Facing these facts allowed her to have a broad enough perspective about herself to accept being "a little bit crazy" and a responsible adult at the same time. Getting clear about these "facts" helped to reduce the anxiety in Mrs. Jones.

As she began to question the origin of her belief that there was a "right" way to be, she traded the anxiety of finding "the right way" to be for the anxiety of realizing one is responsible for determining one's own life course. Since finding "the right way" is impossible to achieve, becoming responsible for her own life course became the goal of treatment.

The second issue that Mrs. Jones needed to face with her parents was the notion that there was a right way for children to behave. Mrs. Jones had decided to raise her children differently than she had been raised. This meant that they sometimes acted the "wrong way" and so would not be acceptable to her parents. Thinking through the choices she had made and the reasons behind them enabled her to be comfortable with her parenting style and to prepare to accept the consequences.

Before she left for the trip to her parents' home, Mrs. Jones planned how she would manage herself during this visit. Her goals were to observe herself and her family so that she could, first, better understand the sources of her reactivity and, second, find a way to increase her level of enjoyment of all her family members. Through observation, she was able to identify her reactivity and respond in a less automatic and more thoughtful manner. As she changed her responses to her family, they in turn changed their responses to her. Mrs. Jones managed to stay somewhat relaxed throughout the visit, which contributed to its success. Her parents even thanked her for coming. Mrs. Jones continues the practice of thoughtful planning before she has telephone or face-to-face contact with her family. She was beginning to transform the relationship with her parents so that it would be less of an anxiety-producing factor in her life.

One day, two years into the treatment, she announced that she was going to attend a family reunion in another state. She said that she had been learning about how some birds learn to sing by listening to others of their species. She thought it would be important for her to "hear" the context in which "her song" was developed in order to have a clear picture of who she was. She decided to make the trip alone, returning for the first time to her extended family as an adult, without her children and husband.

Mrs. Jones has used her thinking about and observations of her extended family to more clearly articulate her own view of herself. The process has meant that she is able to have contact with her family, with enough separateness for herself that she feels able to come away enriched by the contact with her parents and sisters and extended family members.

Defining Herself As a Wife

The "right way to be" thinking had Mrs. Jones convinced that she should be more like her husband. As she began to acknowledge the strengths and weaknesses of both their functioning styles, she gained some appreciation for the useful fit that often occurred between them. This allowed her to acknowledge her strengths and put energy into changing her weaker areas of functioning. She recognized her tendency to overfunction in this relationship, and she announced she would no longer be available as a sounding board. Mrs. Jones's effort to pull back in this area meant she had energy to invest in other ways in the relationship.

Mrs. Jones learned to manage herself in a less emotionally reactive manner in extended family relationships that are at some distance. The learning has had a substantial impact on relationships in her nuclear family, particularly with her husband. She learned to recognize his style of managing his anxiety and was able to see it as separate from her own. She was then able to allow him to take responsibility for managing his anxiety while she focused on her own.

Defining Herself As a Mother

How does the mother of a chronically ill child not overfunction? First, Mrs. Jones shifted some of her focus to her extended family and her marriage as a way to keep from overfocusing on Michael. Second, Mrs. Jones was able to use the experience of her mother's style of overfunctioning for her two disabled sisters to gain a new perspective. At the same time, she gained some appreciation for the stresses and demands with which her mother had to contend. Third, she considered taking an outside job, although the unpredictable nature of Michael's medical condition made that extremely difficult. She recognized that the choices she would have to make would not be easy. Again, she had the realization that there is "no right way."

Mrs. Jones recognized that *every* mother has had to struggle with the problem of balancing the task of providing care for her child while promoting the child's learning to be responsible for himself or herself. Mrs. Jones was able to recognize the ways in which Michael and Joseph drew her into their anxiety. Early in treatment, she described the "right way" for a mother to show she cared for her children: "A mother should be right next to the child and take in his feelings. A good mother should make an effort to get the child not to feel what he is feeling." As the treatment progressed, she began to question the ownership of feelings in the family. Staying out of the children's anxiety meant that she had to learn to tolerate a period of increased anxiety on their part, and she had to learn to manage and contain her own reactivity to this increased anxiety. Once she recognized how she became caught up with the anxiety of her children, she began to see that process operating in other relationships. Her ability to separate herself from Michael enabled Mrs. Jones to leave the country for a trip to Asia with her husband and his relatives.

To understand the origins of her mothering behavior, Mrs. Jones had to look carefully at the history of mothering in her family. Mrs. Jones's mother was the oldest child of eleven siblings. Her great-grandmother had died when her grandmother was six years old, and the great-grandfather had never remarried. This history raised the question of what kind of mothering skills might develop in a child raised without a mother by an older sister and father. When this woman grew up and had eleven children of her own, it seemed likely that the oldest daughter of this mother would develop into an overly responsible sibling. A certain amount of conviction that she was "doing the right thing" may have been a useful attitude to assist with the parenting of often-younger siblings. Understanding how her mother's parenting style may have evolved as a natural response helped her put her mother's criticalness and rigidity in a new perspective. She recognized that her fear of not doing the right thing was a fear of being cut off by her mother. The reality was that she now had a great deal of control over what happened in the relationship with her mother. As she observed her own parenting style, Mrs. Jones would see herself switching from an overly critical style to having no standards at all in an effort to not duplicate what her mother had done. Mrs. Jones was able to become more accepting of her mother's manner and less automatically reactive to it. This knowledge, which helped change her relationship with her mother, was important in her effort to gain some control over her own parenting style.

The Second Year

After frequent hospitalization and much testing, Michael had a heart transplant operation in November 1987. After a very long and unquestionably serious operation, months of testing occurred to see if the body would reject the heart. Several of the early tests showed rejection. This is a time of great tension and anxiety. In addition, it is an extremely trying time for the parents because many of the medical procedures are quite painful to the child.

Mrs. Jones handled the demands of the transplant in a remarkable fashion. They entailed a move to another city, a second apartment, trips between cities, overnight stays in the hospital, and learning how to administer complicated blood tests and injections for Michael when he was not in the hospital. The emotional task was to live with the consequences for Michael's and the family's life due to the decisions they had made. There was the constant recognition that rejection meant an earlier death for Michael.

With these kinds of demands, Mrs. Jones recognized that she would need all her energy to manage the challenging circumstances. One of the hardest situations was learning how to protect herself from the well-meant sympathy of anxious people. Learning to set boundaries went against all her early training of being nice, polite, and always available to others. At one point after the transplant, a large community event was planned in Michael's honor. Mr. and Mrs. Jones were able to successfully set boundaries that would protect the integrity of the family from the overly anxious response of the community.

The therapist's availability for phone contact during the out-of-town stays was important. However, it was imperative for the therapist not to overestimate her importance to the family. The resources of family and friends of the clients had to be recognized as primary.

Sometime after the transplant, Michael met the therapist for the first time. It appeared that Michael had enough "helping people" to integrate into his life so a therapeutic decision was made to keep the focus on the parents' efforts to pull up their level of functioning, knowing this would have an influential effect on the entire family.

At the time of this writing, Michael has celebrated ten years with his new heart. There has been a whole new set of problems that Michael and his family have had to deal with, including some impairment in his functioning that may have resulted from minor strokes that occurred during the operation.

WORK WITH SELF: THINKING ABOUT THEORY AND WORKING TOWARD MORE MATURE FUNCTIONING

Treatment begins with the thinking of the therapist. Successful treatment is based on a sound theoretical foundation and on the personal maturity of the therapist. Solid understanding of Bowen family systems theory requires an extended period of time and investment of much personal energy. A therapist must work to understand how one's functioning in one's extended family is tied to the way in which one's nuclear family operates. The concepts of Bowen theory can be used as a guide for achieving greater maturity in one's important relationships. For most therapists, it is important to operate out of a theory that is consistent within itself and consistent with the experience of life. Bowen theory has been written about in detail by others and will not be repeated in this chapter except to illustrate points in the case study.

The fundamental assumption of Bowen theory is that each individual must manage the dependency and attachment process that occurs between parents and children in the process of growing up. The need to have emotional separateness while remaining emotionally connected is seen as intrinsic in all living creatures. The more individuals are able to do this, the more success they will have in dealing with life's stressful events. This attachment process occurs in all family and other important relationships. The nature of one relationship will greatly influence another in a network of interlocking relationships. Knowledge of the mechanisms that function in these interlocking networks provides the foundation for helping someone to become a more mature person. The learning that Mrs. Jones achieved in her interlocking relationship networks is an excellent example of this principle.

Bowen theory further postulates that the therapist's work on himself or herself is fundamental to successful therapy with clients. The theory states that the nature of man is understood to have evolved from lower forms and is intimately connected with all living things. The ability to think and reason is the most important difference between human and the lower forms of life. The human's emotional functioning can be separated from his or her intellectual functioning, yet the human is seen as governed by the same automatic forces that govern all of life. This includes forces which are thought of as instinctual and which govern the human's emotional and feeling states and his or her relationship systems. Bowen has suggested that the "dance of life" in all living things is governed by emotional system (Bowen, 1978, p. 305).

To manage self in the "dance of life" that is present in treatment, the therapist must know these systems, recognizing how they operate in the therapist as well as the client. The emotional system refers to the underlying, automatic, instinctual system that operates outside of awareness. That system fuels our reactivity. The feeling system allows for some verbal articulation of the internal process inside each person, providing the opportunity to share individual uniqueness. The thinking system provides the objectivity to see the facts and to make plans and take an action that is in one's best interest. When these three systems are in a reasonable balance, one system does not overwhelm the others. However, when a person is emotionally involved in a situation, the thinking response can be overwhelmed by intense feeling and emotional responses (Kerr and Bowen, 1988).

Bowen's description of the emotional system with its basic biological foundation shared with all living creatures is one of the key factors in differentiating Bowen theory from conventional theories of human behavior. The meaning of the emotional system can only be understood by experiencing it in important relationships. The learning cannot be done intellectually. It requires a change in oneself (Kerr, 1989).

I will illustrate how these systems operate simultaneously within the individual. Many years ago, I was on the beach with my son. It was feared that a child had been lost in the water. I remember feeling, "Something terrible could happen to my child." I noticed signs of panic, increased heartbeat and sweating in myself. This was the emotional system and the feeling system in operation. I recognized that I was holding my child's hand. It was a *fact* that he was safe and sound, but that objective fact did not match the subjective feeling state or the automatic reaction of the emotional system. After a few moments, I was able to think clearly enough so that my behavioral response came out of the thinking system. In situations of high anxiety, it is easy to get swept up in the emotional/feeling system and ignore the facts. The style of participation that one has in the "dance of life" is determined by the balance achieved in these internal systems and the balance achieved in the interlocking relationship system. As has been discussed earlier, these two systems are highly interdependent.

This example from the case study will illustrate the process of trying to keep the systems balanced in the head of the therapist. The anxiety related to Michael's illness was always present. However, it was still a shock when the doctors told the Joneses that they could expect to have no more than one year with Michael. Both Mr. and Mrs. Jones came in for the next session. They expressed their grief and sadness about the prospect of watching their son die. They also expressed their comfort in the fact that they were in a therapeutic relationship which would enable them to cope with this loss. The recognition of the trust the patients frequently place in their therapist can be anxiety producing for the therapist.

Two weeks later, Mrs. Jones came in to say the doctors had decided that Michael was a candidate for a heart transplant. This appeared to be the answer—clearly a lifesaving solution. The temptation to automatically grab an easy solution occurred to the therapist. However, the Joneses had been living within the shadow of medical institutions, dealing with complicated medical problems, for eight years—Michael's entire life. They were very cautious and thoughtful, looking at all the ramifications of the decision they were being asked to make. This was an important event in the therapy; it was a very dramatic demonstration that the Joneses were the experts on their lives and the therapist did not have to become one as well. (Of course, the reality that becoming an expert on someone else's life is impossible does not stop therapists from expecting that of themselves.) The parents had the experience and learning that would enable them to make the best decisions they could for themselves and their family. The therapist's job was to manage her anxiety in such a way that a calm and thoughtful setting would be achieved in which the clients could do their best thinking. It was evident that the solutions to their lives' problems would come from the clients and not the therapist. It was important for the therapist to make this point clear to the clients.

The question of what it means to be a responsible therapist is one that every therapist must ask. This entails the ability to be emotionally present to clients and yet sufficiently emotionally separate that the therapist is not caught in the anxiety in the family or does not contribute his or her own anxiety to the family. The therapist must allow the family members to have their own anxiety, to struggle with the important issues, and to come to their own solutions. To do this, the therapist must simply manage his or her own anxiety and operate in a manner to defuse the anxiety in the client. In an atmosphere of lowered anxiety, clients are able to access their life experience and learning as a way to generate options to handle their current life problems. Every living person is a product of some four billion years of natural selection that has produced organisms able to adapt to their environment. In that sense, every living creature is the progeny of survivors—living organisms have a built-in ability to try to find a way to survive. In Bowen family systems therapy, it is the task of the therapist to encourage the natural adaptive survival reflex in clients.

It was useful to recognize the influence of my family history on my emotional functioning to understand the chronic anxiety that might be stimulated by Mrs. Jones's situation. It was also important to understand my own acute anxiety at the launching/separation process with my son, who had just left for college. It was most helpful to use as broad a theoretical perspective as possible to stay objective, not only about the facts of this case, but about my own related anxiety as well.

In an effort to gain some control over my chronic anxiety, I have been studying my family for fifteen years. One of the by-products of this on-going work was the stimulation of many important relationships in my parents' lives that I believe contributed to the reduction of the level of chronic anxiety in my parents and thus, indirectly, in myself. Getting the family to articulate the facts of its family history enabled some members to move beyond the emotional upset that was experienced in the family many years prior to the death of my grandmother. Knowledge of interlocking triangles is important to recognize how the anxiety in a family can be passed around. The key value of my work with my extended family would be that it has provided a reduction in my anxiety and afforded the opportunity for defining myself.

An interview with an aunt provided some information about my great-grandmother that was useful in understanding the process of attachment to children that occurred on the maternal side of my family. My great-grandmother had lost four children, two of whom died in her arms. She made special promises to God, should He allow my grandfather and his sister to live. This helped me understand the intensity that existed in the relationship between my grandfather and his parents.

Second, I recognized that the death of a two-year-old cousin just as I was entering adolescence may have had a significant effect on the feeling/fantasy system I would one day have regarding the children. The death of an older cousin's daughter the summer after her graduation from high school, when my eldest son was four, also added to the feeling/fantasy system concerning separating from parents. My continual work on the attachment system with my own parents and my children has been a useful laboratory for furthering my understanding of chronic anxiety.

Clients frequently come for therapy in a state of heightened anxiety, in which the emotional and feeling state is activated. It is the task of the therapist to not let this anxious state stimulate his or her own emotional and feeling states to an excessive degree. This can be done by (1) understanding how these systems interact to comprise self, (2) learning how to keep the thinking system in the therapist activated to keep the other two systems in balance, and (3) activating the thinking system of the client by helping him or her separate the "facts" from the feelings and emotional reactivity.

Since writing and thinking about a case often provides some objectivity that is important for the course of the treatment, the decision to write this chapter was made at the time of the transplant, when the anxiety and subjectivity were high. In an effort to become clearer about how the "dance of life" operates, parenting behavior in vertebrates was investigated.

ADAPTATION AND SURVIVAL IN FAMILIES

This section describes an evolutionary account of parenting behavior in the animal kingdom to provide a perspective on the adaptation and survival process in human families.

A study of the evolution of parenting behavior indicates that the interplay between the internal guidance system of the organism and the external relationship system is the key factor in the parent-child relationship that determines the survival of the species. In general, the more complex the organism becomes, the more complex the internal guidance system and the external relationship system required for the regulation and preservation of the organism. Evolution has gone in the direction of increasing complexity in this interrelationship, the most complex being that in Homo sapiens.

Adaptation is defined as the process by which individuals attempt to fit into their environment. Survival can be seen as the effectiveness of the fit.

In each species, particular behaviors have been selected for the adaptation process to ensure the survival of the species.

Looking at the evolutionary account of the animal kingdom, one is immediately struck by the fact that all living creatures seem to be driven by the same common need: to produce surviving offspring. Indeed, there is both a fundamental similarity and an incredible variety in the process. Thus, every living animal begins life in the same way, as a bit of proto-plasm covered with an elastic membrane, with a nucleus containing the two entwined coils of the genes of the father and mother. At the moment in time when the genes of the mother merge with the genes of the father to form a new cell, the eggs of most animals are indistinguishable. Astonish-ing as it sounds, the egg of the flea and that of the whale cannot be told apart at this stage of development (Burton, 1987).

The second impression is of the incredible variety in this process. There clearly is no one right way. Survival is determined by the correctness of the fit at a particular time and in a particular place. This rule holds true throughout the evolutionary process, as the direction moves from simple to more complex organisms.

Primitive animals, such as the marine invertebrate starfish, may pro-duce forty million eggs a year. Parental care is limited to depositing the eggs, usually on the sea floor, and letting them fend for themselves. Another marine invertebrate, the giant water bug, lives in freshwater, which has less available nutrition than the sea. These water bugs provide more food for the developing fetus by means of a larger yolk sac. They lay fewer eggs and permit the embryo to remain within the protective environs of the parent body for an extended period of time (Burton, 1987).

The first vertebrates to take the evolutionary step to a land-based life were the reptiles. The absence of water produced basic changes in the egg itself. Hard shells evolved to protect the egg from drying out. The embryos were able to develop within the egg completely and emerge as juveniles, possess-ing all of the physical characteristics of adults except size. The offspring are able to survive independently at birth. Such complexity means fewer eggs are produced. The eggs required a longer time to hatch, hence making them more vulnerable to predators, so reptiles extended their parental involvement by building or locating secure nests and sometimes guarding them.

In birds and mammals, warm-blooded descendants of reptiles, we see a major increase in parental involvement with the young. Examining specif-ic examples of parenting behavior in birds, it is clear that particular behav-iors have been shaped by the environment. For example, ground nest builders whose young are at risk to predators must have all the young hatch on the same day to increase the chance that some may survive a predator's raid. Scientists are unable to explain the process by which this occurs. The mother lays the eggs one a day for two weeks. She then begins incubation. When the oldest bird is ready to emerge, it makes faint clicking sounds that stimulate those laid more recently to break through their shells at the same time.

In the case of the snowy owl, a species that lives in a more mountainous setting, a meager food supply is more of a risk than predators so their eggs must hatch one a day so that each might be fed in turn.

With the evolution of mammals, there occurred a tremendous increase in emotional and physical involvement and interdependence between parents and offspring. In mammals, the egg is fertilized and develops inside the mother and is actively nurtured by her before birth. The nurturing by the mother continues after birth with the nursing process.

Mammal offspring are fully developed at birth but are still dependent on the mother for survival. For example, wildebeest offspring are capable of running at adult speeds within an hour of their birth to keep up with the herd. However, if they become separated from their mother during this juvenile stage, they will die. The audio-vocal calls that have developed in mammals are a way to ensure the connection between mother and child. Separation means that the young do not survive.

Margulis and Sagan (1986) point out that the evolutionary process went in the direction of protective growth in the parental body and has become highly developed with mammals. However, this process seems to have turned around at the point of development of the human species:

> Some apes may have given birth to infants prematurely. The births were easier, since the heads of the infants were smaller. Premature ape infants could have been imprinted with experiences from the harsh outside world at earlier ages, giving them more time to modify their behavior. Experienced ape children can be presumed to have learned better and at a younger age adult survival tricks. (Margulis and Sagan, 1986, p. 209)

The survival of the "immature" human babies requires the longest and most intense postnatal dependency of any of the mammals. It appears that this dependent period allows the brain of the human infant to develop in such a manner as to ensure increased adaptability. After birth, the weight of the average human brain nearly triples in the first two years, from 350 to 1,000 grams. It is informative to look at the evolution of the brain, as it parallels the development of parenting behavior.

The research of Paul MacLean has shown that within the human brain are the evolutionary remnants of the reptilian brain, with its species-specific functions, and the paleomammalian brain, with its more newly evolved mammalian functions of nursing, sensitivity to separation, and affiliation. Within human beings, the cortex becomes greatly expanded into the neomamalian brain with its opportunities for novel, nonautomatic responses, which can be called learning (MacLean, 1975).

Hard wiring is a term used to refer to that neurological structure which is species specific and which operates at the level of stimulus-response. Virtually all the cells in the reptilian brain are "hardwired"; they directly process sensory information (input) or control movement (output). The functioning of the reptilian brain can be said to be programmed by its ancestral past. Little adaptation can be seen in it. In the human brain, there is a large gray area about three-quarters of the cortex called the association area. Because the neurons in this area are not committed at birth to a set function, they are available for learning. They are not preprogrammed and automatic. In mammals, the proportion of hard wiring to the uncommitted areas decreases. The following material examines the processes that influence the way the brain functions.

Acute and chronic anxiety are the signal mechanisms that alert an organism to a threat, real or imagined, to its survival. Thanks to this basic primitive push for survival we are able to respond to acute anxiety fairly successfully. What is more complicated is the functioning of chronic anxiety in our lives. Chronic anxiety can be viewed as a product of the paleomammalian brain with its arousal mechanism that alerts the organism to danger. Danger represents a threat to survival and, increasingly, over the course of evolution, the fear of separation. The organism's ability to function with anxiety appropriate to the situation is greatly influenced by the "hardwired" ancestral past and in later primates by the responses learned from parents. For some, the amount of acute and chronic anxiety transmitted from the previous generation may prevent the organism from doing the kind of learning that contributes to optimum survival. Multigenerational histories of families attest to the fact that not every individual survives and that some individuals have a more successful fit than others. The theory of the emotional system described by Dr. Bowen accounts for these facts (Bowen, 1978).

Clinical observations indicated that the pain associated with death or loss in the parent-child dyad is the determinant factor for the dance of closeness and distance that one can observe in the functioning in nuclear families and in the multigeneration history over time.

Clinical research with human beings has documented the highly connected emotional configuration of the child and the mother and frequently the father. The functional state of each individual shifts constantly, and behaviors change frequently in response to each other and to the environment. The course of the development of the family is characterized by the developing ability of each person to learn for himself or herself and to be responsible for self (Papero, 1988). This process requires the primary care-takers to pull back from their caretaking positions and to allow more and more responsibility for self to rest with the offspring. Optimum survival of the family line seems to occur if this pull back can be managed without a total emotional and geographical cutting off between child and parent.

The research of Murray Bowen suggests that all human beings can be placed on a continuum to describe the degree to which the resolution of the attachment enables the self-responsibility to take hold.

In summary, if we look at nature, we can see that the push to have one's offspring survive to the next generation is in all living creatures. The adaptation of each organism to the environment is specific to the unique characteristics of that organism. Nature provides an infinite variety of adaptive solutions to survival. There is no one right way. Survival is determined by the correctness of the fit at a particular time and place. The unique characteristic of human beings seems to be our highly developed brain with its vast capacity for learning. Survival through adulthood rests on each individual being able to learn for himself or herself. The task of the family can be defined as each person taking responsibility for their own continuing development and for adult members to allow offspring increasing responsibility for their own development. MacLean's research indicates that the most newly evolved part of the brain is the prefrontal cortex. This area, which promotes objective evaluation of the world, is richly connected to the more primitive parts of the brain that have to do with separation. He suggests that optimum human functioning would represent a balanced operation of the old and new brains. Bowen theory has described this task as a lifelong process of continuing the effort to manage the attachment process.

As adults, our survival and the survival of our offspring depends on being able to manage the chronic anxiety from the past to use uncommitted gray areas of the neocortex to learn in the present, and to minimize the amount of anxiety we transfer to the next generation.

Learning from the Evolutionary Experience

I had just finished writing this chapter when I met with Mr. Jones the day before Michael was to have an important surgery to determine whether his body was accepting the new heart. Mr. Jones wanted a consultation on his work system. He was working hard to define himself in a nonreactive manner in an intense, emotionally charged situation. At the end of the hour as he was leaving, having never mentioned his family once, he said, "We will let you know if there are any complications in the surgery." I was affirmed in my decision to let Mr. Jones decide how he would use his time in treatment. I recognized that my temptation at an earlier time in my career would have been to have made sure he "faced important issues" and "did not run away from them." Looking at the variety of responses in nature teaches one to look for and respect unique and creative efforts of clients to cope with their lives.

Later that day, I recognized that optimum survival was a misleading term. In fact, if every living creature were to live, the earth could not support them all. Nature depends on the fact that death is part of the scheme; death must be viewed as part of what constitutes optimum survival of all life on earth.

Looking at the hard facts of evolution, which indicated that survival of human offspring depends on a successful resolution of the intense dependency of infancy, provided useful thinking to balance the emotional reactions to the separation from my college-age son. Successful management of my own life situation resulted in clarity about the clinical issues in the Jones family.

Thinking About Death

Murray Bowen, in *Family Reaction to Death* (1976), suggested that direct thinking about death, or indirect thinking about staying alive and avoiding death, occupies more of humans' time than any other subject:

> Man is an instinctual animal with the same instinctual awareness of death as the lower forms of life. He follows the same predictable instinctual life patterns of all living things. He is born, he grows to maturity, he reproduces, his life force runs out and he dies. In addition, he is a thinking animal with a brain that enables him to reason, reflect, and think abstractly. With his intellect he has devised philosophies and beliefs about the meaning of life and death that tend to deny his place in nature's plan. Each individual has to define his own place in the total scheme and accept the fact that he will die and be replaced by succeeding generations. His difficulty in finding a life plan for himself is complicated by the fact that his life is intimately interwoven with the lives about him. (Bowen, 1978, p. 321)

Bowen emphasizes that every family does not handle death in the same way. The ability to successfully integrate death of family members into the family's life is related to the intensity of the family. He suggested one should strive to get an "easy come, easy go" attitude in relationships. This means not being dependent on a single emotional figure (Reed, 1989). This is at the core of his thinking about differentiation of self. The ability to handle death or, for that matter, life is dependent on the ability to understand and manage the emotional dependence on others and the emotional dependence others have on you.

CONCLUSION

This chapter illustrates the process of therapy with a family whose child has a chronic, life-threatening medical problem. The therapist's use of Bowen theory to inform the treatment was illustrated by her work with the client and her work with herself. Years of study and working to observe the functioning of the therapist's family emotional system provided the foundation for the clinical objectivity necessary for treatment of an intensely emotional family situation such as the Jones family was experiencing. Viewing the human family as part of nature enabled the therapist to ground the parenting process (her own and that of her client's) in a natural process that is basic to all of life.

Recognizing the interdependence of relationship networks, the therapist was able to guide Mrs. Jones's effort to improve her level of responsible functioning in her extended family, her marriage, and her relationship with her children. The increase of anxiety related to Michael's heart transplant operation and recovery provided numerous opportunities for Mrs. Jones to strive for her most responsible functioning. She gained some appreciation and understanding of the mechanisms controlling her behavior in these important relationships, which eventually leads to greater choice and control over her life.

REFERENCES

Bowen, Murray (1976). "Family Reaction to Death." In P. Guerin (Ed.), *Family Therapy: Theory and Practice.* New York: Gardner Press, pp. 335-348.

Bowen, Murray (1978). *Family Therapy in Clinical Practice.* New York: Jason Aronson.

Burton, Robert (1987). *Eggs: Nature's Perfect Package.* London: Roxby Press.

Kerr, Michael (1989). "Darwin to Freud to Bowen." *Georgetown,* Spring.

Kerr, Michael and Bowen, Murray (1988). *Family Evaluation.* New York: W.W. Norton and Co.

MacLean, Paul (1975). "Sensory and Perceptive Factors in Emotional Functions of the Triune Brain." In A. Levi (Ed.), *Emotions—Their Parameters and Measurement.* New York: Raven Press, pp. 71-92.

Margulis, Lynn and Sagan, Dorian (1986). *Microsmos.* New York: Summit Books.

Papero, Daniel (1988). "The Family as a Unit." *Family Center Report,* 9(1).

Reed, Sydney (1989). "Family Reaction to Death." *CFC Review,* 1(2), pp. 1-2.

Chapter 7

Treating College Students from a Bowen Family Systems Theory Perspective

Brian J. Kelly

INTRODUCTION

College students represent a unique group of individuals who seek to know themselves better and to have a better understanding of the world in which they live. Bowen family systems theory (Bowen, 1978; Kerr and Bowen, 1988) offers interesting advantages for working with this population.

Bowen family systems theory has, in my opinion, an appeal to the intellectual curiosity of students. It also allows them to take positive action toward achieving emotional independence while preserving family relationships. This approach to conceptualizing the human experience fits very well with the conflict of autonomy versus dependence that they actually experience, especially in their junior and senior years. Yet, perhaps the main appeal of this approach for college students is that it just makes good sense. The theoretical premise fits logically into the world in which they live. The college students with whom I deal on a daily basis are on the verge of independence. They are dependent on their parents for emotional and financial support, yet they are moving toward a much more autonomous life—one that will involve making key decisions, such as lifestyle, career, and possibly mate selection. Most of these decisions will have a significant impact on them for the rest of their lives. Many of them are anxious about these major life decisions, in addition to other aspects of their future. College years are anxious years!

In our present economy, many students are going to graduate and move back home after having lived independently of adult supervision for several years. What specific advantages does Bowen family systems theory bring to bear on the lives of college students? Beyond all of the aforementioned dynamics is Bowen's concept that each of us is best understood not as an individual psychological entity, but as a functional part of an emotional unit—the family. In expanding the focus from the individual to the family relationship system, Bowen family systems theory expands the perspective of both therapist and client. With this expanded view, a greater variety of applications becomes possible, and a very different way of thinking about a problem emerges. Second, Bowen family systems theory identifies the role of anxiety in the development of any symptom. Bowen described anxiety as an essential ingredient of any symptom and as the individual response to real or imagined threat. Acute anxiety is a response to a threat of limited duration, such as family disasters, fire, automobile accidents, sudden illness, and other emergencies. Humans tend to cope well with acute anxiety. It is not uncommon for the human to function very well during an unanticipated crisis or emergency; neither is it uncommon for them to react with trembling or tears after the crisis is over.

On the other hand, chronic anxiety is a reaction to imagined threats and is experienced as seeing "no light at the end of the tunnel." Humans have a limited capacity to deal with chronic anxiety, which involves itself more with what might happen. As a general rule, specific events trigger acute anxiety, while chronic anxiety appears to be triggered by a disturbance in the relationship system. Chronic anxiety is more closely related to an individual's reactions to the disturbance than the event itself. Symptoms feed on chronic anxiety; they simply cannot exist without it. If a therapist can facilitate the client's efforts to reduce the level of chronic anxiety, symptoms will resolve themselves. Bowen family systems theory, with its focus on the broad perspective of the extended family, offers therapists many new options for alleviating anxiety.

The third aspect of Bowen family systems theory that seems especially attractive to college students is the concept of differentiation of self and the process of defining a self. Students are entering into an adult world, and they want to know what it means to be an adult. The idea of defining a self to the world and especially to important others in a relationship system has great appeal to students. Also, the description of self that ranges from immaturity to maturity seems to appeal to the desire for greater maturity among college students. This theoretical orientation provides food for their thought. Furthermore, the idea that one can, by defining a self within the context of the family unit, enhance one's ability to manage life across the board is appealing.

In summary, this chapter asserts that Bowen family systems theory has both an appeal and unique application for college students. It clearly defines two areas that must be engaged to address a symptom. The first area involves reducing the chronic anxiety that feeds the symptom. The second involves raising differentiation of self. The therapist relies on the theory to guide his or her actions to alleviate chronic anxiety. Family of origin work opens up a whole new vista for managing chronic anxiety. The realization that chronic anxiety is a function of the individual's reaction to an imbalance in the relationship system gives the therapist and the client a map—the family—that can be used to locate the means by which the anxiety is being transmitted through the relationship system to the client. Much of the effort in all therapy is aimed at controlling or limiting chronic anxiety; the long and difficult work of differentiating a self cannot be approached until chronic anxiety has been reduced. In fact, I do not know of any college student who has been able to increase differentiation. I suspect that the number of incidences within therapy of those individuals who take advantage of the available knowledge and actually engage themselves with family in such a way that they improve their level of differentiation is quite small. Certainly, I have not witnessed it with clients. This, however, does not in any way limit the contribution that Bowen family systems theory makes to understanding the human phenomenon and giving people the tools to lower the amount of chronic anxiety in their lives.

So, in dealing with college students, the efforts of the therapist are aimed primarily at symptom reduction through addressing chronic anxiety. The two means by which the reduction of anxiety is influenced are (1) the ability of the therapist to manage self and remain neutral toward the client and (2) the ability of the therapist to think and work from the theory.

It is necessary to identify relationship imbalances and to coach the client to adjust these imbalances. Bowen family systems theory, with its expanded perspective of the extended family as an emotional unit, is the key to keeping the therapist neutral and increasing the flexibility of response within the client. This increase in one's ability to think and act in a variety of ways has a calming effect. When an individual can think clearly, a wide spectrum of responses becomes available. Chronic anxiety is characterized by a kind of tunnel vision that impedes creative responses and free thinking.

Given the fact that all symptoms require anxiety to persist, it is important to understand how Bowen family systems theory is so effective in combating chronic anxiety. Certainly, the role of the therapist is vital to the reduction of anxiety. No contributor to therapeutic literature has demonstrated more clearly than Dr. Bowen just how great the forces of mutual influencing within the client-therapist relationship can be. Bowen was not the first to discover this phenomenon; Freud's concepts of transference and countertransference detailed all of the subtle ways in which humans react to one another and are controlled by the behavior of others.

For an anxious person to encounter a therapist who does not react anxiously is a calming experience. The therapist who is able to think about the client and ask questions that indicate interest rather than reactivity produces a calming effect. Calming effects offer the client a sense of increased self-control.

Knowledge of Bowen family systems theory provides a therapist with a reliable way to think clearly about a situation. When a therapist is trained in this theory, he or she has a way to focus on self and thus monitor tendencies to become emotionally drawn into a reaction. Examples of emotional reactivity or loss of neutrality are losing a systems perspective and focusing on a symptom, being sympathetic or critical, wanting to move in and solve the problem, and failure to see the reciprocity of imbalance in relationships. The task of therapy for the practitioner grounded in Bowen theory is the same as it is for the client and for all humans. All of us will be confronted in life with situations that demand us to conform to the way others want us to be. From the perspective of Bowen theory, the task is always to find a way to be true to self without having to be critical of, or distant from, the forces of conformity. This ability to be different or free without sacrificing relationship is a skill the therapist must demonstrate and one the client can develop.

As mentioned previously, it is important for the therapist to maintain and communicate a systems perspective to see the mutual influence in the client's extended family and to make that influence known to the client. Frequently, the mutual influence can be seen in reciprocal patterns of behavior of which clients are unaware when they begin therapy. Indeed, it was the observation of these patterns of emotional interdependence that persuaded Dr. Bowen that a family could be viewed as an emotional unit. Emotional interdependence can best be viewed in patterns of reciprocity. For example, one spouse intensifies by acting weaker or stronger, while the other will automatically intensify the compensating or reciprocal response so that each one's behavior is affected, even controlled, by the behavior of the other. Other reciprocal patterns that cause family members to rely on automatic behavior patterns include overly adequate and inadequate, decisive and indecisive, leader and follower, emotionally expressive and inexpressive, and overresponsible and irresponsible. These are just some of the reciprocal patterns that may characterize a family.

To what degree family members define any of these differences as a problem may affect the degree of polarization found within the family. The more differences are viewed as a problem, the more polarized the system gets, with members becoming supportive of what they view as the right way of behaving. What began as an interesting difference (potentially a strength) has become a divisive issue. This chapter will demonstrate some clinical principles that mold the intervention strategies. Four brief case studies that view how students have resolved problems while involving themselves in family of origin work are presented. Each example will be followed by an evaluation of the factors involved in therapy that have contributed to successes and failures. The belief is that if one is to learn from experience one must evaluate those factors that encourage or limit progress toward a mature lifestyle. The clinical principles to be kept in mind are the following:

1. The priority of theory in therapy and the importance of changing perception and thinking to effect a more productive individual should be implemented.
2. An individual in distress is a symptom of an imbalance of emotional forces within the family; understanding and correcting that imbalance is the most productive effort that can be made.
3. Knowledge of triangles is a vital tool that students use to gain insight into family functioning and to allow for observation of process. Characteristically, triangles involve two insiders and an outsider, i.e., mother and daughter work together to protect father.
4. One last general concept is focused upon during clinical sessions: behavior can best be understood by examining the functional position of a person within the family system as opposed to viewing a member of the system as sick, wrong, or evil. For example, a mother with a heart condition can function to bring the father and son together in a caretaking effort that includes the denial of real differences and obliterates focus on marital issues. The effort to understand behavior by its function within the system reduces the client's judgmental state and allows for a fresh look at chronic situations. This new perspective comes with new opinions for behavior that are constructive. In all clinical cases, a considerable effort goes into implementing the idea that change in an emotional system occurs when one person decides to change how he or she participates in the family. Many people are not aware of the relationship options they have. Many college students ask their parents for a decision; they do not see the option of asking for ideas instead. Asking for thoughts on an issue allows them to evaluate the ideas for themselves and make their own decisions. Many find freedom in acknowledging dependencies, while requesting to have their point of view considered. Freedom to function can be enhanced when focus shifts from coercive efforts to reach the desired

goal, to being heard and hearing parents' best thoughts. College students are usually financially dependent, and it is important for them to acknowledge that dependency. It also is important for them to explore the limits of dependency. Students, with coaching, have had great success in verbalizing thoughts to parents and eliciting from parents basic ideas that motivate them toward certain decisions. By avoiding a discussion of feelings and working toward an increased understanding of what thoughts might be behind the action, anyone can move toward a more mature relationship with parents. Mature relationships are more flexible in thought and behavior.

CASE STUDY 1

A twenty-one-year-old college junior requested an appointment with the psychologist because she had been depressed for seven months and was not getting better. She was close to failing out of the university. The onset of depression coincided with an abortion. She was still involved with the male by whom she became pregnant; he graduated and entered the Navy. The student is a middle child with two brothers. Her mother is an only child and is described as rebellious in relationship to both her mother and husband. The father is an older brother of two sisters. (The family diagram is shown in Figure 7.1.) When this student entered therapy, she was feeling depressed and was also actively avoiding contact with her family. She had a long history of an intense relationship with her mother, describing herself as being "controlled by my mother" and as "the family handkerchief." She saw herself as unable to control herself with her mother or any boyfriend. She was uninvolved with her brothers. Early efforts in the therapy went toward increasing self-control regarding her mother and bridging the developing distance with her father. She admitted to her parents that she was in academic difficulty, while informing them of her plan to correct the situation. This included a request that they hold off on any comments until the end of the semester unless they observed her violating her plan. Once exams were over, they could talk all they wanted. Part of her plan was to maintain regular visits home while working on efforts to maintain her composure with her mother. She was able to break up with her boyfriend in a constructive manner during this period, although we discussed it only after the fact.

After four months of work with her parents and brothers, the student was more organized in her life (her room was clean, studies organized, and money budgeted). She began working on her relationship with her older brother, whom she had been avoiding for years; she seemed hesitant to do much, but stated that she thought it might be important since there had been

FIGURE 7.1. Family Diagram

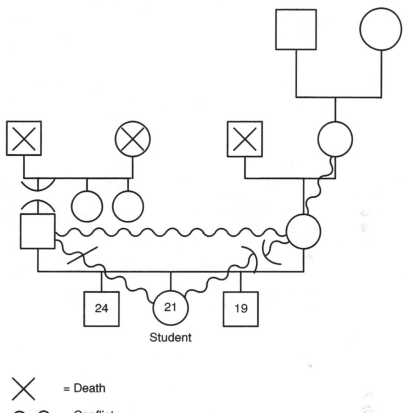

X = Death

~~ = Conflict

~|~ = Distance

)|(= Cutoff

a two-year history of incest between them. Therapy focused on ideas of responsibility within a role, e.g., daughter, sister, granddaughter, and used humor to handle the pushes toward over- or underresponsible functioning. The student then decided that handling her older brother would be a good test for her. After a series of visits with her brother, she recalled that when her brother would make sexual advances she would pretend that she was someone else and blankly comply. When she began dating, all of her relationships were sexually active, and she had complied with her boyfriends' requests in a detached manner, while resenting her sexual partners for not noticing how little emotionally involved she was. Over the summer, she entered a relationship that she described as her first adult relationship. She changed her major course of study to one of her choice rather than her mother's and took the necessary extra courses to graduate on time. No signs of depression have returned. She still lets things get out of control to a degree, but now recognizes what can be done and takes corrective action. She has not yet resolved her relationship with her older brother but has contained her reactivity to the relationship.

In evaluating the course therapy with this student, several factors seem to account for the general success that she experienced. The first beneficial factor was her awareness that her functioning was tied very closely to her mother's intense focus on her as the only daughter. A second factor that had a positive influence on the course of therapy had to do with her father's quick and positive response to increased contact and interest. This was followed by the student's ability, once contact had been made with her father, to see his compulsive, controlled, and withdrawn behavior as a direct reaction to her mother's impulsiveness and emotional outbursts. When she could see that each parent was influencing the other along an impulsive, rigid continuum and that neither represented the right way, this student was able to view her parents' behavior as humorous and see some of the same humorous aspects in her own behavior. A final positive contribution to the outcome of therapy was her brother's willingness and readiness to move into a peer relationship with his sister.

Every therapy situation contains factors that limit or impede progress. Some of the factors that limited the accomplishments in this case follow. First, and perhaps most limiting, was the therapist's failure to get a good grasp of extended family issues. The therapist became as swamped in the nuclear family as the client. When romantic relationships are going well, this client loses family of origin focus and motivation. This is not uncommon, and college students seem predictably more prone to these powerful distractions. Finally, one often can view the process of thinking as it goes from individual focus, to awareness of reciprocity in relationship, to the broader view of family as an emotional unit. Progress can get stuck at any level, of course. I do not believe, in this case, that the second level was as firmly established as it could have been; very little, if any, awareness of family as a single emotional unit was achieved. Without this vision, no further progress could occur.

What did occur was a much calmer emotional environment. This was achieved through increased family contact, increased focus on self, and efforts toward calm relating and an avoidance of distancing.

CASE STUDY 2

This twenty-year-old male junior came into therapy because his fiancée was suicidal and he was at a loss as to how to deal with her. Over the weekend she had cut her wrists slightly. He tried to take her to the hospital, and when she refused to go, he slapped her. He decided then that he needed help. This student has an older sister and two living parents. His father is the only child of a high-ranking Nazi general who died during the final stages of World War II. His mother is the oldest of four children and the only child in that family to live in the United States. (The family diagram is shown in Figure 7.2.) This student's parents have a conflictual relationship, and the father is very emotionally distant. He had an affair with the mother's youngest sister, has hired prostitutes, and has been heavily involved in pornography. These revelations had isolated both his children from him. This student had no answers to questions about his father's side of the story or what may have motivated his father. The student felt that his father was worthless and that his mother required care and support or she might kill herself. Later he did acknowledge some curiosity and a desire to get to know his father but was concerned about what would happen to his mother if he did not side with her.

I joked with him about being controlled and frustrated by suicidal women and suggested he take a first aid course so he would be equipped to handle a suicide if he ever decided to behave independently. During the next session, the student informed me that he had read a first aid book, told his fiancée and mother that he believed he could handle suicidal attempts, and had lunch with his father. By the end of the second semester, he had agreed to work with his father for the summer, was teasing his mother about her depression, and refusing to side with either parent in disputes. He talked about experiencing a new sense of freedom and broke up with his fiancée. After the summer ended, he came in and reported that he was happy at home, he had a new girlfriend who did not seem to need his protection, and he was not compelled to plan a marriage just because he was in love, as his father had done. He stated that his relationships with girls were better although his efforts had been mostly focused on relating well to both his parents.

FIGURE 7.2. Family Diagram

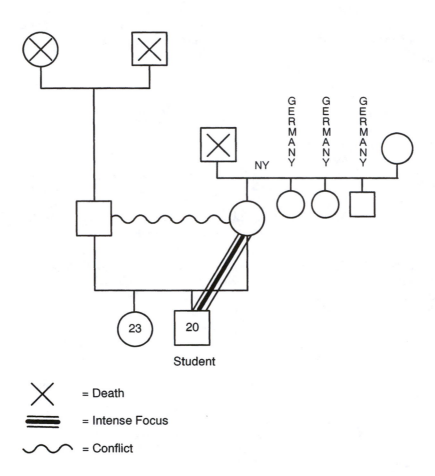

= Death

= Intense Focus

= Conflict

It is difficult for me to evaluate clearly the effectiveness of this kind of therapy. Obviously some things went well, and this is a good story. It is almost as if a technique was used and it worked. I do not think that has much to do with Bowen family systems approach to therapy. I do think that there is great value in reflecting on what the positive aspects were that Bowen family systems theory brought to this situation, and, as in the first case presentation, no evaluation is complete without some attention paid to those elements of therapy that limited or constricted progress.

Perhaps the most significant positive influence in this case was that the student entered therapy focused on what he could do to extricate himself from the situation in which he found himself with his fiancée. He may have been trying to remove himself from the relationship completely. A second factor was that his paternal family history was fascinating, and he longed to know more about his father and his father's family. This curiosity made it much easier for him to approach his father, once he thought that he could manage to continue relating to his mother while building a relationship with his father. Another outcome of therapy was that this student achieved positive results in his relationship with his new girlfriend. This provided him with confidence in his ability to bring about change in relationship by focusing on self. Self-focus was easier to achieve in this situation because, I believe, the investment in the romantic relationship was less intense than usual.

Finally, timing is always important. Summer break, a four-month absence, always must be factored into the equation. On the positive side, therapy coincided with a time when the student had to make arrangements for summer employment. It was significant that he had the chance to work with his father and could be encouraged to do so. However, timing also can be a limiting factor. Summer break is a transitional period. As in this case presentation, it often is difficult to reinvolve students in therapy, especially after four months of summer vacation.

Another limiting factor was that this student went quickly into another romantic relationship. Although this relationship may have been more positive than the previous one, the pattern suggests a need for a relationship that can function similar to an addiction and sap the individual of motivation to focus on self. Nonetheless, the student seemed to emerge with greater flexibility within his family than he previously enjoyed. I believe the freedom to relate to his father had always been there; he was just unaware of it. Without the flexibility, his relationship with his father would have evoked a reaction from his mother.

CASE STUDY 3

The previous case study emphasizes the positive side of the therapeutic spectrum; the course of therapy described next is an example of the other end of the spectrum. This is the case of a twenty-one-year-old female student who entered therapy at the beginning of her senior year. She was the youngest of three sisters and the first person in her family to attend college.

(The family diagram is shown in Figure 7.3.) She had no relationship with extended family and maintained minimal contact with her sisters and parents. Her boyfriend had been her only close relationship. They met and began dating early in their freshman year. She agreed to come to counseling because of his concern with her bulimia. She had a six-year uninterrupted pattern of bingeing and inducing vomiting. The student did state that at one point during her high school years she had gotten so weak from constant vomiting that she had collapsed during basketball practice. She believed that was the only time her problem had gotten out of control. She also

FIGURE 7.3. Family Diagram

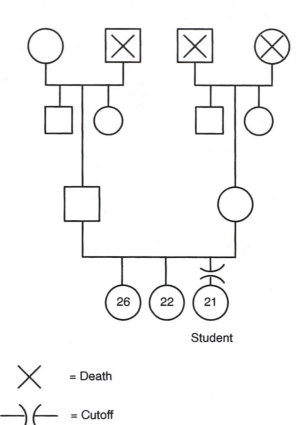

Student

$\times$ = Death

$\dashv)(\vdash$ = Cutoff

believed that her boyfriend was the only person who was aware of the fact that she was bulimic.

This young woman was so emotionally cut off from her family that she was not able to answer any questions about family history or family dynamics. Furthermore, she had no motivation to increase her knowledge or contact with her family. She did not miss having close female friends and had no complaints about her relationship with her boyfriend. I was not able to address family systems issues. To aid the student, I introduced her to biofeedback that aided relaxation training. It has been my experience that this does involve students in self-focus and efforts toward self-control. Often, when an increased level of relaxation is achieved, students are able to explore other issues and focus more on thinking about themselves and their relationships. This did not occur in this instance. In fact, after several weeks, the student reported that she was doing worse, and she believed her efforts to relieve her symptoms were increasing the stress. After discussing the idea that bulimia might be her way to manage stress—allowing her to function—combined with the fact that she could now control her urge to induce vomiting fairly well, all sessions were discontinued with the understanding that she could return to therapy at any time. During this final meeting, it was suggested that becoming isolated physically and/or emotionally from family had negative consequences and that she might think about her isolation as contributing to her problems. Four months later, this student contacted the therapist again. She had had a serious argument with her housemates, and they disclosed that they had known about her bulimia for over three years but felt unable to confront her. To a large extent, their difficulty stemmed from their experience of her as someone who avoided all kinds of contact on emotional issues. This incident convinced the student that she was indeed emotionally isolated from others, and therapy resumed. The focus is no longer on her eating disorder. Although I believe this new effort has a fair chance to succeed to some degree, it is too soon to determine anything. It is useful to remember that Bowen family systems theory is a way of thinking that is filled with hope and cautious optimism. It offers solutions for improvement.

As I have contemplated the factors that have influenced the course of this therapy, I have most often wondered what I missed when I did not involve the boyfriend in the process. After all, he was the one who had the most energy invested in change. He was this student's only intimate relationship. From her perspective, he was more interested in symptom removal than in her. Perhaps four months' time could have been saved.

On the positive side, the client returned with motivation and felt welcomed. It seems all too easy to overestimate the need to resolve a symptom rather than to respect the symptom, and it is vital to understand the function of any symptom. Bulimia is a common problem encountered by college therapists. In its most intense state, it is life-threatening. The Bowen family systems theory perspective of understanding the function of a symptom offers a different perspective that can be productive. I believe that this case is an example of the positive aspects of viewing a symptom from a position of respect and a desire to understand the symptom's functional contribution. Indeed, it is as easy to triangle with a symptom as it is with anything or anyone else. From a functional perspective, any symptom serves to contain a lot of anxiety in one manageable area, thus providing a degree of self-control or at least the illusion of self-control. In this instance, focus on bulimia allowed this student to downplay her inability to relate to others in an adult, intimate fashion. I believe that it was easier for her to focus on eating issues rather than on the isolation. This allowed her to survive college, get accepted to graduate school, and maintain a relationship with a boyfriend. Had the therapist been more aware of the triangle of symptom, client, and therapist and encouraged the symptom, what might have happened? My hunch is that therapy would have progressed more smoothly if the symptom had been encouraged on the basis of its function and that this approach would have produced more reflection and self-understanding.

CASE STUDY 4

This case involves a twenty-one-year-old female student who was active in an Adult Children of Alcoholics (ACOA) group. She is the middle child of five siblings. She has two older sisters and there is a fair amount of extended family contact. (Figure 7.4 represents the family diagram.) Both older sisters participate in Alcoholics Anonymous. There is much talk among the three oldest girls about the father's drinking. This student reports a strained relationship with her father; even when they are together they do not talk.

The ACOA group leader referred her to therapy. Her presenting problem pertained to roommate difficulties that had resulted in her moving out and feeling very anxious and alone as a consequence. Her initial responses to questions in therapy indicated that she also felt isolated in her family. Her relationship with her older sisters was confined to complaining about her father's drinking. She would participate in these conversations but was uncomfortable about it. She was, however, convinced that her father was an alcoholic and dysfunctional. Her mother was her sole link to information about the family and the only person with whom she believed she could

FIGURE 7.4. Family Diagram

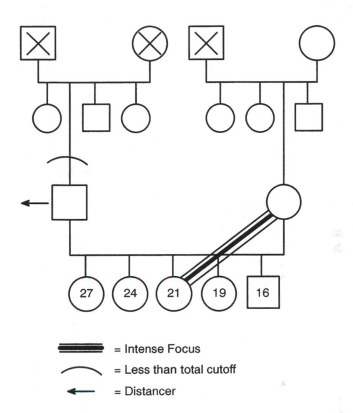

= Intense Focus
= Less than total cutoff
= Distancer

talk. After a few weeks of investigation, this student came to view her housemate situation as similar to the isolation she experienced at home. She began to recognize that her tendency to criticize others was a means for her to distance herself and that this was most typical of how she related to her father. Much of the time was spent on making neutral contact with nuclear and extended family. Mostly she worked at not being critical and at staying in contact with others. These efforts were rewarding and calming and led to more open relations with her father. Most of the therapy sessions involved discussing views of the interdependence of family relationships and ways of remaining neutral or avoiding being critical.

A significant shift occurred after a visit home, during which she had gone out to dinner with her mother and father. Initially, her report of this event described her father drinking and starting a fight with her. Subsequently, she changed her view and announced during a later session that she believed she had become so anxious and withdrawn when her father ordered a drink that his anger was more a result of her behavior than of the drinking. Evaluating this possibility has led to a greater willingness to relate to her father in a calm fashion. She has made progress with her father and continues to relate well to her sisters, brother, and extended family. She is now aware of monitoring her own behavior. When she gets caught in triangles, she rethinks a strategy for the next visit or conversation. The family itself has responded well to her, and she says, "It sounds crazy, but even my grades are better than they ever have been, and I think it has to do with my family work." An interesting side note is that she continues to go to her ACOA group, but not as often and with an ability to pick and choose helpful ideas. Her self-reports indicate increased satisfaction on all fronts, while enjoying her best semester academically.

This is a case of "so far so good." I am not clear which factors may have limited progress. When asked about her experience in therapy, she reported some initial confusion, along with a sense that there was value in understanding herself in relationship to her family. The fact that her two sisters and father began drinking at about the same time helped convince her that it was legitimate to view the family as an emotional unit. She read several articles explaining the theory, and it seemed to help her think differently about herself and her family relationships. I suspect that it was important for the therapist to be supportive of her attending and learning from her ACOA group. Nothing, however, is so significant as the willingness of the client to work to improve her relationships with family members. Her motivation and ability to keep working at focusing on self and her reactivity to others has been interesting to witness. This is a client who seems always to bring some new insight or question to therapy that is a result of previous effort.

The task for the therapist seems to be to let the theory do the work without much interference from the therapist. In other words, keep the focus on the ideas and knowledge contained in Bowen family systems theory and let them work! Bowen theory does not criticize, blame, condemn, approve, or encourage. Bowen theory's usefulness is in its ability to describe what is, and in this description, one can find a prescription for change.

CONCLUSION

This chapter has presented some ideas about Bowen family systems theory that have resulted from years of attempting to think in terms of this theory while functioning as a therapist on a university campus. The author has come to believe that efforts leading toward differentiation of self are rare, if not lacking completely, among college students. It, however, does raise some interesting issues. Hopefully, the reader will find that Bowen theory offers college students many benefits, even though their efforts will fall short of differentiation. Differentiation is an adult task; it requires one first to work to create a calmer emotional unit so that one can manage one's own reactivity to others and work toward a new and difficult conceptualization of self and relationships. This involves a potentially lifelong effort. Systems thinking means that the individual judges the whole world from a perspective of mutual influence and interdependence rather than from right or wrong, good or bad. Bowen family systems theory has the capacity to provide anyone with a different world view, and it can provide a road map for reaching a more productive level of functioning. It is calming for clients to be in contact with a therapist who is making this kind of effort. This chapter illustrates that the theory provides a means for calming any situation, allowing for symptom reduction and increased functioning.

REFERENCES

Bowen, Murray (1978). *Family Therapy in Clinical Practice.* New York: Jason Aronson.

Kerr, Michael E. and Bowen, Murray (1988). *Family Evaluation.* New York: W.W. Norton and Company.

Chapter 8

The Use of Bowen Theory
in Clinical Practice
with the Elderly

James B. Smith

In a Bowen theory approach, clinical practice is grounded in theory. In turn, theory has been, and continues to be, based in the testing of clinical hypotheses in clinical practice. Theory and clinical practice are two sides of the same coin; they go hand in glove. One cannot be adequately understood apart from the other.

The body of knowledge that constitutes Bowen theory evolved from the clinical practice of one individual whose life goal was making the study of human behavior more scientific (Bowen, 1978). His work was based on clinical hypotheses that were tested and revised over time in different clinical settings with different clinical populations. He was reluctant to call his findings a theory until he believed they had met the test of accepted scientific practice. He also emphasized that it is only a theory and not fact. His clinical research has stood the test of time in the clinical practice and research of countless others who continue to use Bowen theory in clinical practice and who work to study and extend it.

Clinicians have tested and applied Bowen theory in a variety of clinical contexts, with a variety of populations and presenting problems. Some have used it in their clinical practice with grown children who function as caretakers for elderly family members (Graefe, 1990; McCullough, 1991). The purpose of this chapter is to illustrate the use of Bowen theory in clinical practice with elderly individuals who as yet are functioning on their own. This chapter will consist of (1) a statement of relevant principles of Bowen theory, (2) a brief discussion of clinical practice with the elderly, (3) a composite clinical case study, (4) a discussion of issues raised in the clinical work, with comments about the clinical process, and (5) a summary.

BOWEN THEORY

There are two key ideas, which, taken together, probably best distinguish Bowen theory from other theories of psychotherapy. First, Bowen theory assumes that the human is a product of evolution and is more similar to, than different from, other life forms. As with all other life forms, the human has been "written in nature." Bowen chose to anchor his theory on the assumption that the human and the human family are driven and guided by emotional/instinctual forces "written in nature" (Kerr and Bowen, 1988, p. 26). Second, individual functioning is seen as a product of the relationship system. Each individual is shaped by the relationships in which he or she lives his or her life. Reciprocally, the individual shapes those with whom he or she lives. Taken together, these two key, interwoven ideas form the fabric out of which Bowen theory was cut.

Emotional System

Much had been "written in nature" long before the human evolved. The human has been written in nature without human intervention. The processes driving human development and behavior do not depend on humans being aware of them for their existence; they operate independently from the human. Just as with other life forms, humans are attracted to each other, court, mate, reproduce; rear young, hurt young; help one another, hurt one another; compete, fight, and make up; become violent; run away, defend their turf; dominate and submit to one another; and prey on other life. The learned ethnic, cultural, and historical variations on these common themes are rich and varied in the human, probably more so than for any other species of life. But, these processes are assumed to be as basic to the human as they are to all other life forms. The human is quick to offer and is often preoccupied with finding explanations for these natural processes that occur elsewhere in life.

These processes form what is called the emotional system in Bowen theory. In Bowen's words:

> Emotional functioning includes the automatic forces that govern protoplasmic life. It includes the force that biology defines as instinct, reproduction, the automatic activity controlled by the autonomic nervous system, subjective emotional and feeling states, and the forces that govern relationship systems. . . . In broad term, the emotional system governs the "dance of life" in all living things. (Bowen, 1978, pp. 304-305)

In Bowen theory, the use of the term *emotional* is virtually synonymous with the term instinctual. Emotion is distinguished from feeling, which is used to describe the awareness the human has of its emotional/instinctual system.

Human behavior and development are significantly governed by the natural processes which comprise the emotional system and which regulate the functioning of all living things. The human is unique in some respects, as are all organisms. The human's highly developed cerebral cortex provides a "thinking brain," giving him or her the capacity to reason and abstract and to regulate internal and external stimuli to a greater degree than probably any other life form. These are probably the major differences between the human and other life forms. However, the largest portions of the human's life are governed by processes that predate the development of the cerebral cortex, as it seems to be true that much more of what drives the human involves those parts of the brain he or she shares with lower forms of life than he or she is willing, or able, to admit. Viewing oneself objectively as one among many life forms on the phylogenetic ladder, with many similarities and few differences, is more difficult for the human to accept than the fact that Earth is not the center of the universe.

Togetherness and Individuality

Bowen theory postulates two basic life forces "written in nature" that are inferred from the observation of human functioning (Kerr and Bowen, 1988). Togetherness is used to describe that which drives an individual to follow the directives of others, to be dependent, connected, and indistinct from others. Biological and psychological systems and mechanisms that direct the human to feel and function as part of a group and to follow the group have evolved over countless centuries. These systems and mechanisms have stood the test of time. "Following the herd" and "circling the wagons" comes naturally to humans and has served them well. Togetherness is rooted in biological processes the human presumably shares with other life forms. The intensity of togetherness in a given individual is heavily influenced by the relationship system in the family in which he or she grows up.

Individuality, on the other hand, directs an organism to follow its own pursuits, to be a separate, distinct, independent entity, and separate biological and psychological systems and mechanisms have evolved to allow the human to feel and function as a separate individual able to follow one's own pursuits. "Striking out on one's own" and "being one's own person" are natural for the human, and although rooted in biological processes, individuality in a given person develops primarily in the relationship system of the family in which he or she is raised.

Togetherness is analogous to the team half of the individual-team dichotomy, and individuality is analogous to the individual half (Kerr and Bowen, 1988, p. 65). The human is probably unique in the ability to be both an individual and a team player, arising from the human ability to be aware of the differences between thinking and feeling in self and to have a choice in how to respond. Although togetherness and individuality have both evolved and stood the test of time, it seems likely that togetherness evolved before individuality. "Following the herd" in response to real or imagined threat is an even more automatic response in the human than "striking out on one's own."

Differentiation

The process by which an individual manages the life forces of togetherness and individuality is called differentiation (Bowen, 1978). Individuals have a variable capacity to be directed by togetherness or to follow their individual pursuits. Differentiation is both a naturally occurring and a learned process in the human, and it is assumed there is a version of differentiation in all life forms. It is more basic to understanding variation in human functioning than other biological, psychological, or sociological variables, such as race, gender, culture, income, intelligence, education, or even genetic makeup.

The higher the differentiation, the more an individual is observed to follow his or her own life course while at the same time cooperating, looking out for others, and remaining in viable contact with important others under internal or external threat. The higher the differentiation, the more a person is able to enhance self-welfare while not impinging on the welfare of others. By not automatically responding to internal and external emotional stimuli, the human has the capacity to restrain selfish, spiteful, violent urges even during times of high stress. These indicators of higher differentiation can be observed at the level of the individual, the family, other natural groups, and organizations, as well as at the level of society.

The lower the differentiation, the more an individual is observed to be automatically driven by what the group wants or says is important. The lower the differentiation, the more an individual has difficulty following his or her separate pursuits while cooperating with others. When threatened, there is regression to selfish, spiteful, aggressive, and avoidance behavior. These indicators of lower differentiation can also be observed at the individual, family, group, organization, and societal levels.

Bowen theory assumes that an individual will carry about the same level of differentiation as the family in which he or she is born and raised. The adage that "the apples don't fall too far from the tree" applies to the human as well as to other life forms. Although there is variability, it is limited. It seems likely that the higher one climbs on the phylogenetic ladder, the more individual variability there is among family members. It is common for some family members to feel they are basically different from other family members and to spend a lifetime pretending to themselves and proving to others they are different. But, it is a fact that they are more similar to the others than different. It does not always appear this way. Individual variation among family members is most influenced by one's functional position, such as sibling position (Toman, 1969), and how one is "emotionally programmed" in family relationships.

Bowen theory hypothesizes a "scale" of differentiation which assumes that each individual is born into a family with a preset level of differentiation. It suggests that what really distinguishes one family from another are not other biological, psychological, or sociological variables, but how well families have adapted to the realities life has presented over multiple generations. In this sense, differentiation refers to a process that has developed over time in a family and into which an individual is born. This preset level of differentiation is more influential in human functioning than most are able to acknowledge.

If one hypothesizes a 100-point scale of variability for differentiation, it is accurate to say that every family falls somewhere on the scale. One can estimate a level of differentiation by examining how its individual members have lived their lives over multiple generations. In other words, how have family members faced the realities that life has presented? By observing over time the "tracks" that people have left, one can estimate a level of differentiation. With enough "facts of functioning" to observe, it is possible to estimate a level of differentiation for individuals, families, other natural groups and organizations, or societies.

Multigenerational Emotional Process

Every individual is part of an evolving family "written in nature" that can be traced back through multiple generations of recorded history. A survey of factual information tracking how one's ancestors have lived their lives provides a good estimate of current differentiation. The further back the survey of a family goes, the greater divergence one would see in the range of level of differentiation among family members. If one were able to survey a sufficient number of branches of one's family tree, one would observe examples of all of the imaginable variations of human functioning.

In the survey of any family tree, some branches would be discovered in which most family members would be moving toward better and better differentiation. More of these individuals would have taken fuller advantage of their occupational and educational opportunities and be less encumbered by serious emotional, physical, and social problems. There would be more intact marriages, with more children functioning at the same or better levels of differentiation than their parents. These families would be less impaired by the predictable stresses of everyday life—children growing up, marrying, raising families, earning a living, growing older and dying. They would be less impaired by the unpredictable stresses as well—floods, hurricanes, wars, epidemics, and financial crises in society.

This survey of multiple generations of any family would also reveal branches of the family tree in which increasingly lower levels of differentiation could be traced over time. There would be more people squandering educational and occupational opportunities. More would be involved in unstable marriages and relationships. More would be distant and unavailable to others in the family who were important to them, moving geographically to solve difficult relationship problems. Individuals in this branch would be more impaired by emotional, physical, and social problems and would succumb to the predictable and the unpredictable stresses of life. Tolerance for additional stress would be minimal. Fewer and fewer children would themselves produce viable offspring, resulting in the eventual extinction of that branch of the family tree.

Individuals are born into the middle of evolving families. They are either in a branch of the family tree that is flourishing or in a branch that is on its way to extinction. Individuals do not have any choice about which family they are born into or whether the family tree is ascending or descending. They have no control over their race, culture, sex, or genetic pool or the emotional climate of the family at the time and place of birth. At the same time, because of the cerebral cortex, the human has the capacity to influence this process. Although making the effort to "differentiate a self" in one's family does not change the human much, it does allow him or her more freedom to contend with life in the best way possible.

A survey of multiple generations of a family can be viewed as a form of family assessment that looks at what families and family members have actually been able to accomplish in life, given their particular life circumstances. This sort of assessment does not prize higher differentiation or belittle lower differentiation; it is neutral as to how families and their members felt about or explained their functioning or the functioning of others. The goal of this approach to family assessment is to objectively survey the "facts of functioning" of the family and its members.

Stress, Reactivity, and Anxiety

In Bowen theory, stress, reactivity, and anxiety are also seen as processes "written in nature." Stress is a threat to an organism resulting from change in its internal or external environment. Anxiety is seen as the variable response or reaction of an organism to a real or imagined threat. With added stress comes the potential for more anxiety. More highly differentiated individuals are less anxious and more adaptive to perceived threat. Less-differentiated people are more anxious and less adaptive to stress. The more anxious a person is, the more reactive he or she is. A person may go through through a period in which he or she is highly prone to angry outbursts, tearful episodes, or constant withdrawal. The anger, tears, and withdrawal are all reactions. The more automatic and intense these reactions, the more they reflect a state of chronic anxiety. When the level of anxiety increases, emotional reactions are triggered more easily and are more intense.

Anxiety is assumed to be present in some form in all living things. As more advanced forms of life evolved, physiological systems involved in anxiety became more complex. As the human evolved, psychological systems and mechanisms developed to cope with anxiety. Probably at every level of life, organisms show increased anxiety and reactivity to threat. Reactivity is manifested along a continuum, from complete emotional shutdown, such as severe depression or catatonia, to emotional frenzy, such as mania or euphoria. Increased anxiety is manifested in various types of emotional reactivity such as the fight or flight response. Subjective manifestations of anxiety include a heightened sense of awareness and a fear of impending doom. Objective manifestations of anxiety include increased responsiveness, higher heart rate, and higher blood pressure. Both emotional reactivity and anxiety have important adaptive functions, but too much or too little reactivity reduces an organism's adaptiveness.

Acute anxiety generally occurs in response to real threats (fear of what is) and is experienced as temporary. Most people adapt to acute anxiety fairly successfully, whereas chronic anxiety easily strains one's adaptive ability. Although there are innate and learned elements in both acute and chronic anxiety, learning that occurs in family relationships plays a more important role in chronic anxiety.

Chronic anxiety is viewed as a system of actions and reactions that, once triggered, seem to have a life of their own, largely independent of the triggering stimuli. The principal generator of chronic anxiety in the human seems to be the imagined threat to a desired relationship. Once a disturbance is triggered, chronic anxiety is engendered more by one's reaction to the disturbance than by the disturbance itself. When one can maintain workable contact with emotionally significant others, one is more likely to successfully adapt to stressful events.

The level of chronic anxiety varies among individuals and in the same individual over time, just as it does among families and in the same family. It varies as well in groups and organizations and probably varies at the level of society as well. The average level of chronic anxiety parallels the basic level of differentiation: the higher the differentiation, the lower the chronic anxiety; the lower the differentiation, the higher the chronic anxiety.

Emotional Triangles

In Bowen theory, the basic relationship unit "written in nature" is the emotional triangle, which has evolved as a social strategy whose function is to bind anxiety. The higher the differentiation, the less one is automatically caught up in triangles. The lower the differentiation, the more one is automatically caught up in triangles. From his observations of different clinical populations, Bowen observed how naturally unstable a dyad is as anxiety in the relationship increases. One or the other in the dyad automatically talks about the other, falls silent, feels anxious, gets angry, or talks about impersonal material as anxiety increases. The triangle (or interdependent triad, as it was referred to in Bowen's early research) is the "building block" of relationship systems:

> A two-person emotional system is unstable in that it forms itself into a three-person system or triangle under stress. A system larger than three persons becomes a series of interlocking triangles. (Bowen, 1978, p. 478)

For most, the parental triangle is the central and most influential one. However, this triangle is always interlocking with the central triangles of one's siblings in the current generation and with the central triangles of one's parents and their siblings in the previous generation and so on up the family tree. The triangle can be observed in, and seems basic to, other natural groups and organizations and probably exists as well at the level of society. It seems likely the triangle or some similar social strategy to bind anxiety might be a basic relationship unit in other forms of life as well.

Clinical Practice Based in Bowen Theory

Clinical practice based in Bowen theory has as its goal the differentiation of self. At the level of theory, this is best described as the effort to "create a situation through which the central triangle . . . in a family . . . can attain a higher level of differentiation" (Bowen, 1978, p. 216). This is the case whether the presenting symptom is in a child, couple, or spouse.

Clinical practice based in Bowen theory initially focused on the entire family unit. Modifications in clinical practice based in ongoing clinical research led to a focus on the two parents and the symptomatic child. Further clinical research led to clinical practice focused on the two spouses and the therapist as the third leg of the triangle. This latter approach provided particularly consistent results.

Based on his efforts to differentiate a self in the interlocking triangles of his own family and the efforts of trainees with their families, Bowen soon concluded that the best overall result in differentiation involved a systematic individual effort to define a self in one's family of origin.

In broad terms, differentiation of self in one's family of origin involves, first, the motivated individual working toward "person to person" relationships with as many family members as one is able. The goal is to relate personally to each one concerning any issue in their relationship, without increasing anxiety, fighting, becoming silent, or talking about others. Second, defining a self involves "becoming a better observer and controlling one's own emotional reactiveness" (Bowen, 1978, p. 541). The goal is to be detached in the observation of self and others in the automatic emotionality of relationships in the family system.

Finally, differentiation of self involves "detriangling self from emotional situations" (Bowen, 1978, p. 542). Developing person-to-person relationships and becoming a better observer of self in family relationships helps to create a more open system and a reduction in anxiety. At this point, there is symptom relief, as well as shifts in important relationships. One can begin to see triangles, and there is the ability to function less automatically and more thoughtfully. One feels less depressed, less anxious, more loved and accepted. Presenting problems in the family system are less intense and one is less impaired by them. One is able to act in more functional ways. But these *functional* changes, or changes in the functional level of differentiation, are not synonymous with *basic* changes, or changes in the basic level of differentiation. A change in the basic level of differentiation involves being able to constantly be in contact with an emotionally charged, high-anxiety issue involving self and important others without taking sides, attacking, or counterattacking and always having a neutral response.

The process of differentiation of self occurs naturally to a greater or lesser extent in all human families. Something akin to this probably occurs naturally in all life forms. Those who are born and raised in families with a higher level of differentiation do it more automatically. Those in families with a lower level of differentiation do it less automatically. But, as Bowen theory points out, differentiation can also be learned. The human can learn to "differentiate a self" within the limits of its biology, psychology, and sociology. One may be born blind, redheaded, genetically predisposed to cancer, rich, black, Dutch, to unmarried parents, with a high IQ, with a learning disorder, schizophrenic, or depressed. Differentiation of self refers to how one lives one's life within these realities, neither exaggerating nor minimalizing them. Bowen describes this process in the following way:

> I believe it is possible, over a long period of time, to increase the basic level [of differentiation] to some degree. Systems therapy cannot re-make that which nature created, but through learning how the organism operates, controlling anxiety, and learning to better adapt to the fortunes and misfortunes of life, it can give nature a better chance. (Bowen, 1978)

CLINICAL PRACTICE WITH THE ELDERLY

Differentiation of self can be observed at all stages of life. In the elderly, perhaps the most crucial viable is the impending fact of one's own death. Bowen observed that the fact of his or her own death will make the human more anxious than anything else (Bowen, 1978). The fact and feeling that "the clock is running out" elicits real and imagined changes in physical, emotional, and social functioning in both self and others, increased dependence on others, and guilt about what one has done or not done in one's life. Differentiation of self refers to how the elderly individual responds to the fact of his or her own death. Responses range from complete physical and/or emotional shutdown in some, to continuing high productivity in others. With most, the response to the stress of their deaths seems to parallel the stress of their own lives. Those who have lived orderly, productive lives seem to continue this way of life until death. Those who have succumbed to life seem to succumb also to death.

There is a small group of elderly who face the fact of death with an extra effort to make basic changes in their lives. This extra effort is often triggered by important shifts in the makeup of the family system, resulting from births, deaths, marriages, and divorces. This clinician has commented elsewhere on the automatic shift toward togetherness in his nuclear family following the deaths of his parents (Smith, 1979). Others have commented on the automatic shift toward greater individuality in a surviving spouse after the death of a mate (McCullough, 1991). Some individuals who have struggled through lifetimes of unacceptable family experiences growing up, unworkable marriages, and bitter conflicts with their now adult children find themselves with the motivation late in life to make basic changes almost in spite of themselves. As one man in his mid-seventies put it, "I can't seem to leave well enough alone."

CLINICAL CASE STUDY

The Condolis (see Figure 8.1) are a composite of more than ten such individuals who illustrate this newfound push toward greater individuality in later life. Of course, none of them would say they were trying to "differentiate a self." They would say, "I am doing what I have to do, even at this late date, because I cannot live that way anymore." In relation to theory, one would say that there has been a shift in later life in the "forces" for togetherness and individuality in which individuality is now more the driving force in their lives. All the individuals comprising the composite case study have the desire to find a better way for self.

The families comprising this composite case were seen over a period of more than twenty years of clinical practice in several different public and private outpatient settings. It is presented in composite form for illustrative and confidentiality purposes.

The Condolis

Mrs. Condoli is a seventy-six-year-old mother of two and grandmother of five. She has been married to the same man for fifty-one years. Her parents emigrated to the United States from their native country in Southern Europe as newlyweds. Her father wanted to earn enough money in the United States to return home and live comfortably. His father had told him he would never amount to anything, and he set out to prove his father wrong. Her mother had no desire to leave her family and native land but reluctantly went along with the idea. She felt she had no choice.

Mrs. Condoli was born within a year after her parents' arrival in a medium-sized Midwestern U.S. city. The youngest of three children, her mother felt isolated, being away from her family and all by herself, and helpless to raise children on her own. In retrospect, Mrs. Condoli said that she felt responsible for herself and her younger sister and brother; her mother seldom left the house and was often unable to accomplish basic household tasks. Mrs. Condoli's father was a skilled artisan who had no difficulty obtaining and keeping work. He saved "every cent he ever made," except a meager amount for the bare subsistence living he and his family endured and, increasingly over years, money he spent at local bars.

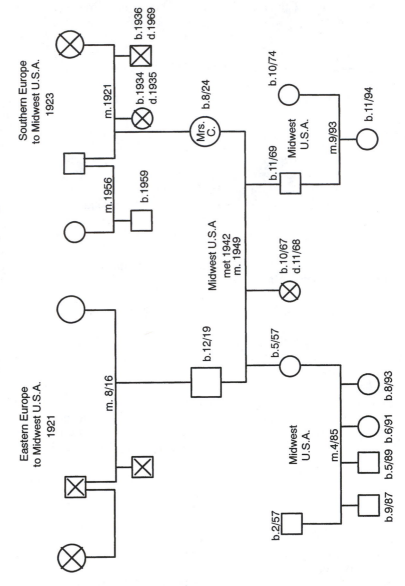

FIGURE 8.1. Condoli Family Diagram

216

When Mrs. Condoli was ten, her sister was born. Taking care of an infant sister became her responsibility "by default"; her mother was too depressed to do it and her father was either at work or at the bar. She said that "someone had to do it." Her infant sister died in her sleep shortly after her first birthday. In her weaker moments, Mrs. Condoli still blames herself. At quieter times, she knows she did everything she could have done for her sister—and more. Her brother was born a year after her sister's death. Taking care of him also fell to Mrs. Condoli because her mother had slipped into an even deeper depression and her father was always gone.

She was not sure where she got the energy to take care of the house, her family, and to complete school. Mrs. Condoli now believes her mother did what she could; at the time though, she greatly resented the lack of help. Through it all, there was never any question whether she could or would do it. With little family support and few friends, Mrs. Condoli felt she was "on her own." She thinks now this is how she became, in her words, a "workaholic." By this, she means that her response to anxiety around her is to get to work. Although others have consistently given her high praise for her strong work ethic, she thinks of it more as a curse than a blessing. As she puts it, "I don't decide to work or not to work—I have to work."

Shortly after Mrs. Condoli graduated from high school, her father decided it was time for him and his family to return to his homeland. Mrs. Condoli "stubbornly" refused to go, as she put it. In spite of all his efforts to change her mind, she "stuck to her guns," saying to her mother and father, in essence, "You can do as you wish, but I'm staying here." In the end, her father did return to his homeland, leaving his wife and children behind. "Forced to choose" between her husband and children, Mrs. Condoli's mother decided to stay with her children.

Having started work the day after her high school graduation at a job her father had chosen for her, Mrs. Condoli spent less time at home. With her husband gone and her daughter at work providing for the family, Mrs. Condoli's mother began to function a little better, taking over the care and management of her son and the household from her daughter. However, shortly after her brother finished high school and enlisted in the Army, her mother died of what Mrs. Condoli describes as a "broken heart."

Mrs. Condoli had only sporadic contact with her brother through the years. To her knowledge, he never married nor had children, nor had he ever returned to the city in which he had grown up. She learned after the fact that he had been discharged from the Army due to alcoholism, had lived in a northeastern city, and had died at an early age.

Mrs. Condoli married, at age twenty-five, a man whom she had met eight years earlier in high school. She had grave misgivings about marriage and children, having seen "what it had done to my mother." Mr. Condoli was the youngest of two boys. His older brother also had never married and died at a relatively young age from alcohol-related symptoms. According to Mrs. Condoli, her brother-in-law "never amounted to much." Her in-laws had divorced before she and Mr. Condoli married. His father had then married a "young girl." His mother died shortly after the death of her oldest son. Mr. Condoli tells anyone who will listen that he "has no family." Mrs. Condoli says her husband and his mother always fought, as did he and his older brother.

Mr. Condoli was employed in a service deportment of a local hospital for all of his working life, eventually becoming department head. He retired at an early age because of arthritis and because of conflict with his superior. Mr. Condoli has recently had a hip transplant and has had difficulty walking. Mrs. Condoli calls her husband a chronic complainer about his health.

Mrs. Condoli says her husband has had "temper tantrums" from the time they were married until shortly before he retired. He "ruled the roost." He made a good living and "made every decision" in the marriage. Mrs. Condoli says he never hit her, but she was always fearful he might or that he would leave her, as he often threatened to do. She has often thought about leaving him and hurting him.

Mrs. Condoli says that her pregnancies went without complication, although she had the "baby blues" after her first child was born. In retrospect, she thinks she has always been depressed. She was "afraid" of her children and felt helpless about raising them, feeling all alone, much as "my mother must have felt." Both of her children have grown up to be "successful." Her daughter is a college graduate with an advanced degree and is married to a physician. They have four children and maintain a lifestyle that for Mr. and Mrs. Condoli is "beyond their means."

All of her daughter's children have been raised in day care settings, which Mrs. Condoli greatly worries about. There is intense conflict between the two oldest sons. Mrs. Condoli is fearful one of them will eventually be seriously hurt. The third child has had medical problems since birth. Mrs. Condoli thinks her daughter is "obsessed" with her career and is not adequately seeing to her children. All of her daughter's children spend time with their grandparents. Individually, there are never any problems; it is only when they are together that problems arise.

Her son is an attorney who only recently married. He and his wife have no children. There has been little contact between Mrs. Condoli and her son since he finished law school, married, and moved to a distant state. She thinks it is for the best because of the intense conflict between he and his father. Her daughter-in-law stays in touch and has proven to be someone Mrs. Condoli can confide in, which she does by phone and the mail. Her daughter-in-law has said that, unlike her own mother, Mrs. Condoli understands and appreciates her.

Mrs. Condoli has worked full-time since her son started high school, until recently. Although she was recently forced to retire because of her age, she continues to work on an on-call basis. She cannot imagine the "living hell" her life would be at home without a job to go to. Without it and her nightly glass of wine, she does not think she would ever sleep. Since his retirement over fifteen years ago, her husband does little except "putter" around the house. Since his surgery, he now seldom goes out and is even more demanding of her. She fears for her own health, wondering whether he would take care of her if needed. She cannot imagine taking care of him if and when he becomes bedridden.

THE CLINICAL PROCESS

Mrs. Condoli was self-referred to therapy after discussing her concerns with a geriatric physician who suggested her depression might be related to family issues. She has been seen a total of forty-four times in a thirty-three-month period. During the first months, she was seen weekly. She was then seen every other week for a few months. Subsequently she has been seen every month or every other month. Her daughter and son were seen as part of an initial evaluation. The clinician has talked with Mr. Condoli by phone, but Mr. Condoli has never come into the office.

Mrs. Condoli addressed a range of concerns in the first year that have continued to recycle. Although fearful of making changes in family relationships and of growing old, she was clear about the driving force in her that said, "I cannot go on the way things are." Through the years, she would almost always start each hour saying things were worse than ever; she was feeling more overwhelmed, depressed, confused, helpless, and hopeless by the latest change for the worse in her life circumstances. As the hour progressed, she would invariably become clearer in her thinking. Initially, she saw very little connection between her family relationships and her emotional state. As time went by, she saw more and more connection between them. She has become more able to achieve some distance on emotionally charged issues involving important family members, particularly her husband and daughter. She has been increasingly able to use the consultation time to clarify her own convictions, feelings, and thoughts and to plan how and when to talk about these issues in important family relationships.

Marital Issues

Mrs. Condoli continues to say that the major issue in her life is how stuck she feels in her marriage. A range of issues have recycled, including her anger, resentment, helplessness, and guilt toward her husband; her depression; her fear he will leave her; her worry about him hurting her or leaving her if she says the wrong thing; her guilt and fear about wanting to leave him or hurt him; her fear of having to care for him as he becomes older and more infirm; and her fear of becoming infirm herself and being abandoned by him and having no one to care for her.

Early on, Mrs. Condoli looked to the clinician to tell her what to do as an "expert" on family relations who could tell her the "right" way to operate in her marriage. His response would be to talk about what he heard her saying, what his views were about the concerns and questions she raised, and what others had told him were successful ways of addressing her concerns and questions. As much as possible, he adopted a "research" attitude, asking question after question in order to (1) gather information, (2) engage Mrs. Condoli's "thinking" brain, and (3) detach from the emotionality. At times of heightened emotionality, the clinician invariably felt he "knew what was best" for her and often had the impulse to tell her. While hearing the intensity of her concerns and questions, he would acknowledge to her that, in his view, the longer one stays in a marriage, the harder it is to reverse an automatic response to the other. However, he also knew that some people were able to make changes no matter how long they had been together, no matter the risks involved.

As the first year went by, the clinician would say to Mrs. Condoli, "This is what our situation looks like to me; what does it look like to you?" He emphasized that her effort toward "making basic changes" had not begun when she had first come to see him, but rather that Mrs. Condoli had obviously long before begun to make changes in the way she had been living. For instance, some years before she had begun to say things to her husband that had been on her mind almost from the beginning of the marriage. Mrs. Condoli said that she did this despite her worst fears because she could "no longer keep her feelings about him to herself." Friends and neighbors, she said, had for years asked why she continued to take his "bullying" and "abuse." In all of the years of her marriage, he had never had anything positive to say about her. The only thing he ever said was what she had not done, how stupid she was, how badly she cooked and cleaned, how lucky she was to have him, etc. Early in her marriage, she thought of leaving but said that "in those days" women were stuck in their marriages, unlike the women of today. It wasn't uncommon with the people she knew for marriages to be this way, and her experience was not much different from theirs. "Women did not have choices in those days," she would say. For years, her daughter worried about her, saying that Mrs. Condoli "should not take what Daddy had been dishing out" to her for as long as she could remember. Mrs. Condoli finally decided to do something. What she found was that, much to her surprise, her worst fears were not realized when she said what she had wanted to say to him for years. She began to gain some confidence in herself. As many times as she did this in the years before and after seeing the clinician, she said it never became easier to do.

Mother-Child Issues

A second major area of concern was multigenerational mother-child issues. Included in this category are conflict and worry about Mrs. Condoli's children, her fears for her grandchildren, issues of being a better mother, her anger and guilt about not being a better mother, her anger with her daughter about not being a better daughter, blaming herself and her mother for not being a better mother—if her mother had been a better mother, she would have been a better mother, and her daughter would have been a better mother—feeling responsible for how her grandchildren turn out, her resentment at her mother for leaving the job of raising her sister and brother to her, and her guilt about not how "badly" her daughter and son have turned out.

There was intense emotionality between Mrs. Condoli and her daughter from the beginning, with each being highly critical of the other. Mrs. Condoli's presenting problem to the clinician was her conflictual relationship with her daughter and the feeling that it was up to her to have a better relationship with her daughter. It was the clinician's observation to Mrs. Condoli that it was very difficult for her to talk about her daughter with any detachment. Mrs. Condoli would berate herself for the job she did raising her daughter. Although acknowledging the clinician's observation that she "probably did the best job she knew how to do," her strong feelings would be that she "should have done better," particularly at times when her adult daughter is critical of her. Although furious at her daughter, she also agrees with her. When criticizing the job her daughter is doing with her children, Mrs. Condoli would say, "If I had done a better job, my daughter would also be doing a better job." When the clinician might suggest that, by most objective standards, Mrs. Condoli and her daughter have done OK, she can hear this faintly, until the emotionality takes over. This is evidenced by her response, "Yes, that is so, but. . . . "

Mrs. Condoli described a trip she and her daughter had taken to her parents' homeland, which was done at the daughter's suggestion before she had consulted with the clinician. Although it was an "eye opener" and "something I had always wanted to do," it did not, in Mrs. Condoli's view, "bring us any closer." If anything, she believes the conflict became even more intense after the visit, at least at first. Mrs. Condoli has remained in touch with several extended family members, who encourage her to return. Her husband has no interest in such a visit. It has always been next to impossible for Mrs. Condoli to leave him for any length of time, although she thinks he would be fine without her.

In her more long-range view of the visit to her parent's homeland, she thinks it gave her a deeper appreciation of both her mother and to some extent her father. For most of her adult life, she was bitter and angry about her mother's inability to be a mother. Visiting extended family members and hearing about her mother and father as children gave her another perspective on them. To hear about her mother from relatives who knew little about her own adult life and trials helped Mrs. Condoli get "a different image" of her. The principle guiding the clinician's observations here was, the more she could climb her own family tree, the more objectivity she would have about herself. The more objectivity she could get about the parental triangle and her functioning in the parental triangle, the more objectivity she would have about her children and their children. In the time he has seen Mrs. Condoli, the clinician has never mentioned the idea of a triangle—not that he never would. With theory as a guide to intervention, he believes that anxiety is still so high that Mrs. Condoli would have difficulty hearing the idea of the triangle. He has never mentioned the idea of "differentiation" in so many words either—again, not that he never would. At some future point, when the level of anxiety is lower in the family, "teaching theory" may become a part of the clinical process. At that point, it might also be possible for Mrs. Condoli to gain a higher basic level of differentiation.

But, it is the clinician's opinion that her functional level of differentiation is higher: Mrs. Condoli has worked at getting to know family members in a more personal and less reactive way; she has become a better observer of her family and her position in it; she is more able to see connections between her mother's depression, her own depression, her worries about her daughter's functioning, and her worries about her grandchildren; she is able to see her own effort to stay busy as a reaction to her mother's shutdown when she becomes depressed; she is less judgmental and more understanding of her mother and father and what motivated them to do what they did and didn't do; she can view her own "busyness" as being no better nor worse than her mother's "shutdown" and her daughter's "obsession with her career" as being no better or worse than her "busyness" or her mother's "shutdown." It is the clinician's opinion that as Mrs. Condoli has become less critical of her mother and father she is less critical of others in general. When he has mentioned this to Mrs. Condoli, she hears it—until the emotionality predictably recycles through the family again.

Other Family Issues

Mrs. Condoli had intense and ambivalent views about her parents. As she related family history and the story of her parents coming to the United States, she portrayed her mother as having "no choice"; she was alternately furious and pitying of her mother. She was typically furious with her father for his spending all the money he earned on liquor or saving it to return to his homeland, for the way he treated her mother and the way he "neglected" his home and family, and for returning to his homeland, remarrying, and having a second family there. (This has softened some since she met and has continued to communicate with a half brother from her father's second marriage.) At the same time, she took obvious pride in his professional accomplishments and "secretly envied" his ability to stick to his plan to return to his homeland. When he decided to return and her mother stood behind Mrs. Condoli's decision not to go, she was obviously proud of her mother. She greatly resented having to stay at home and take care of her infant brother when he was born, and she resented her father's decision that she would go to work the day after she graduated from high school. At the same time, she is alternately furious with herself for going along with this and proud of herself for what she has accomplished.

The clinician's efforts at these times were to clarify what actually occurred, who was involved, and where and when it happened. Questions as to how decisions were made and how events unfolded were asked. Possible connections between generations were explored: In what ways has your marriage been similar to your parent's marriage and different from it? How did your mother's actions in her marriage influence your behavior in your marriage? How did things turn out so differently when it is clear to you that your father wanted nothing but the best for his wife and children?

Over the years, Mrs. Condoli has come to see her mother as less of a victim of her husband. She now believes her mother "had a choice" as to leaving her family in the homeland and coming to the United States with her husband—she talked with women in her parents' homeland of her mother's generation who acted differently than her mother. It is the clinician's opinion that as Mrs. Condoli became more objective about her mother and her marriage she felt and operated less as a "victim" in her own marriage.

Mrs. Condoli felt her brother never had a chance, given the life circumstances into which he was born. Unable to reconcile with his father, he enlisted in the army, and the army "became his family." At times, Mrs. Condoli would blame herself for not having done more for him as a child and adult. She reluctantly took him at his word that he wanted nothing to do with the family. Some of the clinician's questions here were the following: You were born into basically the same life circumstances and seem to have done a bit better in your life than your brother did in his. How did that happen? If your mother had been better able to take care of him, would he have turned out much differently than he did? Mrs. Condoli has never visited the grave site of her brother but is planning to do this in the near future. She believes her son will join her on this visit. It is the clinician's view that her brother's birth shifted her mother's focus from Mrs. Condoli to her brother, which may account in part for the apparent difference in basic level of differentiation. It may be possible to discuss this with Mrs. Condoli in the context of reviewing her visit to her brother's grave site. It may be possible also to discuss further the relationship between the functioning of the oldest daughters and youngest sons across generations.

SUMMARY

The purpose of this chapter has been to illustrate the use of Bowen theory in clinical practice with the elderly person who is functioning on his or her own and is motivated to change. The process of differentiation of self is lifelong. For all of us, it is a process "written in nature" that occurs naturally, with no thought given to it. Those who are born into a family with a higher level of basic differentiation seem to do it more naturally. Those born into a family with a lower level of basic differentiation seem to do it less naturally. For a very few, it becomes a learned and practiced effort. It is the clinician's opinion that all who engage in this work as a learned effort start at a somewhat lower level. Many, if not most, begin such a learned effort after they have started their own families. For some, the effort begins later in life. And, for even fewer, such the the Mrs. Condolis of the world, the effort begins very late in life. However, it is the clinician's opinion that it is never too late. (When he said this to one of the "Mrs. Condolis" in one of their initial visits, she gave him a "withering" look!) It is the clinician's opinion that, as she is getting older and facing death, Mrs. Condoli is experiencing life as never before, with newly discovered and practiced courage of her convictions.

REFERENCES

Bowen, Murray (1978). *Family Therapy in Clinical Practice.* New York: Jason Aronson.

Graefe, Susan (1990). *Empowering Families and the Elderly: A Family Systems Approach.* Pittsburgh, PA: Western Psychiatric Institute and Clinic/Western Pennsylvania Family Center.

Kerr, Michael E. and Bowen, Murray (1988). *Family Evaluation: An Approach Based on Bowen Theory.* New York: W.W. Norton and Co.

McCullough, Paulina G. (1991). *Life Courses in Interaction: A Family Perspective.* Pittsburgh, PA: Western Psychiatric Institute and Clinic/Western Pennsylvania Family Center Conference.

Smith, James B. (1979). *Reactions to Parents' Deaths.* Pittsburgh, PA: Western Psychiatric Institute and Clinic Family Therapy Institute Symposium.

Toman, Walter (1969). *Family Constellations.* New York: Springer.

Chapter 9

Family Systems Treatment of Depression

Bennett I. Tittler

Depression is among the most pervasive and basic emotional symptoms to occur in human beings. Although there is some variation in the form that depression takes and in its severity, commonalities in subjective and physiological experience help define a more general phenomenon.

Current work in the area of depression has concentrated on establishing and diagnosing subtypes (e.g., Prusoff et al., 1980; Steer et al., 1987) and on identifying the physiological processes involved in depression and its treatment (e.g., Noll, Davis, and DeLeon-Jones, 1985; Richelson, 1988). Pharmacological treatments for depression continue to emerge (e.g., Cusack, Nelson, and Richardson, 1994; Preskorn et al., 1995). Recent developments in the psychotherapy of depression have emphasized the cognitive approaches (e.g., Beck et al., 1979; Peterson and Seligman, 1985). The association of depression with factors outside of the individual go back at least as far as Freud's (1986) discussion of depression in relation to loss. Some recent work has begun to examine more closely the significance of key life events and the relationship system in the course that depression takes (e.g., Billings and Moos, 1986; Brown, 1986).

Attempts to elaborate a view of how depression operates within the context of the family have been relatively few thus far. Coyne (1976; Coyne et al., 1987; Strack and Coyne, 1983) has been persistent in his study of the reciprocal relationship between the depressed person and his/her family. In addition, there have been a few descriptions of how to include the family in treatment (e.g., Birchler, 1986; Coyne et al., 1987; Haas, Clarkin, and Glick, 1985) that would qualify as a discussion of depression and its treatment from a more fully developed family systems perspective. In other words, the consideration of depression in relation to the family has been proceeding with very little reference to theory.

My effort here will be to examine the phenomenon of depression from the perspective of family systems theory as developed by Bowen (Bowen, 1978; Kerr and Bowen, 1988). I will attempt to create an interplay between theory and clinical material.

FAMILY SYSTEMS THEORY AND DEPRESSION

Bowen built his family systems theory around a number of concepts that pull together into a coherent picture a wide array of phenomena pertaining to emotional functioning. The following examination of depression proceeds in terms of several of these key concepts. The richness of Bowen's descriptions leaves room for interpretation. What follows represents my own rendering of these concepts based on how I see them and how I have used them.

Multigenerational Cutoff

Psychological theory and research have long acknowledged an association between depression and loss. Family systems theory invites a broad understanding of the effects of loss that includes functional as well as physical loss and the effects over multiple generations. From this broader perspective, loss is seen, not just as the precipitant of an acute depression, but also as a long-term antecedent of the vulnerability to depression. Even more significant, the family systems view suggests that people compound actual loss and other disruptions in life through the tendency at these times to sever or curtail active relationship with segments of the multigenerational family. One implication is that adjustment to loss relates to how the family as a whole responds to the loss and to one another. The ability to retain connection rather than cutoff from family during key nodal points in life is a most significant factor in determining future quality of life.

Where does the tendency to cut off come from and what does it lead to? In both matters, it can be seen as a manifestation of the family fusion, the quantity of tension or chronic anxiety contained within the family. Thus, cutoff is both driven by anxiety and also serves to fix that anxiety in place. Cutoff blocks the possibility of dissipating or resolving family tension through an active, flexible process of interaction throughout the family. One consequence is that depression in various family members, whether in active or latent forms, becomes locked in place.

As one shifts focus from the loss or trauma to the larger family response, an intriguing possibility emerges. Whereas death is irreversible, cutoffs can to some extent be reversed. Indeed, clinical experience supports the theoretically derived notion that depression and the tendency toward depression can be significantly ameliorated through efforts to identify and reverse long-standing multigenerational cutoffs.

Case Study 1

Mrs. A. requested help for her twelve-year-old son in the wake of an angry upheaval in her marriage. Her husband had had a number of extramarital affairs and had finally moved in with another woman. It was apparent upon meeting Mrs. A. that she was significantly depressed. She was gaunt in appearance, admitted to appetite and sleep disturbance, and was painfully slow in her speech and movement. Her family diagram is shown in Figure 9.1.

Treatment took the form of antidepressant medication and psychotherapy for Mrs. A. As her treatment proceeded, her son's behavior problems rapidly improved. However, Mrs. A.'s depression lingered on. Besides her children, to whom she was devoted, she had relied heavily on her husband and his extended family for relationship and interest. Her own family of origin was in England. She had come to the United States with her husband, whom she had met while he was working in England. Mrs. A. was the adopted child of a family with four natural children. She had always felt somewhat peripheral in her family and had allowed squabbles in the family to justify the curtailment of almost all communication with them. Treatment began to focus some attention on this aspect of her life.

Mrs. A. began to initiate communication with her mother, siblings, and old friends back in England. Her efforts were, for the most part, welcomed and reciprocated. She planned a visit back to England with her children for Christmas. Her husband, perhaps fearing she would not return, threatened to prevent her from going. Despite this and last-minute complications with her flight reservations, she had a successful reunion with her family and returned in time for her children to start school again according to schedule. Continued communication with her family resulted in visits from a sister and a cousin. Mrs. A. began to develop a long-term plan—to see both her children complete high school and then return to England to live. As she grew stronger within herself, her husband indicated renewed interest in her. When it was clear to her that he was not relinquishing his girlfriend, she stopped further intimacy with him but maintained regular communication about the children and their care. In order to pay for future trips to England, she began preparing herself to enter the workforce. Despite her apprehension about anything reminiscent of school, she successfully completed a vocational training course. She was delighted when she quickly obtained a

FIGURE 9.1. The A. Family Diagram

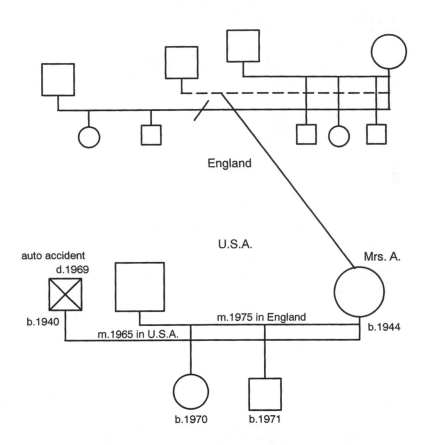

job and realized that she was a valued employee and co-worker. She gradually discontinued her medication and eventually ended psychotherapy. Her progress has not been without setbacks, and her vulnerability, especially to physical symptoms, remains. However, the extent to which she has developed a greater sense of self appears significantly related to her success at reversing the cutoff with her family of origin.

Case Study 2

Mr. B. requested help when he realized he had had the impulse to drive his car off a bridge. He had been placed on a temporary leave of absence from his middle management job, following a series of disagreements with a supervisor. Resolution of this situation awaited the completion of a lengthy grievance process. He and his family were experiencing financial hardship as a result of these events, and his own sense of confidence and self-worth had plummeted. Mr. B. had grown up in an indigent and some-what chaotic inner-city family. He had been proud of his accomplishments and was forlorn at the trouble that had suddenly befallen him. One further piece of information that quite likely had some relevance was the realiza-tion earlier in the year that his wife would probably not be able to have a baby with him. Though she had had a daughter through a prior relationship when younger, there had been several miscarriages since their marriage, and the doctors were discouraging about her ability to carry a baby to full term. The B. family diagram is shown in Figure 9.2.

FIGURE 9.2. The B. Family Diagram

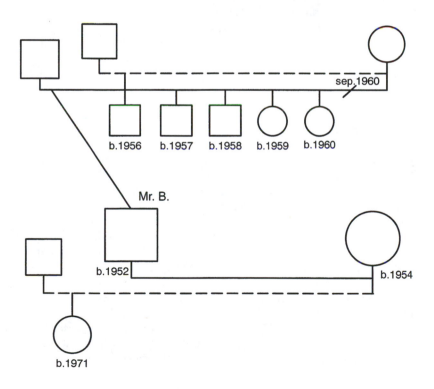

Treatment initially focused on activating the dialogue between Mr. B. and his wife. One result was her decision to get a job, which she did fairly rapidly and which alleviated some of the financial stress. In addition, Mr. B. had the diversion and stimulation of his conversations with his wife. However, he found himself emotionally reactive to the sudden reversal in family roles and also to his wife's advice giving and her limited patience with his expressions of frustration and sadness. At this point, I asked about family of origin, whom he had had almost no communication with for several years. The ultimate cutoff had occurred when he reported his mother to the authorities for neglecting his younger siblings. He said his reputation in the family was that of a "do-gooder." I encouraged him to pick one or two members from his extended family network to contact, without conveying too much emotional urgency. Within a few weeks after initiating these contacts, he had received multiple invitations to visit the family. There ensued several visits back to the family, during which, as he reported, he was lied to, tricked, exploited, and generally taken advantage of. Nevertheless, these contacts necessitated that he stay on his toes and his whole state of being seemed to rise to a higher level of activation. The symptoms of asthma that had accompanied his depression were gone. He resolved to stay out of the inner workings of the family but to remain open to contacts from those who were also seeking a way out of the family malaise or who could maintain some perspective on it. Mr. B. no longer seemed depressed. He reinvested his energies into the grievance process at work and began to prepare for the several contingencies that faced him there. I pointed out that, if he ever needed to recharge his batteries and to reestablish some direction in life, it appeared that increased contact with family of origin served that function for him.

Multigenerational Projection

The fusion or fixed tension of one generation is, with some variability, passed on to the children of the next generation. Some of the children receive a greater portion of this tension than others, but in any family, the tendency is for one generation to transmit to the next a degree of chronic anxiety that is approximately equivalent to the anxiety with which they have lived. The higher the level of chronic anxiety in a family, the greater its vulnerability to dysfunction. Depression and other forms of emotional disorder are one expression of the multigenerational transmission of such vulnerability. Other expressions of the multigenerational projection process fall under the headings of social and physical dysfunctions. The form as well as the degree of family vulnerability tend to be transmitted across generations. Thus, social problems such as delinquency or substance abuse might be prevalent in one family, while physical problems might predominate in another. The vulnerability to depression can be seen as grounded in a multigenerational process that tends toward emotional symptomatology and is fixed in place by physical and emotional cutoffs.

The following clinical vignettes illustrate the transmission of family tension across several generations that results in a clinical depression in one family member designated by the projection process.

Case Study 3

Joey C. was a nine-year-old boy with a younger sister. His mother, who was a schoolteacher, was mainly responsible for decisions that affected the family as a whole. She sought help for a recent onset of depressive symptoms in Joey, following several deaths in the neighborhood. Joey seemed worried and generally lethargic, his grades in school had slipped significantly, and he asked many questions about death. His family diagram is shown in Figure 9.3.

During an evaluation of the family, it was revealed that mother had been brought up by adoptive parents. Although her relationship with her adoptive parents had been relatively harmonious, as an adult she had moved a distance from where they lived and had lapsed into a pattern of little contact. This degree of cutoff was so severe and yet apparently so inadvertent that I immediately suggested she resume face-to-face contact with her adoptive parents. Within a matter of weeks, Joey's symptoms had lifted. His energy returned, his grades went up, and he returned to peer relationships with renewed interest. When, coincidentally, there was an additional death in the neighborhood, Joey and his family had open discussions about it, and Joey accompanied his parents to the funeral. The lifting of Joey's depression and the family's greater openness to the process of death were seen, at least in part, as a result of mother's initiative in reestablishing meaningful contact with the family in which she grew up. The vulnerability inherent in mother's cutoff with her family and her origins had been passed on to her son. The multigenerational transmission process had set the stage for his depression. Thankfully, the depression responded when mother took initiative with the older generation.

Case Study 4

Nancy D. was a seventeen-year-old girl who had been cycling in and out of depression several times a year for the past four years. She had made a suicide gesture during one of her low periods and reported feeling

FIGURE 9.3. The C. Family Diagram

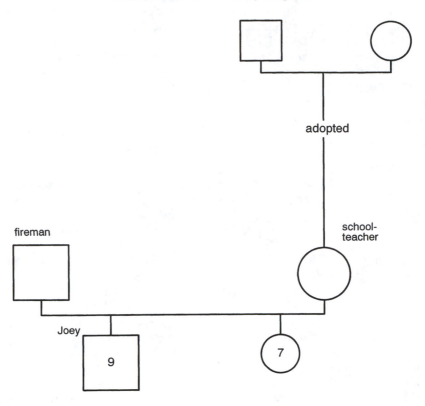

quite despondent during these times. The other clear sign of her distress was her increasing inability to sustain motivation in school or work. When I began to work with her, she had just dropped out of high school for the second time. Her family diagram is shown in Figure 9.4.

The most apparent antecedents to her symptoms were several instances of sexual abuse by a male baby-sitter when she was eight and being raped by a boy she met at a party when she was fifteen. On further examination, earlier origins of her depression could be traced to her mother's depression, which was most acute when Nancy was between the ages of three and six and her parents' marriage was breaking up. In addition, Nancy's contact with her father was curtailed because of his involvement with drugs. The loss of her father replayed her mother's loss of her own father, who had died when she was still young. Thus, the pattern of an early loss

FIGURE 9.4. The D. Family Diagram

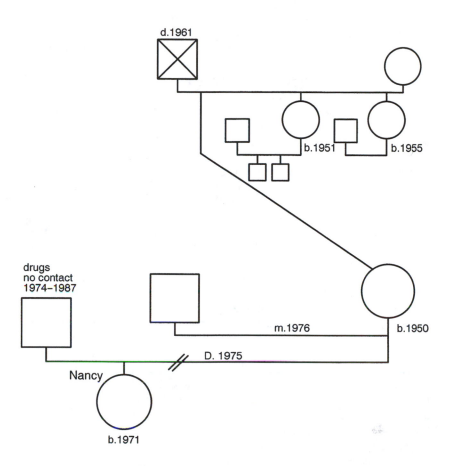

of father and intense involvement with a depressed mother could be seen to encompass at least three generations. When the transmission of multi-generational anxiety moves toward cutoff, a proclivity to depression is one outcome. Treatment in this case has proceeded with the major effort on having mother examine how she might be transmitting her own anxiety and unsureness about self to her daughter. As she did this, mother reawakened her own depression but has been able to comfort herself and to better separate her depression from that of her daughter. The treatment of this case will be described further in the next section.

Nuclear Family Process

If a depression has its seeds in multigenerational cutoff and the projection of chronic anxiety across the generations, nuclear family process addresses who gets the depression and how it is maintained. Symptomatology tends to emerge in those family members most subject to loss of self within the family relationship system. In a given family, one or several persons tend to relinquish self more than the others and thus become designated recipients of the family anxiety. This can take the form of varying degrees of depression in a family that is vulnerable to emotional dysfunction. Loss of self may appear as overfunctioning for the others, underfunctioning for oneself, or a combination of these two. In all cases, there is a loss or a disregard of self.

Self relates to the functioning level of the individual, and it implies a capacity for individuality along with the capacity for effective interdependence. Nuclear family process involves pressures for and against the emergence of self. Anxiety, especially when it is a repeated and long-standing occurrence, tends to undermine self. Conversely, relative freedom from chronic anxiety permits self to flourish. Self exists both as a solid core and as a more changeable property that is affected by current environmental conditions. The nuclear family coordinates and modulates how internal and external tensions are distributed among family members. This is the central process in the development and submerging of self in individual family members.

Just as certain family members tend to give up self, others tend to accumulate self. Accumulation of self within the family occurs in the form of expanding role functions, prerogatives, or degrees of freedom. In some families, the patterns of relinquishing and accumulating self become more and more one-sided over time. In these cases, symptoms become quite fixed and resistant to treatment or any other force for change. This kind of pattern is thought to be a factor in those depressions that have been described as irreversible or intractable.

The more the family focuses anxiety on the symptomatic member or on the symptoms themselves, the more fixed the condition tends to become. The anxious focus may take the form of excessive emotional attention or an exaggerated avoidance of attention to the symptomatic person and his/her condition. Such an arrangement serves to bind family anxiety and becomes an inadvertent investment on the part of the family. For the family to give up this arrangement, others would have to experience and shoulder some of the burden of the resultant anxiety, which, in the cases under consideration here, might mean the appearance of depression in other family members. When possible, the redistribution of family tension among other family members can signal a more flexible adjustment by the family and less debilitation of the more vulnerable family members.

Case Study 4 (continued)

A significant piece of Nancy D.'s treatment has been engaging her mother in a consideration of the nuclear family process. Over the years, her mother's functioning has improved but Nancy's has become increasingly problematic. As mother began to examine her relationship with her daughter and other more general behavior patterns, her own depression reemerged. In contrast, Nancy's functioning has shown signs of improving. Nancy pulled out of a new depressive slide more quickly than in the past and actively engaged her mother concerning issues of separation. She has taken on a more constructive group of friends and has started a more promising job, with enthusiasm for the job rather than just the social contact with co-workers.

At this stage, the mother has been able to articulate several guidelines to help her correct her part in the nuclear family process. These are concerned with her tendency to respond automatically to her daughter in a way that amplifies her daughter's dysfunction. The guidelines include an effort to contain her own excess emotionality when communicating with her daughter, being emotionally available to her daughter when she approaches, but also standing firm against the tendency to condone and reinforce her daughter's irresponsible behavior, especially in financial matters. Awareness about nuclear family process and the role one plays in it has been a central element in the treatment of Nancy's depression.

Case Study 5

Mrs. E. had emigrated from England with her husband shortly after they were married. She had a baby son from an earlier relationship, and Mr. and Mrs. E. subsequently had three daughters after they settled in the United States. Their marital relationship was alternately close and conflictual, with the conflictual mode gradually predominating most of the time. Several years before she began treatment, Mrs. E. had had an abortion, which she remembered as a decision based on her husband's wishes. He did not want any more children. Her depression seemed to have roots in the abortion, the realization that there was an end to her having babies, and the rather constricted pattern of activities in her life. Her family diagram is shown in Figure 9.5.

When she appeared for her initial interview with me, she was quite reticent and clearly feeling very badly about herself. After several sessions, Mrs. E.'s reticence and despondency lifted enough to reveal an angry focus

FIGURE 9.5. The E. Family Diagram

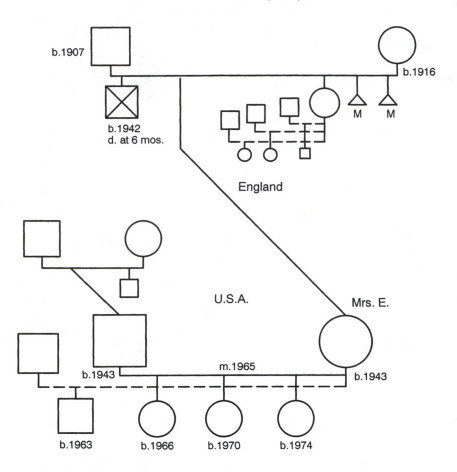

on her husband and her marriage. In their families of origin, Mrs. E. was an older sister of a sister and Mr. E. was an older brother of a brother. The difficulty inherent in these noncomplementary family constellations was apparent in their case. A bitterness between them had accrued from the natural competition for who was in charge. Mr. E.'s role at home had evolved toward less and less significance, and they were unable to maintain the periods of closeness and connectedness at a sufficient frequency and duration. As Mrs. E.'s anger and frustration had grown, so had her tendency to take on excessive responsibility for the household. In effect, she was assuming responsibility for the others at home rather than sharing it with them. Ultimately, this pattern served to increase her loneliness. Her husband and children gravitated toward a passive stance in relation to her. Although the sense of frustration and dissatisfaction with this pattern was most strongly manifested in the marriage, it was also expressed through the children and their periodic difficulties.

Mrs. E.'s rather palpable despair during the first six months of treatment was conveyed more through her bearing and behavior than through her words. At one point, the tension between her and her husband resulted in his striking her and her threatening him with a knife. Mr. E. would occasionally come to therapy sessions when invited but tended to discontinue after a short while and would become negative toward treatment when the intensity in the marriage got higher. The intensity of this process finally lessened somewhat, when I coaxed Mrs. E. to focus some of her energy and thinking on her original family in England. Through a series of letters and eventually a couple of trips and much discussion of these relationships, Mrs. E. faced up to the limitations of her family of origin, while opening up to the possibility of a more active relationship with them. Some of the details of this work included reestablishing a positive relationship with her father at a time when he had become ill. Though they had had some angry standoffs in the past, she had come to have greater respect for him and for his position in the family. His health took a dramatic turn for the better when she arrived on her first visit. Though his health gradually declined after she left, she managed to be back in England again at the time of his death and was able to say good-bye to him. As she came to see her father in a more positive light, she became less inclined to accommodate her mother's and sister's self-indulgent ways. Nevertheless, she maintained more active communication with them and other members of her extended family than she had before.

Besides the effort with her family of origin, the other direction in treatment concerned Mrs. E.'s overresponsible role in the nuclear family. At a certain point in treatment, the pattern of over- and underresponsibility became fairly clear, but Mrs. E. seemed unable to extricate herself from the momentum of the pattern. I wrote identical notes to her husband and each of her children requesting their presence at the next session in order to help Mrs. E., whom I suggested did not know where to turn. Two meetings that included the children, followed by several sessions with just the couple, succeeded in loosening up the rigid pattern and moving the family forward. Mr. and Mrs. E. began to identity some neutral ground from which to share leadership of the family. Problems with each of the children surfaced, but the family seemed better able to coordinate their responses. Eventually, Mrs. E. risked leaving a well-paying manual labor job for an office job that paid less but was more satisfying to her in terms of the work and the social experience it provided. Mrs. E. allowed her life to expand beyond her nuclear family and began enjoying both her family life and her life outside the family significantly more. Despite periodic skirmishes with the children about the extent and limits of their responsibility, each family member had shown some sign of accomplishment and progress in their lives.

Overall Level of Family Functioning

This notion is a derivative of Bowen's concept of differentiation of self. It involves the capacity to think and solve problems about emotional matters and under emotional conditions. It also speaks to the balance of resourcefulness and vulnerability in the family. The many variables associated with style and quality of life tend to be related to this concept. Family functioning level plays a significant part in the course that an emotional disability takes and in the options for treatment. The higher the functioning level of the family, the greater the possibility for attenuating the severity of the disability. Family functioning level is correlated with, but not equivalent to, socioeconomic status. At issue here are a family's emotional resources rather than their physical or social circumstances. In treatment, family functioning level is a foundation for setting realistic goals and expectations.

The case studies that follow illustrate treatment with a family at a higher level of functioning and with a family at a somewhat lower level of functioning. The level of family functioning speaks to which goals are attainable and which are not and also how quickly and to what extent progress can occur. In some cases, one family member will appear to function at a significantly higher level than another family member, or an individual will function considerably better in one sphere of life than another. Optimally, treatment would address the full scope of the family's (and individual's) functioning. By doing so, the tendency to overestimate or underestimate functioning level can be redressed. Assessment of overall functioning level is complex and should remain an ongoing process, always open to new data. Nevertheless, an estimate of functioning level is crucial in setting the direction and pacing of treatment.

Case Study 6

Mr. and Mrs. F. first sought help for their thirteen-year-old son who was underachieving in school and engaging them in battles about decisions such as whether or not he attended private school. Their family diagram is shown in Figure 9.6.

FIGURE 9.6. The F. Family Diagram

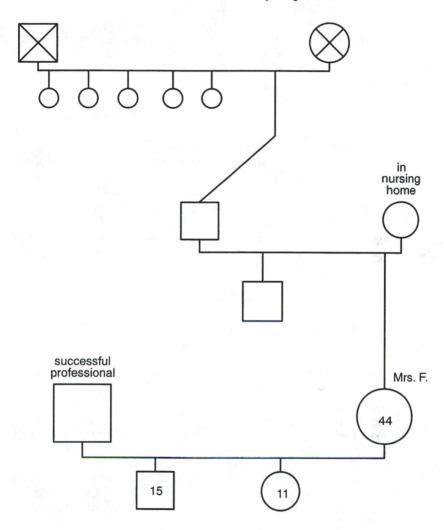

Mr. F. was a successful professional who tended to have high expectations for his son. As he clarified his wishes for his son and gave him more breathing room, the tension in this area lessened, and the youngster began to function better. At this point, Mrs. F. came in by herself asking for help with depression.

Mrs. F. felt she was at a crossroads in her life. She had been occupying herself with the care of the children and assisting her husband in his work but was now sensing that she needed to branch out into a new direction for herself. Her mother had developed the symptoms of senility beginning in her forties, and Mrs. F. was now approaching that same age. She acknowledged an underlying fear that her life would follow the same course as her mother's. At this point, therapy moved in the direction of having her visit her mother by herself, something she had avoided for years, and undertaking a series of interactions with her father in which she politely turned down his requests for special favors. This reversed a mode of interaction that had been prominent in her father's relationships with the family throughout his life.

Though therapy sessions with this family spanned a period of three years, the number of sessions were relatively few. Mrs. F. achieved a greater sense of self-definition in her family of origin and her nuclear family and began to experiment with new vocational interests. She no longer complained about nor showed any signs of depression. Mrs. F.'s sense of her own personal potential had expanded and more clearly reflected a level of functioning consonant with that of her husband and other more successful members of her family of origin.

Case Study 7

Mrs. G.'s depression had been treated for a number of years with medication and supportive therapy contacts. When she began to see me, her youngest son, who was in his early twenties, was experiencing an acute version of her symptoms, and the conflicts between her and her husband were becoming more pronounced. Her family diagram is shown in Figure 9.7.

The son's symptoms subsided more by working with the parents than with him. As they broadened their focus of concern and interest beyond their son, he began to function better. The marital conflict very gradually subsided, after I stopped trying to involve Mr. G. in treatment and worked solely with Mrs. G. Though very affable, Mr. G. did not seem to want to work on himself, and his presence only sparked conflict in the couple. With Mrs. G., I focused on the possibilities for her own self-development, on her relationships with her family of origin, and at times, on her relationships with her children.

Mrs. G. came from a family of modest means and ambitions. Her mother had taken on a greater share of responsibility for the emotional well-being of the family than had her father. As the oldest child, Mrs. G. assumed some of her mother's tendency toward responsibility for others, along with a sense of resentment about this arrangement. Mrs. G. used our discussions to consider and define where the limits were to her sense of responsibility for

FIGURE 9.7. The G. Family Diagram

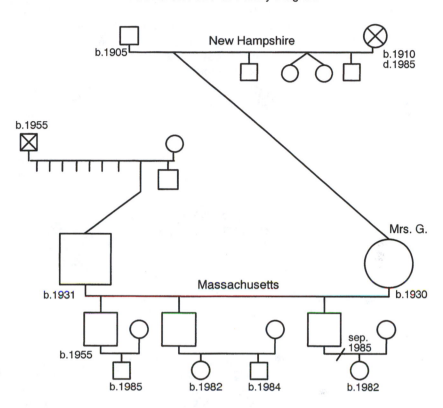

others. For example, in relation to her husband, she gave somewhat less attention to caring for their apartment and sought to go out with friends or her children when he had not invited her out for a while. When conflicts arose among her sons and their wives, she managed to stay relatively neutral, while maintaining some contact with each of them. Although she has remained in contact with a significant portion of her extended family, she is less preoccupied by what she is not doing for the others and correspondingly less resentful of what they are not doing for her. She has experimented with working outside the home to augment the income from her husband's disability payment, but has resisted the sense that this was imperative. She has also taken and shown pleasure in gifts from her grown children, who seem genuinely appreciative of her.

Mrs. G. continues to experience feelings of depression and loss of energy at times. She has made no dramatic shifts in her life during the course of treatment, but she is less preoccupied with her dissatisfactions and seems to have permitted herself a somewhat broader experience and an increase in her sense of fulfillment as a result of family systems treatment. She continues on a maintenance dose of medication and a meeting with me every few months. I believe that Mrs. G.'s progress has to do with discovering and working on goals that were within the reach of herself and her family. This required her own greater appreciation and acceptance of the approximate level at which she and her family functioned and of the fulfillment that was genuinely available to her.

FAMILY SYSTEMS THERAPY WHEN THE SYMPTOMS RESIDE IN ONE FAMILY MEMBER

Family systems treatment largely originated from an interest in schizophrenia and the effort to place this disorder within a wider framework (e.g., Bateson et al., 1956; Bowen et al., 1978; Wynne et al., 1958). Currently, there is a trend to include the family in the treatment of schizophrenia, at least in its earlier stages (e.g., Anderson, Reiss, and Hogarty, 1986; Falloon, Boyd, and McGill, 1984). By the same token, it is generally accepted that families play a role in the origin of children's emotional problems, and this has spawned significant developments in family therapy with children (e.g., Ackerman, 1982; Minuchin, 1974). Finally, those problems that clearly manifest themselves as a disturbance of relationship such as marital conflict have readily lent themselves to a family approach (e.g., Paul and Paul, 1975; Framo, 1982).

In light of the gradual proliferation of family treatments, it is interesting to note that depression and the affective disorders in general continue to be treated very largely from an individually focused framework. Indeed, the same can be said for other forms of emotional dysfunction that present at a moderate level of severity. In these cases, the symptoms draw attention to the symptom bearer. At the same time, that person is usually independent enough to not involve family in issues of daily functioning and caretaking. Indeed, as Coyne (1976) has pointed out in some detail, the depressed person tends to become involved in a process of alienation from his/her closest relations by the very nature of the symptoms. Thus, family tends to distance from active involvement in the treatment of depression, and the treatment approach tends to let the family go.

The theoretical considerations that constitute the main body of this chapter are intended as a basis for pursuing a family systems psychotherapy of depression. The majority of the work may be done with the depressed individual, but the therapy is guided by family systems concepts and will seek out the participation of family when this is deemed useful. The extent to which treatment can proceed through the efforts of the depressed person depends on how much that person has retained areas of adequate functioning. However, even when the overall functioning of the individual remains relatively intact, the focus of the treatment will tend to move toward family, and the availability of other family members for inclusion in treatment can provide an enormous advantage. By grounding progress in a reworking of family relationships, the individual benefits from the presence of family, while gaining some control over the part family plays in the depressive process.

The formulations described in this chapter suggest a series of guidelines for the family systems treatment of depressive conditions:

1. Work to broaden therapy beyond a primary focus on the symptoms of the depressed person.
2. Encourage the symptomatic individual to reclaim a greater portion of self in relation to the family and the rest of the world.
3. Invite significant family members into the therapy and encourage interest in the depressed person but not overinvolvement in his/her symptoms.
4. Encourage the most responsible nonsymptomatic family members to examine and take control of their own tendency to direct excess emotionality to the symptomatic member. Such excess emotionality gets transmitted through a lax, overaccommodating attitude as well as through more visible displays of emotion.
5. Look for multigenerational cutoffs and support the most motivated family members in beginning to bridge cutoffs.
6. Be prepared for symptoms eventually to shift within the family such that other family members experience more of the inner tension originally experienced mainly by the depressed member. Mark these shifts for the family. They generally represent a less pernicious expression of family vulnerability and can be viewed as progress; in essence, the family has learned to distribute its tension more broadly and flexibly.

SUMMARY

Recent work on depression has concentrated on a more precise description of symptoms and on pharmacological and cognitive modes of treatment. These developments continue to reinforce the view of depression as residing in and emanating from the individual. The implications of family systems theory for the understanding and treatment of depression have received scant attention in the literature. Several of Bowen's concepts seem especially useful when approaching the subject of depression. In particular, I have focused on multigenerational cutoffs, multigenerational projection of family tension, nuclear family process, and overall functioning level of the family. This discussion proceeded from the belief that Bowen family systems theory sheds new light on how the symptoms of depression operate. Implications for the family treatment of depression, as elaborated here, were an outgrowth of the primary emphasis on theory.

REFERENCES

Ackerman, N.W. (1982). *The Strength of Family Therapy: Selected Papers of Nathan W. Ackerman.* New York: Brunner/Mazel.

Anderson, C.M., Reiss, D.J., and Hogarty, G.E. (1986). *Schizophrenia and the Family.* New York: Guilford Press.

Bateson, G., Jackson, D.D., Haley, J., and Weakland, J. (1956). Toward a theory of schizophrenia. *Behavioral Science, 1,* 251-264.

Beck, A.T., Rush, A.J., Shaw, B.F., and Emery, G. (1979). *Cognitive Therapy of Depression.* New York: Guilford Press.

Billings, A.G. and Moos, R. (1986). Psychosocial theory and research on depression: An integrative framework and review. In J.C. Coyne (Ed.), *Essential Papers on Depression.* New York: New York University Press, pp. 331-365.

Birchler, G.R. (1986). Alleviating depression with "marital" intervention. *Journal of Psychotherapy and the Family,* 3, 101-116.

Bowen, M. (1978). *Family Therapy in Clinical Practice.* New York: Jason Aronson.

Bowen, M., Dysinger, R.H., Brodey, W.M., and Basmania, B. (1978). In M. Bowen, *Family Therapy in Clinical Practice.* New York: Jason Aronson, pp. 3-15.

Brown, G.W. (1986). A three-factor causal model of depression. In J.C. Coyne (Ed.), *Essential Papers on Depression.* New York: New York University Press, pp. 390-402.

Coyne, J.C. (1976). Toward an interactional description of depression. *Psychiatry,* 39, 28-40.

Coyne J.C., Kessler, R.C., Tal, M., Turnbull, J., Wortman, C.B., and Greden, J.F. (1987). Living with a depressed person. *Journal of Consulting and Clinical Psychology, 55,* 347-352.

Cusack, B., Nelson, A., and Richelson, E. (1994). Binding of antidepressants to human brain receptors: Focus on newer generation compounds. *Psychopharmacology, 114,* 599-565.

Falloon, I.R.J., Boyd, J.L., and McGill, C.W. (1984). *Family Care of Schizophrenia.* New York: Guilford Press.

Framo, J.L. (1982). *Explorations in Marital and Family Therapy.* New York: Springer.

Freud, S. (1986). Mourning and melancholia. In J.C. Coyne (Ed.), *Essential Papers on Depression.* New York: New York University Press, pp. 48-63.

Haas, G.L., Clarkin, J.F., and Glick, I.D. (1985). Marital and family treatment of depression. In E.E. Beckham and W.R. Leber (Eds.), *Handbook of Depression.* Homewood, IL: The Dorsey Press, pp. 151-183.

Jesse, E.H. and L'Abate, L. (1985). Paradoxical treatment of depression in married couples. In L. L'Abate (Ed.), *The Handbook of Family Psychology and Therapy, Volume II.* Homewood, IL: The Dorsey Press.

Kerr, M.E. and Bowen, M. (1988). *Family Evaluation.* New York: W.W. Norton.

Minuchin, S. (1974). *Families and Family Therapy.* Cambridge, MA: Harvard University Press.

Noll, K.M., Davis, J.M., and DeLeon-Jones, F. (1985). Medication and somatic therapies in the treatment of *depression.* In E.E. Beckham and W.R. Leber (Eds.), *Handbook of Depression.* Homewood, IL: The Dorsey Press.

Paul, N.L. and Paul, B.B. (1975). *A Marital Puzzle.* New York: W.W. Norton.

Peterson, C. and Seligman, M.E.P. (1985). The learned helplessness model of depression: Current status of theory and research. In E.E. Beckham and W.R. Leber (Eds.), *Handbook of Depression.* Homewood, IL: The Dorsey Press, pp. 914-939.

Preskorn, S.H., Janicak, P.G., Davis, J.M., and Ayd, F.J., Jr. (1995). Advances in the pharmacotherapy of depressive disorders. *Principles and Practice of Pharmacotherapy, 1,* 1-24.

Prusoff, B.A., Weissman, M.M., Klerman, G.L., and Rounsaville, B.J. (1980). Research diagnostic criteria subtypes of depression. *Archives of General Psychiatry, 37,* 796-801.

Richelson, E. (1988). Synaptic pharmacology of antidepressants: An update. *McLean Hospital Journal, 13,* 67-88.

Steer, R.A., Beck, A.T., Brown, G., and Berchick, R.J. (1987). Self-reported depressive symptoms that differentiate recurrent-episode major depression from dysthymic disorders. *Journal of Clinical Psychology, 43,* 246-250.

Strack, S. and Coyne, J.C. (1983). Social confirmation of dysphoria: Shared and private reactions to depression. *Journal of Personality and Social Psychology, 44,* 798-806.

Wynne, L.C., Ryckoff, I.M., Day, J., and Hirsch, S.I. (1958). Pseudo-mutuality in the family relations of schizophrenics. *Psychiatry, 21,* 205-220.

Chapter 10

Tracking the Emotional Process: Applying Bowen Theory with Phobias and an Obsessive Compulsive Disorder

Donald J. Shoulberg

INTRODUCTION

In this chapter, I describe the principles that enable me to use Bowen family systems theory (Bowen, 1978; Kerr and Bowen, 1988) as a set of hypotheses rather than as a proven theory in my clinical work (Shoulberg, 1985, 1986). I was aware of these principles from the time I began to use Bowen theory to guide my clinical practice, but the way they fit together and how they had to be balanced became clear to me during the first year of clinical work with the Smith family. In the first part of this chapter, I will describe the principles and the first year of work with the Smiths. In the second section of the chapter, I will review the clinical work with the Smith family from the spring of 1985 until the work was terminated in July 1988. The concluding section of the chapter discusses interviews and phone calls from the five-year period following family therapy with the Smiths.

PRINCIPLES GUIDING THE PROCESS OF FAMILY THERAPY

When I greeted Mr. and Mrs. Smith in the waiting room, Mr. Smith shook hands with me. I then extended my hand to Mrs. Smith. She said, "No, the phobias." I nodded, withdrew my hand, and followed the Smiths into my office. I began the session by taking a brief statement from both of them about their reasons for coming to family therapy. I told them what information I had received from the family therapist who referred the Smiths to me.

In July 1985, Mrs. Smith's phobias became so severe that she sought hospital treatment. She left the hospital a few weeks before this interview. During the hospitalization, the phobias did not cause her many difficulties, but since returning home the phobias once again became problematic.

Mrs. Smith began to feel unclean and started compulsively washing her hands in the fall of 1968, shortly before the birth of her third and youngest child, and she had been depressed before the obsession began. In May 1969, she developed a phobia to vomit and became very anxious around infants. She would see white spots and be concerned that the white would touch and envelop her. In the fall of 1982, she saw the imaginary white surround her second child, a daughter, as her daughter entered the coed dorm she would reside in during her second year in college. Mrs. Smith dealt with her concern about "the white" by frequently showering.

One-to-One Neutral Contact with Family Members

During the initial and all subsequent interviews, I employed the first principle that guides all my clinical work—maintaining one-to-one neutral contact with family members. I addressed Mr. and Mrs. Smith separately, dealing with each of them as individuals. Each described the current dilemma that brought him or her to family therapy and his or her view of the history of the presenting problem. By having them speak directly to me rather than to each other, I was letting them know I would structure the sessions. This kind of structure lowers anxiety for clients, since they realize they will be invited to present their viewpoints, and it also lets clients know that they, not the clinician, will have to delineate what is problematic for them. The questions I addressed to Mr. and Mrs. Smith immediately focused them on what was most troublesome for the family.

Neutrality is conveyed when family members are given the opportunity to present their perspectives without others interrupting them. Similar factually oriented questions addressed to each family member shows that the clinician does not favor one family member over another. The ability of the therapist to keep in mind that spouses are at the same basic level of differentiation (Bowen, 1978; Bowen and Kerr, 1988) also helps the therapist dilute feeling and behavioral reactions that favor one spouse over the other. What contributes most to a therapist's ability to remain neutral is coming to a theoretical understanding of the relationship context within which the clinical problems emerged. The second principle guiding clinical work focuses on coming to this theoretical understanding by viewing symptoms and problems in context.

The Relationship Context and Primary Triangles

The relationship context within which symptoms emerge needs to be kept in focus. Determining the primary triangles symptomatic family members participate in is especially relevant.

I conveyed the importance of the relationship context to the Smiths by beginning to construct the family diagram, or genogram, during the first interview. One-third of the way through the initial interview, I said, "For me to understand what is going on I'm going to have to gather some basic facts. I will be constructing a diagram of the family that looks like a family tree. I will record the basic facts on the diagram." I then proceeded to draw the family diagram (Figure 10.1). The diagram was drawn on a large piece of paper that was placed on an easel. This paper can be easily folded and stored in the Smith's file. I began gathering basic facts about Mr. and Mrs. Smith and their children and then some information on their parents and siblings. Name, gender, date of birth, highest level of formal education, occupation, residence, marriages, divorces, pregnancies, medical histories, and deaths were recorded. In all subsequent consultations with the Smiths, this diagram was placed on the easel before the sessions began.

Mrs. Smith believed the phobias were in some way connected with her relationship with Mr. Smith. She realized that possibility during conjoint sessions she and Mr. Smith had with the family therapist who referred the Smiths to me. Mr. Smith neither affirmed or denied the connection between the phobias and marital problems. He had a difficulty focusing on anything except his wife's phobias. From November 1984 through early January 1985, the Smiths were seen for nine sessions. The sessions centered on the severity of the phobias and how Mr. and Mrs. Smith were functioning in the marital relationship, professionally, and with their children. A more detailed multigenerational family history was also collected and discussed.

Since 1968, when the phobias began, there had been periods up to seven weeks, during which Mrs. Smith had been free of phobias, but they always returned. She had been hospitalized nine times, with the most severe episode occurring prior to the last hospitalization in July 1984. That hospitalization was precipitated by her youngest child having her first epileptic seizure. When Mrs. Smith saw her daughter lying on the floor, she thought her daughter was dead. This daughter had become the one person Mrs. Smith trusted to support her emotionally when the phobias were most severe.

The phobias can become so extreme that Mrs. Smith is afraid to touch any of her clothes and has to be dressed by other family members. She takes up to fifty showers a day and insists that any family member entering the home be examined and then shower. She cannot cook and only feels comfortable in a few rooms in her home. At times, the compulsive behavior

FIGURE 10.1. Smith Family Diagram

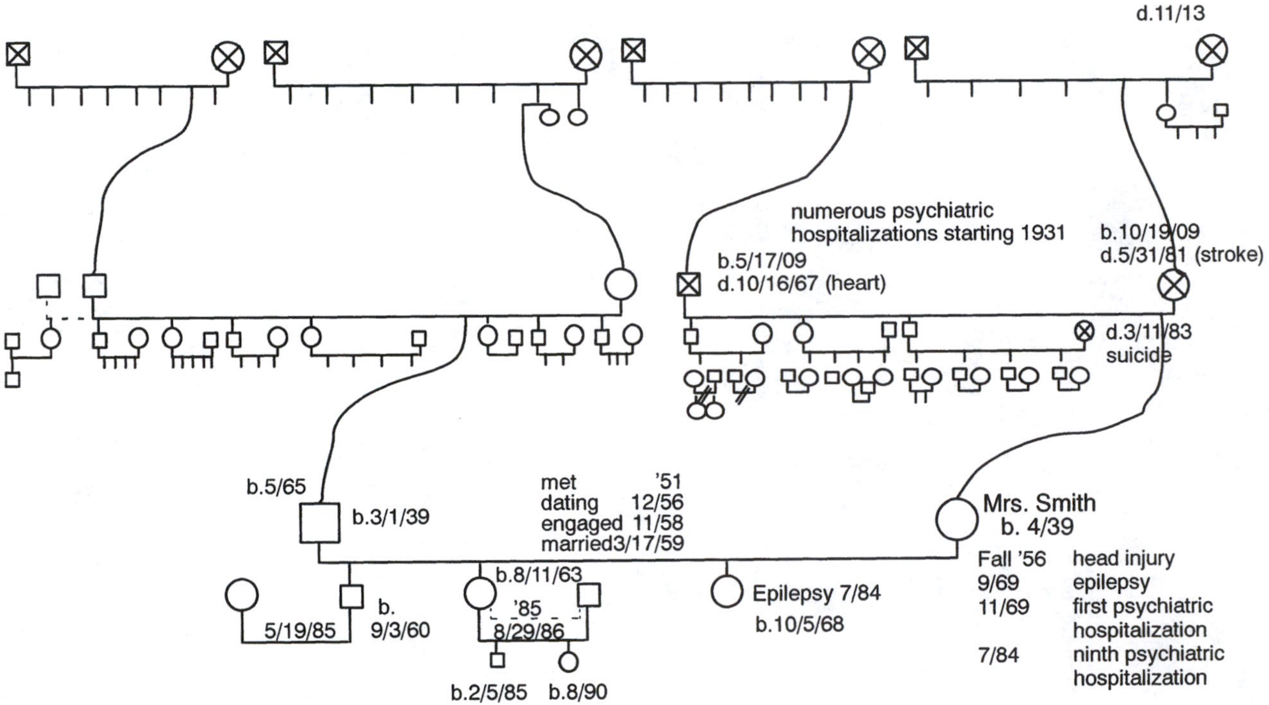

252

is exhausting to Mrs. Smith and exasperating for Mr. Smith and the Smith's other daughter, their second child. Their firstborn son's reaction to the phobias was not discussed. He attended an eastern university in 1979, and after completing his degree, he began work in an East Coast business, where he was employed when the Smiths began family therapy.

Outside of the home, the phobias are not very severe, with the exception of Mrs. Smith having contact with infants. She is able to drive and functions well in a part-time clerical position, and she was a very successful softball coach for a number of years. The phobias are not a problem when she visits with members of her family, but these visits tend to be infrequent.

What became clear during these sessions were shifts in the functioning of Mr. and Mrs. Smith. In the early years of the marriage, Mr. Smith was a full-time student, and Mrs. Smith's salary provided most of the financial resources for the family. She also took charge of running the house and assumed the child care responsibilities. There were some major conflicts in the marriage, especially when Mr. Smith would drink to excess and pay little attention to Mrs. Smith while at social gatherings. In 1965, Mr. Smith completed his degree and obtained a responsible position in a corporation, and the family moved to a large metropolitan area. In addition to Mrs. Smith's emotional symptoms, which became problematic in 1968, epilepsy was diagnosed in September 1969. Mr. Smith ceased doing any excessive drinking that year, and he stopped drinking socially in 1979. He had a one-night affair in 1977 or 1978.

The focus in the conjoint sessions was twofold. Mr. and Mrs. Smith's patterned ways of dealing with each other and their children were discussed. These patterns were then placed in historical context in terms of their marital relationship history. How their current ways of interacting were connected to their patterned ways of relating in their families of origin was questioned but not discussed in depth. Mrs. Smith thought there was a connection between her symptoms and the patterned ways she and Mr. Smith related, but this possibility did not make sense to Mr. Smith.

Toward the end of December 1984, Mrs. Smith became discouraged with her lack of progress. She began questioning the efficacy of the therapy and asked my opinion of an inpatient treatment program for phobias at a prestigious university medical center. I told her that I was unaware of the program, I would be glad to continue working with her and Mr. Smith, and it was my opinion she had an obligation to get what she believed would be the best possible treatment for her problem. She reported in the next session that she called the university hospital and found out the inpatient treatment program had been discontinued.

In early January 1985, Mr. Smith stated that he realized he contributed to the symptoms Mrs. Smith exhibited. He said the more phobic Mrs. Smith became, the more he overfunctioned for her, thus causing the phobias to intensify. He believed that if he could find a way to stay connected with her without overfunctioning she might manage her life more effectively, but he did not think he would be very successful in his efforts. He was entering the busiest time of his work year and would be doing a lot of traveling; consequently, he would not be able to attend many therapy sessions. Mrs. Smith stated that she had increasing difficulties thinking clearly or saying what she was thinking in the presence of Mr. Smith. I agreed to discontinue the regular conjoint sessions, underlined my agreement that Mr. Smith contributed to Mrs. Smith's dysfunction, scheduled individual consultations with Mrs. Smith, and stated I would meet with Mr. Smith whenever he thought it would be helpful to him.

The conjoint sessions were useful in helping the Smiths see that Mrs. Smith's symptoms were in some way influenced by the marital relationship. Their utility though was compromised because Mrs. Smith was so sensitive to the presence of Mr. Smith that she was not able to think clearly or articulate her point of view in his presence. She would alternate between equally anxious reactions of intense criticism or overcompliance to his point of view. When this kind of anxiety is observed in conjoint sessions, it is more helpful to see family members in individual consultations. It is also easier for spouses to become more objective about their families of origin and the influence of their early history in individual sessions. Typically, there is no fundamental change in the way a spouse thinks about the marital relationship until it is placed in a multigenerational context.

In February 1985, Mrs. Smith began reviewing some early events in her life. She was born in 1939 and was the youngest of four children. She remembered that when she was six her mother told her not to touch newly ironed clothes because she was dirty. In January 1952, a number of boys made sexual advances to Mrs. Smith and one of her friends, and in July of the same year, her oldest brother also attempted to engage in sexual activities with her. She tried to tell her mother about not wanting to bathe with this brother, but her mother would not listen to her complaints. In December 1956, she began dating Mr. Smith. When she told Mr. Smith, a few years after they started dating, about her brother's sexual advances toward her, he said that kind of behavior was just part of growing up.

Mrs. Smith was beginning to see some similarities between her mother and her husband. When she told each of them about the inappropriate sexual advances being made toward her, neither her mother nor Mr. Smith was able to understand Mrs. Smith's point of view or intervene with her brother to curtail his behavior. She thought these incidents were connected in some way with her phobias.

In March 1985, I asked Mrs. Smith to describe how she currently made sense of the phobias. She reported that the phobias came out of feelings that were always directed toward someone important to her. Her relationships with these important others would take two forms: She would attempt to get the important other to protect her from someone "who comes on to me," since she could not handle the situation without help. The second way the feelings were transformed into phobias occurred when an important other left her. I helped her see that in both cases she was involved in triangles by diagramming the different forms of the triangles. She would either attempt to get the important other to side with her against a third party, or she would become distant from an important other and that person would move toward someone else. However, when she became overwhelmed by the phobias, there would be at least one important other who would care for her.

The three important others were her mother, husband, and youngest daughter. The earlier triangles were replicated with their two daughters. When her oldest daughter began living in a coed dorm in 1982—a living arrangement her husband supported and she opposed—Mrs. Smith was overwhelmed with "the white." At the time her youngest daughter had her first epileptic seizure, Mrs. Smith's relationship with Mr. Smith was very distant and conflictual, and she depended on her youngest daughter to understand her difficulties with the phobias and to remain available to her. Consequently, Mrs. Smith suffered an emotional collapse when she thought her daughter died during her first epileptic seizure.

Mrs. Smith was now aware of the triangulation that took place whenever she became phobic. She realized that her relationships were linked to the severity of her obsessive compulsive symptoms. She was able to see the connections between the triangles with herself, mother, and brother; herself, brother, and husband; and herself, each daughter, and her husband. She realized that she could not change what was happening in the relationships unless she could observe the patterned way in which family members connected to one another and then modify her part of the pattern.

As Mrs. Smith became more objective about her life difficulties, Mr. Smith became more anxious. In March 1985, he called to say he thought Mrs. Smith might be becoming suicidal and wondered what he should do. I took his concerns literally and outlined various levels of intervention that could be tried. I received no further calls from Mr. Smith, but Mrs. Smith reported that her husband was having major difficulties in his job, his ulcer was acting up again, and for the first time in their marriage, he was narrating his nightmares to her. Within a few weeks, the nightmares stopped, the ulcer was manageable, and no further job difficulties were mentioned.

In April 1985, Mrs. Smith began to discuss her primary triangle with herself, her mother, and her father. She was fairly distant from each of her parents. She viewed her father as totally incompetent and her mother as very domineering. Mrs. Smith realized that she tended to shift between these two polarized positions in dealing with her husband. As she became clearer about the primary triangle, in the spring of 1985, she still had problems with "the white," but despite these difficulties, she stated that she felt better than she had for years, she was able to do some housework, and she cooked a meal for the first time since leaving the hospital.

Theoretically Based Observations of the Relationship System

The third principle that enables me to use Bowen family systems theory as a set of hypotheses, rather than a proven theory is that the clinician consistently reports theoretically based observations of the relationship system to the family. The importance of this principle became clear in the winter and spring of 1985. Mrs. Smith had major problems with clinicians who promised they would help her, giving the impression that they had the answer to her problems. She also had difficulties dealing with clinicians who were nondirective, overly positive, or very critical when she reported things were not improving. It was also her experience that her point of view and her feelings were not very important to most clinicians with whom she previously worked.

By presenting theory-based hypotheses that she could test as she observed what was happening in her relationship system, I was able to avoid some of the pitfalls that tripped up other therapists when dealing with Mrs. Smith. No matter how subjective and feeling-oriented Mrs. Smith's reports might be, I consistently asked factual questions, enabling Mrs. Smith to place her feelings and phobias in an interactional context. I would comment on the patterns of the interactions and frequently diagram the interactions on a chalkboard. She would either challenge me or agree with my hypotheses. Gradually, the patterned interactions, when the phobias were more difficult to manage, became as predictable to her as they were to me. I was constantly inviting her to articulate her understanding of the variables contributing to her symptoms, and I also consistently reported my belief that she was the expert on phobias and knew more about them than most mental health professionals. The give-and-take in this inquiry has more in common with scientific colleagues attempting to account for a particular phenomenon than a traditional doctor/patient relationship. The constant focus on context and interactions enabled her to see patterned ways of relating with her husband and two daughters that replicated ways she, her mother, father, and older sister interacted. This sense of continuity between the present and past diminished her sense of isolation.

FAMILY THERAPY: SPRING 1985 UNTIL JULY 1988

In the late spring and early summer of 1985, Mrs. Smith was able to handle two major transitions in the family without severe reactions. She traveled to the East to attend the marriage of her son in May 1985 and fully participated in the social events connected to the wedding. In June 1985, her oldest daughter moved into her own place. Realizing that her struggle with this daughter replayed her conflict with her oldest sister enabled Mrs. Smith to manage this transition without a major relapse.

In September 1985, Mrs. Smith began questioning whether more frequent sessions might be necessary. From the beginning of September until the middle of October, Mrs. Smith was experiencing much conflict with Mr. Smith, and both were wondering whether this therapy would also fail. During this difficult period, she reported that "the white" occurred whenever someone questioned or disciplined her. She also realized that when she is tired she becomes more symptomatic.

The intensity of her negative reactions to Mr. Smith reminded her of the conflicts that took place between her father and mother. She recalled viewing her father coming out of shock treatment, throwing and breaking things, and striking her mother. She also mentioned that four members of her father's mother's family, all males, committed suicide. In 1983, her sister-in-law, the wife of her brother who was two years older than Mrs. Smith, committed suicide.

Gradually, Mrs. Smith realized that the difficult period she was having in September and October 1985 had as much to do with her youngest daughter's return to school as her husband's criticism of her. She also observed that "the white" was manageable when she immediately dealt with her husband, if she perceived he was becoming domineering or withdrawing too much. She was never able to be that direct with her mother. By the end of October 1985, Mrs. Smith reported the crisis was over. For the first time since 1968, she was able to imagine that something was dirty and the fantasy did not automatically become a reality for her. She was clearly able to distinguish her subjective thoughts and feelings connected with dirt from the fact that the object she was viewing was actually clean. In the past, she would start cleaning the object; this time she refused to begin the compulsive cleaning. Things were calm and open between Mr. and Mrs. Smith, and Mrs. Smith was able to be alone.

During the next few months, things continued to improve in the marital relationship. Mrs. Smith commented, "I'm not pushing him to change; he is doing it himself." They were able to take a trip together without any intense conflict arising. She was becoming preoccupied with her oldest daughter, who was living with a man who became belligerent, tended to abuse drugs, and had a sporadic work history. Mrs. Smith saw her participation in their relationship as a triangle, and I coached her to have more one-to-one contact with this daughter.

Although the phobias returned around Christmas 1985, a typically difficult period for Mrs. Smith, she was not incapacitated by their return. She stated in early January 1986, "The phobias are really bad but I feel a lot better on the inside. They [her husband and youngest daughter] can't see it. All we do is argue. He blames it on the phobias. In dealing with him I don't hold anything in anymore and it's a lot better." They were able to go out for meals together, and Mrs. Smith was using the phone again.

Mrs. Smith continued to focus on triangulation as the way to understand her pattern of interacting that intensified the phobias. When difficulties emerged with someone, particularly her second child, she would try to get Mr. Smith to handle the problem: "He was always my buffer and I'd ask him to take over. Mother was also my buffer." She realized her mother was overfocused on her children and that, unlike her mother, she needed to have interests other than her children. These realizations helped her decrease her advice giving to her middle child. Although she objected to her daughter's relationship, she managed to keep emotionally connected to her daughter.

The time between sessions lengthened to once a month in March 1986. The marital relationship continued to be characterized by little conflict and more open communication. Her daughter married in August 1986. A focal point in many of the sessions before and after the wedding was how Mrs. Smith could continually stay in contact with her daughter without overfunctioning for her. She gradually clarified the wedding expenses she would be responsible for and did not interfere with the way her daughter planned the wedding. The wedding took place without any major problems.

During the next five months, Mrs. Smith continued to shift her relationship with this daughter. She realized she tended to have the same negative reactions to this daughter that she had toward her older sister. As she became more open and direct with this daughter, she observed a shift in her daughter's marital relationship. Her daughter became more direct and open with her husband.

Mrs. Smith was also less influenced by her husband's anxiety. Mr. Smith's work is very demanding during the first four months of the year. As he approached this time of year, he tended to offer Mrs. Smith more advice and to be more critical of her way of managing the phobias. This year was no exception, but Mrs. Smith was able to clearly define to Mr. Smith what she would and would not do. She was able to take on more household chores and be alone more frequently than in the past. She handled the early months of 1987 so well that she requested sessions be extended to once every two months.

In March 1987, Mrs. Smith called me to describe a recent television show on obsessive compulsive disorders that stressed the usefulness of Anafranil in dealing with such disorders. She wanted my help in getting her in one of the experimental programs in which this drug was being administered.

Mrs. Smith met the criteria these programs set for an obsessive compulsive disorder, but she was disqualified from participating in the program because she had a history of a seizure disorder. However, she could receive the medication in Canada. Arrangements were made for her to meet with a Canadian psychiatrist who had years of experience treating patients with Anafranil who were diagnosed with obsessive compulsive disorders.

Mrs. Smith stopped experiencing physical pains in her chest, another symptom she had had for many years, shortly after beginning medication. She realized she was not only modeling symptoms but changing a way of life that had continued for nineteen years. She reported one month after beginning the medication, "It's like learning to walk. I'm like a little baby but I am potty trained."

At the end of May 1987, her youngest daughter graduated from high school. Mrs. Smith compared her view of herself when this daughter graduated with her self-perception when her first two children completed high school: "At graduation I took it all in. I felt this child was the only one to graduate; with the other two I wasn't mature enough to graduate."

She was gradually able to use more rooms in her home as "the white" lifted. She realized she could now think differently:"The medication turns your thinking completely around. It enables you to think rationally." The feeling of being unclean also disappeared. In October 1987, while driving to visit her youngest daughter at college, Mrs. Smith noticed vomit on the road. Although some of the obsessive compulsive patterns remained—she had the car washed—there was no conflict between Mrs. Smith and her husband about how to handle the situation. Her perception of the phobic object reaching out to her was absent, and there was no tightness in her chest. She continued to gain weight, was unable to have orgasms, and experienced some jerky movements in her arms and legs. Given the progress she had made, she requested to extend the time between appointments. It was decided she would have another appointment in three months, and then sessions would be on an as-needed basis.

There were a few brief phone consultations in December 1987 and January 1988. She became very anxious in December, when her vision turned blurry. She went to an emergency room and received a prescription for a small amount of Valium and then spent the night with her married daughter. She believed the anxiety intensified because she was alone while her husband was away on a business trip. The small amount of Valium and staying overnight with her daughter diminished the anxiety and blurred vision.

Her daughter had a son in February 1988. Mrs. Smith was with her daughter when her grandchild was born. She reported in March 1988, one year after beginning Anafranil, that she could handle her grandson's diapers but had trouble caring for him when he would vomit. She believed she would not be able to be that involved with her grandson if she was not on the medication.

Early July 1988, Mrs. Smith called to report she was going through a rough time; the obsessiveness had returned and she was having a lot of flashbacks. She had been caring for her grandson for five days; her youngest daughter was recovering from foot surgery and was unable to shower. By seeing how the return of the symptoms was connected to the pressure she was experiencing due to additional caretaker responsibilities, Mrs. Smith was able to reduce her anxiety. I said her situation was analogous to a recovering alcoholic who was exposed to a week of parties.

On July 20, 1988, Mrs. Smith said, "I graduate today. I don't think I need therapy anymore." The difficulties she reported during the phone call three weeks before this appointment had diminished. The baby vomited on her twice; she gave him to her husband, showered, and was able to go to work. She only takes one shower a day, except on the days she cleans the house. She does some cooking. Even though she dislikes the symptoms connected with the medication, she believes her ability to think clearly is worth putting up with the side effects: "I'm not normal but at least I'm half-way normal. I get stronger as I go on."

When Mrs. Smith terminated family therapy, each member of her nuclear family was functioning at least as well, if not better, than when therapy began in the fall of 1984. The marital relationship was more open and less conflictual. Mr. Smith continued to do well professionally. Mrs. Smith had more contact with her son and her son's wife. Her middle child continued to have a great deal of marital conflict but was not overfunctioning for her husband. She had a part-time job and was in frequent contact with each one of her parents. The youngest daughter had a difficult first year in college. Despite these difficulties, she chose to return to the university and live away from home instead of returning home and attending a junior college.

How Bowen Family Systems Therapy Helped Mrs. Smith

Mrs. Smith consistently reported what was helpful for her in therapy. The focus on who, what, when, and where questions to reveal the factual context within which symptoms emerged was useful. She stated that I was interested in her feelings and not overfocused on the phobias. Since I never asked about feelings, I challenged her observation. What became clear was that Mrs. Smith was invited to present her point of view in the sessions and when her view was different from mine, the differences could be acknowledged. She mentioned during one session, "You are the only doctor I can tell to go to hell." She also found the focus on patterns of interaction illuminating, especially triangles and reciprocity of functioning. As helpful as therapy guided by Bowen theory was to Mrs. Smith, she believed that without the medication her thinking could not have consistently changed. Mrs. Smith believed the ability to think clearly brought about the shift in her ability to function in a more adaptive way.

FIVE YEARS AFTER ENDING FAMILY THERAPY: JULY 1988 TO OCTOBER 1993

Mrs. Smith had three individual sessions at monthly intervals during the summer and early fall of 1990. She continued to manage her phobias and to have as much freedom in her lifestyle as she had when therapy ended in July 1988. She was very anxious about going back to college as a part-time student. Mrs. Smith had gained a lot of weight but has been monitoring her food intake and exercising regularly. Her oldest daughter was about to have her second child. Her youngest daughter was preparing to return to the university she left because of academic difficulties. This daughter had one seizure, but her overall health situation has remained stable.

During summer school in 1990, this daughter was able to earn As in two courses. In July 1990, her oldest daughter had a baby girl. Mrs. Smith visited her son and his family in the East and had no problems with phobias or compulsions during the trip. In September 1990, Mrs. Smith decided she was on course in her life and had no further need of family therapy. I supported her decision. The issues that caused her to resume sessions and her anxiety about returning to college and dealing with her oldest daughter, who was returning to the town where the Smiths live, were now manageable for Mrs. Smith. I supported Mrs. Smith's plan to concentrate on losing weight but told her I had questions about the intense fasting program she was beginning, since long-term results on this kind of program have not been effective.

Mrs. Smith had one additional family therapy session in February 1992. She stated, "I've got a problem with the white." The problem began while Mrs. Smith was struggling with a math class. In high school, Mrs. Smith had no trouble with math, and she is a very competent bookkeeper. Now it is difficult for her to concentrate and remember as she deals with options regarding this class and her academic goals. At the end of the session, we agreed regular sessions were not necessary.

Mrs. Smith called in October 1992 to ask my opinion of someone claiming he could cure phobias and obsessive compulsive disorders. I knew nothing about him and suggested she call an expert at NIH (National Institutes of Health) whose work on obsessive compulsive disorders Mrs. Smith and I had previously discussed. I also discussed this issue with Mrs. Smith's youngest daughter, who called wondering if her mother needed more therapy with me. I told her daughter that Mrs. Smith and I had agreed that she did not need any more sessions with me.

In June 1993, Mrs. Smith called to see if I would be willing to discuss her youngest daughter's career goals in a mental health field. I said I would be glad to see her if she wanted to discuss her situation, and I explained my policy in these kinds of situations is to not charge a fee. As the director of a postgraduate training program in family therapy, I routinely interview persons considering a future in a clinical profession.

During the interview, I reviewed Mrs. Smith's daughter's academic and work history. Her main issue was whether to focus on an advanced degree in special education or to obtain a degree in social welfare. We discussed the pros and cons of each direction.

My most recent telephone conversation with Mrs. Smith took place in early October 1993. Once again she had heard about a new approach to phobias and obsessive compulsive disorders on a TV show, and I posed the kinds of questions I always raise about therapists who promise cures. Mrs. Smith thought the approach might be worth pursuing and clearly indicated she did not think having a family therapy session would be helpful. I did not challenge her point of view.

REFERENCES

Bowen, M. (1978). *Family Therapy in Clinical Practice.* New York: Jason Aronson.
Kerr, M. and Bowen, M. (1988). *Family Evaluation: An Approach Based on Bowen Theory.* New York: W.W. Norton.
Shoulberg, D. (1985). Clinical principles for not intensifying human suffering. *Kansas Association for Marriage and Family Therapy Newsletter.* Spring, 3 (1).
Shoulberg, D. (1986). Tracking the emotional process. Presentation at the Twenty-Third Annual Georgetown Family Symposium, Georgetown University Family Center, Washington, DC, November 9.

Chapter 11

Family Systems with Alcoholism: A Case Study

Anne S. McKnight

INTRODUCTION

Bowen family systems theory is a coherent set of concepts that poses intriguing questions about the nature of the human relationship system and its place in the natural world. This theory holds that human functioning can be understood with the same scientific principles that apply to the behaviors of other living organisms in the web of life.

Dr. Murray Bowen developed Bowen family systems theory over a period of forty years through his research with families and his extensive reading in the natural sciences. He observed families with severe psychiatric difficulties—many with a member who was schizophrenic—at Menninger Clinic in Kansas and then at NIMH, where entire families were hospitalized. As he continued his studies with a broad range of families on an outpatient basis, he strove to develop principles about human functioning that were consistent with factual data recorded about families and with scientific theories about natural phenomena. These concepts provide a framework for viewing and ordering the complexity of human interactions in a relationship system.

From a systems view, the family is an emotional unit, the "emotional system" in which the functioning of each person is a product of the reactions and behaviors of other family members. More complex than the behaviors of its individual members, the family system is an intricately balanced living organism. Its members are constantly adjusting and reacting to one another, shifting emotionally to maintain the stability of the whole.

Family members rely on one another and are sensitive to one another's reactions. Each member operates in his or her life with some kind of "fit" in the family's emotional life. Family members may be uncomfortable with their lives; they may be sick, depressed, or angry. Nevertheless, their functioning position is part of a balance in the family relationship system as a whole.

Some families have members who are experiencing problems, including alcoholism, depression, eating disorders, or marital conflict. These difficulties in one person are interwoven into the relationships in the family. When one person has a problem, it is often an expression of the way in which the family has handled tension among its members.

Family members do not "cause" problems in other family members. However, individuals in a family develop characteristic patterns of relating that perpetuate another's behavior. Sometimes the balance in the family's life is so subtle that it is difficult to understand how it operates; sometimes it appears extraordinarily clear, particularly to outsiders.

Bowen theory describes the development of symptoms in a person within a different framework. From a family systems viewpoint, problems do not develop from a person's intrapsychic conflicts or, in more popular parlance, from his or her head. A breakdown in an individual is seen as an integral part of the interactional process of the nuclear family and of each spouse with his or her family of origin.

This chapter presents the idea that although alcoholism has unique characteristics, families with an alcoholic member operate in ways that fall within the spectrum of human functioning. Alcoholism is but one human problem that exists in some families, along with other difficulties and strengths. This chapter discusses addiction as an understandable thread in a family's life over the generations rather than the crucial variable in the family's current emotional life.

The Case Study of Mr. and Mrs. Swain

Bowen family systems theory will be examined through the exploration of a clinical case—a family that was seen in sessions over a period of several years. Interwoven in the discussions was the theme of alcoholism in the husband, Mr. Swain, and in Mrs. Swain's parents, Mr. and Mrs. Fitzpatrick.

Susan Swain called for an appointment after talking with a lawyer about a separation from her husband. By her own account on the telephone, she did not want to leave her husband but had become depressed and anxious about his drinking.

Mrs. Swain, at thirty-nine, was an exceptionally attractive and verbal woman. She was the mother of two children, nine and seven, and lived with her husband, who was an accountant in a suburban community. Prior to her calling the lawyer, Mr. Swain had been drinking heavily, spending three or four days away from home, his whereabouts unknown to her. He was critical of and angry at her and at times would become physically aggressive. Mrs. Swain worked in a job that she had held since leaving high school, took care of the children, and attempted to anticipate what would anger her husband. How does one understand a bright, articulate, attractive woman living with a drunken, abusive, and distant man?

As Mrs. Swain's story unfolded, her life became more understandable and perhaps even predictable if viewed through a lens of family systems ideas. Mrs. Swain was the oldest of four. Her childhood was characterized by constant conflict between her parents, whom she described as alcoholic. She grew up close to her father, but distant and at odds with her mother. Although her father drank daily, she perceived him as the emotionally available parent. She connected to him despite the drinking.

Mrs. Swain described her mother as overwhelmed by her four children. Alcohol had become a way of distancing herself from their demands and from her husband. Drinking was a means of escaping her mothering responsibilities, which fell increasingly to her oldest daughter. When Mrs. Swain entered her teenage years, she had three siblings, ages six and younger, and a mother who saw herself as inadequate. She assumed even more duties as a teenager and became rebellious as a result, which created a polarized and conflictual relationship between her and her mother. (See Figure 11.1 for the Swain Family Diagram.)

The Concept of the Triangle

Mrs. Swain grew up as a child who was pivotal to her parents' relationship. She functioned as negotiator of the disagreements between her parents; each parent looked to her to manage the tension with the other. When she was a child, her father turned to her emotionally, as her mother distanced herself from him through drinking. She became aligned with him in a bond that left her mother on the outside, more isolated and alone in the struggle with her other children. Mrs. Fitzpatrick reacted to this estrangement by being critical of her daughter, yet still relying on her to help raise the other three children.

Mrs. Swain, her mother, and father form one of the basic units of a relationship system—the triangle. A triangle is a fluid and changeable pattern of interacting among three emotionally connected people. Two people form an inherently unstable relationship. When tensions rise in a twosome, whether in a marriage, friendship, or work relationship, often one person or the other will turn to a third person.

There are many triangles in every family. Each child is in a triangle with his or her parents; a parent is in a triangle with two children; each parent is

FIGURE 11.1. The Swain Family Diagram

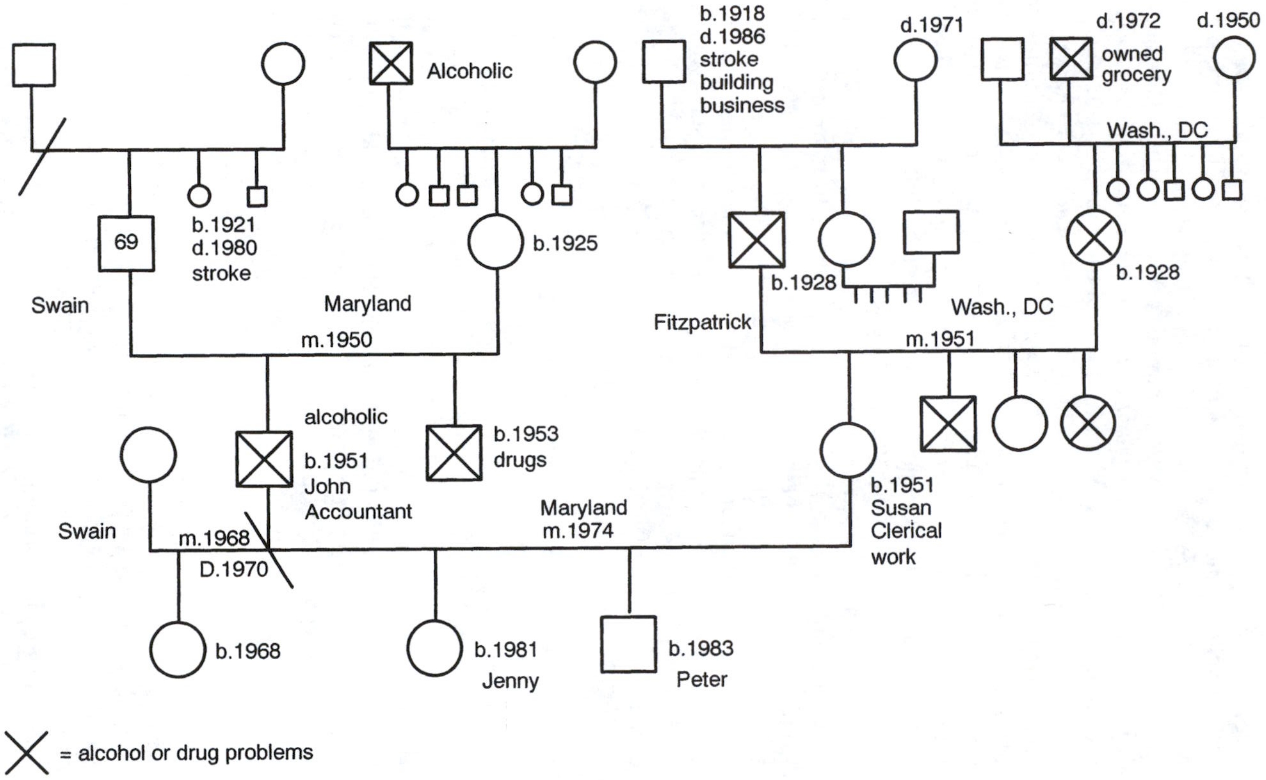

X = alcohol or drug problems

266

in a triangle with his or her parents, and so on. Often people are unaware of the predictability of a pattern of relating until they begin to observe the interactions among family members when tension rises in the family.

When a relationship system is anxious, two people will be close, with the third in the outside position. Mrs. Swain's parents related in a fixed and rigid pattern, in which she mediated the conflict. When tension arose between them, her father turned to her, leaving her mother on the outside emotionally. Mrs. Fitzpatrick became angry at her daughter, pushing her toward her father and reinforcing their closeness. The strain that originated between the parents was reflected in the conflict between Mrs. Fitzpatrick and her daughter.

The closeness between two people in a triangle, as with Mrs. Swain and her father, can be a comfortable and sought-after position when another is on the outside. However, the attraction is based on continued tension with the third rather than on personal one-to-one relating between the other two. When tension is high enough in the triangle, the bonds between the two can become overwhelming, and the most comfortable position becomes the one on the outside.

Another example of the way a triangle operates is when conflict between a couple is rerouted through a child. This is more descriptive of Mr. Swain's position in his family, in which his rebellious, acting-out stance earned him the label of problem child. Although his father distanced himself through work, his parents were in agreement on viewing their son as an intractable troublemaker, consigning him to the outside position in the triangle. Viewing the child's behavior in the context of an interactional process in a triangle widens understanding of the problem in the family.

THE BALANCE OF THE DRIVES
FOR INDIVIDUALITY AND TOGETHERNESS

Each person emerges from his or her own family with variable needs for connection to important others and for autonomous and goal-directed behavior. The drive to develop a separate identity, which is essential for adult functioning, is tempered by deep-rooted automatic responses based on the formative relationships in one's life.

In the course of his research, Bowen (1978) labeled these counteracting forces individuality and togetherness. The drive for individuality is fueled by an ability to direct one's life in a mature and functional way. There also exists in each person a pull for togetherness—an emotionally driven side oriented toward a feeling state based on attachment to others. This side, part of the glue that holds relationships together, can compromise values or goals for the sake of approval or acceptance by others.

The Swain family is an example of how the togetherness force can dictate an individual life direction. Mrs. Swain grew up in a sea of emotionality, in which her parents did not thoughtfully direct the lives of their children. Her life became absorbed in caring for her siblings and mediating the animosity between her parents. So much of her life energy went to holding the family together that she had little left for herself. As in many families in which members function for one another, Mrs. Swain did not fulfill the developmental tasks of young adulthood by separating from the family. She remained at home after high school, both dependent on the family and responsible for it. Only when she found a partner in Mr. Swain, to whom she could transfer her neediness for connection, did she leave the family.

Mr. Swain represents another variation of the balance of togetherness and individuality. Rather than being dependent and overresponsible, as was Mrs. Swain, he distanced from his family through irresponsible behavior. He denied his attachment to his parents, who continually worried about his drinking and social problems. The alcohol was one way to leave his attachments, both to his parents and later to his own nuclear family, and establish a sense of separateness. However, his drinking also interfered with his ability to think and act clearly and promote his own life course. This reactivity to the emotional neediness of another derailed his transition to mature adulthood.

The balance between individuality and togetherness is often described as negating the importance of emotion. Emotions are rooted in deep-seated drives that are essential to human functioning, but part of man's evolutionary heritage is the ability to think and make choices about these instinctual responses.

When emotions are in control, a person's ability to direct his or her life is compromised. For example, a person suffers from depression and is overwhelmed by melancholy and despair; people who are very depressed often cannot direct their lives in a carefully considered manner. Another example is anger. Those who have a solid identity certainly experience anger, but they are not consumed by it. They can examine what made them angry, take steps to address the problem, and move past it. Those whose lives are more dictated by emotion react angrily to events and people; they react to the responses to their anger and function in such an aroused state that they lose the ability to make thoughtful choices. They are run by emotion rather than using it as one of many useful responses in their repertoire.

When people operate in a calm, thoughtful manner, they are in fact more in harmony with their emotions. They have the freedom to recognize their emotional side without being overwhelmed by it, and have the choice to experience emotion without having it dictate their reactions.

The Concept of Differentiation

Bowen (1978) observed a dichotomy in the human between the capacity to make considered choices about life direction—the forces for individuality—and the automatic emotion-based responses that operate in each person at an instinctual level—the forces for togetherness. As each person forms his or her identity through bonds with original caretaking relationships, a balance is achieved between the ability to reflectively direct one's life and the amount of emotion-based functioning linked to the relationship system. Bowen labeled this balance "differentiation of self," a term chosen from the biological sciences for its connotation of an organism's ability to maintain a separateness from the larger system around it. Through his research, he observed that all humans function somewhere on a theoretical spectrum, varying in the balance of these forces in their lives. People higher on the scale are caught in their relationship systems, incapable of separating as independent adults from the emotional forces in their families.

The balance in the forces of individuality and togetherness in an individual is related to the level of differentiation in a family. This balance is influenced by:

- the level of anxiety transmitted from generation to generation in the family,
- important life events such as death or divorce,
- pressures from the environment, and
- the intactness and stability of the present relationship system.

When people experience an increase in anxiety and stress in family life, they become more dependent on one another for support that may bolster their functioning for a short time. However, when the anxiety is chronic and the neediness is constant, family members may become depleted by the demands for togetherness. They may back away from, but also be caught in, the emotionally charged pull of the family. When emotionality runs high enough in a family, the child is unable to make the gradual separation from the family toward a goal-directed adulthood.

A family with alcoholism, such as Mrs. Swain's parents' family, is flooded with emotion. The level of conflict and reactivity is so high, and the involvement of the family members in one another's lives so pervasive, either in being needy or in taking care of others, that they have little opportunity to set a considered course for their lives. Often people are determined to behave differently from their parents but instead repeat a pattern from their own family. Mrs. Swain was caught in her father's desire for closeness and in her mother's dependency on her to manage the house and children. She chose to stay in the family at a time when others were in a transition to independent living through college or moving out on their own.

The balance between emotional neediness and goal-oriented thoughtfulness determines a person's level of differentiation of self. This is not the same as social position or prestige in work, although those factors may be a part of the life of a more differentiated person. It is instead a framework for thinking broadly about a person's life and his or her overall ability to function in physical, emotional, intellectual, and relationship areas.

Courtship—A Doorway into Relationship Patterns

In courtship, two people test each other's ability to meet their emotional needs. They enter the relationship as separate individuals, but as time goes on, each "invests" in the other, or gives up some part of his or her identity for the relationship. Those who are fleeing their own families will begin the courtship process expecting that their partners will compensate for the deficiencies in their own families. People whose lives are more stable and self-directed have less desire to find validation in another.

Often in courtship, attraction is based on finding a complementary relationship with one's partner. One who is shy can be smitten by the outgoing, confident manner of the other. One partner connects to the strong, capable nature of the other, while the other finds fulfillment in being protective.

When they first meet, people have the ability to be more emotionally free with one another, to be relatively tolerant and accepting of the problems of their partner. In fact, what is attractive or appealing about the partner in the initial stages of the relationship may become problematic and difficult in the course of marriage.

The use of alcohol fits into this framework. Although many families experience drinking negatively, in others it serves to promote the viability of the relationship system. To a point, alcohol eases tensions and is a connector in relationships; warm and intimate moments are shared over a glass of wine. Only at a later time, when a person's use of alcohol becomes a chronic coping mechanism does it begin to contribute more tension and problems to the relationship than it serves to allay. For example, before they married, Mrs. Swain and her husband drank together, enjoying the social aspect. She did not experience the negative effects of his drinking because she did not depend on him on a day-to-day basis.

People Marry Those with Similar Levels of Differentiation

The emotional patterns most central to a person's life in his or her own family of origin will repeat with some variation in important adult relationships such as marriage or raising children. A person separating from the intensity of his or her original family reconnects with the same emotional charge to his or her nuclear family, although he or she may believe that the future spouse is entirely different from the family of origin.

A person marries a spouse with "an equal level of differentiation"—a similar need for attachment in the relationship and at the same approximate level of ability to achieve a balanced and productive life.

This is sometimes an unsettling idea. In many families, one spouse is more functional, creative, responsible, efficient, conscientious, or outgoing than the other. In some marriages, one spouse is psychotic, alcoholic, depressed, or otherwise clearly operating beneath the capabilities of his or her partner. For example, the Swains appeared to function at different levels when they first came in for therapy: Mrs. Swain was capable and efficient, while Mr. Swain was alcoholic and abusive.

Many professionals focus on identifying and treating the sick partner without recognizing his or her place in the equilibrium of the family system. Knowing the spouses have similar levels of differentiation removes the focus and blame from either and recognizes that each contributes to the emotional patterns in the family. Two people enter a long-term relationship with a similar kind of expectation for emotional closeness—a mutual degree of need for emotional investment in the other.

When they first met, Mrs. Swain had graduated from high school and had taken the job where she worked while living at home. Mr. Swain was in graduate school at the time. He was the older son in a family in which the father was described as distant. He had been married previously, but the marriage had ended after eighteen months "due to his drinking," according to his first wife's account.

Looking back, Mrs. Swain thought, and her husband agreed, that his drinking constituted alcoholic behavior in the days of their courtship. They dated for three years before he decided that he was ready to marry. They set a date for the marriage, but he did not come to the ceremony, and they postponed the wedding for several months.

The clarity and objectivity of an individual's thinking about his or her life has a context in the stability of the relationship system. Conversely, a high level of emotion in a family can distort an objective view of relationships; a person can be propelled by the intensity of a chaotic family into a relationship that has not been carefully evaluated.

When she met her husband, Mrs. Swain was bound by, yet fleeing, the emotional strictures of her family. Her reliance on her father was an emotional pull to remain in the family in which conflict and lack of organization reigned. As the oldest daughter, she was a stabilizing force both to her father and to the organization of the household, as her teenage siblings were in constant difficulty.

Mrs. Swain had a yearning for attachment when she met her future husband. She saw in her husband, despite his drinking and her knowledge that it had ended his first marriage, a strong person who was capable of making decisions. The support she sought in Mr. Swain was familiar—she could lean on him much as she had on her father.

Mrs. Swain entered the marriage already accustomed to relating to important people in her life who had drinking problems. Despite his alcohol use, her father was an emotional pillar to her. She did not "cause" her husband's drinking, but she did willingly enter a permanent relationship in which it was openly acknowledged. Later, when she commented on his being drunk, he retorted, "You knew my drinking was a problem when you married me." As in many families with alcoholism, Mr. Swain was addicted to alcohol before his wife met him. Each person carries into a marriage a level of immaturity and problems that are related to unresolved attachment to one's family of origin.

So Mr. and Mrs. Swain found a "fit"—each fulfilled unmet needs of the other in the courtship. They established an intricate balance of dependence on each other: Mrs. Swain looked to her husband for leadership and relief from the burdens of her own family, while he attached to her competence and patient tolerance of his irresponsible behavior.

Fusion or the Ties That Bind

Marriage binds and intensifies the emotional patterns that first attract partners to each other. In a day-to-day relationship over time, partners become sensitive and reactive to the thoughts and actions that may have drawn them to each other initially. The more intensely a person seeks to fill the emotional deficits of the other or to have another shore up his or her life, the more fused the marriage relationship becomes.

During the ten years of their marriage, the relationship between Mrs. Swain and her husband changed. Mr. Swain's drinking increased; he became involved with other women and was physically violent; and conflict arose between them.

When individuals with high levels of need for togetherness marry, each partner invests increasing levels of "self" in the other. This fusion becomes more binding as they share the day-to-day responsibilities of managing their lives, children, and careers. They no longer have the emotional freedom to be themselves as they did in courtship. Spouses assume they know what the other thinks, and they begin to behave based on how they think the other will react. They become dependent on each other so that each has difficulty charting his or her own goals. One feels swallowed up by the relationship; the other is drained by it. Some couples begin to look alike physically as the years pass. One spouse may begin explaining viewpoints using the imperial "we" or conversely, by taking an automatic position of disagreement.

The desire for emotional closeness in marriage is influenced by a person's relationship system in his or her own family. People who are fleeing their families will have a very high degree of investment in their spouses and children. They expect the marriage to meet emotional deficits from their own families, but instead find they have married someone with a similar level of neediness. They may become disappointed, lonely, and depressed and experience conflict with their spouses or look to their children for emotional satisfaction.

Pattern of Over/Underfunctioning

In times of crisis, a family can develop a certain adaptability that allows necessary tasks to be transferred from one member to another. This shift can be a mark of flexibility in the family. However, when one member progressively drops responsible functioning, and other members take on what belongs to that member, then a "tilt" develops. With couples, this leaves one in a dysfunctional and the other in a strong position. Although neither of these positions is comfortable, this balance becomes a way of handling the connection between them. One is helpless, the other caretaking. As this tilt becomes progressively more marked, the tension in the family rises, with continual difficulties with the problem member. A spiral of anxiety is created, which pushes the tilt in the balance of over- and underfunctioning in the relationship.

The Swain's marriage illustrated the melding together of their identities so that each was highly sensitive and responsive to the neediness of the other. Mr. Swain was physically violent, absent from the family, financially irresponsible, and negligent of the children's safety when he was drunk. Mrs. Swain alternated between anger and caretaking but could never clearly define a position in response to his behavior. When he was not drunk, she did not want to create conflict or discuss the problems they were experiencing. Although numerous people had told her to leave the marriage, she could not conceptualize how she would cope, even though she worked the more consistently of the two. This is often the dilemma addressed in alcoholic and violent marriages—the identities of the couple are so fused that neither can think about the possibility of separation from the other.

When the Swains married, Mrs. Swain saw her husband as the leader in their relationship. He made decisions about the finances, and he set the emotional tone in the relationship. However, over time, they began to interact with each other in ways that were characteristic of their positions in their own families. In the course of the marriage, Mr. Swain increasingly acted out the role of the irresponsible son. Behavior associated with drinking escapades eroded his accountability. He drank at the office; he drove the car while intoxicated; he did not come home for several days at a time. Mrs. Swain responded to this irresponsibility as she had in her parents' marriage: she shouldered the burdens in the family as he dropped them. The complementarity in the marriage shifted in character. She became "stronger" as he became more unaccountable.

In the tilting of the marital relationship, each side has a part to play—the problem person acts powerless, and the responsible one treats him or her as helpless. One is adaptive, looking to the spouse for strength and capability. The other partner is sensitive to the spouse's weakness. The adaptive one donates self to the one who looks capable. It is as if a certain fluidity exists in the relationship, transferring basic functioning from one spouse to the other.

Each member of a family who functions at an optimum level directs and manages his or her own life. A person taking on another's responsibilities may appear to be a superfunctioner, but in the process, he or she gives up fulfilling his or her own creative potential. Nevertheless, in many marriages, there is a disparity in the level of differentiation between the spouses.

As one spouse becomes more capable, the other is "let off the hook" to drink and act irresponsibly. The dilemma and the challenge for the overfunctioning partner is to find a position that is not accountable to the other, but allows him or her to meet responsibilities in the family and to the self. As Mrs. Swain explained when she considered divorce, she saw her husband as a helpless, irresponsible, yet abusive child.

In families with alcoholism, there are several factors that lock the over/underfunctioning into place and intensify the process of donating and borrowing of self. Over time, the general course of problem drinking takes a toll on the physical and neurological substructure of a person. Blackout, memory losses, unreasonable fear, as well as physical problems such as high blood pressure, sexual problems, and cirrhosis of the liver are consequences of alcohol consumption. Alcohol also reduces the ability to think clearly and be goal-directed, and this too intensifies over time.

There is a cohesiveness in many families with alcoholism. The paradox of the process in over/underfunctioning is that although there is a significant "problem" in the drinker, it is a stable pattern in a family. Many would underestimate the durability of these marriages. For example, there is a recognized frustration in emergency rooms and police stations because wives of alcoholic men often do not press charges against their husbands after they have been physically assaulted.

A problem develops in one member as part of an interactional process in a family unit. A systems view is based on the premise that addiction is interwoven into the relationship system, of each spouse in his or her own family and of their interaction together, and is an essential ingredient in the equilibrium in a family. It is not the "cause" of the family's problems per se, but it does become a focus for anxiety as the family interacts and relates around one person's alcoholism. Each spouse has a part to play in the over- and underfunctioning. To view one as the victim and the other as the problem is simply to reflect the family process.

Shift in Family Patterns with Sobriety

The accuracy of the view that a person's addiction is interwoven in the family's emotional life is revealed when the alcoholic becomes sober. A change in the behavior of the alcoholic, especially when it is a step toward a more functional, defined self, can temporarily throw the whole family off balance.

In relation to the tilt in the relationship, the overfunctioning spouse is in balance with the underfunctioner; they are complementary. When the alcoholic stops drinking and becomes more in charge of his or her life, an emotional shift takes place in the family. The tilt in the marriage begins to move with the "recovery process" of the person with alcoholism. If the spouse cannot refocus his or her own life, the couple may end up in conflict and/or separation. This transitional period is often more stressful for both spouses than the original patterns of alcoholic drinking.

The predictable reaction of a spouse to an alcoholic who is not drinking is to become highly anxious. Spouses often describe this reaction as "walking on eggshells." Some will comment that they were more comfortable when their spouse was drinking, as they knew what to expect. They describe the fear of the new unknown relationship as more intense than their fear of the problems encountered from the drinking. Many have somatic problems and depression. Mrs. Swain stated that once, when problems in her marriage had mounted to crisis proportions, her husband agreed to go for counseling and stopped drinking for six months. She said that this was one of the most difficult periods of her life; she felt constant pressure to be the person her husband wanted her to be in exchange for his not drinking.

A person's sense of self is challenged at many levels when one member changes his or her behavior in a family: One's identity is threatened when one is no longer needed in the same way; the sense of predictability of how one relates to others in the family is altered; the way one experiences closeness—perhaps through conflict or the honeymoon nondrinking periods—and the methods of defining one's space through distancing into silence or alcohol are changed. If one has grown up with alcoholism in one's family of origin, then sobriety in a spouse challenges one to respond differently in many areas of one's life. Patterns of connecting, of processing emotions, and of creating boundaries in a relationship are recreated in different forms and configurations that are new, challenging, and disturbing.

Shift in a Family Creates Anxiety

The strain that develops in a family when the alcoholic has stopped drinking is an indication of how the family's anxiety was absorbed by its focus on the drinking behavior. Certainly, the drinker creates concerns through his or her behavior. At the same time, by becoming preoccupied with the problems of the alcoholic, family members do not manage the issues and dilemmas of their own lives. The drinker becomes the sponge for family anxiety. When he or she stops drinking and becomes more responsible, it is as if the tension is pumped back into the rest of the family.

Family members are vulnerable to other symptoms at this time. The alcoholic may be getting support and gratification from a treatment program or self-help group. While he or she is working on sobriety in a "fellowship" of like-minded recovering alcoholics, the family, on the other hand, is confronted with the reality that the drinking did not cause all the problems among them and that new difficulties are arising.

When anxiety is high in a family, problems will emerge in one of the spouses, in the family's overfocus on a child, or in marital conflict. There are few families that do not experience one of these when someone stops drinking. The reaction may be as minor as the wife being depressed, perhaps not feeling she has an important place in the family life. In other families when the drinker becomes more operational, the other spouse collapses. It is almost as if his or her life course was stabilized by his or her focus on the alcoholic. Thus, the tilt in the marriage tips in the other direction.

The family may also try to refocus the problem onto the alcoholic who has not really changed or has not changed enough. They may find they liked him or her better when he or she was drinking and was more firm or less irritable. For example, a son may openly voice the desire for his father to drink, as the family begins to focus its attention on the son's marijuana use.

However, the most common area of problems for families with a non-drinking alcoholic is marital conflict and divorce. Alcoholics Anonymous (AA) has estimated that 75 percent of its members are divorced and that the majority divorce after the alcoholic becomes sober. Separation and divorce after sobriety are, at face value, paradoxical. Most divorces are initiated by the recovering alcoholic, and there are many explanations. "My sobriety came first" is one. Another is that "both of us were sick when I was drinking. I got well, she didn't." Or "When I stopped drinking, I had the courage to get out." Yet, whatever the explanation of the process, the homeostasis of the family has been unbalanced by the change in the alcoholic. It is as if one-half of the seesaw moved, leaving the other side suspended in midair. The alcoholic establishes more boundaries for self in the relationship, without a corresponding shift in the spouse. In a sense, the overfunctioning spouse cannot "give back" his or her borrowed share of responsibility for functioning to a sober spouse without lapsing into problems himself or herself. The marriage can become unbalanced and break apart.

From a systems view, a problem so pervasive as addiction is only one part of the complicated web of a family's life. Like the tip of an iceberg, substance use is what meets the eye when one first observes the interactions of the family. It is dynamic and absorbing and tends to take the focus off the reactions and life course of the rest of the family.

The most important ingredient in working toward a balanced, functioning family is the ability of each member to take responsibility for the course of his or her own life. To do this, each person must find a way to defocus from the intensity and the neediness of the alcoholic and be in charge of his or her own life in as thoughtful and mature a way as possible. One direction for this work is to better understand how the relationship system in one's own family has played a part in the overall intensity and patterns of relating that have influenced the choices one has made in life.

MULTIGENERATIONAL PROCESS
AND THE TRANSMISSION OF PATTERNS
IN THE RELATIONSHIP SYSTEM

Over thousands of years of evolution, humans reproduced not only genetic similarities in their descendants, but also ways of relating in families and tribes that ensured their survival and the success of their offspring. The emotional forces transmitted from one generation to another are powerful molders of a person's development and attachments to others. The relationship system, which is an expression of the deepest connections among people, is the vehicle for the transmission of differentiation from one generation to the next. That is, a person's overall capabilities, as well as his or her problems, have a context in the formative relationships in his or her life.

Relationships in the family are a forge for one's emotional life and level of functioning that are expressed in the patterns and themes central to one's life. Although individuals seek to make conscious choices about their lives, many of their reactions are feeling responses programmed at an automatic level in their families of origin. For example, a mother may find that she is using admonitions with her child that she heard from her own mother, even though she vowed she would raise her child differently.

The concept of differentiation is of overriding importance in understanding the transmission of patterns across generations. The overall level of emotional maturity in a family is passed on in varying degrees to the next generation. When emotionality in a family is focused on a particular child, he or she is less capable of developing a carefully considered life direction and is more vulnerable to physical, emotional, and addiction problems. At the same time, those families with more chronic anxiety and lower levels of differentiation will in general have a multitude of more serious problems, in which addiction can play a role. The relationship system carries dysfunction such as alcoholism from one generation to the next, although patterns repeated across generations are much broader and more complex than a particular problem.

Over time, Mrs. Swain was the person most motivated to examine her reactivity, her positions in her nuclear and extended families, and the emotional patterns of her life. She began to reach out to friends, talk to her father about her situation, and examine her choices in responding to her husband. She began to recognize how she allowed him to set the tone for the relationship. She made a plan for her actions when he was violent, which she told him about in advance. This allowed her to be less afraid of discussing her concerns with him. He became interested that she was reacting differently; he stopped drinking and came to counseling sessions with her, although their relationship became more conflictual. Therefore, in a paradoxical manner, working toward more individuality can lead to a more balanced, mature relationship.

Although this idea seems fairly simplistic and perhaps obvious, it is difficult to keep the relationship system rather than specific problems in focus when thinking about the recurrence of themes across generations. Often people can observe that a problem, such as cancer or diabetes, reappears in succeeding generations of a family. Certainly, professionals in the field of addiction readily accept that alcoholism runs in families. However, it is more difficult to conceptualize that the relationship system, in which the alcoholism is generated, is actually what is being replicated.

The tendency to view a repeating problem such as addiction as genetically based is common in the medical profession today. However, more and more questions are being asked about the emotional components of the reappearance across generations of hypertension, heart attacks, diabetes, and even cancer. Addiction is a repeating pattern in families, but it has so many facets that the idea that it is exclusively a product of genetic transmission will probably always be challenged.

The relationship system, which is an expression of the basic level of differentiation in a family, is a broader framework for understanding the repeated patterns that are transmitted from generation to generation. The theme of relating through addiction is one way a family's emotional life is organized from one generation to the next. The use of substances becomes an integral part and even a regulator of the members' interactions, while drawing the focus away from underlying issues in the family. Addiction both reflects and influences the emotional life of a family across generations.

There were several important multigenerational themes in the Swain family. Mrs. Swain was an example of one of the intriguing aspects of a multigenerational theme—the daughter of an alcoholic marrying an alcoholic.

The development of alcoholism and attachment to an alcoholic are two facets of an emotional pattern—complimentary positions that are reenacted in succeeding generations. Mrs. Swain brought some of the unresolved emotional dilemmas from her own family into her marriage. The closeness to her father, despite his drinking, and the impact on her life of the conflict with her mother were important influences on the formation of her identity. These relationships formed a context for the choice of her marital partner and her functioning in her adult nuclear family.

The Functional Role of Addiction in the Family

Addiction is a process in an individual that is inextricably bound to the relationship system of a family. One member's addiction becomes a part of characteristic patterns of relating in a family and a regulator of their interactions across generations.

Addiction Creates a Focus for the Family

Addiction is a unifier for family members who can agree that the "problem" is the alcoholic. Focusing on the drinker gives family members an excuse not to concentrate on their own lives. The life of the family gets "caught" in the emotions surrounding the addiction. Becoming absorbed in another's dysfunction allows a person to deny his or her own feelings of neediness, providing the illusion that he or she is managing his or her own life.

Some people only recognize how much their lives are governed by the addiction when the addicted person has stopped the addictive behavior. Mrs. Swain described the depression she experienced about six months into her husband's abstinence: "What I realize now," she said, "is that when I don't worry about him, I question my sense of self, of who I am."

Using Substances Regulates Distance and Closeness in a Family

There are many mechanisms to avoid or promote closeness in relationships. Watching football, having an affair, and working long hours are a few of the ways to regulate distance in a relationship. Mood-altering substances have a unique role in this human process. First, when a person is high, they can be physically present but emotionally absent. They are "tuned out." Sometimes they do not even remember being present. For some, drinking is an outlet for being both emotionally and physically distant.

At the same time, addiction provides a tie to the family. Often the user is quite dependent on others for his or her basic needs, unable to function without the support of the family. Yet at the surface level, he or she appears removed and distant. This is a pattern that is repeated with variations across generations. For example, Mr. Swain, who was raised by a father who was absent due to his preoccupation with work, was equally distant from his family through drinking.

The Family Lives in a Predictable Chaos

What appears to an outside observer to be chaos can have an underlying stability for the family. Although a family is living from crisis to crisis, what is consistent is the way the members are oriented toward solving problems. The addiction can serve to absorb chronic anxiety and has a stabilizing effect on the family unit.

Turmoil is a predictable pattern that leaves an imprint on family life. Children who grow up in this situation find existence confusing or boring when emotions are calmer. They are used to running on adrenaline, and often their self-esteem is bound up with their ability to cope with crises and to manage a chaotic home life. This functions to prevent them from being aware of their own desires and needs as adults.

Alcoholism or Drug Dependency Can Be a Marker of Over- and Underfunctioning in a Family

A person who is dependent on others can further that position in the family by using mood-altering substances. As the dependency develops, other family members take on more responsibility, with the user becoming more helpless.

A child who grows up feeling responsible for maintaining the stability of the family will likely repeat this in important relationships in his or her adult life. A family member can be trained to be a "helper," as much as a person who develops addiction learns to be dependent and helpless. The addiction in the family allows each to repeat a pattern of relating from his or her childhood.

A Person Consumes Alcohol or Drugs to Feel More Independent or Separate, but the Use Serves to Increase the Dependency on the Family

This is most usefully illustrated by an adolescent in a transition from family life to independence. When a child has difficulty establishing his or her own identity, he or she can turn to drugs or alcohol to feel more "grown up." The child is not conforming to the parents' expectations, so he or she sees himself or herself as self-reliant. But the use of a substance undercuts the ability to direct one's own life. Often the teenager does not leave home but remains dependent on the parents, although distant and involved with his or her peers. The paradox remains: although he or she "feels" alcohol and drug use contribute to his or her maturity, they actually serve to block a well-planned exit from the family.

Sometimes, as with Mr. Swain, the route to independence is to transfer the dependency on parents to the relationship with a spouse. Here the chords of caretaking and neediness are played out with only slight variations from the family of origin.

Alcoholism Is a Marker of Emotional Intensity in a Family

Addiction can be a marker of emotional intensity in a family. It can arise in a family in the impaired member, who is most affected by the family's anxiety and least capable of individuating a self. It can also affect the person who is most sensitive and responsive to the difficulties in the family. Often this person may appear quite functional, but his or her life is built around compensating for the deficiencies in others, to the point that he or she becomes "used up." Alcohol tends to shore up these individuals.

Rarely is addiction a random occurrence; it is rather a reflection of the emotional process in a family. Substance abuse is woven into the fabric of the relationship system, which is based on the level of differentiation transmitted from one generation to the next. When addiction is absent in a generation, similar emotional patterns are reproduced through different themes.

In many families, patterns "flip-flop" across generations. A highly competent parent may have an irresponsible child who does not have room to develop his or her own independent, competent identity. This child, as a parent, may produce an overresponsible offspring in the next generation.

Mr. Swain's family has an element of this "flip-flop." Although he was the oldest brother in that family, his behavior did not reflect that characteristic position. He was irresponsible and acted out as a teenager, beginning to drink in his early teens, although he finished graduate school and worked in a responsible job. His mother had worried about his behavior for many years, but never had the ability to address the issue with him in a forceful way.

Focusing on the functional role of addiction in a family is different from an interpretation that a family is "sick" or "needs to suffer." Rather it is an attempt to study the facts of the relationship system to better observe the multigenerational patterns that are lived out by the family members.

Sibling Position

One theoretical concept useful in understanding emotional patterns is the role of sibling position in a family constellation. Walter Toman (1961) has researched and written extensively on sibling position. He states that the development of each child is influenced by his or her order of birth into a family.

The oldest child is the first person to enter the emotional space of the parents so this child spends his or her first few years as the only focus of both parents—they have more time and emotional energy for this child than when subsequent children are vying for their attention.

Oldest children are followed by younger, more helpless siblings. The elder brother grows up as the leader and protector, while caretaking and managing younger siblings often falls to the oldest sister. The youngest, on the other hand, is raised in a family always having stronger and more capable siblings to help and protect him or her. Youngest children may be viewed as "babies" in their families their entire lives.

The family diagram of the Swain family indicates the sibling position of each member. Mrs. Swain was the oldest daughter in her family. She stated that her parents had wanted to marry for five years but were unable to do so because of financial difficulties. Being the first child, the eldest daughter, was a crucial fact in shaping Mrs. Swain's life.

Toman (1961) constructed portraits of each sibling position that are fascinatingly accurate. The general conclusion from his research is that the birth order in a family shapes a person's personality and molds his or her choice of marriage partners and friends.

In every family, birth position as well as important life events in the family at the birth of a child affect the child's development, such as the child being handicapped or ill or the sex of the child being significant to the family. In families where stress or anxiety is high, these factors have a heightened influence.

In families with an alcoholic parent, the characteristics of birth position are somewhat skewed. The oldest daughter is particularly important in a family in which the parents are not shouldering their responsibilities. This child may be pushed to a superresponsible position if one or both parents are immature or absorbed in life's problems. When a father is drinking, the eldest son may inherit the mantle of a family's leadership responsibilities at an early age.

On the other hand, when anxiety is high, the child may not fulfill a birth position in a characteristic way. The oldest may be needy and helpless, and a younger sibling may take on a more responsible position. The most frequent sibling position for people who develop alcoholism is as the youngest child, but the next most vulnerable is the oldest.

Sometimes in a family it is useful to understand how a child does not function in a way that is typical for his or her sibling position. This can often be a clue to the intensity and focus of the emotional forces in the family. For example, Mr. Swain is an oldest brother who did not act responsibly or with leadership in his family. Compensating for the distant stance of his father, he was constantly nagged and protected by his mother. He responded rebelliously, developing a drinking problem in his early teens. Although at times he was fastidious about his work, his general capabilities were undercut by his alcoholism. His becoming so dependent on his wife—not typical of an eldest sibling—is a reflection of the level of emotional attachment in his own family.

Sibling position is one factor that can influence a person's reactions and choices in life. Being a concrete part of a person's experience in a relationship system, birth order affects how an individual relates to his or her children and the way themes develop through the generations. However, the level of emotional intensity and overall functioning of the family are also important ingredients in how sibling position plays a role in family life. No one concept alone of Bowen family systems theory explains the full complexity of relationship patterns across generations.

An individual's life is one moment in the course of a family's history and experience that is generations in the making. The more a person views himself or herself as a product of that process and begins to understand what has contributed to the relationship patterns across generations, the more he or she can begin to make responsible decisions about his or her own life.

Bowen family systems theory provides a means for looking beneath the surface of human interactions to study the relationship process across generations. To begin to observe patterns of interacting, to think about the function of a problem in a family's life, to integrate how events such as birth order have a knowable, perhaps even predictable, outcome over the generations provides a context for a person to make informed and objective choices about overwhelming and emotionally charged issues. A person can widen the lens beyond his or her personal experience and reactions to the broad flow of a family's life of which he or she is one small fragment.

ALCOHOL AND DRUGS: REGULATORS OF EMOTIONAL DISTANCE AND CLOSENESS

One of the basic questions of human existence is how a person maintains a connection to and a separateness from important others in a relationship system.

The emotional dependence of the offspring of warm-blooded creatures has been a cornerstone of survival throughout evolutionary history. Some instinctual maternal forces of attachment are stirred when a child is in the uterus, and the family bonds that are built in childhood are the most powerful forces that a person encounters in his or her lifetime.

A child's attachment to his or her mother, created out of a biological need to survive, forms the core around which other formative relationships with the father, siblings, and grandparents are built. The human young, in contrast to many mammalian species, spend two decades in a dependent position in which they learn the necessary emotional, social, and life skills to survive on their own, mate, and reproduce. In general, the ability to sustain a relationship with a primary caretaker is a prerequisite for emotional stability and balance in adulthood.

However, in the process of maturation, a child moves progressively toward independence and to greater definition of self. This is not a denial of the importance of the attachment, but a recognition of the necessity to carve out an identity, separate and distinct from the parents.

Distancing from Emotional Intensity

In families with high levels of emotional intensity, the partners may lose their individuality in the relationship. They become so interdependent, so fused, that one backs away from the closeness so as not to be suffocated by the emotional demands of the other. To carve out a sense of self in their lives, they move away from the charged atmosphere in their family. Dependency is denied by distancing from those on whom they are dependent. Many who think themselves "independent" from their families often experience a retriggering of reactions from their childhood years upon returning home.

When a person is distant, he or she is often perceived by others as "unemotional" or not involved. However, distancing is an indicator of precisely how sensitive and how caught the person is in the emotional life of the family. A father may appear removed from family life, but this may be his way of reacting to his wife's involvement with the children. A teenager may distance from his or her parents into his or her peer group as a means to establish an identity separate from the parents. The desire to distance confirms just how important the others are in the emotional life of an individual.

The human has devised innumerable ways to distance in the face of emotionality. Many people separate from emotionally charged relationships through geographic distance. For example, one man who was highly successful professionally thought that living in Australia was a comfortable distance from his mother, who lived in New York. People can distance through work, other relationships, and mood-altering substances.

Distancing Through Conflict

Distancing is a mechanism for establishing boundaries for self to diminish sensitivity to the reactions of others. In marriage, each partner becomes overwhelmed by the intensity of the emotions in the relationship and can only preserve a sense of identity by maintaining a remoteness from the other. However, when carried to an extreme, a distant position challenges the bonds that keep a marriage intact. Conflict can become a vehicle for maintaining contact, however destructive or problematic. A common pattern is a heated conflict, resulting in a distant separateness that is resolved by another conflict. However, this process presents a problem itself. When one person moves toward another, his or her sense of separateness crumbles, and the couple is again overcome by intense emotion and the need for distance.

The Swains maintained contact through conflict that escalated to physical, violent confrontation. Their arguments became the means to touch an emotional nerve in the relationship. Although fights were painful, they became a recognition of the bond that existed in the marriage—that tie which provides the glue for so many marriages in which there is alcoholism.

Mrs. Swain described how she did not always believe what her husband said during their arguments, but still, it was the only time her husband talked with her. She in turn found the conflict to be an arena in which she could vent the frustration and anger that developed when he was away from home or passed out after dinner.

In some families, as perhaps with Mrs. Swain, people grow up experiencing conflict as a routine part of everyday life. They are used to connecting with others at high levels of emotional intensity. The challenge for these couples is to maintain their emotional connection without the cycling of conflict and distance.

Drinking As a Regulator of Connection in the Marriage

In some marriages, the alcoholic partner goes through periods of drinking and nondrinking. This cycle can parallel the regulation of distance and closeness in the relationship. Periodically Mr. Swain would curtail his drinking, and Mrs. Swain would describe him as "another person." The closeness she experienced in these brief periods kept her interested in maintaining the marriage. Families describe these periods as the "honeymoon" times, when the alcoholic spouse is eager to please, loving, and sometimes contrite over problems created by the drinking. These periods of nondrinking were in sharp contrast to Mr. Swain's violent and angry outbursts or his absence from home when he was drinking. During drinking periods, Mrs. Swain shut down emotionally so as not to be involved in the "craziness" of his drinking.

What was difficult for Mrs. Swain to contemplate was that this brief closeness and the drinking episodes were all part of the same emotional process in the marriage. She saw her husband as "two people," and she worked to recapture the times of communication and calm by being as helpful to her husband as possible. For some couples, periods of nondrinking are times of conflict in which one spouse communicates the problems and frustrations they have accumulated during the episodes of drinking.

Substance Abuse As a Buffer to Closeness

Alcohol and other substances that are abused serve the role of emotional buffers in a family. In the course of marriage, spouses often look to the other for more closeness; each is seeking to meet needs that were unresolved in his or her own family. Yet the more one seeks emotional gratification from a needy other, the less one receives. Each submerges "self" in the other, and the partners become fused, with little space for their own identities. In this context, drinking becomes a buffer to overcloseness; it provides the drinker with a sense of escape from the relationship and his or her own problems, temporarily offering a sense of emotional space.

Yet drinking also creates many other problems, including alienating the other spouse. Often the drinker will stop for a period after a crisis to move toward the spouse, creating the "honeymoon" period. But the closeness and the drinking are two faces of the relationship, which together are an overall attempt to regulate a comfortable level of distance in the marriage. The distance maintains the ability of each in the couple to preserve a sense of his or her own boundaries and not be swallowed up by the other.

Abstinence As Redefinition of Boundaries in Relationships

Drugs and alcohol provide emotional space temporarily; in the long run, they create more dependency on others. When a person stops using drugs or alcohol, he or she must grapple with losing the connection that is fostered by dependency. "Recovery" is a process of becoming more responsible for self and less reliant on others. Yet in losing the altered state created by substances, one also loses the buffers in the relationships in one's life and can become sensitive and overwhelmed by the emotions of the family. Abstaining from alcohol and drugs shifts the patterns of connection in the family. Paradoxically, the family may experience more distance in the relationships, as the alcoholic's swings between closeness and conflict become less pronounced. The side effects of the drug use create fewer difficulties, but the couple loses the special times of making up after the problems, as they did in the past.

What the couple is experiencing is the redefining of boundaries of self in the relationship. The "recovering" alcoholic usually is focused on rebuilding his or her life without drinking. This effort for self can be perceived as an emotional movement away from the family. For some people in recovery, AA becomes another family, a set of relationships that are more comfortable and accepting than the family. Others distance through work or other relationships.

It is important to remember that the couple maintained an emotional connection through cycles of drinking and nondrinking and the intertwining themes of conflict and distance. Many professionals wonder at the solidity of marriages in which one partner has an addiction. Yet the spouses have worked out a way to be connected through the drinking, albeit it with destructive and problematic side effects. A balance in the intensity of this connection is worked out through distancing, whether through alcohol or in other ways.

The Concepts of Differentiation, Detachment, and Distance

One of the important ideas of Al-Anon is detachment. The goal of detachment is to focus on oneself and one's own goals and to not react to the behavior and mood swings of the alcoholic. The purpose of detachment is to be more defined about who one is, and less responsive to the drinker's ability to dictate the emotional tone of the family.

For many people, this effort to be nonreactive becomes difficult to distinguish from distancing. Certainly, the two may look similar to an outsider or be experienced similarly in the family for a period of time. However, there are some basic differences.

Distancing is a mechanism to preserve one's sense of identity in the face of emotionality. As a chronic solution to emotions and issues in family life, it leads one to tolerate and prolong problems that exist. It is also a regulating mechanism for unresolved emotional attachment in the family. Detachment, on the other hand, is a conscious process of nonreaction to these same issues and problems, with the goal of defining one's position in relation to them. Distancing is a retreat from emotionally laden issues to preserve self. Detachment is a defining of self, who one is and what one believes, in relationship to these same issues and can be a step in the process of differentiation in a family.

Mrs. Swain discussed the difference for her in her marriage. At one point, her husband had hit her during a disagreement, and she had a black eye. In the past, when physical violence erupted, she withdrew from the relationship emotionally and sexually until he came to her and persuaded her to become involved in the relationship again. However, she feared this cycle of violence, withdrawal, and rapprochement.

In a subsequent episode when he became physically abusive, she thought about how to establish a position without distancing from the relationship. She decided to tell him that if he hit her again she would press charges against him. This was her stand, but at the same time, she did not withdraw from the relationship as she had in the past. She did not react to his anger, and she continued to communicate with him. This decision to take a position, but continue to relate, was perceived by her husband as a difference in her that he did not like, but respected. As she maintained a firm, but calm, position, he decided to make some changes himself.

Distancing is a regulator for anxiety generated by emotional attachment. Pulling away from suffocating relationships, through alcohol, drugs, or a myriad of other mechanisms, is simply a confirmation of their power. One's emotional life becomes guided by avoiding charged relationships rather than a determined and thoughtful effort to be a more defined individual.

Differentiation, on the other hand, entails an effort to better understand the reactivity that causes a person to flee a relationship. A person who seeks self-definition attempts to become knowledgeable about the emotional patterns of his or her relationship system and how he or she is caught in them. Those who can work at establishing and maintaining an identity while remaining connected to important others have an increased ability to direct their lives. The boundaries of self are defined by decisions and choices based on their values and beliefs rather than the reactions to their relationship system. The ability to manage one's reactions and to defocus from the behavior of another, which is addressed in the idea of detachment, is a stepping stone in that effort to become more of a person in one's own right.

FAMILY SYSTEMS THEORY
AS A CONTEXT FOR CHANGE

What is a systems view of change in a family? How does a consultant sit with a person or a family group to allow everyone to function optimally? How does a therapist do his best thinking theoretically, with an eye on the way his emotions are caught in the dilemmas of the family?

Bowen family systems theory has a relevance in two separate, but connected, arenas of therapy. The first arena is the clinician and his or her self-management; the second is the family's increased understanding of their interactions and each person's ability to set of life course that is consistent with his or her values.

Theory is a frame of reference for understanding a family's difficulties, as well as a guide for the ways a therapist can become snared by his or her emotions. The anxiety of the family operates as both a motivator and a barrier to change, and the more the therapist can negotiate his or her way through their emotions based on principles, the more he or she becomes a resource for them in their journey to responsible functioning.

The Therapist's Management of Self
in the Process of Therapy

Theory as a Guide to the Therapist's Emotional Functioning

The ideas of Bowen family systems theory pertain to all relationship systems, including that of the therapist to the individual or family in a session. Therapists' knowledge of their own emotional functioning is an essential ingredient in the outcome of their interactions with a family.

Professionals intersect with the life of a family during a particular crisis, at a time when its natural resilience is eroded. Family members are seeking a respite from a flood of anxious reactivity and related symptoms. Therapists have a choice in responding to the anxiety of a family. They can become a part of its emotional system, reacting to members' neediness by helping them or intervening in their difficulties. Also, they can develop the ability to think from theory, while being in contact with their emotions—a path that provides the family with more choices in how members react and interact with one another.

From the viewpoint of traditional, individual theory, the process of forming a relationship with a person triggers a transference or an attachment to the therapist based on earlier, primary bonds in a person's life. This transference becomes the source of insight and interpretation for the course of therapy. The therapist reacts with a countertransference, based on his or her own pattern of relating. The success of therapy from a psychodynamic view can be measured in the ability of the patient to use the transference and the skill of the therapist in recognizing and managing his or her countertransference.

When the focus is shifted from the individual's intrapsychic conflicts to the family's relationship system, as the context of understanding human interactions, then the position of the therapist changes. If the therapist seeks to join the relationship system of the family, he or she will be overwhelmed by the power of its emotions, and unable to manage the countertransference in the triangles with the family members.

Many therapists have a helpful background. Some come from families in which they were trained to be helpers, often in response to a problem in the family. Their advanced studies have augmented this early training by schooling them in techniques and theories that provide strategies and insight for helping people solve the dilemmas of their lives.

The anxiety of a family can trigger deeply imbedded emotions in the therapist. An oldest sister who is a therapist may find herself irritated by a wife who seems to have too many opinions or who is too judgmental of a husband who does not make decisions easily. A professional who has grown up with an alcoholic father may find a mission in reforming a father's drinking.

In the short run, the family members may use the therapist as a temporary reprieve from their interactions with one another. But in the long run, the therapist's helpfulness only serves to prolong their inability to solve their own difficulties. The professional who joins the emotional life of the family becomes part of their process rather than a vehicle to allow them to change. The goal of a systems thinker is to remain in charge of his or her own reactivity, working to stay emotionally outside of the relationship system of the family, while maintaining contact with the individuals within it.

The clinician who has taken the concepts of Bowen theory and applied them to gain a more defined and thoughtful position in his or her own family will bring an increased ability to counsel others without becoming entwined in their problems. The more the clinician has worked to differentiate a self in his or her family of origin, the freer he or she is to use thinking rather than reacting with the family. He or she will have a greater ability to avoid the most common pitfall of the profession—the effort to "help" the family find a better path based on his or her "expertise." Instead, the therapist will be working to thoughtfully manage his or her own emotions. A therapist who brings calm and directed reflection to sessions allows a family greater relief from the spiral of emotions that is fueled by automatic patterns of reacting.

The Therapist As Neutral Observer

Theoretically, a striving for neutrality on the part of the therapist will assist the family members in becoming more objective about their lives. When the therapist sits calmly with a family, not reacting to their emotions, they become more insightful and less blaming of one another. Their feelings have less control over their lives, and they are freer to objectively view their part in the family problem.

Providing an atmosphere of calm in the face of chronic upheaval and reactivity gives a family an opportunity to address long-term patterns of interacting. When the level of anxiety in a family decreases, people have more ability to think about how their relationship system has influenced the nature and direction of their life decisions.

The Understanding of Theory

Families are relationship systems that interact based on principles consistent with other systems in the natural world. Theory becomes an avenue for understanding, for making sense of what has been confusing in the life of a family, the emotions of the therapist, or the process of therapy.

The bulk of this chapter has focused on theory. Much like a Chinese puzzle, one concept does not stand alone, separate from the others, but addresses the complexity of a relationship system from a certain perspective. Triangles can only be fully understood by observing how they interlock in the larger system. The impact of birth order on an individual is intertwined with the focus of the family on a child. The development of a symptom in a family has a context in its overall level of differentiation.

The challenge for a therapist is to manage his or her own reactions, to work toward differentiation of self in his or her own family of origin, to strive to maintain objectivity in his or her clinical sessions, and to pursue an understanding of theory. These are the building blocks of solid clinical work.

The Process of Change in a Family System

Anxiety: A Source of Symptoms and a Motivator for Change

Anxiety based on life's dilemmas is a motivator for change. It is part of the human's repertoire for adaptation to the complexities of one's environment. It mobilizes the organism for action. At one level, pain, crisis, or extreme anxiety can release a family from a chronic debilitating cycle of interacting. It can propel them to take a position regarding irresponsibility in the family.

Some families are able to think about patterns, but are unable or unwilling to change them. Some self-diagnosed alcoholics will not stop drinking, and some workaholics are not interested in cutting back their work schedules. They have achieved a certain comfort in the way they handle their chronic anxiety, and they become stuck, until a crisis propels them forward by providing a motivation to change. When Mrs. Swain consulted a divorce lawyer, Mr. Swain agreed to stop drinking.

However, anxiety has another face: it can also be a constant in a family, transmitted across generations, that fuels symptoms and serves to derail a stable life course. Often the mechanisms that manage the chronic anxiety, such as drug use, a physical symptom, or focus on a child, produce more reactivity in the family. For example, drinking is an escape from the dilemmas that arise from alcohol use, which in turn creates more difficulties and tension in the family. The spiral of problems and anxious reacting produces a progression in the severity of a symptom, which is characteristic of the course of alcoholism.

There were many examples of this in the Swain family. Mr. Swain was arrested for drinking and driving. Mrs. Swain went to the jail in the middle of the night to pay the bond. He vowed he would never drink again and was contrite about his arrest, and she helped him to pay the lawyer and his fine. This crisis only served to heighten the tension in the family and to intensify the problems. When Mr. Swain returned to drinking, his usage and the anxiety in the family intensified.

Researching the Facts

One avenue to pursue neutrality is to research the life of a family across the generations. This research does not focus on how the family felt about one another, but asks questions of fact—how, what, where. A structure for organizing factual data in a family is a family diagram. This is a record of the relationship system over the generations, with pertinent information about a family, including dates of birth, death, and marriage, records of work, health, and geographical moves, as well as other significant, factual data.

A family diagram is a vehicle for exploring and understanding a person's family of origin. Constructing a three-generation chart can be a step toward more objective thinking in the face of emotionally laden issues in a person's life. A person can begin to identify with and understand better the characters of this wider system. For many people, asking about their parents and grandparents gives them a new perspective about their family. They never thought of their parents as the children of their grandparents or wondered how their parents became who they are. Facts become stepping stones out of a cauldron of confusing and overwhelming reactions.

As Mrs. Swain diagrammed the facts of her family, she realized how functioning as the eldest in her own family laid the groundwork for her managing her husband's increasingly dependent behavior. Raised as an overresponsible daughter in a family in which alcoholism was a part of the immaturity of her parents, she looked to a man for leadership, while being accustomed to shouldering a heavy load of responsibilities in the family.

Coaching a Family to Manage Its Emotions

As a person's life becomes less driven by anxious reacting, he or she is more capable of directing his or her life by principles. When a member of a family operates more calmly, other members will often function more calmly. Sometimes the neutral presence of the therapist can dampen the anxiety in the family and give members more room to think about the difficulties they face.

In every person, a reflective, mature side coexists alongside one that is wired with deep-seated emotions from one's past. Most people can find some answers to the problems they face when they are calmer.

Family members often have some "good advice" to give to a neighbor about a situation that they cannot handle in their own family. They "know" the answer—they are aware that they should stop drinking, be less helpful to the alcoholic, or set guidelines for themselves with their child. They simply cannot get free enough from the forces that are driving them emotionally to act on their best judgement.

When an individual is less flooded with emotion, he or she is better able to define a direction in life. As Mrs. Swain became capable of sorting through her reactions to her husband when he was violent, she devised a strategy to approach the problem. Mrs. Swain's problem was not that she did not have enough advice—she had suggestions from every side. What helped her to come to some conclusions was having an atmosphere in which she could think and define a direction for herself.

At other times, the family can benefit from understanding some of the principles of theory. Presenting the idea that a person should observe his or her reactions can provide the impetus to think rather than simply react. Hearing the concept of putting one's head in charge of one's emotions can be a starting point for an individual's attempt to be more directed in life. The idea that a person has choices in how he or she reacts encourages people to begin to manage themselves in emotionally charged relationships.

A therapist can ask some of the following questions: How does one begin to observe how one reacts to important others? When one becomes more objective about one's own functioning, can one begin to identify patterns of reacting? Can knowing one's reactivity help one gain more ability to make decisions about it? Can one choose to be angry rather than swamped in angry feelings? Can one become free enough of one's emotions to make choices about one's actions in the situation that provoked the feelings?

Identifying Patterns in Family Relationship

One of the important ideas of Bowen family systems theory is that the level of differentiation of a person is the outcome of many generations of relationships. An individual's level of functioning with his or her children is a variation of how his or her parents raised him or her, and their parents, them. The family diagram is a vehicle for recording the facts about individuals who comprise those generations. Family interviews and research can help a person have some insight into the emotional forces that have been at play in the family.

Rarely does one broaden the focus from an individual problem or issue in a marriage to discerning the multigenerational themes without shifting the thinking in a person's head. When experiences are seen in a broader framework—as part of a process that has flowed through generations in a family—one has more difficulty in blaming and reacting. When an alcoholic parent is viewed in the context of his or her alcoholic parent, then one gains perspective. The parent's inadequacies seem less personally directed toward the child and more of an expression of the emotional climate in which the parent was raised. When a spouse thinks about his or her over-helpfulness in a marriage as a reflection of taking on parental responsibilities as a child, then he or she has more latitude to address personal patterns of functioning.

As Mrs. Swain strove to understand her parents better, a broader picture of the themes in the family emerged. Her mother was also the eldest daughter in a family of six. Her mother's mother was wealthy and had consigned her six offspring to the care of nannies as they grew up. As Mrs. Swain listened to her mother discuss her childhood, she began to understand that her mother had taken on many responsibilities for her younger siblings—a pattern similar to her own childhood.

Alcoholism can intensify an emotional pattern that exists in a family. Mrs. Swain said the conflict and distance she experienced with her mother hinged on her mother's drinking. However, as she began to talk with her mother in a more personal way, her mother became less judgmental and critical. She found that drinking was not the barrier she thought it was in their relationship. She began to view her mother less through her father's eyes and more as a person who, understandably, had lost her identity in the web of relationships with her husband and children. She became interested in her mother rather than angry at her. The facts of Mrs. Swain's life did not change how Mrs. Swain grew up, but it gave her a different viewpoint about their relationship.

Researching the generations of one's family is a paradox of sorts. On the one hand, one begins to understand how fully one lives out the themes from the past. Choices one seems to have made, such as whom one marries, may appear to be ghosts from another generation rather than autonomous selections. Yet observing these patterns frees one to assess one's options. If a person can understand the emotional legacy of prior generations, he or she has a new freedom to consider alternatives in how to interact with the present.

In addition, each person carries a version of his or her relationship system wired into the deepest part of the brain, intertwined with emotions and triggering automatic reactions that are often outside his or her rational understanding. Imbedded in each person is a variation of mother, father, and the important themes of the family that are retriggered in responses to his or her spouse and children. To become acquainted with these forces, to get to know them, to see them as part of a discernable pattern can free a person from them.

Mrs. Swain sought to gain a broader perspective of her family to more objectively view her own reactions. When she began to see her mother as a vulnerable human who was facing her own dilemmas, and not simply as a critical parent, she began to relate to her in a more personal, adult fashion. She realized her father's perspective less and began to see the part he played in her mother's isolation. She started to feel less "caught" in the family's difficulties and freer to focus on her own life.

Researching and understanding patterns in one's family can be a step toward becoming more neutral and more capable of relating within the intense emotional forces in one's life.

Differentiation of Self

Differentiation of self is a concept that is difficult to define, yet at the core of the concept of Bowen family systems theory. People emerge from their relationship systems with a level of operating self. This is a natural process that exists in other species as well. The ability to differentiate a self is related to a number of questions: Can a person understand and function differently in the emotional forces that affect the very core of his or her being? Can an individual begin to operate less automatically in regard to reactivity, cutoff, and attachment? In what ways can a person become freer to live his or her own life, without instinctively repeating the emotional processes of past generations?

Charting a course for responsible functioning in a family takes a lifetime. No one person can change another. Yet each person, by establishing a responsible position for self, can affect the family of which he or she is a part. How does one not accept responsibilities that belong to another or allow another to function for oneself? These questions are not easily answered, and the process of answering them is often at the heart of change.

Mrs. Swain was trying to be a responsible wife and mother by working and caring for the children, yet she also began to regulate her husband's life. She supervised his behavior, helped him when he had difficulties from drinking, and monitored the finances. He began to act like an unruly child, not a husband. Responsible functioning calls for a definition of self, a sense of one's boundaries, and an idea of one's values.

This is a lifelong enterprise, not something to be determined in a few sessions, or even a few years. For most people, conceptualizing what their lives would be if directed by their thinking and not their emotions requires considerable thought and effort. However, when people begin to define a self, with a clearer sense of boundaries and goals, they function in a way they had not thought possible before.

Mrs. Swain commented that, in all her efforts, her greatest dilemma was that she did not experience a sense of self, a separate identity of her own. She ran her family efficiently and was indispensable to her parents, but her self-definition came from being needed in these relationships. The road she explored in therapy was finding the guideposts for her own separateness in these intense relationships. Her path, as with most people, had many turns and some detours. However, she slowly worked to become freer of the automatic reactions that had determined the direction of her life in the past.

Mrs. Swain strove to become more observant about her reactions to her family. She sought to be less responsive to the needs of her parents, slowly becoming less available for their crises. As she had more personal contact with her mother, she found she was less drawn into sympathizing with her father. She found a challenge with her husband was not to be so absorbed by his difficulties, and yet to be clearer about limiting his behavior, particularly when he was physically abusive. She sought to be calmer, yet more engaged with her children emotionally. In her work, she became clearer about the limits of her job and began to speak up to her boss. Mrs. Swain struggled with themes of depression and lack of self-esteem and experienced great difficulty in developing a focus on her own interests and friendships.

This endeavor to define a self has no blueprint and few guidelines. However, by recognizing the patterns and triangles in which one is caught, one can set an agenda for work toward self-definition. As one learns to manage oneself in the face of emotionally laden relationships, one gains a solidity and a sense of identity that permits a more thoughtful life direction. This is the work a person pursues in his or her family—whether he or she lives with addiction or another of the parade of human difficulties.

The Challenge of Systems Thinking

Bowen family systems theory provides a set of principles for comprehending the underlying connections among people that create predictable patterns of interaction in a family's life. It adds a dimension to understanding human functioning by widening the lens from a particular symptom, to the wider relationship system, to the natural world of which humans are a part.

From a systems view, alcoholism is a human condition that is an outcome of a relationship process across many generations. The anxiety of the family is bound by this symptom, which develops a function in its emotional life. When a drinking problem becomes a starting point for exploring the relationship system as a whole, the family no longer focuses solely on the alcoholic. Rather, the contours of his or her life are seen to "fit" like a piece of a puzzle with the needs, reactions, and patterns of the family. Any person in the system who functions differently can rearrange the pieces of this puzzle.

The Swains were one study of a family that developed across the generations the mechanism of relating through drinking. When Mr. Swain stopped drinking, underlying relationship issues in the family surfaced.

Their handling of neediness through caretaking and dependency, through cycles of conflict and closeness, and through overinvestment in the needs of the other were explored. Alcohol was believed to be one mechanism to regulate emotionality and attachment to important others in their families.

Thinking about the relationship system rather than the defined problem allows a freedom to explore the complexity and richness of a family's life. There are many questions worth exploring: Can alcoholism come to be viewed as a systems issue and not an individual's problem? Can the family regard it as a challenge that will better allow them to understand its relationship system rather than a disease to be fixed in an individual? How do people maintain boundaries in the family? How do they function in under- or overresponsible positions? What is the overall level of maturity in each? What efforts in their lives could family members make to be more thoughtful about the direction they have chosen? How does each person in a family understand what patterns he or she brings from his or her family of origin? How do people think about these themes playing out in their nuclear families? What other ways does a family have of binding the anxiety that travels across generations besides substance abuse?

Life holds many dilemmas. Alcoholism has a compelling quality that invites a focus, a labeling, and a solution for the individual who is experiencing the addiction. However, in confining the problem to an individual, the complexity of the larger system is missed. A push to change the "alcoholic" often exacerbates the problem and denies the family the opportunity to explore the intricate threads of its emotional life. Bowen family systems theory offers principles to begin that exploration, widen the focus, understand relationship patterns across generations, and begin to define a responsible direction in one's life. These principles provide a pathway for people to stay interested and engaged in the process of achieving their most mature potential, regardless of the challenging dilemmas they face.

REFERENCES

Bowen, M. (1978). *Family Therapy in Clinical Practice.* New York: Jason Aronson.
Toman, W. (1961). *Family Constellation.* New York: Springer.

Chapter 12

Incest: A Family Systems Perspective

Peter Titelman

This chapter describes one effort to understand and intervene with families in which incest has occurred, using a version of Bowen family systems theory as a conceptual base. The following topics are discussed: (1) the current social and political focus on sexual abuse; (2) incest and Bowen family systems theory; (3) anthropology and incest; (4) sociobiology and incest; (5) the clinical research perspective: multiple family member access and family systems neutrality; and (6) two case studies.

THE CURRENT SOCIAL AND POLITICAL FOCUS ON SEXUAL ABUSE

In the past several years, the media, social services, and law enforcement have been increasingly outspoken about incest and other forms of sexual abuse. Sexual abuse has been the ultimate secret, the most powerful taboo. The greater focus on dealing with this phenomenon has generally been a plus. Part of the new openness is related to legislation in many states that mandates the disclosure by professionals regarding knowledge of sexual abuse.

Sexual abuse, and incest specifically, are no longer submerged in secrecy. Rather, it is now considered a legitimate phenomenon to discuss, study, and address in psychotherapy. The topic of incest is referred to almost daily in our local and national media.

The negative side of this intense social and political focus on sexual abuse, including incest, is the emotional reactivity that it arouses, not only in the general populace, but also among social service professionals: physicians, nurses, social workers, psychiatrists, psychologists, day care workers, and others. When social service providers deal with incest, whether it involves reporting its occurrence or in clinical work, it unleashes tremendous anxiety for those professionals.

An issue such as incest creates reactivity rather than thoughtfully planned response because of the highly emotionally charged nature of the abuse. Professionals have difficulty developing a research orientation amid all the professional reactivity, and the danger is to lose one's own neutrality and engage in conflict with, or distance from, agencies or individual clinicians. This is certainly the material of which triangles are formed.

INCEST AND BOWEN FAMILY SYSTEMS THEORY

Merriam Webster's Dictionary defines incest as a "sexual relationship between persons related with the degree wherein marriage is forbidden by law." W. Smith (1994) views incest as one form of child sexual abuse.

Incest, similar to schizophrenia and twinship, is a paradigmatic form of emotional and physical/behavioral fusion. It represents one extreme side of the individuality/togetherness balance. Incest is an extreme version of a universal human quality—the tendency to fuse with one or more family members, the desire for oneness.

Insofar as incest is a universal taboo, one that appears to be universally broken, it provides a unique opportunity for linking Bowen family systems theory with the other sciences, particularly sociobiology and anthropology. Incest provides an excellent example of gene-culture co-evolution. Incest cannot be reduced to cultural or individual differences and thus provides an issue of substance about which Bowen family systems theory can contribute a new perspective.

Furthermore, the prohibition against incest serves as one of the central organizers upon which the family as a multigenerational emotional system is constructed. This taboo, as we shall see in reviewing anthropological findings, represents a baseline for normative operation of the individuality-togetherness forces. The prohibition against incest is an elemental bedrock upon which physical and emotional differentiation within the family can occur. The breakdown of this prohibition can lead to a range of social, psychological, and physical symptoms, including the possibility of the extinction of the family.

Finally, incest is a phenomenon that can highlight the differences between Freudian theory, which is the basis for most individually oriented theories of behavior, and Bowen family systems theory. Incest viewed from a psychoanalytic perspective is understood mostly in terms of an unconscious fantasy experience—the Oedipus complex originating in the intrapsychic experience of the child. The focus is on the Oedipal triad. In contrast, a Bowen family systems perspective is more interested in incest as an actual, factual behavior that is real, not fantasized. Through the lens of

Bowen theory, incest is understood in terms of the interlocking emotional triangles in the multigenerational emotional process. Also, Bowen family systems theory combines a theory of the family emotional system with evolutionary biological theory. Bowen theory resides upon Darwinian natural systems theory, and it is both an application and expansion of that theory as applied to the human family. Thus, where Freudian theory would look at the underlying basis of incest in terms of the balance of id, ego, and superego, Bowen family systems theory describes incest as a manifestation of an imbalance of the forces of individuality and togetherness.

A Bowen family systems theoretical hypothesis is that incest is a phenomenon that exists in nature, including man and other animals, and that it does not represent a qualitatively different form of human behavior. If one explores enough branches of any family, it is highly likely that all variations of human functioning can be observed, including incest.

ANTHROPOLOGY AND INCEST

The works of anthropologists Murdock (1949) and Berelson and Steiner (1964) are discussed here to provide an anthropological context that demonstrates the universality of the prohibition against incest and the universal possibility for breaking that prohibition.

Murdock (1949), in *Social Structure,* states:

> In no known society is it conventional or even permissible for father and daughter, mother and son, or brother and sister to have sexual intercourse or to marry. (p. 250)

He draws upon conclusive evidence from 250 societies. Because of the incest taboo, each child is compelled to seek a spouse in another family to establish a marital relationship. The consequence of the incest prohibition is the existence of both a family of orientation (origin) and a family of procreation. Murdock draws the following conclusions from his empirical data: (1) Incest is a universal taboo within the nuclear family; (2) incest does not apply universally to any relative of the opposite sex outside the nuclear family; (3) incest taboos are never exclusively confined to the nuclear family; (4) incest taboos tend to apply with diminished intensity to kin outside the nuclear family; (5) incest is characterized by a peculiar intensity and an emotional quality (incest often carries the death penalty); (6) violations of the incest taboo occur and are reported in most samples of fifty societies; (7) fifty-six societies recognize first-cousin marriage. Inbreeding is viewed as negative if recessive traits are undesirable and positive if recessive traits are desirable.

Berelson and Steiner (1964), in *Human Behavior: An Inventory of Scientific Findings,* also state that every human society has a prohibition against incest. The few exceptions involve ritualistic permission before a hunt or battle or royal or sacred prerogatives.

Berelson and Steiner (1964) support the Bowen family systems notion that man is on the same continuum with other species rather than being a fundamentally different form of life. They point out that the prohibition against incest exists among animals that live in families and social groups and among those that are slower in maturing. These animals tend to be larger and more intelligent, have longer life spans, and exist within a nuclear family arrangement.

The following reasons for the universality and intensity of the incest taboo are presented by Berelson and Steiner (1964). The first is the *genetic reason,* the belief and, in certain circumstances, the fact that intrafamily relations produce deteriorated offspring. The second reason, *maintenance of the family,* is the need to defend the nuclear family and, to a lesser extent, the extended family from intense conflict that would arise from sexual rivalries, passions, and jealousies. The third reason, *mutual assistance,* is the original need to develop a social group larger than the family for purposes of protection and sustenance and the consequent desirability of pushing family members outward in order to broaden alliances. (The major consequence of the incest prohibition is the discontinuity of the nuclear family, which typically contains only two generations.) The fourth reason, *socialization and social integration,* is the need to preserve parents' authority over child rearing by clearly separating the parental and sexual roles and the need to encourage adjustment to the larger society outside of the family. The fifth reason, *accounting for the intensity of maintenance,* is that the taboo is taught early and breaking it is punished severely.

When the incest taboo is broken within the nuclear family, it is much more likely to involve father and daughter than mother and son. In relation to the extended family, the incest prohibition ranges widely among societies in the specific relatives considered out of bounds. It does not apply universally to any one relative, and it goes beyond blood ties and correlates with kinship terminology similar to that used within the nuclear family (e.g., any relative called "mother" or "father"), including stepparents.

The important implications for Bowen family systems theory from the above anthropological findings are as follows:

1. The incest taboo is a universal culturally transmitted mechanism that blocks the genetic, psychological, and sociological damage of extreme inbreeding, with its potential for genetic and emotional fusion. The major consequence of the incest prohibition is that the nuclear

family cannot remain an isolated unit. To avoid the biological destruction of the family that incest would bring about, there is an inevitable connection of the nuclear family with the extended family and larger society. The family engaged in incest would, theoretically, become an extinct family, based on the forces of togetherness overwhelming the forces of individuality to the point where a survival level of differentiation would no longer exist.

2. Based on a large societal sample, the prohibition against incest is found to be universally violated. This author would hypothesize that the universal violation of the incest taboo occurs in families with a sufficient combination of undifferentiation, or emotional fusion, interlocked with intense stressors from the environment in the presence of chronic anxiety and in the context of unresolved emotional cutoff between either individuals and/or segments of the nuclear and extended families.

3. The incest taboo applies universally within the nuclear family, but within the extended family, it is variable.

SOCIOBIOLOGY AND INCEST

Turning to natural systems, the work of C. Lumsden and E.O. Wilson, *Promethean Fire* (1984), and Trivers, *Social Evolution* (1985), will be explored to illustrate a sociobiological understanding of the universal prohibition against incest.

The theoretical underpinning of Lumsden and Wilson's (1984) work is the conception of gene-culture coevolution, summarized as follows: " . . . the main postulate is that certain unique and remarkable properties of the human mind result in a tight linkage between genetic evolution and cultural history" (p. 20). According to Lumsden and Wilson's thesis, the genes prescribe the rules of development (the epigenetic rules) by which the individual mind is assembled. From this perspective, the mind grows by absorbing parts of the culture already in existence. In the words of Lumsden and Wilson (1984), "The culture is created anew in each generation by the summed decisions and innovations of all members of the society" (p. 117). ". . . In sum, culture is created and shaped by biological processes while the biological processes are simultaneously altered in response to culture change" (p. 118). They also state that the purpose of sex is to create diversity: "The primary role of sex is more subtle than straightforward reproduction: it is the creation of genetic diversity among offspring" (p. 28).

Lumsden and Wilson (1984) argue that incest taboos are biologically based and influence the way culture is formed. They use the example that

" . . . outbreeding is much more likely to occur than brother-sister incest because individuals raised closely together during the first six years of life are rarely interested in full sexual intercourse" (p. 20). These authors, drawing upon anthropological material, state that only a very small percentage of individuals prefer to have sexual relations with brothers or sisters (p. 164). Some may harbor thoughts or fantasies of desire toward siblings. However, " . . . the vast majority choose to mate with persons raised outside their immediate family circle" (p. 64).

According to Lumsden and Wilson (1984), studies of the origins of sexual preference in Israel kibbutzim and Taiwanese villages indicate that, even if other members of the society could somehow be neutral or favorable toward sibling incest, young people would still automatically avoid it, by an overwhelming majority. The aversion is based on an unconscious process of mental development. Children raised closely together during the first six years of life feel little or no sexual attraction toward one another when they reach maturity, whether they are close relatives or not. The feeling has little to do with culture or the classification of kin.

Even if a society could somehow begin anew with brother-sister incest as the norm, it would probably develop a cultural antagonism toward the practice in a generation or two. Eventually, the society would incorporate taboos in the form of rituals and myths to justify and reinforce the aversion. In a phrase, "the genetic leash pulls culture back into line." Genes prescribing the most efficient epigenetic rules spread through the population over many generations. The human population evolved toward those forms of learned behavior which conveyed the greatest diversity, survival, and reproductive power. According to Lumsden and Wilson (1984):

> The rule against incest is so strong and pervasive across history and societies that it can be reasonably supposed to have a genetic basis. Of course individuals continue to exercise free will in the matter. They can think about the problem at any depth, down to the epigenetic rules and the genes and with due attention to their own special circumstances. Then they can decide. Most likely they will resist incestuous acts because the epigenetic rules have nudged their minds into forms that are much more likely to receive deep emotional reward from the practice of sex outside the family. (p. 176)

Wilson (1980) describes how other social mammals besides humans avoid incest and the mechanisms they use to accomplish it. Wilson (1980), *Sociobiology*, gives three types of structures against incest among mammals that include the following examples: First, the majority of all lions leave the pride of their birth before joining the lionesses of another pride;

second, the pattern holds true for old world monkeys and apes, and Wilson (1980) reports that, "In the small territorial family groups of the white-handed gibbon, Hylobateslar, the father drives sons from the group when they attain sexual maturity, and the mother drives away her daughters" (p. 38); and third, Wilson (1980) described the following incest avoidance among mice: "young female mice (mus musculus) reared with both female and male parents later prefer to mate with males of a different strain, thus rejecting males most similar to the father" (p. 38).

Trivers (1985), in *Social Evolution,* describes how kin recognition, among some animals, provides another mechanism of incest avoidance:

> Recognition of kin may also be important at the time of mating. Individuals may wish to avoid inbreeding and may, at the same time, be selected to avoid excessive outbreeding, where this breaks up sets of genes coadapted to local circumstances. For this reason Patrick Bateson suggests that birds often *learn* while still young what a prospective mate should look like. An innate system of recognition would not as easily permit the subtle discrimination required, but a learned system permits an offspring when young to imprint on the appearance of its parent or siblings, using this as a standard by which to judge a prospective mate with those who are similar but not identical to those on whom they have imprinted. More recently, Bateson has shown that Japanese quail reared with their siblings later prefer to spend time near first cousins—compare to more or less related individuals—and this correlates positively with courtship. (pp. 134-135)

Trivers *also* implies that genetically there is a fine balance between inbreeding (incest) and altruism. According to Trivers (1985), up to a point, inbreeding is favored by evolution, but when it goes too far, it is harmful to the survival of a given species:

> Inbreeding increases degree of relatedness by increasing the genealogical connections among individuals. In addition, products of inbreeding will find that the two halves of their genome are partly correlated. This will lead products of inbreeding to value themselves relatively more, except insofar as the inbreeding has resulted in reduced reproductive potential for them. (p. 143)

Sociobiology views incest and its prohibition as resting upon a balance between inbreeding and outbreeding (variation). This correlates with a Bowen family systems conception that the emotionally instinctual forces of individuality and togetherness underlie the universal prohibition against incest and the universal breaking of it among humans. From the perspective of Bowen theory, this author hypothesizes that the balance of these two emotional forces expressed through the level of adaptation or differentiation/undifferentiation, in conjunction with the relationship process, accounts for both the universal prohibition against engaging in incest and the universal breaking of the incest prohibition.

THE CLINICAL-RESEARCH PERSPECTIVE: MULTIPLE FAMILY MEMBER ACCESS AND FAMILY SYSTEMS NEUTRALITY

In the theoretical-clinical research perspective of this chapter, the phenomenon of incest involves an interdependence between Bowen theory and clinical manifestation: examining the phenomenon of incest through the theory and conversely viewing the theory through the phenomenon. Theory provides the lens through which one can observe incest as an expression of the family emotional system that has evolved within the interrelated constraints of nature and culture.

Instead of seeing incest only through the eyes of the "victim," or the "victimizer," or the "significant other(s)," a clinical approach based on Bowen theory seeks to access and understand incest from the perspectives of the positions of (1) the child or adolescent who has experienced incest ("victim"), (2) the adult who experienced incest as a child or adolescent ("victim"), and (3) the adolescent or adult who initiated incest (the offender/perpetrator, "victimizer/victim").

Since 1985, this author treated more than forty families in which incest has been either the primary or an important secondary presenting problem. The following configurations were presented: father or stepfather/daughter or stepdaughter incest, grandfather/granddaughter incest, cousin/cousin incest, uncle/niece incest, and father/son incest.

In these families, the access, in terms of the identified patient, included adults who experienced incest as a child or adolescent, adults who initiated incest, and children or adolescents who experienced incest.

Multiple family member access helps to achieve the goal of being emotionally neutral in relation to all members of the family. This involves avoiding sidetaking, fusion, and overidentification with the family member who has experienced incest (the "victim"), the family member who initiated incest (the "perpetrator"), or other family members, while at the same time holding the family member who initiates incest—the "perpetrator"— responsible for his or her behavior. The presence of incest stresses the coach's capacity to be neutral.

Bowen family systems theory addresses the issue of how the therapist becomes fused and triangled into the emotional system of the clients. In turn, there is a general concern for how the therapist gets "unstuck" from the clinical families with whom he or she is engaged.

The family therapist has two main problems in dealing with the fundamental issue of connectedness and separateness in clinical work with incest. The first is overinvolvement, or getting too caught up in the family's problem. The other is distancing, or backing away from the family's problem(s). When the therapist gets caught up in the emotional processes of the clinical family, he or she often can become either *oversympathetic* or *rejecting*.

Approaching incest as a research topic helps to detoxify the clinician's reactivity toward it. Bowen (1978) wrote about how a research dimension adds to the clinical intervention:

> With experience I discovered that research families did better in psychotherapy than families seen only for psychotherapy, and since then have worked to make every family into a research family. (p. 246)

The initial clinical research hypothesis that guided the initial work with incest was that incest is a *paradigmatic form of fusion,* a low level of differentiation expressed as poor boundaries, including the following:

1. poorly differentiated individuals (high degree of undifferentiation between emotionally reactive and cognitively goal-directed functioning);
2. high degree of fusion between parents and children;
3. high level of unresolved attachment between parents/spouses and their families of origin.

CASE STUDY 1: MULTIGENERATIONAL PATTERN OF INCEST—ACCESS THROUGH A CHILD

The presenting issue was incest between seven-and-a-half-year-old Molly A. and her stepfather, age thirty-seven. Sexual interaction between step-relatives is not identified legally as incest in most states, but if a child under eighteen is involved, it is defined as sexual abuse. From this author's perspective, a sexual relationship between a stepfather and stepdaughter who live in the same household qualifies as "residential incest," and it is the emotional equivalent to incest that occurs between a biological parent and child. The siblings were five-and-a-half-year-old twin sisters and a three-and-a-half-year-old stepbrother.

The initial contact with family A. was as a psychologist consultant to a mental health center providing individual psychological evaluations of Molly and her mother. The stepfather was in jail on a charge of assaulting his wife, and he was awaiting trial on the charges of sexually molesting his stepdaughter.

The assessment of Molly indicated a bright child who seemed to function as a caretaker. Her most overt concern was that she had not seen her stepfather and his family for several months. She was very upset that her stepfather was in jail, and although she was glad that he was not living in the home, because of his physical violence toward her mother, she expressed guilt and concern that her stepfather was in jail; she missed him and was upset that she was not allowed to visit him, while her half-siblings had that opportunity. The therapy lasted one and a half years.

The initial intervention was conducted by this author and a female co-therapist (who had had Molly in group therapy for sexually abused girls) by meeting with Mr. and Mrs. A. in the jail. Mr. A. was supported in his desire to plead guilty, against his lawyer's initial advice to plead not guilty. A letter was drafted in support of family therapy and requested that incarceration be limited. At the trial, Mr. A. faced the possibility of a ninety-nine-year sentence to be served in state prison. However, he pleaded guilty, accepting responsibility for his actions, and was given a suspended sentence to run concurrently with his year of incarceration for assaulting his wife while drunk.

The initial sessions with the couple focused on the following: (1) supporting the guilty plea and legitimizing seeing the family inside the jail; (2) setting the grounds for appropriate, nonsexual communication between stepfather and stepdaughter; and (3) taking family sexual and drug and alcohol histories. (Figure 12.1 presents the A. Family Diagram.)

The initial sessions with mother, stepfather, and Molly focused on the stepfather's efforts to apologize to Molly for the incest and to try to alleviate her guilt for disclosing the behavior that led to his incarceration. He was able to express to his stepdaughter that he understood that her telling her mother about the incest was appropriate and necessary. It was clear from the reaction of the child that not only was she not uncomfortable being with her stepfather, but that his apologizing and his nonblaming of her reporting the incest was a relief. She had missed him and was glad to have the chance to see him again. Molly remembered him as he was when in an emaciated alcoholic state, "looking like a pasty white ghost." Molly was glad to see him appearing healthier.

The sessions with stepfather, mother, and daughter were limited to five during the period of a year. They focused on allowing stepfather and stepdaughter to communicate appropriately, having Molly voice her concerns about her stepfather, and speaking directly about what controls step-

FIGURE 12.1. The A. Family Diagram

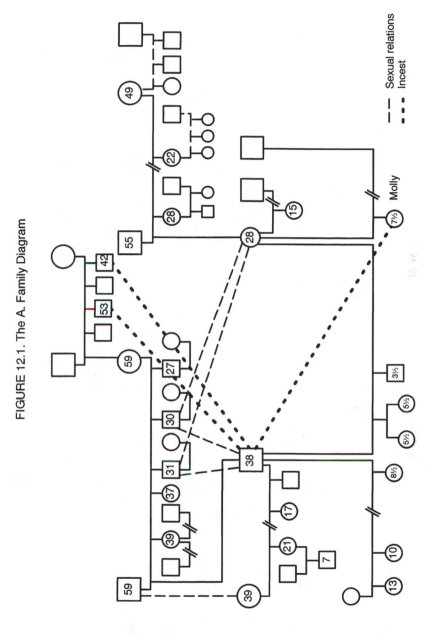

father, mother, and stepdaughter needed in order to be reassured that the incestuous behavior would not be repeated.

The majority of the sessions, usually weekly over a period of almost a year, involved the couple. These sessions had the following foci: (1) helping the stepfather take responsibility for his incestuous behavior; (2) exploring and supporting appropriate boundaries between the stepfather and his stepdaughter (including the format and experience of furlough day and overnight visits); (3) exploration and modification of the marital relationship; and (4) exploring the place and meaning of incest behavior among various members of the extended family.

The stepfather had been sexually abused by two of his maternal uncles with whom he had lived as a child. He described having been anally raped by the two uncles while sharing bedrooms with them. During the sessions with the couple, Mr. A. was able to discuss his being sexually abused by his uncles and later a priest. These experiences had been pushed away and repressed. His being a victim of sexual abuse had taken place when he was six, the same age his stepdaughter was when he began sexually abusing her. The shame and guilt, including feelings of being homosexual, were explored. Mr. A. was able to talk about having forced two of his younger brothers to have sex with him. Mr. A. had been the overfunctioning caretaking oldest brother, who felt he was always being asked to give money to his brothers to assuage his guilt for being sexually involved with them. While Mr. A. was in jail, Mrs. A. had a sexual relationship with those same two brothers.

Mr. A. had had almost no contact with his parents or brothers for a couple of years prior to his incarceration. He was encouraged to make contact with his parents and eventually his brothers. Mr. A. began having contact with his parents and has developed a less caretaking relationship with them. His parents were then able to be more emotionally available for Mr. A.

Mr. A. was paroled from jail after nine months. In addition to continuing the family therapy, he participated in Alcoholics Anonymous, and he and Mrs. A. joined Parents United, a support group for families involved in sexual abuse. Mr. and Mrs. A., who had been in a common-law marriage, had a large formal wedding.

Case Analysis

This case highlights many of the issues and patterns this clinician-researcher has seen in families with incest:

1. *Incest is an extreme expression of undifferentiation in the family.* Another way of characterizing these families is to say that they are

highly emotionally fused, lacking physical, emotional, and social boundaries between individuals. They are stuck together in unseen ways. Families in which incest occurs are characterized by being at the low end of the differentiation-undifferentiation continuum. In the A. family, both spouses were poorly differentiated, and the level of undifferentiation of self of both spouses was comparable. Each of them had difficulty separating emotionally reactive functioning from goal-directed functioning. The boundaries between Mr. A. and Mrs. A. in their marital relationship and their relationship with their respective families of origin were poorly defined. Both families were characterized by a high level of emotional cutoff. The incestuous behavior on the part of Mr. A. with two of his uncles, two of his brothers, and his stepdaughter and Mrs. A.'s sexual involvement with two of her brothers-in-law as a way of retaliating toward her husband for committing incest are markers of the multiple levels of undifferentiation in this family system.

2. *Nuclear family emotional process is characterized by emotional fusion.* Eventually the marital relationship becomes conflictual or distant, and one or more children are triangled into the process. In the A. family, the couple had a stormy relationship, with much conflict and jealousy on both sides. Eventually Molly and her stepfather became overly close, with Mrs. A. on the outside of the triangle.

3. *In incest, the projection process is focused on the child involved in incest.* Sibling functioning position is a factor. The incestuously involved child is in a caretaking relationship with one or both of the parents and sometimes the siblings. In the A. family, Molly was the triangled child. In this triangle, Mr. A. and Molly were in a hostilely fused relationship, and Mrs. A. was in conflictual and distant relationships with both Mr. A. and her daughter Molly.

4. *Incestuous behavior is a mode of binding anxiety, evolving from unresolved triangles, that expresses the interlocking process of emotional fusion and emotional cutoff that exists between the nuclear and extended family systems on one or both of the paternal and maternal sides.* Mr. A. had been cut off from his family of origin, including the several years he lived with his paternal grandparents and was sexually abused by two of his maternal uncles. Further, conflict followed by cutoff occurred between Mr. A. and his younger brothers and his parents in the years after he sexually abused his brothers. Mrs. A.'s parents were divorced and she was cut off from her father. Mrs. A. was in a caretaking position in relation to her alcoholic, underfunctioning mother. As an adult, Mrs. A. would often use distance to deal

with the overwhelming demands of her mother. Thus, Mrs. A., similar to her husband, came to the marriage with a high degree of distance from family of origin. Mr. and Mrs. A. manifested intense conflict followed by distance and cutoff. They would automatically fuse together to meet the severe gaps in self, based on each being highly undifferentiated.

5. *Incest occurs within a multigenerational process.* The victimizer was often sexually victimized, in many cases at the same age as the child he or she is victimizing. The multigenerational transmission process is the continuation of the family projection process carried through multiple generations. It is hypothesized that the chronic anxiety that is experienced by the adult who was subject to incest as a child is automatically bound through taking on the functioning position of the perpetrator of incest. In this way, the adult who has experienced incest as a child escapes from being trapped in the victim position by moving into the functioning position of the adult perpetrator. This is another way of describing how incest in the current generation, or within a nuclear family, binds the anxiety that has originated in the previous generation(s) and is passed down into the next generation. Anxiety can be bound through the transformation of "being done in" to "doing in the other," in this case a child, to project the chronic anxiety from the self of the adult who has experienced incest as a child to the self of the child who is currently "being done in." The projection process in this situation involves a parent projecting through incestuous sexual behavior his or her anxieties onto a child. In this way, the parent functions with less anxiety by transferring certain aspects of self to the child. What begins as an anxiety for the parent becomes an anxious reality in the child's life. In the A. family, Mr. A. was initially a "child-victim" of incest that was initiated by his maternal uncles while he was living in their home. That behavior occurred when Mr. A. was six years old, the same age that Molly was when he initiated an incestuous relationship with her. As a child-victim of incest, Mr. A. had been forced to submit to anal intercourse as initiated by his uncles. As an adult-perpetrator, he was the active initiator of anal intercourse with Molly, his stepdaughter. The binding of anxiety involved Mr. A. moving out of a sexual passive position, in which he was being "done in," to a sexually active position, in which he was "doing in" his stepdaughter, Molly.

6. *Incestuous behavior is frequently triggered by alcohol and/or drug abuse.* Mr. A. had a alcohol and drug problem. His substance abuse peaked at the time he was involved in incest with his stepdaughter.

Alcohol and drugs are believed to be anxiety binders. They mask the experience of previous trauma and stress without dealing with it. Eventually, the anxiety that was not dealt with at its source, in this case Mr. A.'s relationship with his uncles and the priest who sexually abused him, was transmitted through a process of triangling and emerged in the relationship between Mr. A. and his two younger brothers. The mutigenerational transmission, through the mechanism of interlocking triangles, then led to the incest being expressed between Mr. A. and his stepdaughter.

The therapeutic intervention involves working—from a stance of neutrality—with a variety of family units: the couple; mother and daughter; father and daughter; father, mother, and daughter; and all of the above as individuals. When the perpetrator is in jail, it can be useful to see him or her with his or her spouse and family in the jail. Intervention with the A. family involved working with the parents as a couple and with the unit of the parents and the sexually abused stepdaughter.

If the family is separated, the therapist works for reunification of the family when it is clear that the incestuous behavior has ceased and is under control. The family therapy described with the A. family is an example of this approach. This author believes that it is detrimental to support the family's and society's efforts to emotionally or physically cut off the relationship between the perpetrator and the incestuously involved child. Having the father leave the home temporarily, rather than the daughter, is preferable, but banishment or criticism does not solve the problem. Cutoff leads to blame and guilt that are often devastating and do further irreparable harm beyond the activity of incest itself. Maintaining a neutral stance in relation to all members of the family means holding the adults involved in incest responsible for their actions, while at the same time not taking a blaming, guilt-inducing position.

CASE STUDY 2: EMOTIONAL CUTOFF AND INCEST— ACCESS THROUGH THE ADULT WHO EXPERIENCED INCEST AS A CHILD

The following is an example of work with an adult female, Mrs. B., age forty-four, whose father abused her as a child. The therapy included seventy-eight sessions over a four-year period. The bulk of the sessions, fifty-one, were with Mrs. B. individually. Twenty of the sessions included her husband, five sessions included her older sister, one session included the older sister and a younger brother, and there was one session with Mrs. B. and her father. (Figure 12.2 presents the B. Family Diagram.) This case highlights the significance of exploring the covered-over incest experience, dealing with it, and supporting direct contact between Mrs. B. and her father in order to constructively address the trauma and the emotional cutoff.

The following colloquial description was written by the client at the end of therapy. It highlights a family focus that seeks to overcome the emotional cutoff associated with incest:

> My anxieties began somewhere about the age of eleven. I remember having problems breathing and swallowing for no apparent reason. My parents took me to our family doctor, who gave me a shot. From the seventh grade, until I quit school in my sophomore year in high school, I suffered from dizziness, nausea, and hives. My parents and our family doctor attributed all this to school anxiety. This was the reason for leaving school.
>
> I was married at sixteen. My husband, who was eighteen, was unable to cope with my increasing anxieties and the responsibility of having a wife, and later two children. The early years of our marriage, I suffered from terrible bouts of depression.
>
> My parents were concerned about my depression and took me to a medical doctor they had been told was successful in helping people with nervous conditions. I was overwhelmed with a feeling that I was going to harm my children whom I loved dearly. I was treated off and on by this doctor for approximately eight years. Eventually I realized all the drugs I was taking weren't helping me. I was getting worse. I would have bouts of vomiting and lose massive amounts of weight and suffered from terrible headaches.
>
> My husband went out nearly every night. He would come home after drinking and stand next to the bed where I was sleeping. I would wake up and be unable to recognize who he was and be terrified!
>
> My mother-in-law had mental problems which went untreated for most of my husband's life. It was a big secret untalked about outside the immediate family. His father coped by going to a local bar every day after work and on the weekends. Whenever I would have a bad spell, my husband would tell me to snap out of it, or I would be locked up in a mental hospital.
>
> Every time I tried to take a job, I would get so anxious, I wouldn't be able to get out of bed. Suicidal feelings would overwhelm me. My sister called one day as I was looking in the phone book for a psychiatrist. She set up an appointment for a physical with her doctor, and he referred me to one. I would see him periodically. It was

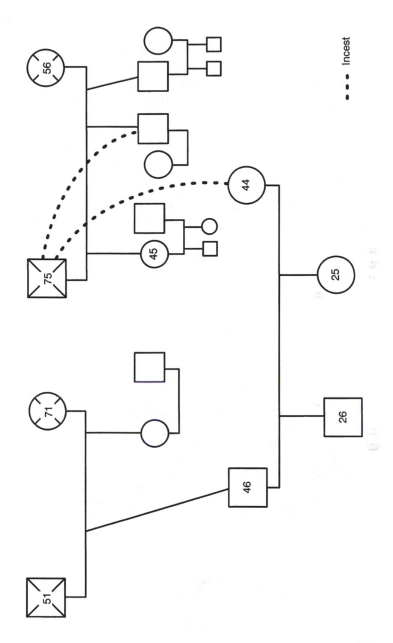

FIGURE 12.2. The B. Family Diagram

●●● — Incest

during this time I was finally able to take a part-time job, which gave me a great feeling and for the first time in my life gave me money of my own.

After my kids were grown, the fear of hurting them was replaced by a fear of being a lesbian. But I was still afraid to be alone and had fear and an unreal anger toward drunks.

I had this recurring dream, where I felt I was more awake than asleep, but I couldn't open my eyes. I could hear someone walking, then coming up the stairs where the bedrooms were. I would try real hard to open my eyes to see who it was, but I couldn't. I knew the doors were locked, and I was home alone in the house. Before I was married, I had this same dream, but at that time, I really thought someone had been there. We didn't lock our doors back then. From the day I was married, and even now, my doors are always locked. When my mother came home I told her someone had been there. All of the above would obsess my thoughts when I was upset.

My brother, who is three years younger than I, had problems of his own from his early high school years until today. He has a terrible phobia of being alone and going to bed alone. His biggest problem has been drinking. His wife left him after eleven years of marriage and no children. He went on this downward spiral of drinking and being rowdy that lasted four years. He would call me in the middle of the night to tell me he was going to kill his wife. I sent him to my doctor, who in turn called his wife to warn her, and my brother never went back to him. It was my brother's drinking and fighting that set in motion the greatest bout of anxiety and depression I had ever endured. I went weekly to my doctor. I couldn't sleep, and I was terrified all of my waking hours. I couldn't stop working, but I was terrified to go to work. (Later I learned it was to be my salvation.) I got claustrophobia and would get anxiety attacks and dizzy spells once I got to work. I needed people desperately, but I was afraid of them.

About this time I got a referral to a family therapist. I felt I could not "play the game" with my marriage and my life anymore. I felt like I was dying inside. I experienced what felt to me like banging into walls. I had no more solutions to problems; I had lost the ability to fantasize (my lifesaver when things were bad). I couldn't feel anger or joy.

My husband was never an active part of any of my medical treatment to this point. I didn't realize how beneficial joint counseling would be. I thought I was the problem, because I was unable to deal with life. I told him if he didn't take part, I would have to leave him because I couldn't deal with our life together anymore. This was another thing that had me confused. One part of me wanted to leave him, while another part felt it would be a mistake. He came to therapy, reluctantly, but he came.

I expected instant relief. I never dreamed it wouldn't come until three years later. Our first session I talked about everything that bothered me. I felt my bad marriage was the direct cause, that if it were to improve I would get better. If not, I would have to get out. It was some time later that I could see my husband's weekend "flus" and foul moods were a result of his Friday night drinking. It became so obvious to my daughter and me he could no longer deny it. My daughter and I would tell him we were leaving for the day to get away from his verbal abuse. Slowly he changed his pattern. He doesn't drink to excess and it doesn't carry over the weekend anymore.

My father and mother had problems in my early teens. My father was heavy into working at this time because they had just purchased their first home. My mother went out with her girlfriends (some butch), and she had a boyfriend who would call the house. My father started drinking more on his off time. He followed her one night, and shortly thereafter, he tried to hang himself in our cellar. We, my sister, one and a half years older than I, and my brother, three years younger than I, along with my mother, were witness to this. He was unsuccessful, but that act left its mark on all of us. But no one ever discussed it. It was like it never happened. My mother became pregnant somewhere during this period of time, and after my youngest brother was born, she just stayed home and never had any friends for any length of time. We all lived in fear of my father trying to kill himself.

After about one and a half years of therapy my relationship with my husband started to improve, but I had to accept that there must be more than that, because I wasn't getting better.

I noticed that when I worked during the week I would be somewhat OK, even though I dreaded going home (for no reason). I would look forward to my weekends off, but I would get so distressed I would get immobilized by irrational fears. After that pattern repeated itself over and over, I realized I was afraid of my husband. My rational mind knew there was no basis for this. He never hurt me physically. Slowly I began to feel less anxious. My husband and I began communicating, and we both seemed to share the same life goals. I had put him through hell the previous year and a half. It truly amazed me that he hung in there (I couldn't even stand myself).

When I wasn't working, I spent a lot of time with my sister and my friend. I tried to keep busy and talking. I know now I was running away from the unknown. From past experience I knew if stopped I would be overwhelmed by my feelings, and it would give me more problems. I was afraid to be alone. The marriage was progressing, and PMS medication had leveled off my drastic mood swings, but the anxiety was awful. It felt like the ground was shaking, but it was me shaking.

We started once again to discuss the men in my life, and the footsteps, and the fear of the stranger in the hospital. I had a conscious memory of a great-uncle fondling my sister and me in our early teens. He had been like a grandfather to us. After talking about this I became extremely upset and cried and cried.

I started having dreams. I felt like I was awake, but my eyes were closed. I could hear footsteps coming up the stairs. These dreams were different than the usual. I was able to think, and seemed to have some control over what I was seeing. They were like short clips out of context with what I was dreaming. The first sexual-type dream was on the floor between twin beds (my sister and I shared a room with twin beds). Someone was getting up off of me. I only got a quick glimpse of a profile turning. I thought of going to see my uncle. But I didn't really want to do this. I did dig up some old photos of my uncle. I hadn't seen him in twenty years. I also asked my mother if she ever remembered anything happening to me, which she didn't.

I tried not to be afraid of the dreams. The people I knew in my dreams would end up looking like someone else. I began searching with a vengeance in my dreams. I got to the point in one dream where I wouldn't look away, and a veil like a curtain was drawn left to right across in front of me so I couldn't see a face. The end result of the dreams was sexual, but not graphic. I had decided I would be able to go to where my uncle used to live (no one knows where he is today).

My anxiety was getting worse. I was having chest pains, terrible heart palpitations, and dizzy spells, but I kept working.

The dreams continued, each time the footsteps coming close up the stairs, before I would snap out of my sleep. It was during this time when my friend who I knew had a nervous breakdown told me that her husband had been having sex with her oldest daughter. She divorced him after twenty-something years and has never forgiven him. Without realizing that what she had said upset me, I started having problems being in her company. I avoided her, but felt so guilty I went to see her to tell her I was having problems being in her company. I was able to see her after this confession, but didn't feel as relaxed as I had.

I got to where I saw someone at the top of the stairs, two teenage boys with a grocery bag. Next time, they walked past the bed where I was lying. Next came the figure of a man in white underwear in my dark bedroom near the foot of the bed. The next dream I turned my head to the left and it startled me that someone was next to me, head on the pillow. I was talking with this person; I could see this. I tried to look into the face but it was wobbly. The next one, the room was light, I was on my hands and knees, and someone was licking my rectum.

The next dream someone was on top of me. This person was talking and the face was wobbly so I decided to listen to the voice, and it slowed to $33^1/_3$ rpm. This time I kept looking, and the face straightened. It was my father!

Even though I knew there was always this possibility, it stunned me. I walked around for days, in a daze trying to put it all together. I didn't tell anyone. This all came about a year or so after we began. My father, who I and my sister felt couldn't have done such a thing, could never live with it. We went away on vacation as planned. My brother's girlfriend and I started talking very personal. I told her what we were working on, and before I could say who it was, she said "It was your father!" Then she said he had also molested my brother (three years younger than I). This made me angry. That evening when we went out I thought I was going to be sick. The girlfriend made me promise not to tell my brother she told me. My brother and I had just recently gotten back together, from three years earlier when I went over the edge. At that time I told him not to visit me when he was drinking.

My father was near death at one point before I discovered the incest. Later, my brother told me he nearly told my mother and my younger brother about what my father did to him, out of anger.

We set up a session for me to tell my brother and sister about my father, with the hope my brother would open up. My brother never showed. I told my sister; all she said was "Oh, no." Not disagreeing, but not wanting to believe it. I was so frustrated because my brother hadn't come, that I told my sister what my brother's girlfriend had said, and why it was so important that he come to the session. This is when my sister told me that when we first started on this subject my brother had confided in her what my father had done to him and said if she felt it would help me, to tell me. She couldn't, because she didn't want it to be true. I was surprised by her confession, but I understood what she was saying.

I went to see my brother and told him what I had discovered in therapy, that my father had molested me, and the dreams, and how our sister had held back, etc. We talked about all the hard issues of our youth, and I asked him to come to the next session, which he did. I did not enjoy the pain associated with the process of discovering my father's identity, but I don't know if I would have accepted that it had happened to me also, if my sister had told me in the beginning.

I had a hard time whenever I went to see my parents. I would get angry at my father over nothing. I stopped going because I would have trouble sleeping, and get the hives, etc. My brother was doing the same.

We set up a session with my brother and me to discuss talking with my father. My brother didn't show. The next session he did. He agreed to join me and do joint sessions. He cancelled on me an hour before my session. Then whenever I saw him he wouldn't discuss it. This is when I asked my father to join me (I had a terrible fear he would overreact and kill himself). I felt it would never end until I did this. I didn't want this to come out in anger, and I felt now that it had come out in the open. Surprisingly, throughout all of our lives, we were a really connected family, and I didn't want this to change.

My father came to the next therapy session. I never felt so out on a limb. My father spoke very honestly, but when I told him he had molested my brother and me, he said no, he could never. I said it was true. He said he had no recall, but if two of his kids say it's so, it must be so. He apologized to me. It was one of the hardest things I've ever had to do. I felt like I had destroyed him. This was not a good feeling, but deep down, I knew he had to take the responsibility for this act, so I could stop feeling like a victim. My father admitted his drinking during this period. This is when he got into alcohol black-outs. I accepted that, and in my heart, I knew he was sorry. The past thirty-something years of pain will never be forgotten, but what's more important to me is the coming thirty. I knew my father needed to see that I truly accepted his apology, so I kept going there to his home. He never told my mom, which to me wasn't important. It was between us. I didn't even get angry at him for trying to deny the incest, like I felt I would. Even the hostility toward my mother lessened.

My brother was avoiding my parents, so I decided to tell him about the session with my father, what he said, and that I accepted what he had to say. He seemed relieved and said he never could have done it.

My mom had a stroke recently and died one and a half weeks later. It was a hard time for all of my family. For the first time in my life I felt I would be OK right at the onset. My family sharing the same pain gave me my strength.

I know I'm not stress-free any more than the next person, but hopefully no more either. I know I will experience down time but that I'll have the strength to pull up out of it. The best compliment I've ever received was from my youngest brother and his wife. They said that "my strength," throughout my mother's sickness and death, helped them get through it. I knew the pain they were feeling. I had been real close to my mom at one point, but had worked hard to become independent. I think that's the best gift a parent can give her grown children, is independence, so they feel secure enough in their own lives to go on when we are gone. I know today, that my mother was a very unhappy person, who had no life outside of her children. My life isn't perfect, and I'm not trying to be perfect anymore; it's exhausting, and not worth the effort. I like the person I am today. I've found that I am a good person; I have a capacity for forgiveness. I'll never forget the past, but it doesn't hurt anymore.

It amazes me how far we've come, as I'm returning my dad's wash, and helping him with his bills, and he casually tells me my brother called just to see how he's doing today. This is my family, the most important people in this world!

Case Analysis

When incest occurs, the breaking of that prohibition is such a strong taboo that the behavior is usually a secret within the family. Not only is the child who is involved in incest often threatened physically and psychologically by the perpetrating parent, but he or she often feels ashamed and guilty and self-blaming, both for the occurrence of incest and also for the presence of a mixture of negative and positive feelings toward the perpetrating parent. The child and the adult who experienced incest as a child often have difficulty remembering those painful experiences. Often the mechanism of dissociation of self from body occurs as a means to live through aggressive sexual experiences at the hand of a parent, uncle, or brother.

In the B. family, it was clear the incestuous experience between the father and both his children, Mrs. B. and her brother, was a family secret. At a conscious level, Mrs. B. had lived many years without thinking about the incest. She "forgot" about it, and in its place, she had many symptoms that were expressed in the marital relationship and in symptoms such as anxiety and depression.

From a systems perspective, all of the symptoms can be understood as involving triangling. Mrs. B.'s anxiety in regard to the incestuous behavior with her father was temporarily, and ultimately unsuccessfully, bound through a focus on her individual symptoms and the interpersonal problems in her marriage.

In other words, the triangle involved Mrs. B. focusing on her emotional symptoms, with her father and the experience of incest being in the distant, outside position in the triangle. For Mrs. B., as in other similar cases, secrecy supported the emergence of physical, social, and emotional symptoms in the individual, insofar as it was a mechanism that kept the family from dealing directly with one another.

The B. family illustrates that in incest, as with the case in all emotional problems, the whole family was involved and affected at different levels. In Mrs. B.'s parents' marriage, there was considerable conflict followed by distance. Mrs. B.'s mother had extramarital relationships with both men and women. Mrs. B.'s father attempted suicide, apparently at least in part in response to his wife's infidelity and withdrawal of intimacy. The father's alcoholism may have been both a factor in his wife's distancing from him physically and emotionally and a mode of responding to his wife's withdrawal from him. The level of emotional maturity, or differentiation, of both parents appears to have been equally low.

In the central parent-child triangle, Mr. B. turned his emotional attention and focus toward his second daughter, Mrs. B., and perhaps to a somewhat lesser degree to her younger brother. Thus, one basic triangle that existed for many years in Mrs. B.'s family of origin consisted of the parents being emotionally and physically distant and the father and Mrs. B. being in an overly close relationship, characterized by hostile fusion. A similar triangle may have existed with Mrs. B.'s brother functioning in a similar position with his parents. Based on subsequent therapy with that brother, undertaken by the same therapist, it was clear that he too experienced severe symptomatology related to being the object of sexual abuse by his father. In the triangles involving Mrs. B. and her parents, and the one involving her next younger brother and their parents, the mother was experienced as distant, unavailable, and unprotective. In subsequent therapy that involved the youngest brother and his wife, undertaken by the same therapist, it became clear that the "baby" brother was infantilized in an overly close position with his mother and in a distant relationship with his father. It appears that Mrs. B.'s mother may have discovered that her husband was sexually abusing one or both of her older children. Her overprotectiveness toward the "baby," including keeping him away from his father, may have been done out of fear that he might also sexually abuse him. In the triangle involving this youngest son, she and the son functioned in a somewhat symbiotically fused relationship, with the father being in the distant position from both his wife and his son. The relationship between the oldest sister of Mrs. B. and her parents appears to have involved some functional distance from both of her parents. She did hide the fact that her brother told her he was sexually abused by their father from Mrs. B. for several years. She disclosed it at the time she became involved with Mrs. B. in family therapy. That secrecy seems related to her desire to protect her parents and to keep a lid on this emotional issue.

As in the case of the A. family, and in the majority of cases in which this therapist as been involved in dealing with incest, alcohol was viewed as a triggering factor in the father's initiation of sexual activity with his children. Mrs. B. describes her father as often suffering from "blackouts." It may be that Mrs. B.'s father did not remember his sexual behavior due to the "blackouts" and the general alcoholic condition that he was in at that time. However, even if that were true, the father was still responsible for his behavior. Saying that the whole family functions as a reciprocally functioning emotional unit in no way abrogates any individual's legal, moral, or ethical responsibility. Rather, it provides a framework both for understanding and intervening in relation to this toxic problem from a position that is more emotionally neutral.

The key factor in this therapy, as in all systems work, was the capacity of the therapist to manage his own emotional reactivity so that he could be emotionally neutral. The therapist was able to accomplish that stance without it being a "pretend" position or posture. He was able to avoid blaming and shaming Mrs. B., her father, her mother, and her siblings. The therapist strove to conceptualize the entire family as an emotional unit whose members were neither devils nor angels. Rather, the B. family was viewed by the therapist as a family struggling with painful relationship issues in the best way it could manage.

Initially, the therapist helped create an environment in which Mrs. B. was able to think more clearly, with less emotional distortion, by being less reactive to the client's predicament and not having to see her as a helpless victim. In this context, her anxiety began to lower. She began to be able to address her emotional symptoms and bring them more under her control. Then she was able to address marital issues with her husband, including his drinking. When the marital relationship was on a more even keel, then Mrs. B., whose anxiety was now lower, was able to begin "to look" at the incest and her relationship with her father. Dreams were the modality through which Mrs. B. began to talk about the "unthinkable" and "unseeable" incest with her father. Dreams were not interpreted psychoanalytically or through any other theoretical conception. Rather, they were the "window" through which Mrs. B. was able to perceive her experience of incest.

This was *not* an attempt on the therapist's part to help the family member to "recover" a memory. Rather, it was Mrs. B.'s effort to clarify her amorphous anxiety and blurred emotions that moved her toward "seeing" her father's face in the dream and identifying him as being involved with her sexually. The dreams occurred as part of Mrs. B.'s movement from the managing of her anxiety symptoms to more flexibility and less fusion in her marriage. She was then ready to begin differentiation work from the parental triangle, in particular the emotionally charged relationship with her father, her mother's distance, and the incest behavior.

When Mrs. A. was calm enough to face the incest and not be too reactive to it, she could have calm sessions that included her sister and her brother. In the presence of Mrs. B.'s lower reactivity, her siblings were able to acknowledge the incest, to break through the silence of shame and familial overprotection. They could affirm the painful reality of incest, but without having to cut off from each other, blame each other, or break up the family.

At this stage of the therapy, Mrs. B. was ready to meet and speak directly to, rather than confront and attack, her father regarding the incest. This was not an effort of catharsis but rather an effort to be more true to self in relation to her family. She was able to be goal directed in the face of her father's original denial that he had had sexual relations with her and her brother. Because she was able to keep from attacking her father and not be overly emotional, Mrs. B.'s posture facilitated her father acknowledging the reality of the incest.

The session with Mrs. B. and her father was not a dramatic event; it was low-key in terms of its emotionality. It was the result of more than two years of constant effort on the part of Mrs. A. to know her self better, to lower her anxiety, to know her family more objectively, and to differentiate a self in the context of both her nuclear family and her family of origin. This effort led to a decrease in fusion with her family, without her having to emotionally cut off from them. On the contrary, as Mrs. B. described, following her dealing directly with her father about the incest, an emotional logjam was broken. She slowly began to have more positive feelings toward her father and to spend more comfortable time with him. Mrs. B. came to hold her father responsible for his sexually abusive behavior without having to nullify that he was still her father. Although she held him responsible for his negative behavior toward her, she could also acknowledge that he cared for her and she for him.

CONCLUSION

The initial theoretical hypothesis in this chapter was that incest represents an extreme form of emotional fusion, an extreme manifestation of undifferentiation. Incestual fusion occurs in families in which emotional cutoff from extended family and cutoff from the larger social group are hallmarks. The expanded hypothesis would be that incest is a form of fusion that develops in response to emotional cutoff from the family of origin or extended family.

It is hoped that in the midst of a trend of seeming societal regression, in which the authorities and mental health community often become emotionally reactive and fused with the families with which they work, a Bowen family systems theoretical perspective may facilitate lowering the level of emotional reactivity to the problem of incest and related issues. In so doing, a somewhat greater ability to be objective and neutral in the presence of intense emotionality may be achieved. This allows for a better possibility of ameliorating cutoff which is often devastating and which does irreparable damage beyond the incest itself. Maintaining neutrality in relation to all members of the family, while holding the adults involved responsible for their behavior, is the best course for stemming the multigenerational transmission of incest into future generations.

REFERENCES

Berelson, B. and Steiner, G.A. (1964). *Human Behavior: An Inventory of Scientific Findings.* New York: Harcourt, Brace, and World.

Bowen, M. (1978). *Family Therapy in Clinical Practice.* Northvale, NJ: Jason Aronson.

Lumsden, C. and Wilson, E.O. (1984). *Promethean Fire.* Cambridge, MA: Harvard University Press.

Murdock, G.P. (1949). *Social Structure.* New York: Macmillan.

Smith, W.H. (1994). Child Abuse and Family Emotional Process. Presented at the 1994 Pittsburgh Family Systems Conference and Symposium. Western Pennsylvania Family Center, Pittsburgh, Pennsylvania.

Trivers, R. (1985). *Social Evolution.* Menlo Park, CA: Benjamin Cummings Publishing Co.

Wilson, E.O. (1980). *Sociobiology: The Abridged Edition.* Cambridge, MA: The Belknap Press.

Chapter 13

Child-Focused Divorce

Edward W. Beal

INTRODUCTION

The nature of contemporary marital disruption in our society is unprecedented. In the past, death was the major cause of marital disruption; today, it is more likely to be divorce. The treatment of the acute and chronic symptoms of divorcing families requires an understanding of this reversal and of the societal, nuclear family, and multigenerational factors involved.

The outcome of any marriage is determined by the functioning of each spouse, their mutual emotional harmony, and the relationship between the marriage and societal influences, including religious and civil laws, economic and medical factors, and the extended family system, all of which influence the capacity of an individual to regulate himself or herself. Similarly, the marital relationship also influences the capacity of an individual to regulate himself or herself. The clinical application of Bowen family systems theory to divorce includes the biological, familial, societal, and multigenerational aspects of marriage and their mutual reciprocity.

The capacity for a stable, functional, long-term emotional bond between two people may be an evolved characteristic. The complexity of the cerebral cortex and the prolonged dependency between parent and child permit more information from earlier generations to be transmitted nongenetically. Children learn directly from their parents and through firsthand observation how to manage marital relationships. This merger of individuals into a functionally interdependent unit centered around the reproductive process—what we call monogamy—reaches a fairly elaborate form in the human family. The factors that influence the mutual emotional harmony in that bond include the physical, social, and emotional well-being of the individuals, their influence on one another, and the societal factors that impact their marriage.

Although there appear to be predictable patterns by which marital bonds are established and maintained, according to anthropologist Helen Fisher, marriage similarly has a predictable cross-cultural pattern of decay. Reviewing demographic yearbooks of the United Nations for sixty-two societies, Fisher isolated a cross-cultural pattern in which divorce peaks between the second and fourth year of marriage—"the four-year itch." This pattern persists despite diverse cultural factors, individual customs, or a low or high divorce rate. The American peak, slightly earlier than the four-year worldwide peak, corresponds with the end of the normal two- to three-year period of infatuation. It is conceivable that those who marry primarily for romance and reproduction divorce when the passion fades (Fisher, 1992).

However, Fisher suggests that the timing of divorce, not the rate, has a biological or evolutionary base. Divorce peaks in the young, within three to four years of marriage, and in marriages with zero to two children. The more children, the longer the marriage and the less likely is a divorce. Pair-bonds are built primarily around romance and sexual reproduction and abandoned through adultery or divorce, but, as she suggests, long marriages require work. Nevertheless, Fisher carefully observes that "the American divorce peak has nothing to do with the rising divorce rate in America" (Fisher, 1992, p. 110). There has been a major decrease in the stability of long-term marital relationships in the United States in the past thirty years. It is unlikely that this represents a simultaneous change in the evolved capacity of individuals to stabilize intimate relationships, but rather, it reflects more the change in society's capacity to regulate marital stability. Although no one in a society founded on self-determination, with its emphasis on civil liberty, would oppose two mature married individuals having the opportunity to divorce each other, the rate of marital dissolution does raise questions about the nature and quality of modern family life. Clinical observations suggest that the highest rate of divorce is occurring in the less mature segment of society and that a highly anxious family with an intense child-focused process is passing on the divorce phenomenon from one generation to another through the process of conflict and emotional cutoff.

This chapter describes the divorce process on a societal, familial, and multigenerational level, with special emphasis on the phenomenon of the child-focused divorce as a mechanism for the multigenerational transmission of emotional cutoff. Concepts derived from Bowen family systems theory (Bowen, 1978) are used to describe these phenomena and to plan strategies for intervention.

DIVORCING SOCIETY

Notwithstanding the observations by Fisher about divorce peaking at the fourth year of marriage, the marital disruption rate in the United States from

1860 to 1960 from all causes remained level except for some minor ups and downs related to issues such as war and economic depression. During that time, however, the divorce rate changed from about 7 percent in 1860 to almost 35 percent in 1960. Therefore, the rising marital disruption from divorce was offset by the decreasing marital disruption from death, due to the increased longevity of the population in general. In other words, the increasing exit from marriage by divorce was offset by the decreasing exit from marriage by death until about 1960 (Castro and Bumpass, 1987).

However, in the past thirty years, the marital disruption rate has soared dramatically. Indeed about one-half of today's youth will have spent some time in a one-parent family; when combined with their own chances of marital success, only a minority of Americans will have a stable two-parent family in both childhood and as an adult (Castro and Bumpass, 1987). Since the majority of men and women who divorce remarry, it is unlikely that this evolved property of the family and individuals is disappearing but rather that families and society are having considerably more difficulty regulating marriage. It is doubtful that the nature of marriage changed drastically or that the level of maturity of those entering marriage changed dramatically. In fact, the average age at marriage has increased considerably. It is quite possible that for such a rapid change to occur, societal factors regulating marriage have been a major influence on the dissolution rate. If stable marriages within society depend on extramarital controls such as religion, civil law, economic variability, and intact relationships with past generations, then it is possible to view the increasing divorce rate as a function of the influence of these extramarital controls.

Societal Factors

Economic

The expansion of the U.S. economy following World War II allowed the entrance of more individuals into the workforce, especially women. Enhanced economic viability of women has led to the perception of enhanced emotional independence between the sexes. This evolution in the thinking about women in the home and workforce led to a change in the traditional division of labor in the marriage and family, in which husbands worked and women took care of the home. Although women have always worked outside the home, the division of labor now is subject to more individual variation and negotiation between couples. More mature individuals will find this an opportunity to be flexible. Less mature individuals may find the lack of clearly defined expectations an opportunity for more conflict than cooperation. The higher divorce rate among women with advanced degrees may reflect their greater economic independence from men and marriage.

Religious and Civil Laws

The influence of religious laws on the divorce rate was highlighted by the Church of England's decision in 1967 to embrace the concept of no-fault divorce. The mutual influence of the mental health movement and the Protestant church is revealed in the church's belief that individuals should not be blamed for behavior that arises from their emotional make-up. Previously, the church granted divorce only for adultery or physical cruelty, but the general thinking of the Church shifted to consider the new idea that a person's marital history may not be the ideal way to judge the state of his/her soul (Stone, 1989). In 1971, California Legislature, quoting the Church of England document for support, was the first to pass no-fault divorce laws that permitted termination of marriages, not for offenses previously considered unpardonable, such as adultery or physical or mental cruelty, but because of temperamental incompatibility or disappointment that married life was not as the couple hoped it would be. These legislative changes have spread rapidly throughout the United States so that now no-fault divorce is the law in fifty states.

The net effect of these societal changes has been to facilitate entrances and exits from marriages. It is arguable that the rising divorce rate, variously estimated from 52 percent to 80 percent for a thirty-year marriage if all trends remain, is more a function of these societal influences than an acute change in this evolved characteristic of the family called the marital bond (Castro and Bumpass, 1987).

Differentiation and Divorce

Individual reaction to these societal changes varies according to one's level of differentiation. Individuals with higher levels of differentiation are less reactive to societal changes; individuals with lower levels would be more reactive. Although individual cases may vary considerably, it is possible that chronic reactivity may be a concept that would describe the stepwise progression in this phenomenon between society and families. The increased divorce rate then may reflect a disturbance or regression in intimate relationships, fostered by increasing reactivity and changes in previously established societal controls. In my opinion, the current decline in the marriage rate, the significant increase in average age at first marriage, and the rising cohabitation rate before marriage and after divorce reflect the chronically reactive manner in which society is attempting to rework and reestablish stable adult relationships. The long-term pattern for divorce appears to be stabilizing at a minimum of 52 percent, although a marriage lasting thirty years has a much greater chance of surviving the next years than a newly formed one (Castro and Bumpass, 1987). It appears those individuals who are emotionally cut off from extended family and from important societal traditions may have fewer resources with which to tone down reactivity from marital interaction and have fewer guidelines available for problem solving and cooperative behavior.

Societal and Family Emotional Cutoff: Death versus Divorce

Although large numbers of reconstituted families have existed for years, the source of the initial family dissolution was more likely to be the death of a parent rather than parental divorce. The precipitating cause of marital disruption affects the functioning of the family and the degree of emotional cutoff of the children. In my opinion, divorce disrupts all family members more than any other event. Most researchers agree it creates a significant regression in all family members, including both parents. When parental death occurs, the surviving parent and children are usually older. Divorce arises out of long-term conflict and leads to greater intergenerational conflict and cutoff. Divorce is voluntary, as perceived by children, and therefore less emotionally forgivable. Subsequent romantic triangles are less tolerated in a divorced parent than in a widow or widower.

Family emotional cleavage in divorce usually leaves children in the custody of their mother, approximately 90 percent of the time, and less emotionally connected to their father and the paternal extended family system. In contrast, the death of a mother or father generates an outpouring of emotional support from both sides of the family and from friends. For the most part, this phenomenon does not happen with divorce.

Divorce breeds divorce. There is a multigenerational emotional process operating in families, coupled with the societal changes regulating marital relationships, that contributes to the current higher divorce rates and higher degree of emotional cutoff from family of origin.

Two studies illustrate that white women whose parents were divorced prior to their sixteenth birthday will be 59 to 69 percent more likely themselves to divorce than women from intact families (London, Kahn, and Pratt, 1988). White males from divorced families have a 32 percent greater chance of divorcing than those from intact families (Glenn and Kramer, 1987). The multigenerational pattern of emotional cutoff in daughters whose fathers had died seems to be less, as they had only a 35 percent greater risk of divorce than did women from intact families. Remarriage for divorcés and widows seems to affect emotional cutoff in different ways. Daughters whose parents divorce and remarry have two times greater risk of divorce than those living with both parents. Widows who remarry seem to protect their daughters from divorce. These patterns persist no matter when the divorce occurs, early or late in the daughter's life, but are most problematic if the child is in early adolescence (London, Kahn, and Pratt, 1988).

Researchers speculate about the mechanisms that transmit the divorce rate. They postulate that early sex, pregnancy before marriage, and delinquency are all linked to higher divorce rates, as is marrying at an early age (Castro and Bumpass, 1987). However, even when these studies control for early sex and premarital pregnancy, there is still significantly more divorce among adults whose parents were divorced. Children of divorce are likely to have not only unsatisfactory marriages, but also less reluctant to end them. Moreover, their courtship patterns appear to be somewhat different from children from intact families. This information suggests that examination of the nuclear family emotional patterns and how they contribute to the emotional cutoff in divorcing families would be helpful.

NUCLEAR FAMILY EMOTIONAL SYSTEM AND THE DIVORCE PROCESS

There is no question that divorce makes a significant difference in how a family functions and how a child grows up. Researchers emphasize the influence of age, gender, custody and visitation arrangements, as well as postdivorce parental and ex-spousal relationships and the influence of remarriage. However, in my opinion, the factors that are most important are the unique characteristics of the child, the parent-child relationships, and more important, the way the family reorganizes itself after the parents have separated. Bowen family systems theory, with its emphasis on the nuclear family patterns of conflict, adaptation, physical or emotional distancing, and child focus, illuminates how the postdivorce family reorganizes itself.

Research demonstrates that a child's age, gender, individual resilience, and the custody arrangements have a lot to do with his/her acute response to parental divorce. These are the symptom patterns about which parents most often consult mental health professionals. However, it is the nuclear family emotional patterns and the degree of child focus before and after the divorce that determine the intensity of symptoms and the long-term adaptive relationship patterns.

Acute symptoms, for the most part, reflect a child's stage of growth and development. The intensity of the symptoms reflects the level of differentiation and child focus present. Young preschoolers often demonstrate rather regressed behavior, especially if the divorce has significantly disorganized their parents. Older preschoolers often blame themselves for the divorce or for driving one of their parents away. School-age children can rely on their peer relationships to stabilize their functioning but, nevertheless, often experience pervasive sadness. The availability of peers for latency-age children for stability is offset by the inability of this age group, in contrast to the younger children, to use fantasy and play as effectively to make their futures seem more palatable. Late-latency-age children are old enough to be embarrassed by their parents' behavior and to be more aware of the obvious loyalty issues and triangulating, particularly evident in highly child-focused divorces. The child's continuing contact with both parents can be drastically undermined by persistent postdivorce marital conflict (Wallerstein and Blakeslee, 1989).

Adolescents who are unable to emotionally disengage from their parents' divorce are vulnerable to regressive behavior such as sexual promiscuity, excessive drug use, and poor academic functioning. Recent studies have shown that even college-age students are significantly affected by parental divorce and that it alters their dating and courtship behavior (Southworth and Schwartz, 1987).

Since most divorces occur before the end of seven years of marriage, the typical case presented to the mental health professional is a conflictual couple with one or two children under seven years of age. The age, gender, individual resilience, and the way the child is caught up in the family emotional patterns will determine the nature and intensity of the symptoms (Beal, 1991b). Approximately 15 percent of all divorces with custody disputes result in some form of arbitration/litigation process. Since 1972, over one million U.S. children per year are involved in divorces, and therefore, the number of child-focused custody disputes could reach 150,000 per year (Beal, 1991a).

EVALUATION AND THERAPY
IN MILDLY CHILD-FOCUSED FAMILIES

Evaluations begin by asking questions that will identify relationship patterns and family emotional processes and by defining the symptoms in the context of the overall family emotional system. It is appropriate to obtain data from both parents, separated or not. Seeing separated parents together depends on clinical judgement as to whether it intensifies the emotional process.

Many child-focused divorcing parents consult about the emotional process and its effect on the children. It is important to determine where they are in the divorce decision-making process and the extent to which indecisiveness may contribute to the child's symptoms. My focus is to delineate the emotional process, define the part each person plays, and suggest ways to change but not intensify it.

In general, the emotional functioning of all family members regresses for a period of two to three years after the divorce. Yet, in my opinion, the predivorce family history is critical in determining how the divorcing family can continue its parental functioning. Spousal conflict continuing postdivorce and involving the children is the most potentially damaging triangle. Therefore, any effort at symptom improvement in the child without concomitant change in the marital conflict is problematic.

After identifying the part each individual plays, the focus is on helping each person to change himself or herself rather than change the other. As the therapist relates to the family, he/she attempts to remain outside the family emotional field to better provide feedback to the family on how their interactional patterns lead to specific dysfunctions in each family member. This approach decreases the intensity of emotional focus on the child and shifts the parental focus to the marital relationship or to each spouse's relationship to his/her family of origin. This shift has the greatest potential for modifying problems and may be relatively easy to accomplish in mildly child-focused families, especially if parents can learn to view the child as an extension of the family. Accomplishing this shift depends on the therapist's concept of the problem and his/her skill in keeping the family involved and often is aided by keeping the children physically removed from therapy sessions. To the extent that a couple is unable to view their divorce at least in part as a function of overall family emotional patterns, this shift is more difficult (Beal, 1979).

Divorcing families with a good prognosis for children can be identified in the initial evaluation. Although the marital conflict may be substantial, it infrequently involves the children directly. These children may be symptomatic secondary to family breakup but less so from family conflict. Conflicting spouses can retain good parental skills, and either both voluntarily attend the evaluation, or one highly motivated parent seeks assistance. In general, these parents believe that more can be accomplished by keeping the family emotional process and decision making out of the legal system. In addition, these parents can minimize the influence of extended family anxiety on the divorce process.

Once the marital conflict has developed significant triangles outside the nuclear family, the therapist must keep them in mind and work with them. These triangles may involve affairs, lawyers and courts, remarriages, or extended family.

CASE STUDY 1

History and Evaluation

Mr. A. was a highly motivated, upwardly mobile professional with an advanced degree. He married a woman who was willing to support him through graduate school. During the first years of their marriage, it became apparent that the husband made most of the decisions involving the marital pair, and the wife adapted to whatever the husband wanted.

A child was born three years after the marriage. The father developed a chronic illness secondary to an infectious process, which forced the mother to be caregiver to both husband and daughter. Once the father recovered, he became progressively more involved in his studies and bored with family life. Because of frequent conflicts, he was often away from home. Despite his enormous sense of guilt, he decided to leave the family and divorce. Following the divorce itself, he maintained fairly regular contact with his daughter.

Although the divorce process itself had been conflictual, the couple had been able to work it out through their respective lawyers. The father sought therapy because of the mother's impending remarriage, her plan to move to another area of the United States, and their daughter's beginning of dysfunction in school. After the initial interview, it was apparent that the father was trying to make a continuous reentry into the emotional life of his daughter, he was becoming progressively more anxious about the close emotional intensity between his ex-wife and daughter (as well as the fact that his ex-wife was planning to marry a man similar to himself), and his ex-wife's anxiety about this decision was leading to considerable dysfunction in his daughter. When Mr. A. attempted to talk about his anxiety, she complained that he was interfering with her life. (See Figure 13.1 for the A. Family Diagram.)

Therapy

After the initial consultation, Mr. A. was advised to contact a highly competent lawyer who would evaluate the possibility that Mr. A. could bring a lawsuit to prevent the removal of his daughter from the area or to obtain custody. No therapy or mediation seemed appropriate unless Mr. A. clearly understood his chances of resolving the situation through litigation.

When it became clear that little could be resolved through litigation, the family was more prepared to resolve their issues within the nuclear family. Proceeding in the opposite direction—working with the family first with-

FIGURE 13.1. The A. Family Diagram

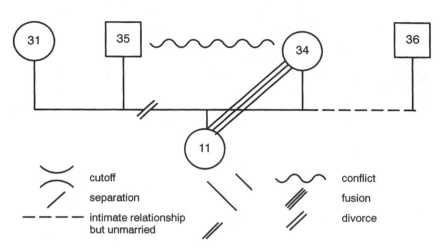

out them knowing the legal options—can often facilitate legal system interference in family decision making, especially when anxiety is high.

Mr. A., his ex-wife, and their daughter agreed to meet. Initially, considerable anxiety was generated by the resurrection of the marital relationship; it became clear, however, that the lack of resolution of the prior emotional relationship contributed to the current symptoms. Although the wishes of the ten-year-old child were considered, I believed resolution would be more complete if the therapy focused on the process between Mr. A. and his former wife. Through several sessions over a number of months, the former Mrs. A. was able to see the similarity between her new relationship and her previous one with Mr. A. She was also able to see how anxiety about the new relationship was being transmitted to her child. When it was clear that Mr. A. would have open and appropriate access to his child, Mrs. A. began to see her ex-spouse as supportive rather than as interfering. The major emphasis was to clarify the general interactional patterns within the family and the part each individual played.

In discussing the practical details of decision making and planning, the family became more aware of the depression and guilt remaining from previously unresolved issues. Together, Mr. A. and his former wife were able to make appropriate plans for contact between their child and both parents. When it was obvious to both parents that they each had a significant contribution to make to their daughter's welfare, they stopped blaming each other and focused on what each of them would do. After the marriage and the move, Mr. A. and his new wife visited in the home of the former Mrs. A. and her new husband. They reported that the social visit went very well. At last report, the daughter had become a very good student and had been placed in advanced classes.

Observations

This approach recognized the major triangles within and outside of the nuclear family, contained the anxiety within the family, worked on previously unresolved issues, and kept the unresolved prior marital problems from focusing on the child. The reduction and containment of the family anxiety and the reduction of the emotional focus on the child presumably enhanced the child's functioning.

With some highly conflictual family problems, the family anxiety cannot be contained, and the therapist may be required to work more closely with nonfamily systems. This process may require therapist-lawyer contact, both dealing from different theoretical frameworks and having differing goals. Legal divorce with emotional separation/divorce is rather different from a legal divorce alone. In my experience, most couples obtain only the latter. The failure to work toward an emotional separation/divorce explains attempts to retain lawyers who reflect one's own emotional bias. It is an unusual lawyer, working within an adversarial framework, who can take a position different from his/her client, maintain the relationship, and still operate within standards in the best interests of the child. The more emotionally biased one spouse-lawyer relationship becomes against the other, the less likely the best interests of the children and the postdivorce family are served (Beal, 1985).

CASE STUDY 2

As anxiety increases, containing the emotional reactivity within the divorcing family becomes increasingly complicated. As blaming increases, motivation to change oneself is lower. A belief that the legal system is highly likely to reinforce one's own emotional bias leads to an overlapping of legal and marital triangles and lawyers who may automatically reflect marital emotional bias. These factors, associated with impulsive decision making, result in less functional divorce resolution and moderate to severe symptoms in children.

History and Evaluation

Two highly competent professionals "fell in love" from the moment they saw each other. Their brief five-month courtship was characterized by intense conflicts. Yet their highly romantic reconciliations focused the relationship on romance rather than on recognition of differences and the need for resolution. Their daughter was born within the first year of their marriage, the second marriage for both of them. (See Figure 13.2 for the B. Family Diagram.)

After the wedding, these intense conflicts were followed by emotional distance and increased activity in their respective professional lives. Both spouses were dominating and inflexible regarding the emotionally based issues between them. Within the first year and before the birth of their child, the parents separated.

After the birth, the marital conflict quickly focused on their differences concerning the well-being of the child. The parents each invited their extended families to move into their respective homes to help with the care of the newborn. When it became obvious that no compromises were possible, the parents each hired a different child psychiatrist to testify to their adequacy as parents. Within one year of marriage, the family emotional triangle overlapped with those of the extended family and the legal mental health systems.

FIGURE 13.2. The B. Family Diagram

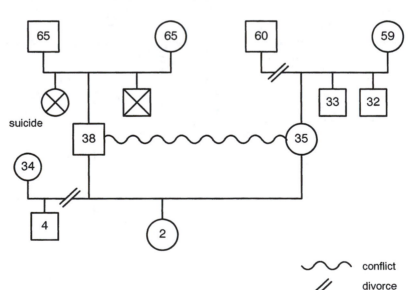

When asked to evaluate the mother-child relationship, I agreed to do so if both parents would be involved or if the husband would indicate directly to me that he refused to be involved. My initial court presentation recommended an appropriate visitation schedule for this young child. Possibly because of the highly explosive nature of the spousal relationship or the judge's own personal preferences, no consideration was given to expert testimony in this initial proceeding. Through their lawyers, the spouses agreed to accept another child psychiatrist as mediator for visitation. However, the psychiatrist was unable to keep the adversarial process appropriately focused between the parents so it quickly disintegrated. The ensuing visitation schedule did not account for the developmental stage of the child. The child began having significant symptoms related to the constant shifting back and forth between parents. Several months later, the mother contacted me again to evaluate the child's symptomatology and asked if I would testify as to the effects of the visitation schedule on the child.

I agreed to see the child, the mother, and the grandmother over a period of time to study the situation. The father refused to be involved. Although information obtained in this manner has a built-in bias, it became apparent that the inability of the parents to cooperate was significantly contributing to the child's symptoms. Moreover, the recent suicide of the father's older sister and the death from illness of the father's younger brother were fostering the child-focused process.

Therapy

In general, I advised conciliation and accommodation between the parents. This relationship style contrasted with the prior organization of the marital dyad, in which conflict and inflexibility reigned. Despite the mother's efforts at compromise, the father frequently took her to court on issues unrelated to visitation. When little responsibility for self, a high degree of blaming, and overlapping marital and legal triangles exist, it sometimes is appropriate to use the legal system to reduce a child's symptoms. Therefore, I suggested the mother hire a new lawyer with a highly adversarial reputation. This intervention strategy made the legal relationship parallel to the organization of the original marital dyad. As the mother realized the difficulty in winning this case through conciliation, she became aware of the new lawyer's ability to reduce the harassment. Through advocacy, although unhappy about the child's contact with the father, she was able to take a position with the child regarding the importance of visitation. Without filing any further motions, this new lawyer "persuaded" the father to cease his frequent visits to court. Consequently, the child's symptoms regarding separation anxiety quickly improved.

Although an adversarial process is not generally recommended for the resolution of these problems, it is increasingly apparent that, in some highly conflictual marriages with little focus on personal responsibility and high focus on blaming, the court system may be used to contain the intrafamily emotional process so that it can be worked on in therapy (Beal, 1985).

CASE STUDY 3

This case presented as a periodically symptomatic child-focused process that was activated by extended family contact and remarriage, yet the long-term family relationship pattern was most problematic. Peaceful divorces do not necessarily lead to peaceful postdivorce family functioning. A highly adaptive child with immature adaptive parents may, under significant stress, exceed parental adaptive capacity. Too much flexibility may lead to a spineless position. Asymptomatic during and immediately following the divorce process, a child may become highly symptomatic later, when differences between the parents are less easily dissolved through adaptiveness. Extended family reactivity or remarriage of one of the ex-spouses may require real choices rather than compromises.

History and Evaluation

Two spouses assumed primarily adaptive positions in relation to emotionally based issues. The husband was the oldest of ten children; the wife, the older of two sisters. In the husband's family, his father made all the decisions and his mother complied. In the wife's family, her mother assumed a very protective role toward the children, with no overt conflict appearing between her parents.

While dating in college and becoming best friends, they "fell in love." During the first six years of marriage, they began to have sexual difficulties, "discovered" they had nothing in common, and developed significant emotional distance from each other. They considered separation but stayed together. Later they decided to separate but again changed their minds. As the relationship evolved, it was obvious they had trouble differing from each other. (See Figure 13.3 for the C. Family Diagram.)

Spouses often have difficulty adapting their solidified marital relationship to parenting, especially when their first child is born more than five years after the wedding. Hiring someone to care for their child, who was born six years after the marriage, both parents continued to work. Nevertheless, the husband knew the marriage would end eventually because of the

FIGURE 13.3. The C. Family Diagram

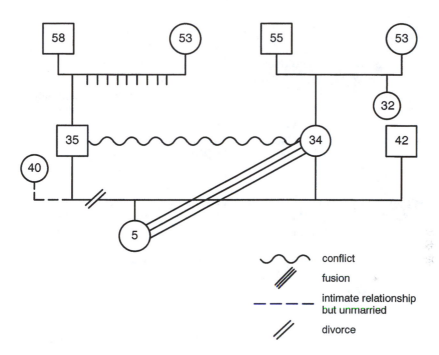

excessive adaptiveness in negotiating differences. Yet he said he would feel guilty about initiating a separation, by either deserting his wife to avoid further contact or promoting an affair by her so she would leave him. Correspondingly, the wife indicated it was all right for the husband to have an affair to deal with their marital problems as long as he did not tell her.

When their child was four and a half years old, the parents made a firm decision to separate. Both acknowledged the good parenting skills of the other and handled the separation in a complex but responsible manner. The child experienced some developmentally appropriate anxieties but these were changed by working directly with the parents and the parents working with the school. Symptomatically, this child appeared a mildly focused one. However, she clearly had been the major reason for the continuation of the marriage, an emotional burden for any child. The mother decided to let the child live with the father because, in her opinion, the child liked the father best and he was an excellent father. The mother characteristically made this and other decisions without consulting her extended family.

After she informed them, her family was so upset that she changed her mind.

Therapy

Although there was no open conflict, they contacted me about the best plans for the child. With little difficulty, they outlined the type of structure the child needed and the appropriate visitation and residential arrangements. They agreed to joint custody, equal time with the child, no alimony or child support, and an equal division of additional costs incurred in raising the child. It was clear they found it easier to make decisions as parents than as spouses. Although this couple attended several sessions, worked hard, and had no overt conflictual issues, their mutual adaptiveness presented a long-term problem for them and ultimately for their child. While making appropriate arrangements for the child and separating, they had not recognized or resolved their marital differences. A divorce that does not resolve the marital problems under the aforementioned arrangements will predictably resurrect itself as a child-focused problem when one of them remarries or moves away and wants to take the child along. They were unable and unwilling to discuss this problem.

Two years later they called. The mother remarried, and the father was planning to. The mother's new husband was being transferred to another city and she wanted to take the child with her. They wanted advice as to what they should do about the child. A significant consideration was who would do best without the child. The mother indicated that she needed the child more than the child needed her. The father thought he would function better without the child than would the mother. As a part of the decision-making process, I helped them decide on a visitation schedule regardless of with whom the child lived. They had to decide who would be the primary custodian.

This family had turned an initial strength into a liability; their adaptiveness to each other had led to an inability to make or take responsibility for decisions. After several sessions, it was apparent that neither would compromise on this matter so the father engaged a child psychiatrist to see both parents. After an evaluation, this expert decided in favor of the father; the mother then engaged her own child psychiatrist, who subsequently decided in her favor.

In my opinion, the child probably would have done reasonably well with either parent. A decision by an outside expert is only a decision; it does not resolve the basic paralysis between the parents. The therapeutic and legal system to some extent contained the anxiety of this family and minimized the child's symptoms, but the pre- and postdivorce family emotional patterns shaped the child's emotional attachments for the future. In my opinion, when these child-focused children become adults, they are likely to develop problems in establishing and maintaining intimate relationships (Beal, 1985).

EVALUATION:
SEVERELY CHILD-FOCUSED FAMILIES

The Bowen family systems theory orientation to severely child-focused divorcing families offers a way of thinking about the family and legal system that maximizes a flexible approach and enlarges criteria by which decisions can be made. Referrals often come directly from family members but also from lawyers or directly from the court. The therapist's orientation to the problem can flow along a continuum from therapist to mediator to arbitrator. This pathway maximizes flexibility and individual responsibility among family members and minimizes responsibility for decision making by the therapist, insofar as anxiety, differentiation, and the system permit.

As family anxiety and blaming increase and maturity and personal responsibility decrease, the therapist will be pulled along the continuum from therapist to mediator to decision maker. However, regarding custody decisions, society relegates the final legal decision to the judge when parents are unable or unwilling to do so. Less mature individuals in a highly charged atmosphere are unwilling to compromise or negotiate differences if they believe a judge is likely to decide in their favor.

Clarifying the reason for referral before the initial visit—whether for therapy for self, spouse, or child, divorce mediation, or custody evaluation with "expert testimony"—highlights sources of family anxiety and exposes specific triangles. Although the family is often unsure what it wants, besides "please help my child," lack of prior clarification can lead to polarization and enmeshment in triangles in which the therapist conducts an evaluation under the most adverse circumstances. In some states, it is actually against the law to perform a nonemergency medical/psychiatric evaluation on a minor child when requested by a noncustodial parent (Bernet, 1995). Clarification of the task before beginning the evaluation actually reduces the number of families seen but makes the triangles more workable later.

As discussed earlier, the more frequent and easier cases are the mildly child-focused families in which the family seeks help for a spouse or a child. Yet a request for marriage or divorce counseling is only a question about direction. Each involves a focus on self-definition that is critical in both decision-making processes. Although the content of the discussion may be different, the process of self-definition is similar. Disputes over

custody, visitation, property division, and alimony frequently are complicated by family emotional processes. A Bowen family systems approach
with a focus on self-definition over continuing conflict can be helpful to
separating spouses. Lawyers can commit to writing what couples can agree
upon. Again, a legal divorce without an appropriate emotional separation/
divorce is a decision but not a resolution of the marital emotional residue.

The more complicated cases involve referrals in which the family with
declining maturity, a low level of responsibility, and high levels of blaming wants help in custody decision making but "agrees to accept" the
therapist's recommendation if they cannot resolve it themselves. Although
often denied and infrequently stated, the agreement to accept the therapist's decision has a caveat, including "as long as they think the therapist
was fair and decided it their way." The most advantageous position is to
have the parents and their lawyers choose one professional to work with
all four adults, to have a written document detailing the task, and to obtain
a court order appointing the therapist to work with the family. This written
procedure, although subject to court scrutiny, clarifies the task, minimizes
triangling, and when anxiety rises, it allows the therapist to have active
contact with all sides of the triangles. It is arguable as to why mental health
professionals should be involved in the family's procedure of child custody litigation. However, it is a part of society, and in my opinion, a professional with the broadest orientation to a child's emotional universe is in the
best position to determine how the emotional cleavage in a family occurs
(Beal, 1985).

The American Psychiatric Association's Task Force on Clinical Assessment in Child Custody recommends gathering information on four areas
when evaluating severely child-focused families: (1) the reciprocal attachment between a parent and a child, (2) the child's preference, (3) the child's
needs and the adult's parenting capacities, and (4) the relevant family dynamics (APA, 1988). Additionally, I recommend assessing (5) past marital history, (6) the contact a prospective custodial parent will permit between the child
and the other parent, (7) the nature of the relationship between each parent
and the extended family, (8) gender of the child and prospective custodial
parent, (9) any possibility for remarriage by either parent, and (10) the willingness of a parent to accept a reasoned decision. When spouses believe a
decision by someone else is the best and only way to resolve their problems,
their family is in trouble. This abdication of personal responsibility, coupled
with high-level marital conflict, major emotional focus on blaming the
other, and a court-ordered involuntary evaluation, suggests immediate and
long-term problems in children. In general, these spouses have minimal
ability to tone down marital emotional reactivity or to minimize the influ-

ence of the extended family or legal system on their own decision making, and they have minimal responsibility for resolution of custody and visitation problems.

CASE STUDY 4

History and Evaluation

Mr. and Mrs. Z. were separated and divorced when their daughter was seven and their son was two. Mr. Z. had been married twice before and had one child who was emancipated. Mrs. Z., who was married once before, had no other children but had retained custody of their two mutual children. A highly charged, bitter divorce led to intermittent contact between Mr. Z. and the children. Over the next five years, Mr. Z. alleged that his former wife systematically obstructed his relationship with the children by, among other things, tape-recording phone conversations, denigrating the father in front of the children, and preventing scheduled visitation through feigned illness. He returned to court to have his visitation rights enforced, and the court appointed a psychiatrist to work with the parents and advise the court regarding an appropriate visitation schedule. The psychiatrist met separately with all the parties who agreed to a schedule that included a provision for phone calls and a note from a physician if illness prevented visitation. Moreover, the mother was to notify the school that in case of emergency, when she could not be contacted, the school was to contact the father. (See Figure 13.4 for the Z. Family Diagram.)

Although the initial evaluation was not a custody determination, the following observations were made: The children had an emotionally close, overly protected relationship with their mother and a distant, hostile relationship with their father. Too young to have their preference make any difference, the children nevertheless strongly indicated they wanted to live with their mother. The conflict over visitation was simply the latest battle in an unresolved, highly conflicted child-focused divorce.

Mr. Z. had a long history of emotionally cutting off from family members and had recently married for the fourth time but kept fairly regular contact with his own mother. Mrs. Z. alleged close family ties but almost never visited or phoned her extended family. Mrs. Z. denied much responsibility for the visitation problems, talked mostly of how it interfered with the children's schedule, and thought regular contact between the children and her former husband was of little value to them. Mr. Z. claimed he really wanted a relationship with his children, but it was initially unclear

FIGURE 13.4. The Z. Family Diagram

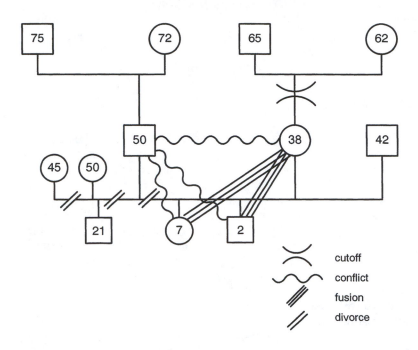

how much this contact served the function of simply harassing his former wife. In my opinion, it is appropriate to put into place a structure that allows a postdivorce family to most closely re-create the best aspects of the predivorce parent-child relationships. The court asked that the psychiatrist have ongoing contact with the family from year to year to determine how the visitation was going and to make recommendations. Parental disputes could be processed through the mental health professional without further litigation.

The next several years were eventful. The older daughter developed a relationship with Mr. Z.'s new wife, her stepmother, her hostility to her father decreased, and she began dating, which caused great problems between her and her mother. The prior emotionally close relationship between mother and daughter had focused on their mutual dislike of men and Mr. Z. in particular. Mrs. Z.'s anxiety surfaced in her increasing battles with the daughter and her overprotection of her son. The latter missed several visits with his father because of illness, but no physician visits were made. The son had become a good athlete, but he was not allowed to participate in athletics, and peers were not admitted to their home. Depressed, his school performance deteriorated. As the relationship with his daughter improved, Mr. Z. was given a different factual picture of what went on in the home of his former wife. Efforts to get Mrs. Z. to modify her behavior were met only with allegations that her children's difficulties were a product of the contact with Mr. Z. As these rigid emotional patterns became more entrenched, the daughter ran away from home to live with Mr. Z., who petitioned the court for custody of both children. By this time, there was a new judge, several new lawyers, but the same psychiatrist.

Therapy

When the legal system becomes this enmeshed in the family triangles, the mental health professional becomes more a fact finder and advisor to the family and court, with a focus on reducing anxiety. An evaluation indicated acute symptoms in both children that were a product of the intense child focus in the mother's home, with significant cutoff from extended family, her own friends, and the children's peer relationships. Mr. Z. seemed genuinely interested in taking care of the children, and his new wife had established a sufficient relationship with the children to facilitate the possibility. There were clearly some advantages to a stable two-parent home over an unstable one-parent home, and there is much current research that supports the idea of children functioning better with the same-sex parent. Moreover, other research illustrates that most families recover within two to three years postseparation and divorce and reach a stable reorganization. Highly child-focused families are at risk for not being able to do that, and Mrs. Z. seemed unable to do so. Her refusal to accept any responsibility other than blaming Mr. Z. compounded efforts to change the patterns.

After a lengthy trial, the judge ordered a transfer of custody of both children to the father's home. Additionally, he ordered the same psychiatrist to work with all parties and to develop a visitation schedule for Mrs. Z. This decision was made despite Mrs. Z.'s efforts, which resulted in another psychiatrist testifying that leaving the children with Mrs. Z. was in their best interest. At this level of acute and chronic anxiety, it is difficult for the mental health professional to maintain a balanced relationship with all members of the family. However, meeting separately with all family members, focusing on specific tasks, and attempting to reduce reactivity facilitate continued contact and reduce acute anxiety.

For several years, the children lived in their father's home. The deterioration in the mother-daughter relationship was such that contact was limited.

Mrs. Z. viewed her daughter's interest in dating boys and in her father to be an act of disloyalty difficult to abide. Following the move, her son's significant improvements in school functioning, peer relationships, and athletics were impressive. Moreover he managed to maintain contact with and loyalty to his mother. Although some acute problems persisted, father, stepmother, and both children worked on them in therapy. Mrs. Z. minimized contact with the psychiatrist.

In the middle of a child-focused family conflict, in which the mental health professional or the court takes a position deemed unfavorable to one side, the emotional process then refocuses and the court, judge, or mental health professional becomes the problem. The more rigid the emotional process, the more fixed is the opinion of the "maligned" parent. Ordinarily, these families involve multiple lawyers, jurisdictions, court systems, and other mental health professionals. In the service of saving their children, a parent may spend the equivalent of a college education or have to declare bankruptcy to finance this process. The degree of reactive emotional irresponsibility seen in these families is highlighted by a similar case in which two children were kidnapped by a custodial mother from their elementary school to keep them from their "dangerous" father. After spending several days with their mother in the basement of the grandparents' home, the children finally persuaded their mother to let them return to school.

More than ten years after their divorce, the conflict between Mr. and Mrs. Z. continued. Mrs. Z. petitioned the court to have another "neutral expert" of her choosing evaluate the record. The court granted her request. Psychiatrist number two extensively interviewed her and psychiatrist number one and made an exhaustive review of the records, the psychiatrist's opinion, and the basis for that opinion. This latest psychiatrist concluded that the court and the first psychiatrist had reached an appropriate conclusion.

Hiring a new lawyer, Mrs. Z. appealed the case to the state court of appeals, which ultimately reaffirmed the lower-court decision. For a while, the emotionally driven conflict shifted from custody and visitation to filing petitions regarding alimony and support payments. Subsequently, it shifted to the credibility and objectivity of the original judge, and the higher court was again petitioned, asking that the lower-court judge be recused. The higher court affirmed the lower-court judge's decision. When this judge retired, Mrs. Z. petitioned to have psychiatrist number one removed from the case on the grounds of failing to remain objective. This petition was also denied.

This extensive triangling, fostered by the "maligned" parent and fueled by the adversarial system, replicates within the society the family's emotionally based child-focused process. This replication is seldom helpful to the child. Currently, accusations of child sexual abuse in the context of child custody litigation are almost an epidemic in the United States. The emotional reactivity associated with this issue greatly facilitates this triangling outside of the family. Appointing one objective, competent, systems-oriented mental health professional can reduce acute symptoms in the children and the overall reactivity in the family and legal systems.

Although the Z. children suffered a great deal, they have remained functional members of society who have obtained good educations and employment. One might argue that containing the emotional process within the legal system may have helped their family adjustment. Nevertheless, this adjustment has been maintained at the expense of very polarized relationships between the children and each parent. It is this emotional polarization and chronic reactivity that will significantly influence their subsequent adult intimate relationships.

ADULT CHILDREN OF CHILD-FOCUSED DIVORCES

Adults who have grown up in a family using emotional cutoff and child focus as mechanisms for dealing with family anxiety have difficulty establishing and maintaining intimate mature adult relationships. The important task is to emotionally extricate themselves from their parents' marriage and divorce and identify the family emotional processes and their part in them. Studies indicate that parental divorce, regardless of when it occurs in a child's life, enhances anxiety in courtship. It correlates with earlier and more premarital sex, more cohabitation, and earlier marriages. Additionally, if the divorce had been highly conflictual or if the parent-child postdivorce relationship deteriorated, the adult children were less committed to relationships and quicker to threaten to end a relationship if it was not working. Children who are the product of child-focused divorces have more of these problems (Beal, 1991a).

CASE STUDY 5

Evaluation

Mr. M., a thirty-year-old lawyer who had been living with his girlfriend for five years, started having an affair about a month after she suggested they get married. Instead of working on the relationship with his girlfriend, he sought reasons to travel on business. Confronted by a suspicious girlfriend, he denied the affair. Gradually, his agitation built and got the best of him. His first psychiatrist told him it was a developmental crisis, that he was afraid of responsibility. Mr. M. thought it was a more fundamental problem. A careful history revealed that he was an intensely child-focused product of a divorce of which he was unaware. (See Figure 13.5 for the M. Family Diagram.)

He had a vague notion that his maternal grandparents had divorced when his mother was eight and his uncle was six. He also knew that his grandmother had remarried and died several years later and that his uncle had died a year after that. Upon questioning, he realized the deaths were something his supposedly close-knit family never talked about. He did not know that his grandmother committed suicide upon the discovery that her new husband was having an affair and that his uncle committed suicide a year later, despondent over his mother's death.

FIGURE 13.5. The M. Family Diagram

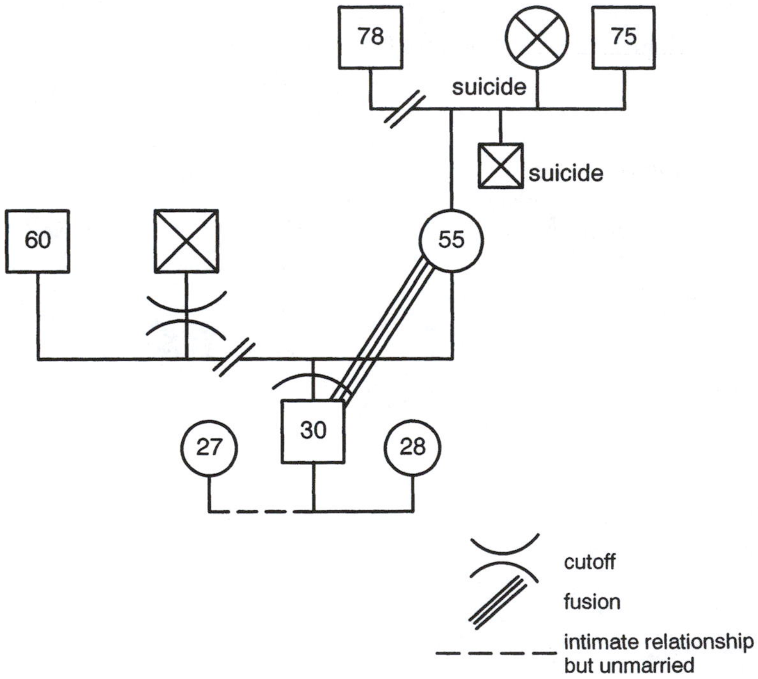

Mr. M.'s mother delayed marriage for over a decade following these tragedies. Later she married a man who came from a large, happy family, the kind she wanted for herself. They agreed they would have one child and dedicate their lives to him/her. Within a year after his birth, Mr. M.'s parents had divorced; his father felt deserted by his wife's strong attachment to their son. She quickly remarried, and Mr. M. was raised by her and his stepfather. However, Mr. M. knew nothing of these cutoffs and divorces before he came for consultation about the troubling effects of his own affair.

His mother thought life's problems would be too painful for her son and saw her job as protecting him from pain and anxiety. When there was a problem between Mr. M. and his stepfather, his mother intervened, thinking it was her job to raise him. He grew up distant from his stepfather and dependent on his mother, who managed his emotional life for him. He thought he was close to his extended family but had to admit that he had not been allowed to attend family funerals. His mother had not even told him of his biological father's death when Mr. M. was twenty-two.

Mr. M. began to realize that he expected women to compromise their feelings and please him, to take care of him emotionally and not place demands on him. However, life with his girlfriend, emotionally cut off from her and himself, became rather boring, uneventful, lifeless. When she suggested the greater commitment of marriage, he responded with anxiety, emotional and physical distance, and by having an affair. Paradoxically, the woman with whom he had an affair seemed the opposite. She insisted that he talk with her intimately. She demanded that he try to know her better, reveal himself, and discuss his feelings. He had little experience in doing that, yet was attracted by it, especially in the absence of a committed relationship. While working on these issues in therapy, he realized this was not a developmental crisis but rather a reflection of the way he experienced his mother and that his current relationship problems were a product of his past.

When Mr. M. said he could not leave his problems behind him, he was referring to his family of origin. He was the product of a child-focused marriage, in which his mother's anxieties about divorce and suicide were focused on him. By centering on him, sheltering him from pain, she was able to avoid her own. Unable to extricate himself from her emotional life, he was her mirror image: she took care of emotions for everyone else, and Mr. M. got everyone else to take care of emotions for him.

Therapy

Mr. M. was encouraged to spend more time with his mother and stepfather separately. If he could get a better perspective on how he functioned in past relationships, he might be able to be more effective in current ones.

It was through his efforts to learn about their courtship, how they met, and the decision to marry that he learned about the divorces and suicides. Initially, his efforts led to reenactment of old patterns. His mother, instead of talking about herself, focused on him and his needs. Mr. M. would return from these visits having "talked about all the right things" and having learned nothing about himself and how he operated in relationships. He said he wanted to tell his mother who he was, but she kept providing the answers for him. The parallels in his current relationships became clearer. When things became tense with his girlfriend, she dealt with his emotions for him or he distanced. The woman with whom he was having the affair would not do this for him. He liked that, but she complained she did not know who he was; neither did he.

By most standards, Mr. M. was a successful member of society, having recovered from the acute trauma of parental divorce and being raised with a stepparent. Although he had always known where he was going in life, only when ready to establish intimate adult relationships did he realize knowing himself was also important. Adults who are the product of highly child-focused parental divorces have predictable difficulty with this task. He made a sustained effort to reconnect with this multigenerational emotional process focused on him. It was important for him to be as objective as possible in understanding how this pattern operated and to define his part in it. The extent to which he could extricate himself from it would determine how he functioned emotionally as a mature adult (Beal, 1991a).

SUMMARY

This chapter identifies societal changes regulating marital relationships. After contrasting marital disruption from divorce versus death, it suggests that the concepts of differentiation, emotional cutoff, and nuclear family emotional system, with a specific emphasis on child focus, illuminate the current divorce phenomenon. Divorcing clinical families with cooperative, conflictual, and adaptive marital relationships and child focus are presented. As anxiety increases and regression occurs, these families triangle with the legal and court systems as well as the mental health profession. Suggestions are made on how to contain acute symptoms and work toward long-term resolutions. Bowen family systems theory offers ways for the helping professions to conceptualize the roles of therapist-mediator-arbitrator in the child-focused divorce process. A final case illustrates how a "successful" adult child of divorce can continue to work on self in the context of these multigenerational processes.

REFERENCES

American Psychiatric Association Task Force on Clinical Assessment in Child Custody (1988). *Child Custody Consultation.* Washington, DC: American Psychiatric Association.

Beal, E. W. (1979). Children of Divorce: A Family Systems Perspective. *Journal of Social Issues,* 35:140-154.

Beal, E. W. (1985). A Systems View of Divorce Intervention Strategies. In *Divorce and Family Mediation,* Eds. J. C. Hansen and S. C. Grebe. Rockville, MD: Aspen Systems Publications, pp. 16-33.

Beal, E. W. (1991a). *Adult Children of Divorce.* New York: Delacorte Press.

Beal, E. W. (1991b). Adult Children of Divorce: An Epidemic? Paper presented at the 144th Annual Meeting of the American Psychiatric Association, New York, May.

Bernet, W. (1995). Running Scared: Therapists' Excessive Concern about Following Rules. *Bulletin of American Academy of Psychiatry and Law,* 23:367-374.

Bowen, M. (1978). *Family Therapy in Clinical Practice.* New York: Jason Aronson.

Castro, T. and Bumpass, L. (1987). Recent Trends and Differentials in Marital Disruption. Monograph available from Center of Demography and Ecology, University of Wisconsin-Madison, June.

Fisher, H. E. (1992). *The Anatomy of Love, The Natural History of Monogamy, Adultery, and Divorce.* New York: W.W. Norton.

Glenn, N. D. and Kramer, K. D. (1987). The Marriage and Divorces of the Children of Divorce. *Journal of Marriage and the Family,* 49:811-825.

London, K. A., Kahn, J. R., and Pratt, W. F. (1988). Are Daughters of Divorced Parents More Likely to Divorce as Adults? Paper presented at Annual Meeting of the Population Association of America, New Orleans, April 21-23.

Southworth, S. and Schwarz, J. C. (1987). Post Divorce Contact, Relationships with Father and Heterosexual Trust in Female College Students, *American Journal of Orthopsychiatry,* 57:371.

Stone, L. (1989). A Short History of Divorce. *Family Therapy Networker,* November/December: 53-57.

Wallerstein, J. S. and Blakeslee, S. (1989). *Second Chances.* New York: Ticknor and Fields.

Chapter 14

Treating a Remarried Family System

Katharine Gratwick Baker

This chapter applies concepts from Bowen family systems theory to the clinical treatment of a remarried family system. Components of the treatment model are drawn from the work of Kerr (Kerr and Bowen, 1988) and Bowen (1978). Effective clinical treatment always involves a concurrent interweaving of assessment, self-observation, development of directions for change, anticipation of reactions to change, and implementation of change. Although assessment is presented as a separate component of clinical treatment, it continues throughout the course of treatment and provides the building blocks for all therapeutic intervention. The family diagram is used in this treatment model as a tool for recording family information throughout the process of assessment and treatment. It provides active rather than static visual images of the evolving family relationship system.

The first part of the chapter reviews ten aspects of family functioning: the symptomatic person, sibling position, nuclear family emotional process, stressful events, emotional reactivity to stress, nuclear family adaptiveness, extended family stability and intactness, emotional cutoff, therapeutic focus, and prognosis. These concepts from Bowen family systems theory (Kerr, 1987), including the creation of a family diagram (see Figure 14.1), are applied to the remarried family generically and to a specific family in treatment (the Robertsons). In the second part of the chapter, the Robertson family is followed through its five-year course of treatment.

The term *remarried family* is used to refer to families in which at least one member of an adult pair has had a previous marriage that ended with the divorce or death of a spouse. Remarried families can include minor or adult offspring who may or may not be living in the household. The remarried couple may or may not have custody of minor children. *Remarried family* is the descriptive term chosen for this family form because of its neutrality. In the view of this author, terms such as *stepfamily, blended family,* and *reconstituted family* either carry a negative bias or imply that some kind of relationship melding is a necessary part of the description.

Bowen family systems theory is useful in the assessment and treatment of remarried families because its scope encompasses the considerable relationship complexities of such families without imposing one-time married family models or expectations on them. By focusing on the factual realities of even the most complex families as emotional systems, rather than focusing on the individual pathologies of family members, this approach moves away from a focus on the "problem" and toward providing remarried families with skills for managing a range of life events with equanimity. Through an attention to *process,* Bowen theory avoids the concrete, measurable outcomes or goals for treatment that so often generate further anxiety rather than creating a sense of calm competence in the family and a readiness for handling the unexpected vicissitudes of life.

DEMOGRAPHY OF THE REMARRIED FAMILY

The remarried family is a well-established family form in the United States at the end of the twentieth century. Estimates suggest that 35 percent of American children growing up in the 1990s will live with a stepparent at some time before the age of eighteen. Although historically remarriage has been fairly common in the United States, until the 1950s, it usually followed the death of a spouse. The divorce rate was relatively low until the mid-1960s, when it more than doubled, from 2.2 percent of all marriages in 1960 to 5.2 percent in 1980. Since then, the rate has remained relatively stable, but approximately half of all marriages contracted in the 1990s are likely to end in divorce (McGoldrick and Carter, 1989).

Approximately 65 percent of divorced women and 70 percent of divorced men remarry, with the median length of time between divorce and remarriage at about three years. Remarriage for widowed individuals is also high, although widowed men remarry at a rate five times greater than widowed women. Remarriages are reportedly somewhat less stable than first marriages, with a second divorce rate at about 55 percent. Divorce and remarriage rates are even higher for those marrying more than twice (Furstenberg and Spanier, 1984). Marriage as an institution is apparently not being rejected in contemporary American society, but its statistical stability is far less assured than in earlier times. One can assume that remarried families will form a significant part of family clinical practice in the 1990s, such families will function along a continuum of adaptability, and a model of treatment that focuses on these families as nonpathological emotional systems may be useful.

Dr. Murray Bowen initiated a focus on family systems assessment in 1979 and 1980, when the American Psychiatric Association's third Diagnostic and Statistical Manual (APA, 1980) was being revised. At that time, Bowen hoped to develop a family diagnostic manual. The manual was never completed, but work on a family diagnostic approach culminated in the publication of *Family Evaluation: An Approach Based on Bowen Theory* (Kerr and Bowen, 1988). Kerr (1987) first outlined the approach in an article titled "Family Diagnosis," which appeared in the *Family Center Report*. This chapter follows Kerr's ten-faceted assessment model.

The Symptomatic Person

In medical and psychiatric diagnosis, the symptomatic person receives the primary focus. In family diagnosis, the same is true, as the clinician initially focuses on which family member may be dysfunctional and what may be the nature of the dysfunction (Kerr, 1987). When a clinician meets with a remarried family, as with any family, the symptomatic person could be any member of the family (a child, a parent or stepparent, a grandparent or stepgrandparent). The symptomatic person is the reason the family calls for an appointment. He or she may even initiate the process. Although he or she may not be the most anxious person in the family system, his or her symptoms are distressing enough for someone in the family to want to do something about them. The symptoms may be emotional, physiological, or social. In remarried families, the symptomatic person is most often identified as one of the children from a prior marriage, since these children are frequently resistant to the idea of a remarriage and the parents may project their anxiety about their new adult commitment onto their children.

In the Robertson family, the symptomatic person was Mrs. Robertson, a twenty-eight-year-old woman who had married for the first time three months prior to her first appointment. Mrs. Robertson had a master's degree in economics and worked for a government agency. Her husband, age forty-one, had a PhD in economics, taught at a university in Washington, DC, and had three prior marriages, with three noncustodial children, ages fifteen, thirteen, and eleven, from his first marriage. (A family diagram of the Robertson family is shown as Figure 14.1.)

The symptoms that inspired Mrs. Robertson to set up an appointment were her intensely angry outbursts toward her new husband, anxiety attacks when her stepchildren came to stay with them, jealousy of her fifteen-year-old stepdaughter's close relationship with her father, and some sleep and appetite disturbance. Mrs. Robertson frequently thought of leaving her new husband because she was so upset by her reactivity to his children. However, she had not contacted a lawyer nor had there been any marital separations. Shortly after her first clinical appointment, Mrs. Robertson had an abortion because she was so uncertain about the long-term

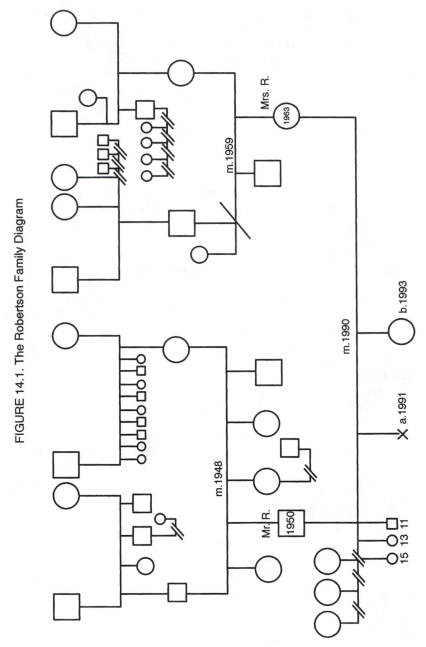

FIGURE 14.1. The Robertson Family Diagram

358

future of her marriage. Other family members did not experience symptoms to the degree that Mrs. Robertson did, although her older stepdaughter suffered from migraine headaches, her eleven-year-old stepson functioned poorly in school, her husband had some sleep disturbance, and the family had chronic financial problems.

Sibling Position

Sibling position as a component of family diagnosis is drawn from the research of Walter Toman (1961). Toman theorized that certain fixed adult personality characteristics, as well as marital choices, are grounded in the family relationship environment in which a child grows up. His findings have been found to be valid in a number of different cultures and were incorporated into Bowen family systems theory in the early 1960s (Kerr, 1987). In assessing a remarried family, the sibling configuration of the children's generation is most often the focus of concern. Toman's models have not yet been systematically adapted to the study of complex stepsibling relationships. His research is based on sibling relationships in simple biological one-time married families. One assumes from Toman's research that if there is a four- or five-year gap between the birth (adoption or arrival) of new siblings, each child will function pretty much as an only child, since he or she will have had a sustained period of parental focus without the competition of same-age or peer siblings. If, however, stepchildren are the same age as their new siblings or older than a prior oldest (thus disrupting a natural hierarchy that the biological siblings have established), what impact does this have on future relationship formation for the children involved? For example, what kinds of outcomes would result if an older stepbrother marries a younger sister of a half brother and a stepbrother, if the half brother never lived in the same household with his younger sister and the older stepbrother joined the household when the sister was twelve years old? These are research questions that remain to be studied.

The weight of key sibling variables has not been established in the research, but one might assume that the younger the children are at the time of a remarriage and the more exposure the stepsiblings have to each other, the more impact a new sibling configuration will have on future relationships. In other words, young children living together in the same household rather than relating to each other through weekend visitation will develop many of the sibling relationship patterns typical of one-time married families. Later additions of stepsiblings might be more similar to peer friendships, which tend to wax and wane, depending on other social factors. When children have the option of moving out and living in another parent's household, the sibling relationship will also have less emotional impact.

Sibling position may or may not be very important in an overall assessment of a remarried family, but it can be a point of focus in reflecting the smoke screen of complexity that often attends the evaluation of a remarried family. If these complex configurations also exist in the parent and grandparent generations, the family diagram may be particularly challenging. As will be seen, drawing the family diagram may be one of the most useful initial interventions a Bowen-trained clinician makes in clarifying remarried family relationships and calming the system through fact gathering.

In the case of the Robertson family, Mrs. Robertson was the younger sister of an older, unmarried, low-functioning brother who barely finished high school and had heavy involvement with marijuana, alcohol, and cocaine. Her mother was also the younger sister of a cutoff, dysfunctional older brother. Her father was the low-functioning older brother of a cutoff younger brother who was a college-educated, successful businessman. The pattern on both sides of her family seemed to be that younger siblings did better than older siblings, although at some cost to their adult relationships.

Mr. Robertson was the second of five children, with an older sister, two younger sisters, and a youngest brother. His mother, a registered nurse, was the youngest of ten children and the only one of six daughters to marry and leave home. Mr. Robertson's alcoholic father was the oldest of four, with two younger brothers and a younger sister. His paternal grandfather had died when his father was eleven, leaving his father in charge of the younger siblings. Mr. Robertson's father had apparently tried hard (with the encouragement of his mother) to be the boss of these younger siblings, and he approached his own five children in the same bossy style.

According to Toman's (1961) model, Mr. and Mrs. Robertson should have been compatible in terms of oldest-youngest complementarity and their familiarity with opposite-sex siblings, although Mrs. Robertson might have had the expectation that a man in the older sibling position would be low functioning or at least irresponsible.

Nuclear Family Emotional Process

The nuclear family emotional process describes patterns of emotional functioning in nuclear families. In examining this process, the clinician broadens the diagnostic focus from the individual to the wider nuclear family relationship system (Kerr, 1987). When assessing nuclear family emotional process, the clinician tries to understand the relationship balances among family members who live together. In a remarried family following divorce, this is often difficult because the people who live together may shift frequently, as children move back and forth from one household to another. If one defines the nuclear family as "those relating to each other around an emotional nucleus" (Bowen, 1988), the nuclear remarried family might include all the married and formerly married adults who are emotionally tied to a given child or group of children.

In a first-marriage nuclear family, the emotional nucleus is usually the married couple. But in a remarriage, the children often take emotional center stage. They may have become the "functional" emotional nucleus for their biological parents who have developed an allergic reactivity to each other. As in first-time married families, one of the patterns frequently seen in a remarried family is the process of passing adult "allergies" through the children to other adults in the system, a triangling or projection process that perpetuates hostility or cutoff between formerly married parents. The formerly married parents may continue to be a "basic," though split, emotional nucleus, whereas the children may be the central emotional organizing core of the remarried family on a functional level. This pattern can also occur in remarriage following the death of a spouse, when the dead parent and the first marriage are idealized to the extent that there may be little emotional space for the remarriage to become a new emotional nucleus. Another aspect of the nuclear family emotional process is observable when one spouse becomes impaired and develops psychological, physical, or social symptoms. A third manifestation of nuclear family emotional process can be observed in the marital relationship itself, which may be harmonious, conflictual, distant, or mixed.

In a remarried family, one frequently encounters combinations of all three of these patterns. A remarried family may initially attempt to be extremely harmonious if family members are driven by a need to overcome past marital failure or to perpetuate the idealization of marriage following the death of a spouse. The only reason all the people in the household live together is because of the relationship between the newly married couple. This couple will often attempt to present a united front to all the children to reinforce the emotional fusion of their relationship.

However, remarriages can swiftly deteriorate into armed camps, with reactivity to an overly harmonious marriage being projected onto the children if the parents attack their stepchildren and protect their biological children. This process is especially common when the children are adolescents who are developmentally preparing to leave home but are also being pulled back into the remarried family emotional fusion. The anxiety generated by this process may also lead to the development of psychological, physical, and social symptoms in a spouse.

In the Robertson family, Mrs. Robertson's aversion to her fifteen-year-old stepdaughter seemed to have more to do with her concerns about the long-term stability of her marriage than her stepdaughter's behavior. She felt on the outside of emotional triangles that included herself, her husband, and his daughter, and herself, her husband, and his first wife. In the first triangle, she perceived her husband and his daughter excluding her from their closeness. In the second triangle, she perceived her husband and his first wife excluding her as they made financial and parenting decisions. She had difficulty being comfortable in this outside position (she had always been in an inside position with her mother in her own family), and she identified the stepdaughter as her primary antagonist rather than taking on her new husband. The marriage had not become overtly conflictual, but the relationship was distant, and Mrs. Robertson had developed psychological symptoms that were beginning to impair her functioning.

Stressors

This component of family diagnosis refers to stressful events that occur in the life of a family. The magnitude and number of stressful events, as well as their duration and the timing between them, determine the level of stress a family is experiencing. The family's reaction to stressful events may also increase stress, as "emotionally driven chain reactions" may cause even more stress than the original event (Kerr, 1987, p. 2). Stress for remarried families is often particularly intense within the first two or three years of the remarriage. The changes that a remarried family must adapt to may include moving a household, absorbing new family members, adapting to changed visitation and custody schedules, changes in financial arrangements such as child-support payments, changes in family traditions, eating patterns (two stepsiblings are vegetarians and the other two will eat nothing but TV dinners), and even pets (the new stepfather breaks out in hives when he is in the same room with his stepfamily's cat).

Many of these changes can hardly be called stressful "events" because of their intensity and extended duration. Thus, a family member's resistance to change or lack of adaptation may become a new stressor that impinges on the family system's capacity to respond flexibly to its new realities. As noted by Kerr (1987), the family's response to events may be much more stressful to the relationship system than the events themselves.

In the Robertson family, stressful events included the remarriage in October 1990 (to which Mr. Robertson's children were not invited and which his parents and siblings refused to attend since they did not think a fourth marriage could be serious); Mrs. Robertson's mother's diagnosis of breast cancer in December 1990; Mrs. Robertson's decision that same month to refuse to permit her husband's children to visit her home, except one at a time; her abortion in January 1991; Mr. Robertson's difficulty getting tenure in his university position in February 1991; Mrs. Robertson's father's major heart attack in November 1991; the collapse of their roof during a snowstorm in January 1992; and the ongoing demands of Mr. Robertson's ex-wife for more financial assistance. All of these events were factual, but intense. The family members' responses to these events led to a marked increase in anxiety.

Emotional Reactivity

An assessment of the emotional reactivity to stress in a family includes identifying the number and intensity of the symptoms, as well as the amount of functional impairment that goes along with the symptoms. It also includes an assessment of the distance, anxiety, and/or conflict in the family's relationships. According to Kerr (1987, p. 2), "a clinician usually assesses [the emotional reactivity] in a particular family on the basis of comparisons with many other families," since there are no statistically objective standards yet for measuring this aspect of family functioning.

Since at least one partner in all remarried families has been through the ending of a prior marriage through divorce or death of a spouse, one can assume that a fairly high level of chronic anxiety exists, particularly with regard to the long-term viability of the new marriage in its early years. Therefore, potential reactivity to even minor stressors is ready to kick in at a fairly intense level, with physical, social, or psychological symptoms being common among both children and adults. As previously noted, even relatively minor stressful events can generate major "emotionally driven chain reactions"; in particular, a focus on the behavior of nonbiological children may lead to marital conflict that can split the family into loyalty alliances. Emotional reactivity may also be expressed in impaired professional and school functioning for members of newly remarried families. The degree of impairment must be taken into account when completing an overall assessment of the family. It is important, however, that clinicians not compare the functioning of remarried families with that of first-marriage families, since the emotional reactivity of remarried families is normally high in the first three to four years of the marriage, whereas recovery to former levels of functioning is also common in more mature families.

In the Robertson family, emotional reactivity appeared to be an ongoing pattern among the adult generations. The stepgrandparents developed serious illnesses soon after the marriage, and Mrs. Robertson developed the previously described symptoms: angry outbursts at her new husband, appetite and sleep disorders, and reduced professional functioning. The older stepdaughter's migraines, on the other hand, were not chronic and subsided several months after her father's remarriage.

Before this marriage, Mr. Robertson had managed his anxiety with pro-longed heavy marijuana use. After the remarriage, he regularly diverted marital reactivity into conflict with his first wife over child care arrangements and child support payments. In addition, he became embroiled in a tenure struggle at his university shortly after the remarriage.

Nuclear Family Adaptiveness

Nuclear family adaptiveness parallels "level of differentiation." It is assessed by examining the family's emotional reactivity to the stress it is experiencing. A high level of reactivity in response to minimal stress would indicate a lower level of adaptiveness. Conversely, a low level of reactivity to severe stress would indicate a higher level of adaptiveness. In determining the degree of nuclear family adaptiveness, it is important to examine the entire history of the family and not just its recent experience of stressful events (Kerr, 1987).

In a remarried family, one can assume a high level of stress associated with the immediate life events that have preceded the remarriage. Stress can be equated not only with change, but also with the impact of that change on an emotional system. The changes experienced by all remarried families are inevitably momentous on every level—social, physical, and psychological. How the family responds to those changes is determined by (1) the family's perception of its own competence in dealing with change, (2) the family's ability to see a range of choices or options for responding to change, and (3) the family's history in managing past changes. In assessing the adaptiveness of a remarried family, the clinician must examine the response of the original families to the death or divorce, bearing in mind the range of possibilities for experiencing loss or conflict while minimizing or maximizing reactivity.

For remarriages preceded by divorce, a family's perception of its own competence may be impaired by what it has experienced as prior marital failure. In addition, the divorce may have established a pattern for managing stress through conflict, distance, and cutoff. For remarriages preceded by the death of a spouse, idealization of the dead spouse and emotional fusion with canonized images of death through illness or accident can interfere with the establishment of a flexible new relationship system.

The stressors affecting the Robertson family have already been described, although it is not completely clear whether the serious illnesses of Mrs. Robertson's parents were stressors or manifestations of reactivity to the remarriage. Probably her parents were reactive to their daughter's marriage, they developed physical symptoms, and then the seriousness of the symptoms became stressors to their daughter. In this way, manifestations of reactivity can become stressors themselves, in a kind of emotional chain reaction. The collapse of the Robertson's roof was a stressor, but Mrs. Robertson's decision to have an abortion was driven by reactivity, as were Mr. Robertson's professional difficulties and the stepdaughter's migraines. Mr. Robertson's standard response to stress in the past was to leave his marriage, as he had done on three previous occasions, most recently after a six-month third marriage. Mrs. Robertson had never been married before, but she had been cut off from her father and her older brother for many years. Both families of origin had experienced a number of marital separations, divorces, early parental deaths, alcohol and child abuse, and other forms of violence.

Extended Family Stability and Intactness

A nuclear family is not a closed system but is part of a larger "multi-generational emotional matrix." Assessment of extended family stability and intactness involves understanding the average level of functioning of all significant members of the wider family system. These combined levels of functioning can give an overall, though imprecise, sense of the extended family's basic level of differentiation (Kerr, 1987).

In a remarried family, an assessment of the wider cast of characters, identifying who is alive and available to the family system as well as their average levels of functioning, is often a complex task because there are so many people. These people include not only the immediate biological relatives on both sides of the remarried family, but also the prior spouse and his or her relatives, who may continue to be involved with the children while reacting with hostility to the remarried couple.

The assessment of extended family levels of functioning is intensely bound to the family's reactivity to the remarriage. A central organizing event for the extended family has been the ending of a previous marriage by divorce or death. In the case of divorce, extended family members may have taken sides, offered opinions and advice, provided financial assistance or other help with the children, and become emotional advocates for their relatives. Those who had been most involved usually experience the greatest sense of personal failure when a marriage ends. This may affect their availability to the remarried couple, if they remain bound to their memories of the original family as an enduring emotional unit.

When a first marriage has ended with the death of a spouse through illness or accident, many of the same factors occur, although usually with less focus on marital conflict. Extended family members may have been deeply involved in caring for the dying spouse, dealing with the emotional shock following an accident, helping with the children, and providing financial assistance. They face similar challenges of flexibility and emotional availability to a subsequent marriage, especially if they too remain bound to memories of the first marriage as an enduring emotional unit.

Thus, extended family stability and intactness for a remarried family may be assessed not only through information about prior generational functioning, but also in responses to the remarriage, which may range from cutoff to distance to acceptance to renewed involvement.

In the Robertson family, prior generational functioning had been somewhat erratic. For example:

1. Mrs. Robertson's maternal grandfather, whom she described as a poor rural farmer, left his wife and children for a fifteen-year-old girl. Mrs. Robertson's father also left his wife for a teenage girl, when Mrs. Robertson herself was a teenager.
2. Mrs. Robertson's grandparents, parents, and uncle had been divorced. Her older brother was unmarried.
3. Mr. Robertson's extended family had experienced two divorces, his paternal aunt's and his younger sister's.

Mrs. Robertson's family appeared to be less intact and more fragmented than Mr. Robertson's, but her mother was the only extended family member from either side of the family who was available to and connected with this couple. Mr. Robertson's parents and siblings did not come to the wedding because they did not take the idea of a fourth wedding seriously. Mrs. Robertson's father and brother did not attend the wedding because they were still caught in a reactive loyalty split following the separation of Mrs. Robertson's parents, which had occurred fourteen years earlier. At that time, she and her mother had fused into an emotional unit that cut off from the fused unit of her father and brother.

Emotional Cutoff

This component of family assessment refers to the amount of unresolved emotional attachment that people have to their parents and to their wider extended family systems. The more unresolved the emotional attachment, the lower the level of differentiation (Kerr, 1987). Emotional cutoff is a common way of dealing with the discomfort associated with fusion or intense unresolved attachment in all human relationships.

Remarried families following divorce often exist in a web of emotional cutoffs that may reflect a conflictual response to the emotional fusion of the prior marriage. Cutoff may be part of a family's multigenerational pattern for dealing with anxiety, but it can also be reinforced by the adversarial nature of the American legal system, societal views on the nature of divorce, and the intense reactivity that often accompanies marital dissolution. Emotional cutoff seems to evolve most commonly among extended family and friend networks when people take sides and discontinue contact out of "loyalty" to one former spouse or the other. Reactive cutoff can also occur following the death of an ill spouse, particularly if care for the dying family member led to more "togetherness" than was comfortable for the family.

Of course, many couples (with or without children) continue to be actively negatively involved with each other long after divorce and even remarriage have taken place. In these cases, physical distance has occurred, but emotional connection is generated through conflict. Periods of cutoff can fluctuate with periods of negative attachment, often generated by ongoing coparenting issues. Events such as bar mitzvahs, graduations, weddings, and the births of grandchildren can raise high anxiety in cutoff ex-spouses who are forced into contact with each other to celebrate the achievements of their children. When formerly married parents do have comfortable relationships, the comfort level is usually maintained through invoking child-focused triangles.

Many remarried families that are cut off from significant extended family members create substitute extended families through the "experts" they involve in their lives. These may include friends, neighbors, lawyers, judges, therapists, school systems, welfare workers, probation officers, and others who fill roles that have been abandoned by extended family. Assistance in decision making, problem solving, and the search for resources can engage these outsiders in support of the remarried family, while reinforcing emotional cutoff from extended family.

Mr. and Mrs. Robertson described many cutoffs of long duration in both their extended families that preceded their having met each other. Both Mrs. Robertson's parents were cut off from their only brothers, and she had little contact with either her brother or her father. Mr. Robertson's father was cut off as an adult from the younger siblings he had "raised." Mr. Robertson was significantly connected to only one of his four siblings. Only one relative, Mrs. Robertson's mother, came to their wedding. Mr. Robertson was completely cut off from his second and third wives. He maintained an intensely conflictual contact with his first wife, focusing on parenting issues and child support payments. Mrs. Robertson was cut off from all of Mr. Robertson's prior wives and had no relationship with any of them.

Therapeutic Focus

There are two clinical goals in therapy based on Bowen family systems theory: the first is the reduction of anxiety leading to symptom relief; the second is a long-term effort to increase the basic level of differentiation, thus improving adaptiveness. The clinician chooses a therapeutic focus that will most effectively lead to a reduction of anxiety and an enhancement of basic level of differentiation (Kerr, 1987). As in clinical work with any family, therapeutic goals with a remarried family are to reduce symptoms, reduce acute and chronic anxiety, and enhance adaptiveness in family members and the family system as a whole.

Remarried families are in some ways similar to families from exotic cultures in that they present a smoke screen of complex aspects that can confuse the clinician and make a clear therapeutic focus particularly challenging and elusive. In initial sessions with a remarried family, the clinician may be bombarded with a confusion of names, relationships, practical problems, and a lack of routines and agreement in the basic areas of family life. Often anxiety and reactivity are so high that adults are not making reasonable decisions about child rearing, finances, living arrangements, and maintaining relationships. Extensive emotional cutoffs from significant family members may exist, and outside experts such as lawyers, judges, therapists, and school systems may have been triangled into decision-making roles.

The areas of stressful events, extended family stability, emotional fusion, and reactive cutoff are particularly intense for many remarried families, but certainly, the usual range of functioning and adaptiveness exists in these families, as it does in other kinds of families. In developing a therapeutic focus with remarried families, it is important to emphasize those commonalities with other human families rather than the differences. Scraping away the overlay of complexity and concentrating on the natural systems relationship patterns of all families may contribute to an immediate reduction in anxiety and symptoms. Issues of differentiation are approached as they would be with any family over time. The therapeutic focus developed with the Robertson family is explored later in this chapter.

Prognosis

Prognosis in traditional medical diagnosis emerges from an estimate of the severity of symptoms within the individual. Prognosis in Bowen family systems theory is based on multiple factors in the relationship system which are limited to the underlying emotional system and which affect all clinical dysfunction to some extent (Kerr, 1987).

Based on the relationship variables discussed in the Robertson family assessment, their initial prognosis could best be described as "guarded." Many aspects of their functioning at the time of their first appointment created doubts that they would be able to sustain their marriage, maintain professional achievements, and raise their children to mature, responsible adulthood. The course of treatment for the Robertson family (as described in the next section) addresses only the short-term prognosis. The long-term prognosis over several generations was beyond the scope of this study.

COURSE OF TREATMENT

The Robertson family was seen for a total of twenty-six sessions over a five-year period. The couple decided when they wanted to attend sessions together and when they wanted to come in individually. Initially they were seen almost weekly for ten sessions between the late fall of 1990 and the early spring of 1991. Sessions then became less frequent, and they were seen monthly until September 1991. They returned for ten sessions in the spring and summer of 1995. At that time, they had had a baby girl of their own, and Mrs. Robertson's mother had moved to the area to help with child care. Since 1995, the Robertsons have had occasional telephone contact with the clinician, with reports of continuing marital stability and effective problem solving.

Mrs. Robertson was initially the self-defined symptomatic person. She made the first telephone contact and attended almost all sessions either alone or with her husband. She appeared to be the most flexible and available family member, the one most open to hearing family systems ideas, and the one most capable of implementing them.

Defining and Developing a Relationship with the Family: Clarifying the Approach

The first treatment task for the Bowen-trained clinician is to clarify the nature of the therapeutic process and the role of the clinician in that process. Families that have experienced prior individual psychodynamic therapy or more traditional family therapy find the Bowen theory approach quite different.

Mrs. Robertson had not had any prior clinical treatment and brought no preconceptions or expectations to the initial meetings, other than her desire to feel better. Throughout the sessions with her, I maintained a friendly, respectful, inquiring stance, providing information about family systems ideas, asking questions, and structuring the sessions so that she set the agenda. I also encouraged her to track her own change and begin a process of self-regulation by keeping a journal to record her ideas, thoughts, plans for change, and observations of her own anxiety and reactivity. In addition, after her initial anxiety had decreased, I gave Mrs.

Robertson relevant articles and books on family systems from time to time, depending on her interest.

I also coached Mrs. Robertson in further efforts at self-regulation, including such relaxation exercises as deep, slow breathing, visualization, and progressive muscle relaxation. Visualization involved imagining herself in a quiet place (for Mrs. Robertson, this was a secluded beach where she used to play during her childhood), breathing quietly, listening to the sounds of the water, and feeling the warm breeze on her skin. She practiced these exercises daily and gradually acquired the skills to calm herself physically when she was particularly agitated.

I used the same approach with her husband when he attended his own individual sessions. He was less interested in family systems ideas, nor was he interested in reading books or articles. He asked for concrete suggestions for behavioral change. When his elderly mother was killed in a car accident in the summer of 1995, he was deeply distressed and asked for a number of individual sessions. He used these sessions to plan a memorial service for her that included many family members from whom he had been cut off since his remarriage, including at that time his older daughter from his first marriage.

When the couple was seen together, they listened to each other's issues, talked about their thoughts and feelings with regard to the remarriage, and addressed important areas of decision making, particularly when core stepfamily triangles had been reactivated. My primary goal in couples sessions was to maintain neutrality, manage myself with a minimum of bias, and sustain a direct, open relationship with both husband and wife.

Listening to the Client's Statement of the Problems: Asking Factual Questions

During my initial contact with Mrs. Robertson, I listened to her account of her family situation. At that point, she was a relatively new bride, and she was frantic at the unfamiliarity of her stepchildren's behavior when they arrived at her home every weekend. She said:

> I go crazy when the kids are there. They take over the place. They are rowdy and incredibly messy. They drop their stuff everywhere. Melissa [fifteen] thinks she can run the show. She tells everyone what to do, including me in my own kitchen! And then she struts around in her bra and panties, just showing off to her Dad that she's a great big fifteen-year-old. And he just gives all the kids free rein. He never disciplines them. He feels so guilty when he hasn't seen them all week, that he can't say no to them about anything. I think

they are being outrageous on purpose just to see how much they can get away with, but I don't think he'll ever blow the whistle on them. I can't stand it; I really can't. I am literally going crazy! I scream at my husband. I can't sleep or eat because I'm so upset about this whole nightmare. I was so in love with him. I never dreamed marriage would be like this.

In listening to Mrs. Robertson's distress, I made clear to her that I was hearing and understanding what she was saying, but I maintained a calm position and began asking follow-up questions that would engage her thinking about the situation. My questions initially focused on facts about the children's visits—when they came, how long they stayed, and what activities were planned for them. I then moved to gathering facts about the decision-making process: Who decided when the children would come and how long they would stay? How were these decisions negotiated? Was the decision-making process the same or different after she and Mr. Robertson married? Was she comfortable with the decision-making process? What options did she have for making an impact on the process? The next area of inquiry related to Mrs. Robertson's management of herself during the visits: What did she perceive as her responsibilities during the visits? What choices did she have about participation in activities with the children? What opportunities did she have for spending time getting to know the children individually? Did she and her husband make joint plans for the visits?

In thinking about the answers to these questions, Mrs. Robertson became calmer and more reflective. When she was able to joke about the ridiculousness of some of the children's behaviors, she could then be more objective in her search for solutions, and her anxiety began to abate.

Broadening the Lens: What Are the History and Context for the Problems?

As the Robertsons' treatment proceeded, the questions became broader: How long had this situation been going on? Had things been this bad from the start? What other events might have contributed to the current intensity? What did Mrs. Robertson know about how her husband had left his first family and the kind of contact he had had with the children since then? What did she know about the children's reactions to their two previous stepmothers? When and how did she and her husband meet? When did he first introduce her to his children? What was her prior experience with teenagers? What were her expectations of these children? Did she know other people who had teenage stepchildren? What had she heard about being the stepmother of teenagers? How had she prepared herself for these relationships?

Mrs. Robertson had heard all about her husband's conflicts with the children's mother, whom she described as "the Wicked Witch of the West." She also knew that the children had been a primary cause for the ending of Mr. Robertson's second and third marriages; they had been disruptive, rude, and uncooperative with their first and second stepmothers. She had heard that the children frequently carried messages between their parents, told their father to send their mother more money, and sometimes refused to visit him if their mother was angry with him. She knew little about teenagers, but remembered being a strong ally of her mother's when her father had an affair with a fifteen-year-old neighbor. She also remembered that her maternal grandfather had married a fifteen-year-old girl after divorcing her grandmother. As she recalled these events from her own family history, she began to understand her own reactivity to her husband's fifteen-year-old daughter.

Making a Family Diagram:
A Tool for an Ongoing Assessment

The drawing of the family diagram usually begins in the first or second session. The clinician asks the family to provide family information in a more systematic way, asking for the years of birth and sex of siblings, parents, aunts, uncles, cousins, grandparents, and even great-grandparents if they have this information. The present location, education, health patterns, marital status, religion, and occupation of each of these adults can also be useful. Fortunately Mr. and Mrs. Robertson had comprehensive information about their families (see Figure 14.1), even though they were emotionally cut off from many relatives.

Remarriage as a pattern in the family over generations can be an interesting area for information gathering. As can be seen from the Robertson family diagram, Mrs. Robertson's parents separated in 1978 when she was sixteen, and her father formed a relationship with a fifteen-year-old girl. Although her parents never officially divorced, they both had numerous cohabitant relationships after their separation, which their daughter had observed and been affected by. After her paternal grandfather died in 1933, her paternal stepgrandmother, a singer and model, had had three or four subsequent husbands. Her maternal grandparents had separated and divorced when her grandfather was found with a fifteen-year-old girl (whom he later married). Her mother's older brother had had four wives.

All four of Mr. Robertson's grandparents had only one marriage. He had one uncle and a younger sister who had remarried following a divorce. Remarriage then was a more familiar phenomenon in Mrs. Robertson's family than in her husband's extended family, although Mr. Robertson himself had been married and divorced three times before the current remarriage. One might assume that these multigenerational patterns of separation, divorce, and remarriage increased the Robertsons' anxiety and reactivity to their marriage and led them to wonder if they could sustain their connection through the ups and downs of their relationship.

In the process of drawing a family diagram, the clinician also explores the nature of the relationships between key members of the family: What kind of contact is there between the family member being interviewed and his or her parents and siblings? How often do they spend time together? How open is their conversation? What is the gossip or rumor mill like in the family? What is the contact like between former spouses?

This last question is particularly relevant for remarried families, and the answer often serves as an indicator of the basic adaptability or maturity level of the family. Variation in contact might range from continuing positive or negative emotional fusion to cutoff, constant conflict about money and child rearing, limited contact relating to child rearing, or a more neutral, responsible ability to deal with common concerns without being drawn back into old conflicts.

The Robertsons were cut off from Mr. Robertson's second and third wives, but he was actively engaged in ongoing struggles with his first wife, Suzanne, about money and child rearing. Multiple interlocking triangles including the children and grandparents continued to keep the conflict alive despite Mr. Robertson's attempts to respond more calmly and neutrally to his first wife. For example, when the Robertsons were discussing with Suzanne summer camp plans for the children, Suzanne's parents (who lived in a nearby state) insisted that the children spend July with them.

The family diagram is treated as a living document throughout treatment. New information is recorded as it arises. Often xeroxed copies of the diagram are provided to the family so that they can take it home with them, study the patterns, add to it, and think about it.

Encouraging Self-Observation of One's Own Part in the Development of Problems

The next ongoing component of treatment involves shifting the focus from the "other" to the "self." During the early treatment sessions, most families tend to look for scapegoats, blaming parents, children, or ex-spouses for all the family's problems. Learning to observe their own part in the problems is tremendously difficult for most people, although they may understand intellectually that they can only change themselves and not the "others." Most people enter treatment perceiving themselves as helpless victims of another person's behavior. As Mrs. Robertson said, "These children are driving me crazy. If only they would behave or if only their dad would lay down the law with them, then everything would be fine."

It was very difficult for Mrs. Robertson to begin to observe herself during the stepchildren's visits and to see her own participation in the escalation of their behavior. Her journal was useful for her in implementing a shift in focus. She began to write down what she said to her stepchildren and to her husband at the beginning of the visits and noticed that she was ready for things to go wrong from the moment they walked in the door every Saturday morning. She asked them "why" questions every time she saw them: Why haven't you made any plans for the weekend? Why can't you hang up your jacket? Why can't you ask before you just help yourself to cookies? Why haven't you finished your homework yet? She began to see how she was a factor in the adversarial tone that had been established very early in her relationship with the stepchildren. Mr. Robertson, in turn, began to observe his part in triangles with his wife. For example, every time she asked the children a question, he jumped in and defended them to her. Over time, both became acutely sensitive to their own reactivity in triangles with the children and with Mr. Robertson's ex-wife.

Developing Alternative Ways of Managing Self in Relationships

Many families can improve their self-observation skills but continue to hold onto a helpless stance in problematic relationships. Mrs. Robertson would connect her own reactivity to the stepchildren to what she perceived as her husband's passivity with his children and to the demanding phone calls of his ex-wife. Then she would sigh and say, "But what else can I do? They are all impossible people!" She felt helpless about considering options for changing her own behavior, perhaps because she did not believe that if she changed herself other patterns in the family relationship system might also change. She had to experiment with small changes before she was willing to risk a whole new way of thinking about herself as a participant in what she saw as the "family chaos." This somewhat disengaged stance is often seen in stepparents who define themselves as outsiders, new to the "stepfamily mess," having made no contribution to how it got that way.

Mrs. Robertson had to start by setting a personal goal for herself to feel more comfortable in the family rather than trying to change the whole system. This way she could define what was important to her, which issues she would take on and which she could let go, as well as what alternatives she had when the children visited. When she gave herself permission not to try to be a substitute mother and not to try to maintain absolute order, she became more relaxed with her stepchildren, often choosing to have lunch with a friend when they came over, but also planning separate activities with each stepchild so that she could get to know them better individually. She began to develop the ability to shift gears when the children arrived and to respond to them more flexibly.

Mr. Robertson had more difficulty developing alternate ways of managing himself in relation to his wife, children, and ex-wife. He saw himself as right in the vortex of a mass of interlocking triangles (for example, the triangle including himself, his children, and his wife interlocked with the triangle of himself, his wife, and his ex-wife, and the triangle of himself, his children, and his ex-wife). He could hardly define alternatives for himself, much less implement them. He considered himself responsible for all the unhappiness around him and was determined make the situation better for everyone, but meanwhile, he developed a rather severe sleep disorder and became embroiled in a tenure struggle at his university. The tenure struggle distanced him from the family triangles but did not calm him down nor lead him toward new options for managing his reactivity at home.

Over the course of treatment, Mr. Robertson began to make efforts to tone down his reactivity to these triangles. For example, when Mr. Robertson's first wife called to demand increased child support payments and threatened to go to court if the money were not forthcoming, Mr. Robertson usually gave in to her demands. Mrs. Robertson would then become enraged that he had not discussed the decision with her, and he would become angry with her because of her reactivity. I coached Mr. and Mrs. Robertson to do some long-range financial planning, as well as to strategize ahead of time about how Mr. Robertson would respond when Suzanne demanded money. They learned to anticipate when these demands would come (usually after an upset between Suzanne and her boyfriend or following a change in the children's activities), and Mr. Robertson would respond to her requests in writing, clarifying his understanding of their long-term financial arrangements, as also agreed to by his present wife. Suzanne initially escalated her demands but eventually ceased to threaten court action, as Mr. Robertson toned down his reactivity.

Anticipating Reactivity to Change

An important part of planning changes in one's own behavior relates to anticipating how family members may react to the changes and then preparing for those reactions. Mrs. Robertson assumed that if she became less provocative and demanding, her stepchildren would raise the ante and increase their outrageous behavior until she blew up and went back to her old reactive style of stepparenting.

This turned out to be true. Despite her best intentions, Mrs. Robertson frequently found herself reverting to old patterns and wondering how much more she could take. Gradually, she came to understand that she had been changing her behavior as yet another "technique" for managing the family chaos, imagining that if she changed her behavior, other people would automatically change theirs. To make more solid moves in the direction of a higher level of differentiation, Mrs. Robertson began to understand that she would have to make changes for her "self" rather than as an indirect effort to change the others. When she was clear that the changes were for, in, and of herself, they became more sustainable.

Again the journal writing helped her in this process. She planned a specific change for herself (for example, greeting each child warmly and personally when they arrived on Saturday morning). Then she thought through how each of them might react to her greeting (for example, ignoring her, making a face at her, grunting sullenly, or perhaps actually greeting her in return). Then she planned the range of options she had in responding to their reactions (for example, screaming at them and demanding respect, walking away, grunting back at them, laughing at them, or maintaining a friendly position). She learned Bowen's three recommendations for managing one's "self" in a difficult relationship: "Don't attack, don't defend, and don't withdraw." However, she realized that she would have to create positive actions for herself which would express a calm, neutral, available, interested position in relation to the children and which would be comfortable for her over the long term.

Implementing Change and Sticking to It

Mrs. Robertson worked intensively over a nine-month period to change her reactivity. Her husband attended several sessions with her and had several sessions individually, but he was not as motivated to change as she was. He tended to come to sessions when the family was in a crisis. When things calmed down, he would lose interest in the process of personal self-management, assuming that everything was all right again. He preferred to define his wife as the one who "needed" therapy and missed the fact that she was managing herself increasingly effectively with his children and in the marriage.

After working intensively on her family relationships for an extended period, Mrs. Robertson began to come to therapy less often, touching base with me every three to six months over a four-year period. In 1995, she returned for a series of sessions that focused on her relationship with her mother. Mrs. Robertson had felt confident enough about her marriage to have a baby in 1993 (unlike her first pregnancy, which she had aborted in early 1991). This "mutual" child was a blood relative of every member of the remarried family, and her birth was initially an affirming and stabilizing element in the family. Mrs. Robertson's sixty-one-year-old mother came to live with the Robertsons shortly after the new baby was born to help out with child care while Mrs. Robertson went back to work.

At first the Robertsons had adjusted to the two-person expansion of their family, but two years into the new arrangement, Mrs. Robertson was beginning to unravel. Mr. Robertson was distancing into his work. Several new and intense triangles had evolved, which Mrs. Robertson could observe, but she was having difficulty managing her anxiety in the midst of them. One triangle consisted of Mr. Robertson, Mrs. Robertson, and her mother. Her mother had become very critical of Mr. Robertson and appeared to be trying to turn Mrs. Robertson against him. Her mother had also become increasingly dependent on Mrs. Robertson. Mrs. Robertson supported her mother financially but was tiring of her mother's demands and her inability to set limits with their very active two-year-old daughter, Samantha.

Another difficult triangle consisted of Mrs. Robertson, her mother, and Samantha. Her mother insisted that Samantha call her "Mama" and acted as if she were her "real" mother, while Mrs. Robertson had a kind of older sister role.

Yet another triangle that Mrs. Robertson observed included Mr. Robertson, the children of his first marriage, and Samantha, the only child of the present marriage. Mrs. Robertson thought her husband preferred the older children and criticized him for this, insisting that he spend more time taking care of Samantha. Mr. Robertson resisted her demands, saying he was too busy to run after a toddler.

Mrs. Robertson had learned to implement change and stick to it with her stepchildren, but under the long-term increased stress of having her mother and a new baby in her household, she began to lose her ability to manage herself effectively. New life events and new stressors can challenge even firmly held positions in anxious emotional systems.

Because Mrs. Robertson had implemented change and learned to manage herself effectively in an earlier set of stepfamily relationships, she was able to think through fairly rapidly the kinds of personal changes she needed to make within the new triangles. Of course, defining a self with one's mother can be far more difficult than defining a self in almost any other relationship. Nevertheless, over a six-month period, she worked on managing herself less reactively when her mother criticized her husband. She also rented a small, nearby apartment for her mother and set up a bank account for her so that her mother would function more independently, while continuing to provide part-time child care for Samantha.

Indicators for Anxiety and Symptom Reduction: When Do They Begin?

In the case of the Robertson family, anxiety was apparent at many levels. All family members experienced acute anxiety in response to the remarriage. Symptoms included health problems in the grandparents and a teenage stepdaughter; social/behavioral symptoms in the stepchildren, their newly married biological father, his first wife, and his present wife; and psychological symptoms in many family members, including worry, rumination, feelings of helplessness, apprehension, irritability, difficulty concentrating, muscle tension, and sleep disturbance. *Chronic* anxiety could be observed across several generations in family patterns of marital disruption and cutoff and substance abuse.

Symptom reduction related to *acute* anxiety could be observed in the very first session, as Mrs. Robertson began to talk about her reactivity to the remarriage. Self-regulation through relaxation exercises, visualization, and journal writing also reduced Mrs. Robertson's symptoms of acute anxiety. Acute anxiety is as contagious in a family as an infectious virus, but it also tends to dissipate throughout a family when one family member becomes calmer. This was apparent in the Robertson family; as Mrs. Robertson calmed down, the rest of the family's symptoms gradually abated.

Indicators of Long-Term Increase in Levels of Differentiation

Kerr (1987) has noted that "assessment of a family's functioning in response to highly stressful periods and/or evaluation of the level of stress on a family during unusually symptomatic periods provides an impression about the family's overall adaptiveness" (p. 3). He also suggested that the "level of adaptiveness parallels level of differentiation" (p. 2).

For a remarried family such as the Robertsons, the early months of a remarriage can be highly stressful and may be concurrent with an unusually symptomatic period. The Robertsons did not manage the stressors of remarriage calmly, nor did they consistently maintain good health or high levels of professional functioning during this period of adjustment. Kerr (1987) noted that "a clinician usually assesses a particular family on the basis of comparisons with many other families" (p. 2). This author would add that comparisons with other *remarried families* may be particularly useful in assessing the adaptability of a remarried family, since the adjustments and demands for flexibility in this family form are often unusually emotionally intense and follow long periods of family disruption associated with divorce or death.

Differentiation may be assessed on two levels: basic differentiation and functional differentiation. Basic differentiation is "functioning that is *not dependent on the relationship process*" (Kerr and Bowen, 1988, p. 98). It is "determined largely by a multigenerational emotional process" (p. 98). Functional differentiation is "functioning that is *dependent on the relationship process*" (p. 98). It is "influenced by the level of chronic anxiety in a person's most important relationship systems" (p. 99).

It would be highly unrealistic to expect changes in *basic* levels of differentiation to be observable during a short course of treatment of a remarried family system. However, changes in *functional* levels of differentiation could be observed in Mrs. Robertson during the first year of her marriage. She was able to make changes in her behavior and functioning that stayed solidly with her over the next four years. When new stressors developed after the birth of her baby and the arrival of her mother, she managed relatively well. When she came back into treatment, it was for only six months. Thereafter, she sustained a fairly mature and adaptable level of functioning through numerous subsequent family events. One can assume that other family members increased their levels of differentiation concurrently with Mrs. Robertson, although she provided the leadership and the direction for the wider family effort.

SUMMARY

In conclusion, the Bowen family systems theory approach to clinical treatment of a remarried family system follows the same course as treatment of a one-time married family system. Assessment is concurrent with treatment and includes the same ten components: observation of the symptomatic person, sibling position, nuclear family emotional process, stressful events, emotional reactivity to stress, nuclear family adaptiveness, extended family stability and intactness, emotional cutoff, therapeutic focus, and prognosis. Treatment includes a continuing process of education, self-management for the clinician, broadening the focus, encouraging the client in self-observation and awareness of self-participation in problems, self-regulation of reactivity, developing alternative ways of managing self in relationships, anticipating reactivity to change, implementing change, and sticking to it.

In contrast to a one-time married family, a remarried family system often manifests higher levels of chronic stress and anxiety because of its legacy of family disruption surrounding the divorce or death of a spouse. The same patterns are observable, but often at a higher level of intensity and with more serious physical, psychological, or social/behavioral symptoms. Biological divisions can create complex interlocking triangles as family members ally with their blood relatives against their steprelatives. Projection of anxiety from the parents to the children is also very common, as the remarried parents create a kind of fused pseudoharmonious "united front" in their effort to make this new marriage work. Cutoff may be intense and fueled by the distress of previous marital failure. Depending on their own reactivity to the divorce or death, extended family members may or may not be emotionally available to the remarried family system.

Despite these observations about common patterns in remarried families, it is important to remember that they are generalizations. These patterns do not occur in all remarried families, and when they do occur, the level of intensity is not uniform. Remarried families, similar to one-time married families, function along a continuum of adaptiveness. Some families are able to manage the stressors of remarriage more flexibly and calmly than others. Some families react to the stressors of remarriage with intense upset, and they may rapidly re-divorce. The Robertsons were probably somewhere in the middle of the continuum. Their reactivity to the stressors of remarriage was high, and they manifested many symptoms during the months after the wedding. However, they remained married, they reproduced after three years of marriage, and they began to reconnect with many members of the extended family that had cut off from them. The prognosis for the Robertson family was initially guarded but is now fairly good. Bowen family systems theory provided a useful framework for understanding their experience of remarriage and served as a road map for guiding their self-management through the complexities of their family relationship system.

REFERENCES

American Psychiatric Association (1980). *Diagnostic and statistical manual of mental disorders,* Third Edition. Washington, DC: American Psychiatric Association.

Bowen, M. (1978). *Family therapy in clinical practice.* New York: Jason Aronson.

Bowen, M. (1988). Personal communication. Washington, DC.

Furstenberg, F. F., Jr. and Spanier, G. B. (1984). *Recycling the family: Remarriage after divorce.* Beverly Hills, CA: Sage Publications.

Kerr, M. E. (1987). Family diagnosis. *Family Center Report,* 8(4), pp. 1 - 4.

Kerr, M. E. and Bowen, M. (1988). *Family evaluation: An approach based on Bowen theory.* New York: W. W. Norton and Company.

McGoldrick, M. and Carter, B. (1989). Forming a remarried family. In B. Carter and M. McGoldrick (Eds.), *The changing family life cycle: A framework for family therapy* (pp. 399 - 429). Boston: Allyn and Bacon.

Toman, W. (1961). *Family constellation.* New York: Springer.

Chapter 15

Bridging Emotional Cutoff from a Former Spouse

Stephanie J. Ferrera

Few people would have the courage to contact an estranged former spouse and attempt to communicate about unresolved issues. Of those who would be willing to undertake such a project, few would be able to manage the emotional reactivity that would inevitably arise in a way that would allow productive communication. The conventional wisdom in regard to such a situation is "Let sleeping dogs lie." Implicit in this adage is the understanding that the emotional attachment between former spouses is, in most cases, very intense, the passing of years and the avoidance of contact do little to reduce this intensity, and renewed contact between the two carries the risk of reactivating hurtful misunderstanding and impasse.

Maureen Stone (pseudonym), the subject of this case study, made contact with her former husband through an exchange of letters. Into these letters she put information and reflections that she had not communicated to him over their twenty-year divorce. She told him her story and invited him to respond and, if he wished, to tell his story. He did respond, and although his letters were brief and contained views that were hard for Mrs. Stone to hear, they gave her a base of fact and reality that allowed her to resolve within herself emotional issues that she had not resolved in the twenty years of distance and silence.

Central to this chapter is Mrs. Stone's own report of the effort to bridge the cutoff from her former husband. Her report includes the events that led up to her decision to do this, what she hoped to accomplish, the input of the therapist as coach, the letter-writing process, the outcome, and her assessment of the effort.

Mrs. Stone's report is preceded by the therapist's report, which addresses three areas: theory, the therapist's own differentiation of self, and the clinical process. From the viewpoint of Bowen theory, these three elements are a seamless garment. The therapist's theoretical knowledge of emotional systems and his or her own effort toward differentiation of self are the foundation of clinical work. Only to the extent that he or she has understood his or her own family as an emotional system, has understood his or her own emotional functioning in that family, and has worked to become a clearly defined, thoughtful, and responsible self in that family can he or she accompany his or her clients in their effort to do the same.

The chapter concludes with some reflections by the therapist about this particular case and about the larger questions of human conflict and resolution that were raised by work with this client.

THERAPIST'S REPORT

Theory and the Therapist's Own Differentiation of Self

Learning the theory of the family emotional system is far more than an intellectual exercise. The learning process is amazingly slow and must be so because, first, this way of thinking is very different from conventional, individual-focused thinking about human behavior and, second, because every detail of the theory must be taken home, observed, and experienced within one's own family and one's self before it can be known to be accurate and become part of one's own base of wisdom. By the time Maureen Stone first entered my office, I had spent well over ten years grappling with Bowen theory. My primary value to her, I believed, would be whatever level of wisdom about human emotional functioning and human relationships I had attained by that point. What follows is a summary of my knowledge of emotional systems and my own learning process. I have interwoven what I learned conceptually from Murray Bowen with what I learned experientially within my own family and described some of the differences this learning made in my life. This is a selective summary, focusing mainly on the concepts from theory and the experiences from my own life that were most relevant to my work with Mrs. Stone.

From earliest memory, I had been curious about family relationships. The tension levels in both the family I was born into and the family I created with my husband had been uncomfortably high much of the time, and I had searched the universe for solutions to this problem. I managed to graduate college as a psychology major with honors, but with little self-awareness or understanding of human relationships. At twenty-one, shortly after graduation, I married the twenty-three-year-old man I had dated during college. I entered marriage with the overconfidence of one who knows little about what she is getting into. Before long, my husband and I were submerged in the typical problems that arise when two people who are emotionally reactive to each other and unpracticed at working out differences face the demands and responsibilities of marriage and family. By our first anniversary, we were parents of a daughter. Five more children followed in the next twelve years. Our lives were blessed and complicated by active involvement with both our families. In the sixth year of our marriage, shortly after the birth of our third child, my father died, and in the sixteenth year of our marriage, my husband's father died following a long illness. The pace of events—marriages, births, illnesses, deaths, worries, and conflicts—in our two families of origin was such that we were constantly challenged to adapt. As we dealt with various pressures, each of us tended to look to the other with expectations and demands and to be keenly disappointed when the other fell short. The cumulative effect of this over the years was considerable emotional distance and conflict in our marriage.

In my mid-thirties, I decided to professionalize my long-standing interest in the human dilemma by becoming a social worker. In graduate school, among the wide array of subjects encompassed by social work, two courses on "family systems" were available—introductory and advanced. For me, they were by far the most interesting courses, but they barely scratched the surface of my curiosity about family life. Reading Bowen's "On the Differentiation of Self" (Anonymous, 1972) was a turning point in my personal and professional life. I first read it in graduate school and have periodically reread it in the twenty years since. With each reading, I grasp a bit more of the vast mystery Bowen calls "family emotional process" and of the theory he developed to penetrate and illuminate this mystery. Michael Kerr has said about his first encounter with Dr. Bowen, "I didn't understand a lot of what he was saying about the emotional system, but I knew he was describing what I had lived in all my life" (Kerr, 1990). My response was similar.

As I entered the field of social work, I knew that my specialization would be family therapy, and I knew that I needed to learn a great deal more if I was ever to be adequate to this task. At the earliest opportunity, in 1978, I applied to the training program that Bowen headed at Georgetown Family Center. The program met in Washington four times a year for three days each time. Leaving home and going to Washington every three months was no small feat but doing so was an important part of the training. Each time the plane lifted off the ground in Chicago, I was lifting myself physically and emotionally up and out of the intensity I lived in and moving into "thinking space," a degree of distance from the emotional field that makes it possible to find a new vantage point, gain a broader perspective, see people and events in context, and think a bit more clearly and objectively about one's own functioning and relationships.

I carried a heavy agenda of family problems to the training program. My younger sister had been diagnosed with multiple sclerosis in 1972 and had declined rapidly in the following six-year period. As she lost physical mobility, she lost personal freedom. I was grieved to see the quality of her life going downhill in her late thirties, a time when mothering tasks were lightening and she could think about expanding her interests outside the home. When I was not running to my sister's house to help her, I was on the phone with my mother discussing how my sister and her husband should be handling the problem and how their children should be behaving. A secondary focal point for anxiety was my younger son, who was having school problems. Here I was invested in getting my son to take academics more seriously, while at the same time dealing with my husband, who saw *me* as the problem and who believed our son would be all right if I stayed out of his way.

Overresponsibility, my lifelong companion, went with me to the training program. My expectation was that I would learn in a year, or two at the most, what Bowen knew, and with this I would be able to solve the problems in my family. I found the first session at Georgetown a sobering experience. There was a notable absence of the cozy togetherness I had come to expect in mental health programs. Instead, I encountered, conceptually and *in vivo,* the phenomenon Bowen calls "differentiation of self." The idea of differentiation was not new to me, but the living experience of it was. Here were people, Dr. Bowen and the Family Center faculty, who were seriously engaged in an effort not only to teach differentiation as a concept, but to live it as a principle. It soon became apparent to me that the faculty would not join me in my view of my family, my anxiety about it, or my efforts to change it. Rather, they would offer a radically different way of thinking about family, and my supervisor would offer coaching in application of this thinking to myself, my own family, and clinical families.

Bowen viewed the human family as a natural system. His thinking was strongly influenced by his years of reading about a wide spectrum of living systems, from cells to animal colonies to ecosystems. When Bowen arrived at the National Institutes of Mental Health in 1954 to head a research project in which whole families were hospitalized, he had the opportunity to observe the interaction between mother, father, and child from day to day over long time periods. A field of observation that had not previously been accessible to researchers was opened to him. His study of natural systems had prepared his mind to see the family as a system. One of his first realizations was that the family could not be adequately conceptualized as a collective of individuals, each operating for the most part autonomously, while interacting with one another. So deep were the attachments among family members, so responsive were they to one another, so greatly was each member's thinking, feeling, and behavior influenced by the others, that it was accurate to think of the family as an emotional unit or system rather than a group of separate individuals. This does not deny the individuality of each member. Indeed, each one is a self; each has a boundary that separates him or her from the surrounding world, and each has an internal guidance system or ability to think, feel, and act for self. However, the individuality or "self" of each member does not emerge apart from the family; it develops within and is regulated by the togetherness of the family as a whole. Self is not possible in a vacuum; one becomes a self by defining one's self in active relationship with others who are important to self.

Thinking of individuality and togetherness as basic life forces within individuals and families led Bowen to the concept of differentiation of self. He recognized that people vary in the way they work out the individuality-togetherness balance. An optimal balance would be seen in an individual who is able to be for self without being selfish and to be for others without being selfless. Less differentiated people, which includes most of humankind, will easily get caught in the polarities. Those who are motivated to do so can work at conducting their lives within the middle ground.

As I went forward in the Georgetown training program, I assessed myself as being in the fair-to-middling range on the scale of differentiation. Of the many ways one can be undifferentiated, I saw myself primarily taking the path of overresponsibility—focusing on others, taking on every problem as my own, trying to get others to do as I thought best. Overresponsiveness is perhaps a better word for this than overresponsibility, since it is a blind, automatic way of functioning, and the outcome is that one is neither responsible for self nor responsible to others.

The training program helped me see the connection between the emotional intensity in my nuclear and parental families, in which I was deeply embedded, and the emotional cutoff from the larger extended family. My supervisor suggested that I might be able to think more objectively about close-to-home relationships if I could see them as part of the larger multigenerational family process. I set about studying the larger family, both by gathering family history and by cultivating relationships with more distant family members. This brought me face-to-face, conceptually and *in vivo,* with emotional cutoff.

Bowen formally defined the concept of emotional cutoff and added it to his theory in 1975 (Bowen, 1976). In the original six concepts of his theory, completed in the mid-1960s, Bowen had defined the family emotional system as a product of two interrelated variables—level of anxiety and level of differentiation. The 100-point scale of differentiation had been worked out, describing the emotional functioning of individuals and families at different points along the continuum. The "adaptive mechanisms" that are activated as emotional intensity in the family increases had been identified and described. The theory encompassed all levels of family functioning: the reciprocal functioning of the two-person system, the more complex three-person system or triangle, the network of interlocking triangles, and the continuation of the process through multiple generations (multigenerational transmission process).

In adding emotional cutoff to the theory, Bowen stated the need to have a separate concept for the process between generations. Emotional cutoff was the term he chose "to best describe this process of separation, isolation, withdrawal, running away, or denying the importance of the parental family" (Bowen, 1976, p. 84). Emotional cutoff, which is accomplished by distancing physically and/or emotionally, is a way of managing the unresolved attachment to parents. It can give the illusion of having resolved problems in the relationship without truly doing so. This is sometimes recognized when the same problem, or some version of it, develops in new relationships.

Cutoff solves one problem, removing the participants from the difficulties of contact with one another, and it creates another problem, putting people at risk for equal or greater intensity in future relationships. The more intense the family emotional process, the more frequent and intense the process of cutoff is likely to be. The sense of crowding and encroachment may be such that people see no way to preserve themselves other than by severing contact. Doing so gives short-term relief but carries a long-term cost. With each cutoff, one loses an opportunity to deal with, resolve, and learn from the differences and conflicts that are inevitable in relationships. Over time, with repetition of this pattern, one's ability to sustain relationships may be diminished, and one may ultimately be left isolated.

The emotional cutoff in my own family and self was not readily apparent to me. My concept of family included parents and siblings and expanded to include spouses and children of siblings, as these arrived, and my own in-law family. I had active contact with all who were inside this circle. Beyond this were "relatives" on both mother's and father's sides with whom I had occasional polite visits. The possibility that this extended family contained information and perhaps even relationships that could be enlightening and enriching simply did not enter my mind until I studied family systems theory. Theory, plus my supervisor's encouragement to get "up and out," gave me the impetus I needed to take some of the energy that had been riveted on the home front and put it into learning more about the bigger picture.

As I began a series of calls, letters, and visits to members of my mother's family on the East Coast, I came into contact with the version of emotional cutoff that existed in my family and self. It was like a deep undercurrent that I had not known was there until I began trying to swim upstream against it. Initially, the road was smooth. Being my mother's daughter opened doors for me with aunts and cousins who had a positive relationship with her and had heard good things about me. All of them were, similar to my mother, good talkers and storytellers. I gained both information and relationships. Theory was my guide to knowing what information to look for and how to sort out fact from fiction. As I moved on to try to make connections with a branch of the family I had never met, I encountered a rougher road and more dead ends. Some family members expressed doubts (why would you want to bother with "them?") and fears (be careful what you get into with "those people"). It was hard for me to admit they were expressing the same reactivity that was stirred in me by this reconnecting effort. I was moderately successful in moving past my own resistance and other obstacles. I succeeded in contacting several descendants of my maternal grandfather's siblings, from whom I gained valuable information.

With an expanded picture of my family, I was able to see the emotional cutoff more clearly, and I began to understand what produced the cutoff, and what it, in turn, produced. The primary factor seemed to be a propensity to place people into the categories of good and bad. The family was populated with "saints" and "devils," and not many in between. Saints (primarily female) were cheerful, helpful, generous, and considerate of others; they worked hard and faced life with will power. Devils (primarily male) were fighters, hell-raisers, drinkers (lacking will power), and incompetents. To be in the "good" category made one a trusted insider in the communication network; to be in the "bad" made one, for the most part, an outsider who would be talked about but not talked with. As I looked at the historical information I was getting and the observations I was making through the lens of theory, the good/bad polarization gave way to a more systemic view of the family. I began to see the reciprocity between the harmonious closeness of the insiders and their conflict with and distance from the outsiders. I began to see sainthood and devilhood less as the inherent characters of people and more as products of the relationship process and to grasp how each family member might be playing a part in feeding the stereotyping process.

The coaching I was receiving at Georgetown confronted me with a hard lesson: when you see a pattern of thinking or behavior in your own family, *look for the same in yourself and work on it in yourself.* Learning how projection and cutoff worked in my family and how these processes were fueled by overpositive and overnegative subjectivity gave me a new level of understanding of my own emotional functioning and an awareness of what I had to work on. Gradually, I became more alert to my judgmental and critical side; my automatic overpositive/sympathetic reaction to some people and overnegative/blaming reaction to others; my fear of mistakes, fault, and blame; and my need to keep myself in the right/good/insider position.

During my two years in the training program, the seeds were planted for two new directions that have become increasingly important and valuable to me over the years. One was a focus inward to my own thinking process. The other was a focus far outward to the world of nature.

Differentiated thinking is an essential part of differentiation of self—knowing the difference between objectivity and subjectivity within self, knowing the difference between what you know and what you do not know, distinguishing between facts and interpretations, facts and assumptions, and facts and opinions. Dr. Bowen continually challenged people to examine their own thinking. When a statement was made, he often asked the speaker, "How do you know that? What's the evidence for that?" Bowen invited trainees to write papers on "My Beliefs and Where I Got Them," to send him the papers, and to read the papers to the training group. He invited the group to listen without comment as individuals came forward to state their beliefs. I found the task terribly difficult. It forced me to recognize how much I had borrowed "my beliefs" from others. After a fruitless struggle to define my beliefs about the global issues of life, I decided to reduce the assignment to manageable size by simply trying to put into words my thinking about current issues in my own family. I began by identifying some of the spoken and unspoken assumptions and beliefs that I saw operating in my family and went on to describe, in factual terms, the current problems. I then described what a calm and thoughtful response to each of those problems would look like. This effort was quite fruitful: it yielded for me a "working paper," a way of thinking and a set of principles that could guide me as I steered my way through the labyrinth that my family was at that very anxious time.

The other new direction sparked for me by the training program was the discovery of the natural world and the natural sciences. I had always been interested in the humanities, especially philosophy, psychology, history, and literature and equally disinterested in nonhuman forms of life and the sciences. Although I had enjoyed and appreciated the beauty of nature, I had also cut myself off from nature by undervaluing and avoiding the study of its workings. Bowen's natural systems theory, rooted in the facts of evolution and the continuity between the human and all other life on earth, awakened me to the vast possibilities for understanding human behavior that opened up when the human was viewed as descendant, heir, and relative of other species of living organisms. My curiosity raised, I began to read books on biology and evolution, focusing especially on animals and their patterns of family and social life. I began to see evolution as family history writ large. I then came to realize that an evolutionary perspective was necessary for an adequate understanding of the family and that the depth and scope of Bowen's thinking which had originally attracted me came from its foundation in evolution.

With these efforts, I was moving toward natural systems thinking. When my thinking was clearest, I could see the family as a system: I saw how the overall unit shaped the position and functioning of each member and also how each member shaped, in different ways and degrees, the structure and functioning of the overall unit. *Natural* systems thinking meant I could see the relationship process of the family in an evolutionary context, as the product of countless generations of humans and their mammalian ancestors adapting in ways that were necessary for survival and reproduction. An outgrowth of systems thinking is emotional neutrality, defined by Bowen as the ability to be in the presence of disharmony without taking sides. Natural systems thinking allows one to see human situations in their many-sided complexity, thus reducing bias and blame. As I began to experience the neutral state of mind that came with systems thinking, I found it highly rewarding. I could achieve neutrality only occasionally, but when I did, I found that I could think about situations (including personal, close-to-home matters) in a way that was far freer and that offered far more options for response than my usual biased state of mind.

I had not gone far toward natural systems thinking and neutrality when a development arose in my family that would test this newly emerging way of thinking and responding. Following several months of increasing distance in our marriage, my husband informed me he was in a serious relationship with another woman. Although painful, this information helped me make sense of the tension in the previous months, and it opened up some communication between my husband and me. Neither of us wanted to initiate separation or divorce. His position was that we no longer had a "personal relationship"; we were, in effect, separated, but he would continue to live at home so as not to disrupt the children or incur greater expense. My position was that the marriage had a long history and great value to me, and therefore, I would do what I could to understand the problems and work them out.

The year that followed was difficult for our family. Each of us—my husband and I and our children, then ranging in age from twenty-two to ten—lived with the stress and uncertainty of the situation. For me, the challenge was to keep my thinking somewhat free and neutral and to relate to my husband as calmly as I could in an emotional field in which the affair triangle was generating reactivity. Much of the time, I was in the position of outsider in the triangle and the object of intense two-on-one projection. Support was available to me from family and friends, but I found my best resources to be theory, consultation with my supervisor, and input from a few colleagues who were both friends and trained systems thinkers. Neutrality was more valuable to me than allies. At a time when I was feeling an urgency to "do something," the supervisor's response was, "It's premature to make a decision. Pushing your husband into an either/or choice could blow it up. I hate to see a marriage with this much history get decided emotionally. You do not have to do anything but calm down and try to understand the forces that are driving this. You are missing the overview that would give you the prescription for what to do." This perspective had a calming and clarifying effect on me. I postponed taking action in favor of allowing more time for a decision to evolve within the system. This constraint was no small thing for an overresponsible oldest daughter with a life pattern of moving in and taking charge. I put energy that had long been invested in analyzing my husband and trying to change him into focusing on my side of the marriage. Slowly I recognized and described the many ways in which I had functioned in reaction to my husband rather than as a defined self. This project (later published, Ferrera, 1983) opened my eyes to the part I had played in creating and maintaining patterns in our marriage. It had always seemed to me that his being the way he was made it necessary for me to be the way was. Now it made almost as much sense to me that my being the way I was made it necessary for him to be the way he was.

Almost a year after my husband first told me about the affair, he moved away from home to live with his new partner. From our conversations, it was clear that he had thought about what it would take for him to remain with me and that he saw no way to do so and also that the pull he felt toward her was strong. As with many people who face the choice of holding on or letting go, I saw letting go as the lesser of the evils, even though it went against my strongest emotional current. It was clear we were headed for divorce.

Divorce, in simple terms, is the outcome of the emotional equilibrium in the marriage moving from an original positive state to an eventual negative state. The change may be subtle and gradual or more obvious and dramatic. The process goes far beyond the divorcing parties. As with all important family events, nothing less than a multigenerational context is adequate for understanding a divorce, as people struggle to understand what happened. Most divorcing parties and their family members can offer explanations of how the divorce came about, explanations which range from highly subjective (often focusing on one or two variables) to more objective (encompassing many variables with some grasp of the relationship among the variables). The temptation to blame one person is strong, but once one has been introduced to systems thinking and neutrality, one's thinking brain will not let one off that easily.

Once a decision to divorce has been made, the next question is, "What kind of divorce will it be?" The level of emotional reactivity between spouses, and in the larger family, that leads to the breakdown of a marriage is, in most cases, intense. Understandably, emotional cutoff often follows. Our society tends to equate divorce with emotional cutoff and to promote the process with the attitude, "Get over this and get on with your life." Bowen theory, based on an understanding of the depth and complexity of human attachment, takes a different position. It knows that divorce does not end the relationship between spouses. Rather, divorce substantially changes that relationship and requires the spouses, their children, their parents, and others important to them to reorganize the relationship system. Emotional cutoff can be minimized if the husband and wife and their families work to resolve the many issues and decisions of divorce in ways that are the least costly and disruptive to all involved. People struggle, with varying degrees of success, to keep thoughtfulness and responsibility predominant over impulse and reactivity. Mechanisms such as legal decrees, physical distance, and separate households can aid the process if used wisely or can escalate it if not used wisely. Divorces cover a broad spectrum, from those that are extremely anxiety-driven and costly to those that are relatively reasonable and cooperative.

In dealing with my own divorce, I knew I had many choices to make about my own functioning and many opportunities to try to relate to my husband differently in the divorce than I had in the marriage. My global goal was to protect the long-term stability of the family. I would try to have that priority guide all decisions. I wanted to function in a way that would minimize loss and cutoff and would preserve the aspects of our family life that were working well. To achieve this, I would need a set of carefully defined principles to which I could refer at times of high intensity.

One principle was to think of and relate to my former husband as a member of the family, an insider, not an outsider. His track record as a provider had been solid and consistent. He had been a rather distant father but greatly invested in the children, being both empathic and generous to them. A statement that Dr. Bowen had made—"Fathers get as close to their children as mothers allow"—seemed especially relevant for me, although I also understood the other side of that story, that distancing fathers promote overclose mother-child relationships. That valuable message went through my mind often as our family was reorganizing around the divorce. I tried to manage my part in the mother-father-child triangles carefully, mostly by staying out of the way, as father and children worked out new modes of connecting with one another. My former husband was available for frequent visits home, and I valued his continued presence. However, each of his visits presented me with a painful reminder that the marriage was over, that he was not available for a personal relationship with me. I found myself dealing with the phenomenon I call "looking for something that isn't there." It took me a long time to sort out the difference between what was still possible in our relationship and what was no longer possible.

Another guiding principle was to keep my membership in good standing in the Ferrera family. My relationship to my in-law family had been long and enjoyable, and no divorce was desired on either my part or theirs. However, triangles were ever-present and could be activated by a divisive comment or question (which, at moments of intensity, I was tempted to do). My effort here was to avoid putting pressure on them to take sides. As time passed, I came to realize that the family reorganization meant that my in-laws would be developing a new relationship with their son/brother and his new partner. The reality was that there would be occasions when the family, including my children, would gather, and I would not be included. My choice, then, could be cutoff, or it could be to create a different way of thinking about and relating to my in-laws.

Then there were the members of my own family. How would my divorce change my relationship with them? Early on, I recognized that the divorce offered me an opportunity to shift my position in the family a bit and modify old patterns. For one thing, I could "blow my image" as overre-sponsible caretaker, come out of hiding, and be a more real person with real problems and needs. I could level with them, ask for help, and have some confidence in their ability to support me.

My siblings' reactivity to the divorce was mild, and my mother's, predictably, was intense. In contrast to my attempt to "think systems" about the divorce, my mother saw, without a shadow of doubt, that my husband was the wrongdoer. If I became reactive to her view, I could find myself in the ridiculous position of actually defending this man who had left me; defending him, of course, was no more objective than blaming him. In my discussions with my mother, I came to realize that here was the opportunity of a lifetime for differentiation of self. Here was a serious, life-changing event, and here I was thinking about it and managing it in ways very foreign to her. The departure from the "we-ness" that we had woven over the years and the reality of two separate "I's" was evident each time the subject came up. Again, the choice could be cutoff or it could be learning to respect the differences. I believe each of us has done some of both. The difference remains: I have not converted her to my view, nor has she converted me to hers. Although we think differently, she has been a resource to me in many ways—her own example of survivorship, her confidence in my ability to survive, her consistent interest and support.

Over the years since our divorce, my former husband and I have been in fairly regular contact and have kept talking to each other. Much of the conversation has been about our children, finances, family news, and decisions, but we have also talked periodically about our own relationship. The ongoing contact has been immeasurably valuable to me; it has given me the chance to move in and out of an intense relationship system, to see its fine points and nuances, and to come to know my own part in it. Contact with him provides me with a base of reality that corrects my overactive projection process. I have come to know him as an individual separate and different from me, with his own context and his own reality. I have slowly gained a level of neutrality which sees that his acting for self, for what he believed to be his own necessity and best interest, was never an act against me. As a consequence of the choices and changes he made for himself, my life and the lives of our children and other family members were disrupted, and we were pushed to adapt. We were not abandoned by him. He did not act to hurt us; he regretted disturbing his family. In a calm state of mind, this is clear. In an anxious, self-referential state of mind, it is difficult to see.

As one gains a systems perspective on a divorce, one's thinking moves from partial toward comprehensive, from simple toward complex, and from blind spots toward objectivity and neutrality. My understanding of my marriage and divorce has slowly grown to include the multigenerational context in which it took place; the families of origin in which my former husband and I grew up and formed our images and assumptions about marriage; our sibling positions and functional positions; the degree of attachment we had to those families and the differing ways we managed that attachment and separation; the degree of attachment to each other; the reciprocal patterns we developed as we dealt with decisions, conflicts, and responsibilities; the ways we each adapted and compromised; and the consequences of this; the parenting that unified and divided us; the impact of stresses and losses that came into our lives; and the deep drive for individuality that each of us appeared ultimately able to preserve in the face of the pressures in our relationship. My initial negative and pained reaction to the divorce has been replaced by an acceptance that recognizes the opportunities and gains which the event opened up, as well as the losses.

The goal of this section has been to illustrate how theory is learned in the context of one's life and how theory guides the effort to be more differentiated, that is, more aware, mature, and responsible, in the way one lives. Theoretical knowledge of emotional systems, the ability to be an observer at the same time one is a participant, and consistent work on one's own functioning are the ingredients of the differentiating effort. Three circular processes are involved: knowing the system, knowing self as part of the system, and defining self within the system. This human process is identical for the clinician and for the client.

The Clinical Process

Maureen Stone heard about my clinical practice through friends we had in common. In her conversations with these women, she had been introduced to Bowen's ideas, had been intrigued by what she heard, and had decided to pursue it in therapy. She was functioning well, and her life was free of serious problems, but she saw room for growth and improvement. We agreed to meet every other week at the beginning and then less frequently, in accordance with her needs and interests as the therapy progressed.

As of this writing, it has been over four years since I first met with Mrs. Stone. She is an organized thinker and articulate informant, and we covered a lot of ground in that first session: presenting problem ("my mother is the problem"), initial history of her family of origin, a brief overview of her two marriages (past and present), some information about her two sons (one married and one in graduate school) and her relationships with them (close and positive), and some information about her career as an artist and teacher. By the end of the second session, she had provided abundant facts, along with a number of opinions about her family, and I had drawn a fairly detailed four-generation diagram (see Figure 15.1). With theory as my guide, I looked at all that information, thought about the facts of the emotional system that lay hidden within it, and began to raise questions that would bring these facts forward.

I defined for Mrs. Stone my roles as a guide in exploring the emotional process in her family and self and as a coach in whatever changes she decided to make. I told her that I operated from a theory, that this theory was available for her to learn, and that some clients found learning theory to be a useful adjunct and catalyst to therapy. Similar to most of my clients, she never became as fascinated with theory as I have, but she read some literature, discussed ideas in sessions, and presented interesting questions and observations. In the fourth session, she made an observation distinguishing between thinking and feeling within herself: "I can think one way but still

FIGURE 15.1. The Stone Family Diagram

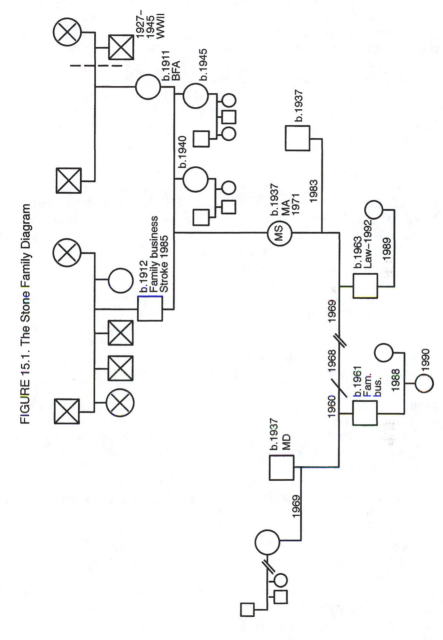

feel the other way." Knowing that the ability to separate a thinking state from a feeling state is central to differentiation of self, I took note of this.

The area of concern that Mrs. Stone focused on initially in therapy was her relationship with her mother. She was the oldest of three daughters; she was in her early fifties, and her parents were in their upper seventies. Her father's serious health problems over the past few years had raised the family anxiety level. Her relationship with her mother had been difficult most of Mrs. Stone's life, with criticism and feelings of rejection running both ways. Father had been the opposite, the source of understanding and nurturance: "My father is my mother."

Mrs. Stone was concerned that she was becoming more similar to her mother. She saw her mother as an unhappy and unproductive woman, bogged down in physical and emotional problems, and when she saw some of mother's traits in herself, it alarmed her. I did not see Mrs. Stone's being similar to her mother as a problem; I saw it as a fact of nature. Given the facts of genes and environment, people will have traits similar to their parents. My hypothesis was that if Mrs. Stone could be a little less reactive and a little more objective about mother, the problem would resolve.

What would enable her to get beyond the reactivity to mother so that she could accept herself (with the traits that were similar to mother's and those that were different) and perhaps also become more accepting of mother? If the level of reactivity was an indicator of the level of fusion between the two of them, what would it take to gain the degree of emotional separation that would allow for a calmer, more flexible relationship? A comment Dr. Bowen had made about difficult relationships came to mind: "There are hazards in trying to bridge a gulf of this magnitude within a small two-person system" (Bowen, 1984). I thought that encouraging Mrs. Stone to move closer to mother was probably not the solution. Pushing people to "communicate" when reactivity is high is often a setup for failure, leading to even more anxiety, discouragement, and continued impasse. Systems thinking suggests that it is better to go in the opposite direction—up and out to the larger system. The rich family history that Mrs. Stone possessed was used to construct a broad, factual context in which to place her mother. We started looking at the facts of mother's life—the family in which she grew up, the people and events that influenced her, the challenges she faced, the way she adapted.

The therapy had not progressed very far along this path when Mrs. Stone's focus shifted from her mother to her former husband. Two things occurred to shift the focus to him: First, she began to see parallels between the relationship with him and that with her mother; the themes of anger, misunderstanding, and rejection were present in both. Second, and more decisive, she learned through an item in the financial news that her husband and his partners had sold a business for a large sum and that he was a wealthy man. This information had great emotional impact, triggering for Mrs. Stone a deep sense of injustice and bringing to the forefront all that had never been resolved in the divorce.

Mrs. Stone had married Dr. Stone when they were both twenty-three. Both had graduated from college, and he was beginning medical school. Their first son was born ten months into the marriage, and their second son two years after that. The marriage ended after eight years, just as Dr. Stone was finishing his medical education. He became involved with another woman and left to be with her. No plans or preparation had been made for a separation, and Mrs. Stone was left, at least initially, with no means of support. She left the East Coast city where she and Dr. Stone had been living and moved with her sons back to her parents' home in the Midwest. Dr. Stone took the lead in procuring a legal divorce, and the financial settlement was based on the low income he was earning at that time. Mrs. Stone became a single mother, working days and taking graduate courses in the evenings, providing most of the care and financial support for her sons. Years later, when the boys were in their teens, she found a new partner and remarried.

Listening to Mrs. Stone describe the ending of the marriage, I saw many of the features of intense emotional process: accelerated pace of change, breakdown in communication, unilateral rather than negotiated decision making, distance, triangles, and finally, a deep emotional cutoff. My impressions were that the divorce had been traumatic for her, that she had been pushed by necessity (and probably also by her own inclination) to move ahead quickly to adapt and survive, and that she had never fully processed or resolved the experience.

How does one come to terms with such an event? One way is to try to understand what has happened and how it happened. People frequently think about the experience for a long time afterward, despite efforts to put it out of their minds. Frequently, an explanation or story is constructed, based on a mix of fact, speculation, and bias. Over time, the story may take on a life of its own, as people become invested in thinking about the event in this way.

When a high level of emotional intensity and emotional cutoff surrounds divorce, it becomes harder for people to arrive at a reasonably complete and objective story, one that includes all sides of the events. When former spouses keep contact and communication as minimal and impersonal as possible, they avoid some obvious problems, but they pay a price. In losing touch with the person who was on the other side of the marriage, one loses touch with the single most important source of information (outside one-self) about the marriage. Without this information, one's view tends to remain myopic and one-sided. Thus, cutoff reduces one's opportunity to learn more about how the reciprocal process in the marriage worked and how it evolved to the point of divorce. In my view, an ongoing effort to relate to and deal with one's former spouse is the high road toward under-standing and ultimately resolving the divorce. Family and friends, thera-pists, and self-help books can contribute comfort and some enlightenment (as well as bias), but no one can offer the kind of learning opportunity that the one other person who lived the experience can offer.

When Mrs. Stone and I began to discuss her options in relation to Dr. Stone, I knew that the aforementioned view was one I held strongly. It was based on my understanding of the emotional system and differentiation of self and had been tested by my own experience. I also recognized that my personal position on this might or might not be useful to her. With the therapy moving into territory that was close to home for me, I recalled a concept from social work school—"overidentifying with the client"—and thought that it would be wise to take time out to clarify within myself the boundary between myself and my client. With caution signals flashing in my head, I reminded myself that the facts of her marriage were quite different from the facts of mine, her goals and interests were different, and the solution she might find was likely to be different from mine. To be responsible to her, I needed to be alert to the danger of my becoming overinvested in having Mrs. Stone see and do things my way.

Mrs. Stone and I began to discuss what options were open to her and what she was invested in doing. I presented my view on what could be gained, in terms of differentiation of self, from an effort to bridge the cutoff from her former spouse and also outlined what such an effort, if it were to have a chance of success, would require. She saw a value to this. The communication between her and Dr. Stone since their divorce had been minimal. She had many unanswered questions about the events twenty years ago that had so drastically altered her life. She was motivated to make contact with him for the sake of getting information that would expand her understanding of those events.

However, the larger agenda, the one which provided the strongest impe-tus for Mrs. Stone to take on this difficult project, was the fairness issue. During the marriage, she had joined her husband in the hard work and sacrifices necessary for his medical education. With the divorce, she had lost not only the personal and emotional security of the marriage, but also the financial security. The divorce settlement had been more dictated by Dr. Stone than negotiated between them. In the divorce process, she felt seriously disadvantaged, as she lacked the time and money needed to engage in an interstate legal case, and she found little encouragement from attorneys or others she consulted to pursue a better settlement than that offered by Dr. Stone. She accepted what was decreed in the settlement but with a strong sense that it was unfair. Following the divorce, an undercurrent of victimization accompanied her even as she moved forward with her life, established herself professionally, and saw her two sons grow up and become accomplished young men. With this history, it was understandable to me why Mrs. Stone had a strong reaction when she learned about the wealth that Dr. Stone had acquired.

Mrs. Stone made several decisions. She decided to make contact with Dr. Stone by letter, the form of communication she saw as best suited to a thoughtful presentation of complex information and issues. She had two agendas for the letter: one was to describe her life with her sons after the divorce, giving Dr. Stone information she had not given him over the years, and the other was to state her view of the fairness issue and make a claim for belated financial reparation. She agreed with me that the tone of the letter should be as neutral and objective as possible, although the content would address serious issues between them. Her ability to say what she wanted to say with a reasonable level of emotional neutrality would be the key to establishing communication.

Mrs. Stone worked on the letter over a six-month period. The writing took her back to revisit, reconstruct, and reflect upon the experiences and events of her relationship with Dr. Stone. My consultation time with her during this period totaled eight hours and focused on two primary tasks: One was to gain a deeper understanding of the emotional process, and especially of her own emotional functioning, in the marriage; the other was to define as clearly as possible her goals for self in the letter writing. I had some concerns about Mrs. Stone pursuing financial reparation. I saw her standing on solid ground as long as she was pursuing knowledge and a better understanding of the emotional process, goals which I believed were within her reach through her own efforts. I saw her moving to shakier ground if she became invested in monetary compensation, a goal that depended on Dr. Stone's agreement and cooperation. My conversations with Mrs. Stone about these questions made clear to me that she understood well the distinction between the "emotional" goal and the "financial" goal and that the gains for self she was realizing in the letter-writing process provided reason and motivation enough to make it worth her effort.

Mrs. Stone's letter went through several stages and revisions as the writing and reflecting process moved her through stages of change in the thinking-feeling balance within herself. When she had achieved a statement that satisfied her own standards of honesty, clarity, and objectivity, she sent the letter. Over the next several months, an exchange of letters between her and Dr. Stone ensued.

From my standpoint as coach/consultant to Mrs. Stone's work, I felt that I was witnessing, and hopefully contributing to, something significant. I knew enough about the power of family emotional systems to appreciate the courage and conviction it took for her to attempt to bridge the cutoff from her former husband. I knew the level of thoughtfulness that she had put into the effort, and I also knew that writing was a useful vehicle for stimulating her thinking. I believed that others, including myself, could learn from her experience. With these things in mind, I asked Mrs. Stone to consider writing about this experience. With little hesitation, and in her characteristic "can do" spirit, she agreed to do so. Her own report follows.

CLIENT'S REPORT

Gaining Freedom
Maureen Stone

Although my relationship with the man I married more than thirty years ago is no longer a significant influence in my life, for twenty years after our divorce this was not so. As do many people, I carried the burden of hurt and anger for a long time. I am writing this to shed what light I can on the process of differentiation or what I call getting free.

As a twenty-three-year-old bride in 1960, I was well prepared by my family and by society to be a wife, homemaker, and mother. My same-age husband, whom I had met in college, was in medical school. I worked briefly until our first child was born ten months after our wedding. At that time, most women were not taking "the pill" for birth control until their families were complete, as its effects were not entirely known. We intended to have a family so this was, although earlier than we had planned, a happy event. Our second son was born two years later. We lived on an income below the government-declared poverty level but with plans for a comfortable future. There was money only for bare necessities, but we didn't mind too much because we knew it was a temporary situation.

After my husband completed four years of medical school, we moved to another city for a one-year internship, to a third city for a three-year medical residency, and to a fourth city for a two-year medical fellowship. We lived in eight different dwellings. His life revolved around his professional training, and mine was focused on the home and children. I had my hands full creating a pleasant home again and again with very little money, while caring for two active boys. There was no question of my working outside the home, as my husband felt strongly that my job was taking care of the children. I became a creative cook of macaroni and hamburger dishes, learned to recover old furniture, and made curtains of muslin. We had no resources for entertainment, but we both enjoyed hiking in the woods and walking on the beach with the boys. I would describe our marriage as quite traditional and satisfactory. I felt lonely at times, but if he did too, he never said so.

After eight years of marriage, just as the end of my husband's long education was in sight, he became romantically involved with a nurse at the hospital where he was training. I was unhappy but realized that for doctors in training this was not unusual. They were known to have affairs with nurses, although I never thought my husband would do so. I was willing to wait it out and go on with our marriage. I had no thought of divorce and felt that this was one of the tribulations of life. I had married him for better or worse. This was worse, but better was in the future. It was a very difficult time emotionally, compounded by the fact that the nurse was married with two children herself, and her mother called me on the phone almost every day to vent her feelings about "this terrible situation." My husband and I talked often about the situation, and he assured me at first that it would pass. Later he said he was thinking about divorce but he just didn't know. I did my best to keep the children happy, but I was devastated. I alternated between berating him and clinging to him in tears. I had no emotional support, as my family was 1,000 miles away; we had not lived in the area long enough to have close friends, and I had never heard of a "support group" if, in fact, there was such a concept then. After close to a year, I needed to get away from the situation to regain some strength. In my distress I had lost twenty pounds, and I now weighed less than one hundred.

During the summer, the children and I spent a month visiting my parents. While we were there, my husband informed me that he would not be living with us when we returned. He left it to me to tell the children that he would not be home. After our return, he visited us on Sundays, and in some ways, it was better than it had been for a long time. We walked in the woods and had nice dinners at home together. For one day a week, his attention was focused on us again. One Sunday, about six weeks after our return, just as we were sitting down to dinner, the phone rang. I answered and recognized the voice of the nurse's mother. She did not identify herself but asked for my husband. He took the phone, listened briefly, and told me he had to go to the hospital. After that, he stopped coming to see us, and he gave me no money for food or rent.

Suddenly I was left with two children to care for and no resources. The neighbors supplied food until I could get some money from my parents. I did not want a divorce because I still hoped eventually this would pass and because I was desperately frightened of life without him. I went to see a lawyer who advised me to get a legal separation so that I could take the children out of state and return to my hometown, where I would have help to care for the children and to get back on my feet. We went to court. The financial settlement was based on his fellowship income, which was still poverty-level, and the judge refused my request for a provision for future increase. It became evident to me that I was to be responsible for the support of myself and our two children. This seemed entirely unfair, but I felt there was no recourse.

My sons and I returned to my parents' home just before Christmas; I felt like an utter failure. I was the only person in my entire extended family ever to fall under the stigma of a failed marriage. The children and I lived with my parents for eight months while I found a job, enrolled in graduate school, and found a place to live. In June, I was served with papers saying that I had been divorced. My husband had gone to Reno and divorced me, leaving us with the same meager financial settlement. The lawyers in my family were not encouraging about the prospect of improving the financial arrangement. They could do nothing themselves. They said it would entail using a lawyer in the state where we had lived and that I would have to be there and postponement tactics could be used. I could not afford to do that, either financially or emotionally. My primary concern was repairing the hurt of my children.

While I appreciated my parents' help, living with them was difficult. Although the house was large enough for all of us to live comfortably, the situation was trying. My mother was emotionally distressed. Not long after we moved out of their house, my mother had some sort of breakdown and refused to see me. She told others that she wished I had never been born. My father suggested that I not call or come to the house for a while, although he came to see us almost every day. This was an exceedingly difficult time. Having been rejected by both my husband and my mother, I began to question my own worth as a person. Fortunately, my two sisters and their families were very supportive. It was several years before my mother spoke to me again, and she now denies that this ever happened so it is impossible to talk with her about it. My father continued to be supportive and spent a great deal of time being a substitute father to his grandsons.

For the next two years, my life had a rigid routine. In the morning, I got the boys up, dressed, fed, and off to school and myself off to my typing job. I rushed home at noon to have lunch with the children and then got them back to school and myself back to work by one o'clock. At three o'clock I called home to make sure the sitter had arrived, and after work, I drove thirty miles to take night courses for my master's degree in education. I would get home close to midnight, and the next morning I would get up to do it all over again. On weekends, I cleaned the house, did laundry, grocery shopped, studied, and spent time with my sons. In the summer, the children were enrolled in day camp. I managed to get my degree in two years while working at a full-time job and being a full-time mother and father for my two active boys. I did not have time to attend my graduation ceremony.

I obtained a job coordinating the art program for an elementary school district. I chose a profession in education because the hours and vacations coincided with my children's schedule. After two years, my position was eliminated due to a budget cut. After several months of near panic, I was very fortunate to get a college teaching position.

The children were wonderfully cooperative through all of this, and I feel exceedingly thankful for that. I know they were hurt and fearful for a while that I would leave too. Much reassurance was necessary. They spent a few weeks with their father in the summers when they were invited. He lived 1,000 miles away. He sent airline tickets when he wished them to visit and deducted half their support payment while they were there. He had remarried immediately after our divorce and now had two stepchildren. I had very little contact with him. We spoke only occasionally on the phone.

Although I showed the world a pleasant face, the underlying theme of my life was a pervading anger. I often woke up in the morning feeling an inexplicable rage and would rise quickly and get on with my day in order to evade the feeling. Possibly the anger fueled my life and gave me the energy to accomplish what I did. It is just as possible that had I not been using up energy carrying that rage, I might have accomplished much more. I realize now that I was tied to my former husband for twenty years even though we seldom saw each other. At the time, however, I thought there was no way I could be tied to someone that I didn't even like. I was so busy going to school, keeping house, making a living, parenting two young boys, and trying to "keep my head together" (as we phrased it in the seventies), that I didn't have much time left to deal with anything else.

In looking for a way to ease the pain of rejection and unworthiness that I felt, I eventually found my way into the human potential movement. I meditated, pounded pillows, cocounseled, and met lots of interesting people, which restored some of my self-esteem and released bits of my anger but never really resolved the underlying issues. Although I ultimately earned two master's degrees, became a college professor, and was successfully raising my children, I still felt angry and hurt. However, my sense of self-worth was improving as I became successful in my profession and at providing for my children. Intellectually, I knew that it was necessary to forgive and forget, and I was often able to fool myself into thinking that I had done so. But now and then, the rage and pain would reassert itself.

Not long after reaching my fiftieth birthday, I became concerned about health issues relative to aging. My mother had been in poor health for a long time, and I did not want to follow her pattern of deterioration. I suspected that some of her problems might be emotionally based. For this reason, I consulted a psychological counselor hoping to counteract any negative patterns I might have assimilated from my mother. We discussed my mother briefly, and I began to see similarities between my relationship with her and that with my former husband. Both had rejected me, I couldn't talk to either one, and I was angry about what I felt had been done to me. The focus of our discussions soon became my unresolved feelings of anger at him. I realized that I needed to find some way to finally resolve this issue. My counselor asked if I had ever told my ex-husband about what our life had been like after the divorce. I decided, at her suggestion, to write him a letter describing some of our difficulties during those years, hoping that telling him might relieve the feelings.

At this time, I saw an article in the newspaper stating that the company that my former husband owned with several others had been sold for over seventy million dollars. Having received from him minimal support payments, based on his poverty-level fellowship salary, to support two growing boys until they were eighteen years of age, and having also contributed to their college educations, I was shocked to realize how wealthy he was. My anger resurfaced. Now at age fifty, I was trying to begin to put together a retirement fund, and he had become a multimillionaire. I was nine years behind my same-age colleagues in earnings and in contributions to the state retirement fund. I had endured the years of poverty during his education with him and had been the major financial support of his children. I thought now that he had this substantial wealth he might be willing to recognize the injustice of the past and to make reparation for the financial inequity. I decided to include this in my letter because the purpose of my letter was to resolve my anger, and I was very angry about that.

It took me six months of rewriting and refining before my letter was ready. I learned to write factually and not use emotionally loaded words that would make him defensive and shut off from what I wanted to communicate. I described my life for the past twenty years supporting and raising the children. I told him that I had not gone to court earlier for more support money because I had neither the time nor resources to do so and because I was afraid that he would have instead taken the children from me. Now that the children were grown, that fear no longer existed. I also made my request for financial reparation and explained why I felt it was deserved. After I mailed the letter, I felt immense anxiety.

He responded with an emphatic "no" to my request and said that he had little sympathy and felt he owed me nothing. I was not surprised by the negative response to the request for money. That was consistent with the past. I knew that it was unlikely that he would agree. But I also knew that he had read the letter and now he knew of our hardships and that I felt financial reparation was deserved. In his letter he said many women successfully raise children alone and that my low-paying career was my own choice. Finally he praised my husband of the last seven years for his contributions to raising the boys and didn't acknowledge that I had anything at all to do with their development.

I had been a single parent for fourteen years. I finally realized that for a long time I had secretly hoped for an expression of appreciation from their father for raising such fine young men in spite of the hardships. Now I knew this would never happen. With the loss of that expectation my emotional tie with him dissolved. I had been looking for approval from him, just as I had from my mother, having never felt accepted just for myself. At last, I did not need their approval, only my own.

I composed my second letter in less than two weeks. I thought it an excellent letter, responding unemotionally point by point to what he had said, and restating my position. The knot of anger had begun to ease, and I could think much more clearly. Two months later I received a brief response. It restated his monetary "no" and ignored everything else mentioned in my letter. He said he did not want to exchange a series of letters but in the next paragraph said he was willing to discuss any issues.

There was an event in our past for which I longed for an explanation. To me it was the precipitating event in our final split. It was the phone call from the mother of the woman for whom he left us that Sunday never to return. The mystery of that phone call and what it was about had haunted me for twenty years. Now I had hope of an answer. I carefully composed a letter acknowledging that we each saw the money issue differently and thanking him for his willingness to discuss issues of the past. I described the events of that fateful day and requested his explanation of what I had perceived as behavior totally alien to his character. For three months, I heard nothing. Then our first grandchild was born. I took that opportunity to write a letter describing the birth and saying that I hoped we could have a more amicable relationship than we had in the past. I also reminded him of the preceding letter saying that no response was a kind of answer but that I would still appreciate an actual answer to my question about the phone call. He responded promptly saying that he was sorry but he had no recollection of the event that I had described. I was disappointed not to have a solution to the mystery, but that somehow no longer matters either.

Although his responses to my letters were less than satisfactory, he did respond. I received neither affirmation nor financial compensation, but I gained something much more valuable. I gained my freedom from the anger and fear I had carried with me for twenty years. I had tried many ways to resolve those feelings, but until I addressed him directly, the feelings always returned. I said (wrote) unemotionally and nonaccusatively: "This is how I see it. You may see it differently, and I accept that, but you now know how I see it." I no longer feel as if I have to prove something to him. Several years after the last letter, I had occasion to spend a day with him at our son's commencement from graduate school. I cannot say that our relationship is friendly; socially polite would be a more appropriate description.

I am no longer angry with my former husband or with my mother. I believe I understand now what was similar in the two relationships. Both of them had been in the position of caretaker to me, my mother when I was a dependent child and my husband when I was pregnant and caring for infants. Neither gave me the care or the approval I thought I needed from them. I discovered that I would survive, and in fact thrive, without their providing much of what I once wanted from them, and even without their approval. It is amazing to me that, after so many years of dwelling on the past, I seldom think of those events anymore. They are no longer a troubling part of my life, and that is a great relief.

My relationships with the other members of my family were always good but are now more relaxed as well. I find I am more accepting of all of our differences. Perhaps this is because I feel personally stronger and stand more firmly on my own two feet. I feel blessed with my present husband who is patient and accepting, and I am grateful to my counselor who got this whole process started and to my friends who gave generously of their attention. I especially appreciate my two sons who accompanied me on the entire journey. And I feel proud of myself for taking the sometimes difficult steps to get untangled and gain my freedom from that heavy burden of the past.

CONCLUSION

In reading Mrs. Stone's personal narrative and talking with her, it was evident to me that she was satisfied with the effort she had made and the result she had achieved. She had reached a closure on a long and arduous journey. For me, however, she had opened a door to new learning. She had stimulated me to think more deeply about human conflict and the varying ways that humans work out their conflicts.

I presented Mrs. Stone with the following statement of my view of her effort and my questions about it:

> I believe that in dealing with your own experience of divorce and cutoff, you have addressed issues that are significant for many people. Many divorced people are left with anger and a sense of having been betrayed by someone they loved and trusted. The general advice in society about resolving a painful divorce or other estrangement is get in touch with your feelings and express them, and then let them go and get on with your life. What I think you are describing here is a different alternative.
>
> My understanding is that (1) you spent years cut off from Dr. Stone, dealing with the repercussions of the divorce on your own and with help from family and friends; (2) in the past two years, you undertook a careful process of reconnecting with Dr. Stone; (3) he did read your letters and respond, but he offered little acknowledgement of your views and he disagreed with and refused your claim for monetary compensation; and (4) despite this, you gained a new perspective on the relationship and a resolution of anger that you had not achieved with your previous efforts.
>
> My questions are the following: What is meant by resolution? How do you account for the resolution you achieved? What changed for you in going back to Dr. Stone and addressing the unresolved issues? How was this different from the cutoff approach or trying to get a resolution without dealing with the other person?

Mrs. Stone found these questions interesting and was willing to go a certain distance with me in exploring them, but for the most part, she left them up to me. She did very well, I think, in drawing her boundaries and staying within them. She knew what she had experienced and was willing to describe it but not to explain it. She stated, "I want to tell the story, not explain the process. I'm not equipped to do that." On the question of what resolution meant, she "knew" her long-carried burden was gone, her internal state was one of peace, and she no longer thought much about the past. On the question of how this resolution had come about, she was satisfied simply to say, "The telling of the story was the resolution." The rest, she believed, was best left in the realm of mystery.

Although I agree that there is much mystery in human relationships and perhaps always will be, I believe that the theory of the emotional system and differentiation of self developed by Bowen sheds considerable light on this mystery. As I came to know Mrs. Stone, Bowen theory was the lens through which I "saw," to a limited degree, the emotional process in her and her family. Theory suggested a number of hypotheses that guided me in working with her, and theory also gave me a way of understanding the gains she made. The following are my thoughts and hypotheses.

First, because a marriage is a fragment of a larger system that includes the families of both partners, one needs to start with those families to understand the marriage. The partners bring into their marriage and replicate with each other the basic patterns of adapting that they have developed in their families of origin. In Mrs. Stone's case, my impression is that the emotional state of her mother and her father's sensitivity to mother were central factors in the family as she was growing up. Taking cues from father as well as mother, she became adept at accommodating to mother's moods. As the oldest, she adapted by helping with the care of her two younger sisters and minimizing demands on her parents. In working out her own balance of togetherness (being what her family seemed to need her to be) and individuality (being what she needed to be), she developed the qualities of resourcefulness, competence, and independence, qualities which served both herself and her family well. The degree of her reactivity to parents—positive toward father and negative toward mother—suggests that she had a moderately intense level of involvement in the parental triangle, yet not so great as to impair her own development in any serious way.

Second, with the family of origin background in mind, I try to understand a marriage in terms of three central questions: What did the two people bring to the marriage (level of maturity and personal stability, level of adaptability)? What did they have to deal with in their marriage (events, responsibilities, stresses, problems with each other)? How did their relationship evolve as they faced the challenges of married life (degree of reactivity to each other, ways in which each adapted to the other, and the relationship patterns which arose from these ways of adapting)? Mrs. Stone, in her report, gives some answers to these questions. Certainly, the eight years of her marriage to Dr. Stone were eventful. His being in medical school, the birth of two children within the first three years of marriage, the geographic moves, the financial constraints, and the relative isolation of living in places where they had no family were factors that would have tested the strength of any marriage. My impression is that, in the marriage, Mrs. Stone probably became the more adaptive of the two; that is, she probably compromised and accommodated more to Dr. Stone than he to her. As she had been a good daughter, Mrs. Stone was invested in being a good wife and mother. I suspect that she operated in the mode of "adaptive overfunctioner," one who "knows" the needs and comfort level of others, sometimes before they know it themselves, one who automatically functions to relieve discomfort in others and to preserve harmony in the relationship. This way of adapting would have worked well for Mrs. Stone and for the marriage up to a point, allowing her to live up to her standard of a good wife by creatively and flexibly meeting the needs of her husband and allowing him to focus his energy on his work. The cost of such a pattern is the degree of self that each partner gives up by relating to the other in this way. To the extent that the marriage is maintained by spouses adapting automatically to each other, the inner self of each is hidden from the other. There is little impetus for each to "define a self," that is, to reflect upon his and her own thoughts and feelings, to formulate ideas and beliefs, and to take positions on issues. There is little impetus to communicate a "defined self" to the other. There is little development, within the marriage, of an ability to identify, discuss, and negotiate differences. Under a surface of harmony, often distance and lone-liness, and resentment too, are growing.

This is the context in which I would understand the breakdown of the Stones's marriage. The appearance of the symptom of Dr. Stone's affair could be seen as both an outcome of the process in the marriage and an escalator of that process. An affair adds considerable stress to a marriage, and in many cases, this stress pushes the spouses to even greater reactivity to each other, thus intensifying the very patterns that have created the problem between them.

Third, with some knowledge of the emotional process in the marriage as a background, I try to understand the emotional process in the divorce. My impression is that, for the Stones, the pattern of dominant husband/ adaptive wife became a primary way of relating in the marriage. This pattern carried over to the divorce. At the time of the separation, Mrs. Stone's feeling intimidated by Dr. Stone, her deep sense of personal failure about the divorce, and the emotional overload of having lived under high stress for a long time left her in a seriously compromised position. At the same time, she had to deal with the necessity of quickly reorganizing her life and providing for her children and herself. The way she responded, as I see it, was to play from her strong suit: she turned to the resources which had worked for her in the past and in which she had the most confidence. The primary one was her own competence and resourcefulness; the next most important was her father. An alternative way of responding would have been to relate more actively with her husband, to be more forceful in making her needs and requirements clear and visible to him, to negotiate more effectively for a fair settlement, and to enlist whatever family and legal support was needed to do so. This, as Mrs. Stone explained in her report, was an avenue which she considered and explored but which did not prove to be viable for her. Under pressure to provide a home for herself and her sons, she made the decision to move back to the Midwest, where she focused on parenting, school, and work, and to a great extent, lost contact with Dr. Stone.

Fourth, knowing something of the emotional process in the marriage and divorce provides a foundation for understanding Mrs. Stone's effort to bridge the cutoff from Dr. Stone and what she gained through that effort. I believe that when one can make contact with a person whom one has found difficult and can deal with difficult issues without getting caught in attacking the other person or defending self, one gains "self." Bowen described this in detail in several papers (Bowen, 1978). The gain of self comes from addressing issues, defining one's own position clearly and firmly, and communicating it to the other. This gain does not depend on the other person's agreement or support. One must be prepared for the real possibility that the other will not support and may not even understand one's position.

Mrs. Stone put a lot of "self" into her letters. She did not pussyfoot around the issues. At the same time, she wrote carefully and thoughtfully, with consideration for the impact that the information and viewpoint she was expressing would have on Dr. Stone. My hypothesis is that Mrs. Stone, in contacting Dr. Stone, in finding her voice and communicating things that had gone unspoken for years, and in relating to him differently, more as a defined self, than she had in the past, found a way to reclaim "self" that had been lost over the course of the marriage and in the overwhelm of the divorce experience.

From what I understand about differentiation of self, an effort such as this is one step, nothing less and nothing more, in a lifelong process. It seems that it is far easier to lose self than to gain it. The gains one makes in differentiation of self are hard won and come in small increments. Yet each gain is significant in the difference it makes in one's life. Whatever gain of self that Mrs. Stone made in this effort goes with her into her present marriage, her relationship with her mother and father and all her other relationships, her work as an artist and teacher, and her ability to "be for self without being selfish, be for others without being selfless."

Mrs. Stone did not continue in therapy beyond the effort to reconnect with her former husband. When I asked about her original reason for seeing me, the difficulties between herself and her mother, she said that she saw no need to return to that focus. She was satisfied that this, too, has been resolved. It made sense to me that, if indeed something had changed within her on a basic level, she would be different in relationship to her mother. We left the whys and wherefores of this in the realm of mystery.

The fifth and final comment I wish to make brings this chapter full circle back to theory. My work with Mrs. Stone stimulated hours of reflection on the questions of human conflict, injury, injustice, compensation, and resolution. Human relationships are inevitably conflictual to varying degrees, and people search for ways of resolving conflict. The way one thinks about relationships and conflict strongly influences the way one will go about resolving the conflicts in one's own life.

In *Family Evaluation,* Michael Kerr makes a distinction between two avenues of resolving conflict that come from two ways of thinking about relationships. One avenue is forgiveness; the other is neutrality:

> If people become convinced that blaming self and/or blaming others is an *inaccurate* perception of the way relationships operate, many feelings about self and others resolve automatically. This is a process different from that involved in "forgiving" oneself or others. Forgiveness is usually based on feelings about what is "right" or "good" or about what one "should" do. Changing a way of thinking involves moving from a cause-and-effect model to a systems model, insofar as that is possible.
>
> People can develop more emotional neutrality by studying their own and other people's multigenerational families to a degree sufficient to convince themselves that human beings have limited emotional autonomy. If human beings are linked together emotionally across the generations by a process that is fueled by automatic reactions and reinforced by subjectivity, who does one blame? Getting beyond blame does not mean exonerating people from the part they play or played in the creation of a problem. It means seeing the total picture, acquiring a balanced view—not feeling compelled to either approve or disapprove of the nature of one's own and other people's families. (Kerr and Bowen, 1988, pp. 254-255)

Forgiveness is a way of resolving conflict that is universally understood; it is highly valued in most religious and moral traditions. It arises from a cause-and-effect view that sees one individual (or group) as wrongdoer and the other as injured. When the problem is seen in this way, the logical solution that follows is apology and reform on the part of the wrongdoer and forgiveness on the part of the injured one. Thus, it is hoped, the wrongdoer will be freed from the feelings of guilt and remorse, the injured one from the feelings of anger and resentment, and the relationship will be healed. If both sides view their problem in this way, there may be a reciprocal offering of forgiveness and apology. If only one sees it this way, that one is free to offer forgiveness or apology independent of the other's response.

What commonly occurs is that both sides view the problem in cause-and-effect terms, but both view themselves as the injured one.

Forgiveness and apology are frequently effective, at least in the short term, in reducing tension and restoring harmony. However, in the longer term, this way of resolving conflict tends to perpetuate conflict. It offers only one option for change: the "cause" of the conflict must change, either voluntarily or under pressure. The one viewed as the cause becomes the focal point of the system, and all efforts are directed to changing this individual.

Neutrality arises out of a very different way of thinking. Emotional neutrality is the natural companion of systems thinking. Systems thinking looks at both sides of a conflict and the reciprocal process between the two. But it takes more than two to keep a fight going, and so systems thinking goes beyond the dyad and places the conflict into a broader context, looking at the triangles and interlocking triangles that have operated over time to bring the conflicting parties into opposition with each other. Viewed through this broader lens, conflict is understood as a process in which many people and events have played a part. Any member of the system who can think about conflict this way can then become more aware of the part self has played, directly or indirectly, in fostering and perpetuating conflict. Every member of the system is a potential agent for change and conflict resolution.

The closer to home an issue is and the more it affects one's own interests, the more difficult it is to be neutral about it. Clearly, it was difficult for Mrs. Stone to be neutral about her divorce, but in the course of months of reflective thinking and writing, I believe she moved in that direction. She gained a systems perspective sufficient to allow her to see new options for self in that relationship. As I understand it, her resolution came when she moved out of a long-standing cutoff, contacted her former husband, and communicated a carefully defined stance in regard to the issues between them. Neither forgiveness nor apology was part of this resolution.

In clinical practice, one frequently observes the shift from emotionalized, subjective thinking to more neutral, objective thinking. A client can be expressing considerable affect as he or she describes the hurtful actions of a family member toward him or her and then can visibly move into a calmer state, as he or she begins to think about that other person in that person's own context and begins to recognize the realities the other is dealing with. This kind of a shift may be facilitated by a clinician who can listen to an emotionalized report without becoming anxious or biased. When the clinician, in an interested and nonanxious way, raises the question, "What is the other side of the story?," the client is often able to respond with a remarkably accurate account of the positions and viewpoints of others. People do know that every story has many sides.

A climate of neutrality begins with one person who is capable of remaining calm and maintaining a systems view of a problem in the presence of others who are reactive. A climate of neutrality develops when the thinking of the neutral one engages the thinking of one or more members of the system. When such a climate is established in clinical sessions, there is a predictable sequence of change. First, people become calmer, and fixed patterns of thinking about the problem are interrupted. Puzzled, thoughtful looks appear on faces. The problem becomes less tragic as people see various sides to it, perhaps even a humorous side. Ultimately, one or more family members begin to shift from an immobilized position, which sees the solution to the problem depending on change in others, to a more autonomous position, which sees options for self (Ferrera, 1986). The clinician's ability to manage self in a way that fosters a climate of neutrality is the hallmark of the theory-based psychotherapy developed by Murray Bowen.

REFERENCES

Anonymous (1972). "On the Differentiation of Self." In *Family Interaction: A Dialogue Between Family Researchers and Family Therapists,* J. Framo, Ed. New York: Springer, pp. 111-173.

Bowen, Murray (1976). "Theory in the Practice of Psychotherapy." In *Family Therapy: Theory and Practice,* P. J. Guerin, Ed. New York: Gardner Press, pp. 42-90.

Bowen, Murray (1978). *Family Therapy in Clinical Practice.* New York: Jason Aronson.

Bowen, Murray (1984). Personal correspondence.

Ferrera, Stephanie (1983). "Defining a No-Self: A Reverse Approach to Differentiation." *The Family,* 11(1): 18-22.

Ferrera, Stephanie (1986). "A Climate of Neutrality." *The Family,* 13(2): 3-7.

Kerr, Michael E. (1990). "Reflections on Twenty-Five Years with Murray Bowen." Lecture to Center for Family Consultation Postgraduate Training Program, Chicago, Illinois.

Kerr, Michael E. and Murray Bowen (1988). *Family Evaluation: An Approach Based on Bowen Theory.* New York: W. W. Norton.

Index

Page numbers followed by the letter "i" indicate illustrations; those followed by the letter "t" indicate tables.